Prison Journal, 1940–1945

EDOUARD DALADIER

Prison Journal

1940–1945

with a foreword
by Stanley Hoffmann

compiled and annotated
by Jean Daladier with Jean Daridan

translated by Arthur D. Greenspan

Routledge
Taylor & Francis Group
LONDON AND NEW YORK

The translation of this book was funded in part by the French Ministry of Culture.

First published 1995 by Westview Press, Inc.

Published 2019 by Routledge
52 Vanderbilt Avenue, New York, NY 10017
2 Park Square, Milton Park, Abingdon, Oxon OX14 4RN

Routledge is an imprint of the Taylor & Francis Group, an informa business

Library of Congress Cataloging-in-Publication Data
Daladier, Edouard, 1884–1970.
[Journal de captivité, 1940–1945. English]
Prison journal, 1940–1945 / Edouard Daladier ; with a foreword by Stanley Hoffmann ; compiled and annotated by Jean Daladier with Jean Daridan ; translated by Arthur Greenspan.
p. cm.
ISBN 0-8133-1905-6
1. Daladier, Edouard, 1884–1970—Diaries. 2. Statesmen—France—Diaries. 3. World War, 1939–1945—Prisoners and prisons—Diaries. 4. France—Politics and government—20th century. I. Daladier, Jean. II. Daridan, Jean. III. Title.
DC397.D25A3 1995
940.5'7244'092—dc20
[B] 94-35523
CIP

ISBN 13: 978-0-367-28426-8 (hbk)
ISBN 13: 978-0-367-29972-9 (pbk)

Contents

Foreword, Stanley Hoffmann, vii

Preface to the English Edition, Jean Daladier, xv

June 1940: The Departure for Morocco, 1

1940, *3*

1941, *45*

1942, *101*

1943, *183*

1944, *247*

1945, *305*

Appendix A: France's Principal Modern Weaponry, 343

Appendix B: The Riom Trial, 345

Appendix C: Biographical Timeline, 357

About the Book, 359

Name Index, 361

Foreword

Stanley Hoffmann

Edouard Daladier was one of France's most important statesmen between the two world wars. He had been the Prime Minister who signed the Munich Agreement in September 1938, at Czechoslovakia's expense, and he was also the Prime Minister who, one year later, declared war on Hitler's Germany after the Nazi invasion of Poland. When his government fell in March 1940, during the "phony war," he remained Minister of Defense in the final cabinet of the Third Republic, the cabinet headed by Paul Reynaud. This government presided over the collapse of France in seven catastrophic weeks in May–June 1940, split over whether to seek an Armistice, resigned, and was followed by the Pétain government, which promptly signed the Armistice, summoned the French Parliament, obtained full powers from it, and set up the Vichy regime.

Daladier was a member of a small but distinguished group of parliamentarians who were led to believe, or tricked into believing, that the Pétain government would keep waging war from North Africa, and who left France on a boat—the *Massilia*—that went to Morocco. There, they were promptly arrested and returned to France. Daladier was among the political and military leaders Vichy threw in jail and decided to try for the responsibility in France's defeat—it was never too clear whether they were being blamed for France's military incompetence or for having wanted to resist Hitler. A special court was set up in Riom (Auvergne) to try Daladier, Léon Blum, and the Generalissimo of 1940, Gamelin, along with a couple of minor figures. Even before the trial, Pétain condemned the accused to be detained in a fortress. The trial, in early 1942, was a disaster for Vichy and had to be suspended. Imprisoned now in another fortress (Bourassol), Daladier and Blum were delivered by Vichy to the Germans, who locked Daladier (along with Reynaud and Gamelin) in a "castle" in the Tirol. Daladier's diary covers these events, until his liberation by the Americans at the end of the war.

Few French politicians have had a more fluctuating reputation. Daladier was often seen as "exhibit A" of the kind of social ascent the Third Republic fostered. The son of a baker in Carpentras (Vaucluse), he was the typical *boursier*—the boy whose brilliance in school results, first in scholarships, and later in obtaining an *agrégation* in history and geography, a degree won through competitive examination, that allowed him to teach in high schools. He soon entered politics, as a Radical, and became mayor of Carpentras at twenty-eight, in 1911. He fought in World War I as a Sergeant and became a Deputy in 1919. The Radical Party was the very loose political force that dominated French politics from the beginning of the twentieth century to 1940. It was ideologically on the Left—the ardent champion of representative and (above all) secular government, of the public school system, and of the "principles of 1789"—and socially quite conservative, in line with the wishes of an electorate of peasants and petits bourgeois. Being a party of the Center, it could form coalitions either with those to its left (including the Socialists) or with more right-wing parties. Daladier, in the 1920s, was the leader of the left-leaning elements in the party and became its President in 1927. The rivalry between the younger Daladier and his former teacher, the mayor of Lyons, Edouard Herriot, who had been the luckless Prime Minister of the leftist Cartel des Gauches in 1924, but later agreed to take part in more conservative cabinets, marked the history of the party for many years.

Daladier, several times a Minister in the 1920s, specialized in foreign and defense matters. His reputation was that of a "Jacobin"—a tough and austere defender of the Republic, with a taste for action and (unlike Herriot) a distaste for rhetoric and sentimentality. There are two kinds of southerners in France: the sunny and loquacious ones (whose seriousness General de Gaulle, a man from the North, always questioned) and the taciturn, more melancholy ones. Daladier was clearly one of the latter. His reputation suffered when his first two experiences as Prime Minister turned out to fall far short of expectations. His nine-month-long Cabinet of 1933, following the 1932 elections that had favored the Left, proved, like its predecessors and successors, incapable of defining a clear financial policy to cope with the Great Depression. It fell when Daladier, under pressure from the Right of his party, took deflationary measures that those conservative Radicals deemed insufficient and that the Socialists, whose votes he needed, rejected. After the scandalous Stavisky affair, in which several Radical politicians were compromised and widely denounced as corrupt, Daladier became Prime Minister again—a week before the violent antiparliamentary riots of February 6, 1934, provoked by far-right "Leagues." Daladier, at first, seemed to want to react firmly in order to restore and maintain law and order; but some of his closest supporters abandoned him, and he resigned on February 7—a decision one historian has called the collective suicide of the Republic.[1] It led to a shift from left to right, which lasted two years; during that period, Marshal Pétain joined the Doumergue government and Pierre Laval became the Prime Minister of deflation.

It was at that time that the Popular Front emerged, at first as a popular reaction to the riots of February 6, 1934, later as a laborious alliance between three parties: the Communists, who adopted a stance of moderation and cooperation with the Socialist rivals and Radical bourgeois they had spent years denouncing, Léon Blum's Socialists (who had never been in power), and the Radicals. The latter were as usual divided, with Herriot at first quite reluctant. It was Daladier who led the Radicals into the Popular Front and went to rallies with Blum, Thorez (the Communist leader), and Jouhaux, the head of France's largest union, the CGT. Daladier became Minister of Defense in Blum's government after the Popular Front's electoral victory in 1936. Quickly, the Radical Party began to back away from Blum; overthrown by the Senate, he was replaced by a Radical (Chautemps). After the fiasco of a very brief second Blum Cabinet, the President of the Republic, Albert Lebrun, turned once more to Daladier in April 1938. This last Daladier Cabinet remained in power almost two years—an exceptionally long time in the Third Republic.

It was an important government. Gradually, within a few months, Daladier moved away from the Popular Front: By the fall of 1938, his Cabinet was an alliance of the Radicals and the moderate Right, strengthened when one of the more impressive (and unorthodox) conservative leaders,

1. Serge Berstein, *Histoire du Parti Radical*, vol. 2 (Paris: Presses de la Fondation Nationale des Sciences Politiques, 1982), p. 287.

Paul Reynaud, became Minister of Finance. Daladier and Reynaud reformed the 1936 legislation that limited work to forty hours a week (thus slowing down rearmament), and when the CGT imprudently called for a general strike, the government faced it down and prevailed. Daladier, for a while, became as widely popular as Poincaré had been in the mid- and late 1920s. He was seen, once more, as a man of firmness and authority; he was treated as a hero when he returned from Munich, having saved peace (but he, unlike Chamberlain, had no illusions about its duration and is reported, upon meeting mobs of enthusiastic well-wishers at the airport, to have exclaimed, in somewhat more pungent language: Fools!), and also when he reasserted France's rights and rule in Algeria and in the colonies, against Mussolini's claims. He was the first to launch an ambitious and coherent "family policy" in order to cope with France's demographic decline; and he heeded the public mood in trying to stem the flow of refugees and put many of them in camps.

After Hitler, violating his promises, occupied Bohemia, Daladier insisted on guaranteeing Poland's integrity. When the Hitler-Stalin pact made war inevitable, Daladier's steadily growing hostility to communism became more intense—after all, he had been in the process of negotiating an alliance with Stalin when the latter turned to Germany. After the declaration of war, Communist deputies were expelled from Parliament. Daladier, and much of the political class, championed a strategy of attrition against Germany. Daladier wanted to avoid at all cost a repeat of the bloodletting of World War I, in which 1.5 million Frenchmen—largely peasants and those other *petits* whom the Radicals represented—had been killed. Like Pétain in 1916–1918, he wanted to minimize French losses; hence the passivity of the French Army, locked in the Maginot Line, while Hitler destroyed Poland. The dominant strategic notion was that of a "peripheral strategy" that would go after supplies indispensable to Hitler: iron ore in Scandinavia, oil in the Caucasus. The French Right seemed more eager to fight Stalin (and help Finland, attacked by him) than to fight Hitler and help Poland. Daladier was accused—especially by the pacifist Laval—of not waging the war energetically enough. Sensing that his majority was waning, Daladier resigned, once again, as Prime Minister.

The diary shows what his main concern was after Vichy denounced and jailed him. He wanted to show that ever since 1936 he had launched an extensive rearmament program, and that France had in many areas (although not in aircraft) as much matériel as Germany. This is what he argued in Riom, where he and Blum turned the tables on Vichy: he, with his figures and facts, Blum with his eloquent defense of the Republic. Again and again, he pointed out that the defeat of France resulted not from a lack of preparation but from the incompetence of the High Command. Battling against Vichy's accusations, he had no time for self-criticism: Alas, the military leaders who proved so timid, unadapted to motorized warfare and *Blitzkrieg*, wedded to a defensive strategy that met the public's battle fatigue, yet contradicted France's alliance policies, were men Daladier had appointed or promoted or protected (like the mediocre Gamelin, whom he shielded from Reynaud's wrath).

For many people in France and abroad, he remains the man of Munich. This is, in a way, unfair. He signed that infamous agreement in part because Chamberlain insisted on appeasement and France alone wasn't strong enough to wage war on Hitler, in part because he was sensitive to the Sudeten Germans' demand for self-determination and critical of the way in which President Benes had handled them. But unlike many other *Munichois* who were either pacifists pure and simple or convinced that settling accounts with the Left, or with the Republic, in France was far more important than resisting Hitler, Daladier wanted to use the "reprieve" Munich represented in order to strengthen France's armies and to restore national unity and resolve. One problem, here, was the presence at the Quai d'Orsay of another Radical, Georges Bonnet, a genuine appeaser whose goals were quite different, and whom he didn't remove from the Foreign Ministry until after the war began. Daladier, whose instincts were often excellent, was frequently a willing victim of the Byzantine coalition politics of the Third Republic (and of his own party), and there was a constant battle between firmness and caution in his actions.

The diary shows a man who both relives a heavy past and defends his role in it, who blames those who took France out of the war in order to indulge in dreams of a reactionary "national revolution"—and also worries about the future of his country and of the world. He has nothing but contempt for *both* Pétain and Laval and gives a devastating account of the third great man of Vichy, Admiral Darlan. He realizes that the war cannot be won without American participation; but he is often morosely pessimistic about the course of the war—unlike Blum—and increasingly anxious about an outcome he foresees with great lucidity: Soviet domination of much of Europe (although he exaggerates the risk of a Bolshevized Germany, on the Polish model). He compares unfavorably the Allies' "abandonment" of Poland with what had happened in Munich. His references to de Gaulle in London and Algiers, to Gaullist propaganda, to the trials and political debates that took place in Algiers in 1943–1944, are often critical; he is clearly afraid that trials occurring while the war goes on will be anything but fair, and he wishes that the French people be consulted before any great political and social changes are carried out; in this respect, he remained a man of the Third Republic.

His combination of humanity and lucidity is evident in his remarks on Germany. He is far more distrustful of Germany than is Blum; but he acknowledges the force of German nationalism and condemns any policy of dismemberment (which de Gaulle pursued for a while). His reaction to learning about the atrocities in concentration camps is moving and strong, but he is not a seeker of revenge.

The reader of this diary will be entertained by Daladier's references to his relations with his many guards and jailers and with his companions of captivity: His sympathy for Blum and for the tennis champion, ex–Vichy Minister–turned–resister Borotra; his fairness toward the baffling and waffling Colonel de La Roque, the head of the largest right-wing League (and later party) in the 1930s—a man whose wolfish rhetoric scared the Left, but who turned out to be a sheep, and who supported Pétain after the defeat yet worked for the British intelligence service; and his old hostility toward Reynaud are all in evidence.

Two other points are worth noting. Daladier's captivity did not isolate him from what was happening. While jailed in France, he received lawyers and other visitors who kept him informed of the latest rumors and gossip, of the latest stories about that quaint Vichy regime that I once described as a pluralistic dictatorship, a conglomeration of feuding factions. In the Tirol, he had access to an extraordinary array of newspapers and radio programs.

Moreover, among his visitors in France there was the infamous René Bousquet, the head of Vichy's police and close collaborator of Laval, who played a large and sinister role in the deportation of Jews. Bousquet had been a "Popular Front Prefect," close to the Radicals. His conversation with Daladier on September 16, 1942, is triply fascinating. First, it reveals the calculations of many Vichyites, for whom German victory was likely: France in order to survive had to fit into the "new European order" and in the meantime could do no more than bow to German demands and plead for some of them to be softened. It is Bousquet who comes and tells Daladier that Vichy had to yield to the German demand that he be deported to Germany. Second, it shows that Bousquet did not want to burn his bridges with the leaders of the "old regime" (as Vichy called the Third Republic): He cultivated Daladier just as he established contacts with the Resistance (he befriended, among others, the young Mitterrand, then en route from his Pétainism of 1941–1942 to his resistance of 1943–1944). All these contacts helped him survive and prosper after the war—until his assassination by a madman in 1993. Third, it is clear from the tone of Daladier's entries that he kept some respect for Bousquet, unlike the strong dislike he had for Bousquet's bosses.

The publication of the diary in English should accomplish at least two things. It should revive interest in a man whom history has not treated very well—an imperfect politician, to be sure, part of a system of government whose vices overwhelmed its democratic merits (see for instance Daladier's account of press corruption), but a man of intelligence, integrity, patriotism, common sense, and culture (cf. his interest in Church history). And it should inform the reader about the extraordinary complexity of a period in which rival contenders fought murderously about France's direction and soul, in which uncertainty about the future obliged men and women to make an existential gamble about the outcome, based in part on what they expected but also on what they desired. Daladier never had any doubts about what he wanted for France, even when he wondered how long it would take for victory to come, and he lamented the fate of much of Europe when it finally occurred.

able to function at capacity. He knew that it would take the French, too, at least four years, as it would the British.

But the crisis erupted in September 1938, when Hitler called for the Germans in the Sudetenland to be reincorporated into the Reich. There has surely been no paucity of statements about the Munich Agreement—acclaimed when they were signed, maligned ever after—but rarely are such pronouncements accompanied by fact.

At the end of World War I, it was Clemenceau who insisted that the Sudetenland be made a part of Czechoslovakia. The Czech President, Tomas Masaryk, was opposed but eventually yielded. Out of a total population of 13.5 million in Czechoslovakia, there were only 6 million Czechs (44 percent) and 3.5 million Germans. There were also Slovaks, Hungarians, and Poles, who more often than not were hostile to the Czechs. (Just recently, barely three years after it was liberated from the Soviet bloc, this same nation split in two.)

France had been so unwise as to guarantee Czechoslovakia's sovereignty on its own. The illusions that were born of the victory of 1918 lasted a very long time.

When Germany remilitarized the Rhineland in 1936, Daladier favored armed intervention. Merely a Member of Parliament at the time, he urged General Maurin, the War Minister, to intervene. Once that moment had passed, he felt that the balance of power had shifted: Germany's rearmament was an established fact.

In September 1938, the British were opposed to any form of armed intervention; in truth, they did not possess the force with which to intervene. Chamberlain, moreover, felt that an agreement could be reached with Hitler. The United States was still an unarmed nation at that point and wedded to its isolationist policies. The Soviets, in spite of what has since been claimed, kept equivocating and proposed to bring the matter before the League of Nations. France knew that it could not by itself oppose Germany, that it would take a multinational alliance to save Czechoslovakia and some two to three years to reestablish the balance of power.

Daladier signed the agreements—an act that would haunt him for the rest of his life. When he returned to France from Munich, he did not proclaim, as Chamberlain did, that he had brought "peace for our time."

Looking down on the crowd that had gathered to welcome him, he simp muttered, "Goddamn fools!" and went back to Parliament to ask for a even greater rearmament program. These are the facts; they speak fo themselves.

In 1939, Daladier was to go even further. To avoid war, and in agree ment with the Poles, he was prepared to negotiate the return to German of Danzig and the Polish corridor. This time, it was Hitler who refuse He attacked Poland, with the help of the Soviets. The same recognition o France's vulnerability was to move Daladier to do everything he could t avoid major battles in the months that followed. (Note that it was not unt 1942–1943 that victory finally swung over to the side of the Allies, and tha it had effectively required an international coalition to turn the tide.)

By 1940, the rearmament objectives had been fulfilled. Shortages per sisted in certain areas, but overall, France was armed with a considerabl stock of modern weaponry. The French, for example, had the same num ber of tanks as the Germans, approximately 2,800. Note, moreover, tha when they were led into battle, the French troops fought bravely. Som 100,000 men died in action, in just a few weeks' time.

The Germans attacked at Sedan. Pétain had refused to defend thi portion of the Ardennes region. General Billotte, in contrast, had long ar gued that this was the sector through which the Germans would send thei armored divisions. He believed that France was capable of sending a equal number of tanks to blunt their attack and that it was time to reorga nize France's defenses. The French High Command would have none o it. On the eve of the German offensive, the command did not even believ the pilot who reported the nighttime movement of huge numbers of en emy tanks, driving on Sedan, headlights ablaze. The confidence tha reigned was so great that certain military leaders even removed the ob structions that had been set up along one of the main access roads.

Most of these Generals had performed admirably in World War I They were still basking in past glory, maneuvering to outdo each other i pride and ambition, as they looked across the border to their young Ger man counterparts. Like the Prussian Generals at Iena before them France's military leaders proved incapable of adapting to the unexpected Their mood swung from excessive confidence to utter panic, and fron there to the absolute certainty that the German Army was invincible and would crush the British in a few weeks' time.

Even as late as 1942–1943, Pétain and the principal leaders in France were convinced that the Anglo-Saxons and the Russians would never be able to defeat the Germans. Pétain saw himself as one of several negotiators in a compromise peace settlement, as is clearly brought out in Daladier's journal. But the truth is that when the likes of Buisson, de Gaulle, and Perré were provided with the necessary firepower, France's young military leaders were able to score clear victories over the Germans. The story was much the same for the Air Force, which was supposedly outnumbered. The facts show that in the few weeks when pilots organized their own missions in the absence of orders from the retreating High Command, they shot down 900 enemy planes while losing only 400 of their own. One wonders what would have happened in the 1940 Battle of Britain had Göring's superior numbers been further reinforced by those 900 aircraft. Whenever able leadership was there—in Africa, Italy, and in France—French soldiers fought valiantly.

But instead of conferring the responsibility for regrouping France's forces to these younger leaders, Prime Minister Paul Reynaud called on Pétain and Weygand, both of whom were convinced that England would be overrun. They had no sense of America's strength and rejected out of hand the possibility of carrying on the war from North Africa. This is an issue that went unquestioned for years and years. We now know that putting up resistance in North Africa, with the men and matériel already in place, bolstered by whatever could have been transported from the mainland, was fully within the realm of possibility. France's fleet ruled the Mediterranean, seconded there by the British fleet. By then there was even an assembly plant for American planes in Casablanca. This was the most unforgivable error of all, the one that has been so carefully hidden over the years and that prefigured the total surrender of the Unoccupied Zone in November 1942, Pétain's and Weygand's refusal to leave for Algiers, and the absurd decision to scuttle the fleet rather than sending it off to join forces with the Allies.

In fact, Daladier, along with several Members of Parliament, left France in June 1940 to carry on the fight from Morocco. He was forcibly brought back, imprisoned, and indicted, first for having declared war on Germany, then for having failed to rearm the nation. His diary offers a scathing depiction of the scandalous Riom trial, suspended by Pétain once it became clear that it was proving detrimental to Vichy. Subsequently, Pétain allowed Daladier to be deported to a prison in Germany. The Riom trial proved that France had indeed been rearmed, a fact that the parties directly involved were to continue to deny for the next fifty years.

While in prison, Daladier wrote about the happenings and people in Vichy with an exactness and a lucidity that are bound to surprise. Even when he was isolated in Germany, he made observations on events past and present that are no less striking. And he gave voice as well to his profound disappointment as he witnessed the inadequacy of Anglo-Saxon policies and the skill with which Stalin went about colonizing all of Eastern Europe, including the very Czechoslovakia that Churchill had claimed he wanted to save in 1938. Following the war, countless people criticized the Munich Agreement, whereas those who expressed opposition to Soviet occupation were far less numerous. The leaders of the French Communist Party tried to obscure the statements they had made in Berlin in 1933, when they called for the liberation of the Sudeten Germans in Czechoslovakia. The Right added its voice as well. Between the end of the war and the early 1970s, former Pétainists and Communists were appointed to ministerial posts. The country began congratulating itself more and more openly for the approach adopted by Pétain, which, it was said, had spared France considerable suffering and paved the way for the Resistance. Others simply pretended that all of France had been in the Resistance. The state of confusion that reigned was the direct result of the country's general unwillingness to examine the past objectively.

Daladier was finally liberated, almost by miracle. As German soldiers were about to execute the remaining prisoners, an American detachment came to the rescue, aided by a German officer and his men. Daladier looked on in horror as this German officer, who had come to defend the lives of enemy prisoners, was killed before his eyes, when the war was in effect already over.

Back in France, Daladier became the scapegoat of both the Right and the Left, and above all the Far Left. He was nonetheless reelected to Parliament. "Munich! Munich!" they shouted, when he voiced his opposition to the war that was beginning in Indochina. They condemned him for having left France unarmed, even though the facts and figures were available to everyone. They condemned him for just about everything, and then some.

Remarkably, he never responded to the attacks and the slander. The consumer society—the world of mass media, advertising, and money—elicited from him only reactions of irony and indifference. He watched as veritable "collective memories" were forged, each by the design and within the limits of the prevailing interest groups or political parties. In Western democracies, there is simply no place for a lone individual and perhaps not even for grand principles. One has only to consider the way electoral campaigns are now financed and how mores have evolved.

In the trenches and in Parliament, in Ministries and prisons, this was a man who fought for republican ideals. For him, being a democrat involved a lifelong political and personal commitment tantamount to stoicism. He needed little to get by and left behind neither money nor possessions. He was emotionless when he testified at Pétain's trial, although Pétain had sentenced him to life in prison, slandered him, and handed him over to the Gestapo. He used to say, "Vengeance is just so much silliness." Those who betrayed him during his years of captivity shamelessly continued reaping benefits from it. He never said anything about it. Perhaps he had arrived at a true experience of freedom and found some form of hope for the future.

One morning in 1970, I listened as he scoffed at the hopes expressed by his physician and offered his farewell with a smile. He died the following day without the slightest fear, and without a word.

I came upon the old notebooks that made up his prison diary long after his death, in the bottom of a dresser drawer. When the book was published in France, I was surprised to receive so many letters from simple folk who had not forgotten him, and who perhaps shared with him the same almost indescribable form of hope.

June 1940: The Departure for Morocco

Jean Daladier

The British had offered Daladier refuge in London, but he preferred to leave for Morocco and continue the struggle from there, as France's leaders in Bordeaux[1] had agreed to do. He wrote the following:

"The government had stated that it would set up its base in North Africa and move all government offices there. Some members were to leave via various Mediterranean ports. Others, including myself, were to go to Le Verdon, where we would board the *Massilia* en route to Casablanca.

"I was anxious to meet with General Noguès.[2] I had appointed him Governor-General of Morocco and wanted to encourage him to carry on the fight.

"In Le Verdon, half of the Deputies who had been present in Bordeaux boarded the *Massilia*, along with General Michel, government personnel, and even Herriot's suitcases.

"We set sail on June 21, in spite of the German mines and the problems we had with the crew; they wanted to return to their families.

"We learned of the Armistice while at sea. The ship's commander categorically refused to alter his course and make for England.

"When we arrived in Casablanca, we were forced to remain on board. It was during that time that the official turnaround in France took place. In the radio and press campaigns mounted against us, we were being accused of desertion.

---

1. In the face of the German advance, the French government had moved from Paris to Tours and from there to Bordeaux in June 1940.

2. General Charles-Auguste Noguès. After having requested and been denied permission from Pétain's government to organize an insurgent military, General Noguès aligned himself with the Marshal. In 1942, Noguès's forces put up armed resistance to the Allied landing. He later sided with Admiral Darlan when the latter came to Algiers. He sought exile in Portugal.

"I finally met Noguès on June 27, in Rabat. 'The Army didn't lose the war,' he said. 'They never went to war.' We both thought that it would be possible to carry on the fight from North Africa, as did all the other leaders, even those in Black Africa and the Middle East.

"We had 270,000 men at our command and the capacity to mobilize them rapidly. We had arms, and even 1,800 top-flight warplanes. Airplanes I had ordered from the United States were to be delivered to Morocco, where assembly plants had already been set up. The Franco-British fleet ruled the Mediterranean. Five admirals had come to Casablanca, among them Laborde and Marquis. Darlan[3] had asked Noguès to set up a command post for him in Rabat.

"Spain was certain to remain neutral, given the exhausting civil war it had just been through and its need for American aid. On Tunisia's border with Libya, there were the Mareth fortifications I had had built.

"Noguès had already cabled Bordeaux several times. He was seeking government authorization to break with official policy and fight on, even if the government had to disavow its involvement in the process.[4] He agreed to send one final cable; it too went for naught.

On June 30, Members of Parliament were prevented from boarding ship and returning to France. They would not be allowed to do so until July 10, in order to deny them the possibility of voting in Vichy, where Pétain was granted plenary powers."[5]

---

3. Admiral François Darlan, who had become Commander in Chief of the Navy in August 1939.

4. While in Morocco, my father and I tried to meet up with the British and leave for London. A submarine was sent to pick us up off the coast of Casablanca. We were betrayed, however, and never found the skiff that would have taken us out from the beach. Other escape attempts failed as well. The Governor-General's office in Rabat managed to foil them all. We were eventually forced—with Noguès's consent, obviously—to leave Morocco under police escort and return to France, where my father was arrested.

General Noguès would later order his troops to fire on the Americans as they landed. He went on to align himself with Darlan and, subsequently, Giraud. After the war, he went into exile. Strange fellow, this General Noguès, who felt he had to ask the government for permission to rebel.

5. General de Gaulle pushed strongly for Noguès to refuse the Armistice and come to London to serve under him.

1940

September 6, 1940

We were having lunch at La Vernue, deep in the countryside near Vichy. André Borie and his family had been my warm and generous hosts for several days. I said to my friends, "It won't be long before I am taken into custody," but they were a little skeptical. "Why would they bother arresting you? The trial is being held right here in Riom.[1] The authorities will know exactly where to find you, since you notified the Minister of the Interior yourself."[2]

I had been warned two or three days before that I could expect to be arrested. The leaders at Vichy had already made up their minds, and there was no time to lose if I hoped to get away. Nonetheless, in view of General Noguès's decision not to make a stand in North Africa and the failed British attempts to spirit me to London, I was determined to face the ordeal in France. On September 3, a young inspector from the *Sûreté* even came to warn me that they would be coming to get me very soon. He offered to take me to Switzerland within a few hours. I thanked him but refused to go.

On September 4, the press published a statement issued by the government in which it claimed "the right to place in administrative detention those individuals deemed dangerous to national security or public safety."

---

1. Site of the court established by the Vichy government, where Daladier and other leaders of the Third Republic were to be tried.

2. Daladier notified him because the Ministry of the Interior is primarily concerned with matters of security and law and order. It oversees general administrative matters within France, such as elections, and virtually all administrative matters for France's territories overseas, but its principal function remains that of governing the nation's various police forces.

Nothing happened for the following two days. In fact, my friends at La Vernue were somewhat amused at my having gotten my papers together and carefully arranged them in two leather briefcases.

I harbored no illusions as to the impartiality of this supreme tribunal[3] —my sentence would undoubtedly come down directly from Pétain—but I felt I owed the people of this country an explanation. Had France been betrayed and if so by whom? And how? I was also afraid that by staying with Borie, I would be endangering him, but he absolutely refused to let me leave.

We went on with our meal. Suddenly, the little blonde serving girl came running up, all excited. "Madame, several cars have pulled in and are stopping in front of the house."

Brochet, the Director of the State Police, strode in. Looking important and solemn, he read aloud an order signed by Porte, the Subprefect of Monluçon, who had run for office in the Nièvre as a Popular Front candidate. In accordance with the law of September 4, 1940, and by virtue of the authority vested in Adrien Marquet,[4] Minister of the Interior, I was to be placed under house arrest in the château in Chazeron.

I dictated and signed a statement of protest, denouncing them for arbitrarily resurrecting a law intended to punish plots against the nation and acts of sabotage against the defense industry.

With the help of my son Jean and Dr. Mazé,[5] and in the presence of a kindly but talkative policeman, I quickly packed two suitcases. I took leave of Mme Borie and her daughters, who had received me in their home and been so gracious and considerate. When I started blaming myself for not having left sooner, they stopped me and hugged me. I told my son Jean to

3. La Cour Suprême de Justice: a Vichy institution created to try Third Republic Ministers et al. for entering and losing the war against Germany, in other words, to find scapegoats for the humiliating defeat of France.

4. Adrien Marquet had a hand in organizing Pétain's government in Bordeaux, where he was Deputy and Mayor.

5. Pierre Mazé, Secretary-General of the Radical-Socialist Party. As one of Daladier's close personal friends, he organized several attempts to rescue him. He played an important role in the Resistance and was eventually arrested by the Germans. He was liberated in 1945.

notify his brother, Pierre, and my sister so that they wouldn't be brutally shaken by reading the news in the morning papers.

We went outside. In spite of the gasoline crisis, there were five cars parked at the door, each of them packed with policemen. So much for the propaganda promoting a return to the land.[6]

One of the policemen, a pale, round-eyed, fat and fleshy fellow, tried to take a picture. Jean and Dr. Mazé lashed out at him, and he put down his camera.

I would never have guessed I rated a five-car procession. Marquet was doing things up right. We drove through Gannat, Aigueperse, and Châtelguyon, with people stopping in the streets, staring at us as we went by. One of the cops began telling the story of his years on the force. I lit up my pipe and sat back.

When we came into Chazeron, I could make out in the distance the château tower, the crenellated ramparts, and the old black walls surrounded by pine trees, all of it taken over now by ravens and owls for a nesting ground. The gate is rather handsomely crafted, but the courtyard, with its well and a few dilapidated buildings, is overgrown with weeds. The grounds were teeming with state troopers and inspectors from the *Sûreté*, strolling about and puffing on cigarettes. Dozens of workers were repairing and patching things up, nailing in doors, boarding up windows, and installing lovely, brand new, sharply pointed bars. Their prisoner had arrived before they'd finished readying his prison.

I was told that the illustrious M. Marquet, the Minister of the Interior, had graced this run-down château that the government had requisitioned by visiting it personally.

That was to be his last official function. A few days later, he was removed from office by Pétain and replaced by Peyrouton,[7] a fitting reward

6. To counter what Pétain claimed to be the decadence that had brought about France's downfall, he promoted a return to the simpler, purer values of life in the countryside.

7. Marcel Peyrouton, Governor-General of France's overseas territories prior to the war, Pétain's Minister of the Interior in 1940, and Governor-General of Algeria after the Allied landing in North Africa. He was incarcerated at the end of the war.

for having betrayed the government in Bordeaux and having helped Pétain come to power. Word has it that he immediately set out for the Occupied Zone to spew out his rancor and offer his services to the Germans.

I sat down in the courtyard, with a policeman still right behind me. The gate opened and a limousine rolled in. Policemen and troopers ran up to greet it, but it turned out to be just Chavin. Several years ago I had named him Prefect of the Vaucluse and then Prefect in Constantine, after having decorated him with the *Légion d'honneur* in between. He is now Director of the *Sûreté*. With a crowd milling around him, our M. Chavin pretended not to see me, even though our eyes met several times. He walked by, passing just a few feet away, on his way to a tour of the château and what passes here for gardens. Then, once he had finished visiting the grounds, he headed back toward the gate at an angle, and doffed his hat in my direction from as far away as he could. I replied by tipping mine.

I was officially welcomed by M. Bartelet, the warden of this Bastille. We chatted for a while. He is a veteran from Lorraine, twice wounded and twice decorated in 1914. Briefly and discreetly, he shared his feelings with me about France's collapse, our surrendering in Bordeaux, and the path the Vichy government had taken since. Then he headed off to oversee the construction work.

Once the iron bars were finally secured, I moved into my cell, that is, my room. I was given two candles, since they hadn't finished wiring electricity for lights. A policeman and a state trooper settled in outside my door. I was free again, alone at last with my thoughts.

This is where I shall have to muster my strength. Ever since the capitulation in Bordeaux, life has left little more than an ashen taste in my mouth. In Morocco, when I realized that all was lost, I occasionally had thoughts of putting an end to it.

I'll have to fight the press, Laval's[8] slimy arrogance, and the Cour Suprême de Justice, even if I have to fight them on my own. I am alone with

8. As Vice Premier, Pierre Laval effectively shared power with Pétain in what was at best an uneasy association and at times an openly hostile one. He was the principal architect

the lions; it's up to me to charge forward and do battle without worrying about the outcome, so that the truth can be known.

It would have been criminal for France not to respect her commitment to Poland at a time when England was finally allied with us in a common cause, as opposed to the way things had transpired over Czechoslovakia. With Hitler reigning over Europe and Italy anxious to get in on the kill, he would have attacked us anyway, in which case the British would have stayed out of it. They would simply have looked after their colonial interests, confident that the United States would back them.

No one has yet said in so many words that France was responsible for this war, but that too will come. In the meantime, they are emphasizing what they call our state of military unpreparedness, for which I am supposed to be responsible. When the time comes, I'll show them figures that prove that the French Army was far better prepared in 1939 than it was in 1914. I'll point out the disastrous errors committed by our military commanders, whose superiors are now blaming my government. They are the ones who betrayed the trust we placed in them, that could have been placed only in them.

Night has fallen, a calm, starry night. I can hear the troopers and police inspectors changing shifts. Outside, the rain is coming down. If only it would go on raining for months, so that England might be spared the bombings and a German invasion. England is my only hope.

September 8, 1940

No visits and no mail since my imprisonment. Peyrouton, the Interior Minister, has gone too far. Even condemned men have those rights. Of course, since he is indebted to me for a good part of his career, the poor fellow won't dare lift so much as a finger to grant authorization.

---

of both the dissolution of the Third Republic and the implementation of the policy of collaboration. Because of his closer ties with the Nazis and his more overtly anti-Semitic acts, he has remained a far less controversial figure than Pétain. He was tried and executed at the end of the war.

Paul Reynaud,[9] who is also under arrest here at Chazeron, asked one of the guards if there had been bars on the windows before he got here. He hadn't noticed they were brand new. Typical Parisian.

When Lebrun[10] first made the decision to call upon Reynaud, I told him that he was turning to a man who would lead us to disaster. Not long after that, in London, Reynaud wondered aloud before a flabbergasted Jean Monnet,[11] "What would have happened to France had there not been those two votes that got me elected?"

He scornfully discarded my policy of temporizing until war supplies could arrive from the United States and until our own industry could swing into gear. He absolutely had to go to war, had to do what Clemenceau had done and make his mark on history. He ran off to London and within fifteen minutes had agreed to send an expeditionary force to Norway and to mine German canals and the Rhine with newly invented British explosives.[12] I was against the idea of an expeditionary force; I preferred blockading Norwegian ports. I opposed the use of floating mines at that juncture and said I would resign if they went through with it. I was convinced there would be retaliatory strikes against our aviation industry. Chamberlain sent me a kindly worded letter to persuade me, and Churchill came all the way to Paris to work on me, but I held out.

In the Senate, Reynaud hailed the naval victory the British won at Narvik and proclaimed: "Hitler's colossal strategic miscalculation."

Even before the truth about the Norwegian expedition was known, Reynaud set about assigning responsibility for the fiasco to Gamelin.[13]

---

9. Paul Reynaud, lawyer and statesman. He was Finance Minister in Daladier's government in 1938 and Prime Minister from March through June 1940. Imprisoned in France in 1940 and subsequently in Germany, he was liberated in 1945.

10. Albert Lebrun, President of France, 1932–1940.

11. Jean Monnet, later called "the father of Europe," presided over the Franco-British Economic Coordination Committee.

12. These floating mines proved to be ineffective.

13. General Maurice Gamelin. First in his class at the Saint-Cyr Military Academy in 1893, he rose to the rank of General at age forty-four. His leadership helped forge the victory at the Marne in 1914. He performed brilliantly as a commander, first with a brigade,

Reynaud brought a list of charges against him in meetings of the Cabinet and the War Council and discredited him in the eyes of public opinion. Twice Gamelin tendered his resignation, but Lebrun refused it each time.

In May, after a series of military setbacks, Reynaud finally managed to relieve Gamelin of his command, but he kept Georges[14] in charge of military operations in the Northeast. After declaring that he would defend Paris in house-to-house fighting if he had to, he cleared out of the city without warning by eight o'clock that night. I can't figure out why he resigned in Bordeaux while he still had the backing of the majority.

To top it off, he has just sent me a message that I should put the blame on Gamelin during the pretrial proceedings.

September 9, 1940

Just finished reading Voltaire on judicial errors in the eighteenth century. I learned this morning that General Gamelin is here. He had been at his friend Gaboriau's when they picked him up. Gaboriau walked out with him to the car and told the arresting officers: "The man you have taken into custody and who is leaving with you is alive. I assume he will be alive when he gets to Chazeron."

The Vichy mafia has probably hatched this plot to "save the honor of the Army," as they used to say back in the days of the Dreyfus affair.

According to the terms of Pétain's decree, only the "immediate subordinates" of Ministers can be held accountable. Gamelin, head of the Joint Chiefs for National Defense, was directly under me in the War Ministry. If he were to disappear, no other General could be charged. Only civilians would be tried, and they would be overwhelmed by Generals who would triumph in the courtroom—after failing on the battlefield.

---

then a division. He was named Chief of Staff in 1931, Inspector General in 1935, Supreme Commander in 1938. He held the position of Chief of Staff for National Defense until May 1940. He was imprisoned by the Vichy government, tried in Riom, and subsequently imprisoned in Germany. He was liberated in 1945.

14. General Joseph Georges, Commander in Chief of Operations in Northeastern France and Army Inspector General.

General Huntziger,[15] who was the first to suffer defeat in the war, the man who lost in Sedan, is today War Minister in the Vichy government.

My "head waiter" here, the policeman who brings in my meals, is an aviator from Lorraine with 1,500 hours of flying time. He has four children in Occupied France, two of whom are prisoners. "Weather like this," he said, watching the rain come down, "is a real problem for bombardiers. If only it could keep up and protect England."

Some of the policemen were in the last war, just as I was. One of them said to me: "Why shouldn't they hold out? Didn't we hold out at Verdun under the heavy artillery shelling?"

Tuesday, September 10, 1940

No newspapers and no visits. Peyrouton has really gone too far. There's a biting, cold wind; it's already autumn. If we stay here through the winter, this room will be ice cold. Even now I have to work with my hat on and blow on my fingers.

I spotted General Gamelin from my window. He seems to have aged considerably. The guards saluted him as he passed by. I first met him in 1933 in the War Ministry, when he was Chief of Staff and Weygand[16] was head of the General Staff.[17] I found him to be cultured and amiable and gifted with a sharp, clear mind. When I went before the Supreme War Council, he joined me in supporting a plan to extend fortifications up to Dunkerque.

---

15. General Charles Huntziger was named to the Supreme War Council in 1938. In 1939, he was put in charge of the Second Army, then of the Fourth Combined Armies Sector (the Ardennes region, where the Germans broke through). He headed the French delegation at the signing of the Armistice. Pétain appointed him War Minister in 1940.

16. General Maxime Weygand, who was Marshall Foch's Chief of Staff during World War I, became Commander in Chief of the French Army in 1930. Having retired in 1935, he was recalled to active duty in 1939 to head military operations in the Mediterranean. In May 1940, he replaced Gamelin as Supreme Commander. He was Minister of National Defense under Pétain from June to September 1940 and Pétain's representative in North Africa in 1940 and 1941. The Germans had him relieved of his duties, after which, in 1942, he was imprisoned in Germany.

17. The Chief of the General Staff was responsible for preparations for war. Command in time of war was the province of the Vice President of the Supreme War Council.

He had been an officer on Joffre's command staff, both in Charleroi and at the Marne, after which he brilliantly commanded a division and an army corps. He was the Poincaré brand of republican, neither Fascist nor Royalist like some of our Generals. After he was named to head the General Staff, by either Piétri[18] or Maurin,[19] our paths crossed again in 1936. I readjusted his budget requests upward and worked out a 14 billion franc rearmament program. I got Blum to back the plan, telling him that I would not go back to the War Ministry if he refused to release the funds.

In 1937, Chautemps[20] and Bonnet[21] turned down the increased budget requests that I judged necessary for our Air Force and our antiaircraft defenses. When I became Prime Minister in 1938, I insisted that we adopt a 20 billion franc program.

Now Marshal Pétain, General Maurin, and Fabry,[22] who was War Minister then, are holding me responsible. What did *they* do between 1934 and 1936?

I tried to lower the retirement age for Generals, but President Lebrun opposed it. Out of kindness or a sense of diplomacy, General Gamelin must have intervened with Lebrun and certain Members of Parliament. The fear of "jumping into the unknown" is a veritable disease in France. It's the Commander in Chief, and he alone, who names the members of the Supreme War Council who lead our armed forces, and he alone is responsible for them.

18. François Piétri, left-wing republican Member of Parliament, several times a Minister. He aligned himself with Pétain, who appointed him Ambassador to Spain from 1940 to 1944.

19. General Joseph Maurin, War Minister in 1936.

20. Camille Chautemps, Radical-Socialist, elected Deputy in 1919. He subsequently served as Prime Minister several times prior to 1938. He was a member of both Paul Reynaud's and Marshal Pétain's Cabinets in 1940. Having been sent by Pétain on a mission to the United States, he remained there for the duration of the war.

21. Georges Bonnet, Radical-Socialist Deputy who became Minister of Foreign Affairs in 1938 and Minister of Justice in 1939. He sided with Marshal Pétain.

22. Jean Fabry, Minister of War and National Defense under Daladier in 1934.

The tenure of men over sixty-two should not have been renewed automatically. I had drawn up reform measures, but with the coming of the war, I had to put them aside.

Gamelin favored intervening on the side of Czechoslovakia in 1938. Contrary to what has been reported in the press, it was in the face of England's reluctance and the frightening inferiority of our Air Force that he gave up the idea. If Reynaud wanted to relieve Gamelin of his command on May 19, 1940, why replace him with Weygand, who had never even commanded troops between 1914 and 1918? He would have done better to choose someone with combat experience.

I see Gamelin heading back to his cell, followed by police inspectors. He never speaks to them.

I've heard he has begun writing. He should keep in mind that the best defense is an aggressive offense.

Wednesday, September 11, 1940

Worked all day, reading through articles published by either Georges Bonnet or his cronies—Berl[23] perhaps, since he was appointed by him. They're signed XXX. "We lost the war, England is being showered with bombs; the time for discretion is over." Bonnet alone saw things clearly; Bonnet alone was a "true" pacifist.

After the Germans had abruptly broken off negotiations at 8 P.M. on August 31 and invaded Poland that very night, I always assumed that they were responsible for starting the war. Now it seems that the responsible parties were England and Lord Halifax, whom Bonnet used to call his friend.

None of these articles mentions the countless memos and statements by Bonnet in which he declared that France would intervene if Poland were attacked. Even I never went that far. I stated in March that I would

23. Emanuel Berl, writer and Editor in Chief of the left-wing weekly, *Marianne*, from 1933 to 1937. In 1940, he collaborated with Pétain, penning several of the Marshal's speeches.

not go to war over Danzig, that I would do so only if Poland were threatened with destruction. Beck, the head of government, relented and said that he would not undertake any military action if Danzig proclaimed itself a part of the Reich.

Bonnet is acting in the interests of the Vichy government and its deep-rooted hatred of the English. Last winter, when I offered Bonnet a position in my government, Pétain told me that the British didn't particularly care for him. The Vichy leaders are living under the illusion that a properly orchestrated hostility toward England will earn them better treatment from the Germans. As for Bonnet, he had schemed to get himself named Vichy's Ambassador to the United States, but Bullitt[24] saw this coming and made it known that the American government would not support the nomination.

Bonnet is now singing the praises of Mussolini and Ciano,[25] probably maneuvering for the vacated ambassadorship to Rome. These articles I'm reading could not have been published without the authorization and perhaps even the assistance of the government. Nowadays, *L'Action française* is France's *Journal officiel.* They ran an article setting forth Pétain's views on education. They would do better to set forth his views on the military: his opposition to armored divisions, his belief in fixed fortifications, and so on.

All the shopkeepers in France are being asked to place a portrait of the Marshal in their windows, and *France Soir* apparently wants to organize a contest!

As for Déat,[26] he claims our imprisonment was long overdue. He was

24. William C. Bullitt, American Ambassador to France from 1936 to 1940. He was a close personal friend of both Roosevelt and Daladier. In 1944, he enlisted in the First French Army.

25. Galeazzo Ciano, close associate and son-in-law of Mussolini; Minister of Foreign Affairs.

26. Marcel Déat was elected to Parliament as a Socialist in 1932 but broke with the SFIO to launch a reformist party in 1933. He favored appeasement with Germany and authored the well-known article "Die for Danzig?" in the daily *L'Œuvre*, a vehicle for German propaganda that he took over in 1940. He headed the pro-German movement in France and as such was opposed to even Vichy's policies.

Air Force Minister under Sarraut.[27] What did Déat do on March 6, 1936, when Germany marched back in to occupy the Rhineland? How many planes did he leave us with? In 1939, he added his signature to a defeatist tract and then claimed that he had merely acceded to a request made by Lecoin[28] and signed a blank page. Frossard[29] came and pleaded with me to let the matter go, and Monzie[30] intervened on his behalf, too.

One of the workers here told me that he had seen soldiers who cried from shame when they were captured, others who laughed and sang *Madelon*, and others still who climbed on the backs of German motorcycles. Then he said: "Who knows? The people who have put you in jail just might someday end up taking your place here."

It's not for me to undermine the wonderful optimism that allows him to go about his work with a light heart.

Mandel[31] got here Tuesday night. He is ill and confined to bed.

The weather has, unfortunately, been absolutely beautiful for the last three days and London is a patchwork of smoke and flames. To be sure, the death toll is not especially high, but what about the factories, the war industry, and the landing fields? Will the mass destruction be followed by an invasion?

---

27. Albert Sarraut, Radical-Socialist, several times a Minister beginning in 1914, including Interior Minister during Daladier's third government (1938–1940) and Education Minister under Reynaud (1940). He was first named Prime Minister in 1933, then again in 1936, and was in power when Hitler moved to occupy the Rhineland. He was imprisoned in Germany in 1944 and 1945.

28. A conscientious objector.

29. Ludovic-Oscar Frossard, journalist and Socialist politician. He was Public Works Minister in Daladier's third government and Information Minister under Reynaud in 1940. He sided with Marshal Pétain in 1940.

30. Anatole de Monzie, Deputy and Senator from the Lot, several times a Minister, including Public Works Minister in Daladier's third government (1938–1940). He had a hand in bringing the Vichy regime to power.

31. Louis Georges Mandel had been Georges Clemenceau's Chief of Staff before being named Minister of the Colonies in Daladier's third government (1938–1940) and Interior Minister under Reynaud in 1940. Pétain had him imprisoned in 1940. He was subsequently deported to Germany, then in 1944 brought back to France, where he was assassinated by the Vichy Militia in Fontainebleau Forest.

I admire the British. After France fell, they could honorably have signed a peace treaty. If they can hold out three months and the United States comes to their aid, maybe the idea of a French resistance force in North Africa will crystallize again. But haven't we already given away all our planes and disarmed our Navy?

Churchill will defend England village by village, house by house. His speech was an admirable display of courage, restraint, and dignity. He has reached a height of true grandeur. Roosevelt's speech was a poor one, at least from what I can gather from the summary in the newspapers. Obviously, he has to deal with the isolationists. England is my only hope. I am filled with admiration for their pilots, who every night have to fly through heavy antiaircraft barrages on their missions over Berlin, Hamburg, and Munich, whereas the German fighter pilots have the benefit of an elaborate warning system.

Is the British Air Force being supplied by the United States? In dealing with Curtiss and later with Glenn Martin in 1938, I was struck by their low production capacity. In the contract we signed, I even agreed to pay a share of the costs for expanding their factories, their retooling, and their hangar construction. I wanted to order 10,000 planes from them. I was opposed by Paul Reynaud and those working under him. They wanted to hold on to the greater part of the Bank of France's gold so as to bolster the franc. Now that France has surrendered, I hope the Americans have given Britain the airplanes I ordered from them. It buoys me to think that the French orders placed in 1938 and during the war significantly increased America's industrial potential, and that England might be reaping the benefits at least of this French initiative. But is their industrial base up to it? That is the main issue. It takes a good year to move from putting out a prototype to factory-line mass production.

When I look over these figures, when I consider the current situation of their industry and the time it will take to increase its capacity, and then the peril that now threatens England, I am overcome with a feeling of anguish.

September 12, 1940

Everyone's bustling about. The policemen in the next room are being moved out of their quarters.

They had a real sawmill going next door. There'll be a lot less snoring coming out of there now, but there must be some reason for the change. I wonder who the next prisoner brought in will be. Léon Blum?[32] All those vicious hatchet men writing for *Le Jour* and *Le Petit Journal* have been clamoring for his arrest. It might be someone else, but not a simple General, and certainly not one of those colonels I passed on the road up from Bordeaux, who were speeding south in their sedans to save their skins.

It's raining here at the château. If only a storm could rage and never die down! Nature could level the playing field that way. If she doesn't, the battle will become more and more lopsided.

I came across an excerpt from a speech Weygand made on July 2, 1939: "I believe that the caliber of the French Army is higher today than at any other time in its history. We have the highest-quality matériel, first-rate fortifications, excellent morale, and an outstanding High Command.

"No one among us wants war. But I state firmly that if we are forced to win new battles, win them we shall."

A pity he wasn't forced to win them.

There has been a complete turnover of the policemen working here. After a full week together, we had gotten used to them. Some of them shared our views and didn't especially try to hide it. One was a former student of mine from my days of teaching history in Marseilles, a fine young man who kept telling me, "Don't let your spirits drop, keep them up." I certainly hope I'll be able to keep them up, but learning to live in the absence of freedom is a painful experience.

32. Léon Blum was a Jewish intellectual and Socialist politician who is primarily remembered as the first leader of the Popular Front government in 1936. He was deeply involved in journalism, first as one of Jaurès's collaborators on *L'Humanité* and subsequently as founder of *Le Populaire*. Following the trial in Riom, he was handed over to the Germans and deported to Buchenwald. After liberation, he returned as the head of *Le Populaire* and became Prime Minister again in 1946, concerning himself then with establishing the institutions of France's newly formed Fourth Republic.

September 13, 1940

London subjected to massive bombings. German field communiqués. German war analyses. Excerpts from German newspapers. *L'Œuvre, Le Jour, Le Petit Parisien, Le Journal*, etc., how abject our newspapers are. I'm not sure which one of them takes the prize. Only Alexandre Varenne's *La Montagne* has maintained its dignity, and I can't figure out how he's managed to keep from being arrested.

I went for my usual walk in the courtyard. When I got back, I learned that my son Jean and Dr. Mazé had been granted permission to visit me. The order stipulates that M. Jean Daladier can see his father without a police inspector present, whereas one will have to be there when I speak with Dr. Mazé. The order is signed by the illustrious Chavin, Director of the *Sûreté*. But how is that going to work, since they'll come together? Am I supposed to ask the inspector to kindly step outside when I address my son and then ask him to come back in when I turn to Mazé? And why hasn't Dulot[33] been authorized to come and see me as well?

At around 6 P.M. three automobiles pulled into the courtyard. The idea flashed through my mind that it was Léon Blum. Looking out through the barred window, I watched a wide brimmed hat, a broad mustache, and a pince-nez emerge from the lead car. Blum calmly surveyed the château. His face looked weary. It's a long drive up from Narbonne. He climbed up the steps slowly, said a few words in the room next to mine, and that was all. They've hunted down the Jew and the Socialist, the man who was responsible for the agreements signed at Matignon.[34] The fact is, there is absolutely no reason for him to be charged with anything. The plutocrats are simply paying him back for having struck fear into them in 1936.

---

33. Charles Dulot was an economist writing for the daily *Le Temps*. He was a close personal friend of Daladier.

34. In June 1936, shortly after the Popular Front came to power, Blum presided over the signing of these agreements between labor (represented by the Confédération Générale du Travail [CGT], the Communist trade union organization) and management. Management agreed to recognize labor unions and union delegates and accepted the principle of collective bargaining. Loosely used, the "Matignon agreements" refer as well to the forty-hour workweek and paid vacations, which became law at the same time.

We created the Popular Front to fight off La Roque[35] and his Croix de Feu. We took them seriously. In 1934 they were well on their way on the road to power. The Popular Front did its most effective work before 1936; after that, they were undone by the Communists. Blum's mistake was in not forcing them to listen to reason, and yet he could easily have run the government without them. But he is a Marxist who believes in the existence of social classes and in the necessity or at least the inevitability of the struggle between them. He used to love it when he was called "comrade" by those clowns from the Metal Workers' Union who refused to put in additional hours for national defense until I put an end to their factory sit-ins and their strikes. Organizing sit-ins in factories that were turning out arms for the war effort was unconscionable. The forty-hour workweek was applied much too automatically and inflexibly for a time when the Germans were working far longer days and more productively.

I think that's the key. Blum could not conceive of a Socialist leader who didn't have the backing of every workers' group, especially just after the working class had finally been able to make some claim to unity. Yet he knew full well that the Communists were insidiously maneuvering to undermine what he was doing. He could have demanded that they toe the line and they would not have put up a fight.

He was often critical of me; in fact, he twice forced me out of power, first in October 1933, then in March 1940, and both times with Flandin's[36]

35. François de La Roque, an antiparliamentarian who became president of the Croix de Feu, a right-wing veterans' association that became increasingly politicized under his leadership. He participated in the riots of February 6, 1934. When the Croix de Feu was dissolved in 1936, along with the other Fascist leagues, he founded the French Social Party (PSF). He sided with Pétain in 1940 but was subsequently imprisoned in Germany and then again in France at the end of the war. (Cf. diary entries for January 1944.)

36. Pierre-Etienne Flandin, President of the right-wing Democratic Alliance in the Chamber of Deputies. He was several times a Minister beginning in 1924 and Prime Minister in 1934–1935. He was a Minister in Marshal Pétain's government (see the diary entry for December 15, 1940). Having been forced out of the government by the Germans in 1941, he left for North Africa in 1942 and was arrested in 1943. In 1945, he was sentenced to five years of national disgrace but won a reprieve for his role in the Resistance.

approval. But he is an upright, courageous man. If any of the people now slandering him had been in his shoes the day following the Armistice, they would have taken off for the United States or South America. I learned a thing or two about such matters from Bullitt.

I haven't seen Blum since June 17 or 18, when we were together in Pomaret's[37] office. We were both very shaken by the misfortunes our country was suffering, and we hugged each other in a mutually spontaneous gesture.

I can hear him walking about next door; I can hear him very clearly. We could communicate through Morse code if we wanted, but both of us have better things to do.

September 14, 1940

The sky is clear and illuminated by the insolent brilliance of the moon. Two days from now we'll learn about more bombings and perhaps the invasion of England.

Letters mailed September 8 have just reached me today, many of them bringing words of encouragement from good, simple folk.

I got a lovely letter from my son Jean. The ordeal he's going through is making a man of him, as I had fervently hoped it would. Many of the doors that used to open for him at the slightest touch are now bolted shut. He'll learn how low men can stoop and that, in the end, nothing ever comes easily.

If Doumergue,[38] Flandin, and Laval, who knew of and in fact denounced Germany's massive rearmament, had made a serious effort to rearm the nation, it wouldn't have fallen to me, beginning in 1936, to organize the war industry and produce all the equipment with which our armies went into battle. Everything had to be built from the ground up. I

37. Charles Pomaret, Socialist Labor Minister under both Daladier and Reynaud, then Interior Minister under Marshal Pétain. He sought refuge in Switzerland.

38. Gaston Doumergue, Radical-Socialist President of France from 1924 to 1931. He took over from Daladier as Prime Minister in February 1934 and later appointed Marshal Pétain to his first Cabinet position, Minister of War.

had to fight certain management groups and certain union leaders. We explained to them how serious the situation was and that the Fascist and Nazi movements they were fulminating against in their meetings weren't going to wait for us to draw up statistical charts and debate over them.

I can still see them snickering while Belin,[39] the Vice President of the CGT, looked on approvingly, as they awaited the publication of *Syndicats*, financed with money from secret funds.

September 15, 1940

Sometime near midnight, I was awakened with a start by howling winds. To the north of us, they were twisting trees and pulling pines and cedars right out of the ground. The sky was pale, the way it is just before daybreak. Policemen stood watching the storm through windows facing south. I hope the Nazi planes ran into this weather over the Channel.

At 8 A.M. a peasant cleaning woman said to me, "What horrible weather!"

"It was a beautiful night for England," I said.

"Oh it was," she replied. "In that case, I'm all for it. They're our only hope."

In spite of her errors and her shortcomings, England has never been as popular in France as she is today. Baudouin,[40] the financier turned Minister, our man of Fascist business matters, has been making speeches that so reek of the most mindless obsequiousness toward our conquerors that they have probably reinforced our admiration for the British. Somebody must have told him, and now he has stopped. Too bad.

September 16, 1940

This was a happy day. At 10:15 this morning, my son Jean and Dr. Mazé came into my room, preceded by the stuffy, solemn warden of this Bastille.

39. René Belin, left-wing union leader who in 1940 sided with Marshal Pétain. Pétain appointed him Labor Minister.

40. Paul Baudouin, Director of the Indochina Bank. Although Paul Reynaud had appointed him Secretary of the War Council, Baudouin went on to betray Reynaud by helping to bring the Vichy regime to power. Pétain named him Minister of Foreign Affairs.

We embraced each other. So many things have happened since I was arrested at La Vernue. I asked about Dulot. Mazé said that he was infuriated with the people at the Interior Ministry who refused to grant him permission to come and see me, which tells me that he is fine.

The three of us headed down to the vegetable garden for a stroll. In a gesture of tact and sensitivity that their chief would have severely reprimanded them for, the inspectors from the *Sûreté* sat apart on a bench, smoking and chatting together idly. With his keen doctor's eye, Mazé pointed out that, as was the custom many centuries ago, the château walls had been reinforced with animal bones embedded in the sand between the stones. "Too bad they weren't human bones," my son said. "That would fit in better with present-day local color." I gave him an affectionate slap on the back and we continued on our walk around the courtyard.

Near morning's end, the warden came in to say that Jean and Mazé could stay and have lunch with me, but in the presence of an inspector from the *Sûreté.* That was not about to keep me from saying all the lovely things I had to say about the honorable Minister of the Interior and the head of the *Sûreté,* our friend Chavin, whom I had once named Prefect of the Vaucluse.

Finally they had to leave. I said good-bye to them from behind the bars, as they were crossing the courtyard. They turned several times to wave back and disappeared behind the trees near the gate. I spotted them one final time after that.

That evening, the old police inspector who had accompanied us at lunch came into my cell, smiling. "I just got back from the village. There's a wine merchant there who picks up British broadcasts. They said that the English had shot down 185 German planes. You'll see, we're going to win this thing."

Tuesday, September 17, 1940

They do what they can to jam the radio, but there's always one frequency they don't manage to block out.

This morning, a carpenter working in one of the rooms repeated to me what they were saying about our arrests on British radio. He also recited several brief passages from one of de Gaulle's speeches. "Hell of a speech!" Then he added: "Before the last war, Laval was a revolutionary and a Socialist. Now he's rich and he owns a château and a few newspapers. Contractors direct us to buy our supplies from his company."

Looking out my window, I saw Mandel go by with his topcoat open and his hands, in the gray gloves he always wears, hanging freely at his side. I could hear his clipped speech resonating in the courtyard.

He has been accused of plotting against national security. They claim he tried to foment a rebellion in Africa, financed by Jewish Moroccans, and get himself named Proconsul or something of the sort. That was just a web of lies that he tore apart in Meknès, where he was initially interrogated. I heard that the Examining Magistrate from the military, who was in charge of the case, wanted to have it thrown out.

September 19, 1940

Every newspaper is running front-page headlines announcing that General Gamelin and I have been indicted. It's a press release from the Ministry of Justice. The tactic doesn't surprise me at all. They've got to keep the Krauts and their pals happy.

September 20, 1940

Received a letter from Roger Génébrier,[41] my friend in need, as I used to call him.

Over a three-year period, from 1937 through September 1, 1939, I earmarked more than 65 billion francs for national defense, 39 billion of that to the Air Force. If the various Prime Ministers and other Ministers directly involved, General Maurin, Fabry, and those who succeeded them between 1934 and 1936, had committed just half that much to rearming the nation, the situation would have been entirely different, but it was left to me to build from the ground up and produce all the modern weaponry we had at the time of the mobilization. Needless to say, the Generals who

41. Roger Génébrier, career public official. As Daladier's associate and faithful friend, Génébrier helped him throughout his captivity and took part in Daladier's various attempts to escape.

were defeated, prodded on now by Weygand, are all doing what they can to relieve themselves of their own responsibility and place it at my feet. But not one of them ever voiced a complaint, neither on August 23 nor after that, and especially not during my visits to the front. I defy them to show me one single letter in which they expressed reservations.

One of my regrets at being locked up here is that I can't put together a dossier made up of the firsthand accounts of those who actually fought in the war. How can I be expected to prepare my defense under these conditions?

September 21, 1940

I went to Riom at 2:30 P.M. and for three hours answered questions put to me by M. Lagarde, a member of the High Court of Appeals and the Examining Magistrate[42] for the case. His mind is already made up; he shares the government's opinion. Of course they had no trouble turning up all the accommodating souls they needed: Bonnet, naturally, the Army Generals, Weygand and Alibert,[43] Baudouin, and so forth. Barthe[44] did his part by rummaging through the trash and fishing out scraps of paper.

The prosecution's argument holds that the French government in power at the time was responsible for the war. I listened to M. Lagarde tell me how I should have insisted that England begin conscripting soldiers in 1936, and that in the face of their refusal, I should have signed a treaty with Germany and Italy! What a pity M. Lagarde wasn't Foreign Minister back then. Of course, our defeat is all the explanation they need. The same M. Lagarde was surprised when I read him a series of Bonnet's declarations in which he stated that any German threat to Poland would immediately

42. For criminal matters in the French legal system, an Examining Magistrate (*juge d'instruction*) is appointed to carry out an investigation and ultimately make the determination whether to indict. In U.S. terms, he is part police detective, part Grand Jury, and part pretrial prosecutor.

43. Raphaël Alibert, member of the Conseil d'Etat, France's highest juridical body. Prior to the war, he had close ties with right-wing extremists. He had a hand in the conspiracy in Bordeaux, helping and counseling Marshal Pétain, who subsequently appointed him Minister of Justice.

44. Edouard Barthe, Socialist Deputy who aligned himself with Marshal Pétain.

trigger France's intervention. He hasn't read the blue book, or any diplomatic dispatches or documents for that matter, only the Fascist newspapers that are subsidized by the Germans: *Gringoire*, *Candide*, *L'Œuvre*, and *L'Action française*.[45]

I have no illusions. I know they've already worked out the sentence to be rendered by this special tribunal, but I have to make a stand and let the truth come out.

September 22, 1940

The bombing of London has not let up; I read a statement issued by the Lord Mayor of the city. The important question is whether England is being supplied with significant numbers of aircraft from the United States and Canada. Without that support, they'll soon run out of fighter planes. The United States seems increasingly preoccupied with Japanese imperialism. Will Japan play the part that Berlin expects it to? If England should fall before winter comes, the fleet would head for Canada, Churchill said. We might see a huge Anglo-Saxon coalition that would include the United States and the nations of the Commonwealth.

Some of the members of the *Sûreté* have been dismissed, in particular two inspectors who had said hello to me and shaken my hand. Another inspector was dismissed for having committed the grievous crime of remaining in my room with me for a few minutes while I was having dinner.

September 23, 1940

I had been looking forward to a visit from Mazé and my son Jean but spent the day waiting for them in vain.

September 24, 1940

I was doing my best to get some work done when Jean and Mazé showed up, loaded down with packages like a pair of Santa Clauses. They had been

45. All four newspapers were politically far right, antirepublican, and pro-German. Before 1939, *Gringoire* had launched a series of attacks against Daladier that featured doctored photographs.

in the South: Orange, Carpentras, Marseilles. My sister is undaunted as always, preparing for the coming winter and doing whatever is necessary to see to my son's education. They saw our friends in Orange, who have remained faithful to me.

September 25, 1940

It rained all night. Water is seeping through the roof, spreading over the parquet floors.

The Japanese have landed in Indochina and taken over the airfields. Their planes will take off from there on bombing runs over China. A communiqué from pitiful M. Baudouin explains that our realistic approach to foreign policy *is* really the best one. General Catroux[46] has been relieved of his position as Governor-General of Indochina for simply trying to defend France's interests in Asia.

De Gaulle has been beaten back in Dakar.[47] The attack was poorly organized. He must have been misled by people in his entourage.

Alibert, the Minister of Justice, whose home had been searched by the police back when the Cagoule[48] was active, hasn't lost any time. He has put through one of those good old laws that was popular during the Second Empire, a statute approved by the Marshal, instituting a court-martial at which they can try de Gaulle's accomplices. It is, needless to add, a despi-

46. General Georges Catroux, Governor-General of Indochina in 1939. In 1940, when he tried to join forces with de Gaulle, Vichy dismissed him. He commanded the Free French forces in Syria and Lebanon. In 1945, he was named Governor-General of Algeria.

47. De Gaulle's Free French forces were repelled by Vichy's military as they attempted to seize the port city of Dakar.

48. The Cagoule was the name given by the press to the Secret Committee for Revolutionary Action (CSAR), an organization operating clandestinely, under the leadership of Eugène Deloncle and the patronage of Marshal Franchet d'Esperey. They possessed large arms supplies and boasted some 10,000 military and civilian members. The organization had close ties with Commander Loustanau-Lacau (see "1944," n. 9), who, while serving as Pétain's aide, helped organize an insurrection within the Army.

cable and outrageous piece of legislation. The spirits of Trestaillons[49] must be dancing with glee.

I've heard that a piece of property in the Indre belonging to the La Rochefoucauld family has been converted into a detention center for about sixty Socialists and Radicals. They were chosen from among those who voted against dictatorship at the National Assembly session held in Vichy. Pétain is on the job and giving a good imitation of Monck.

Friday, September 27, 1940

Ribet,[50] my lawyer, came to see me this afternoon, accompanied by his wife, who is also a member of the bar. He told me that the charges against me are grotesque, that they don't stand up in the light of day. He took a great many notes, as did Mme Ribet, who is lovely, alert, and resolute, and very patriotic as well. Whereas pimps and murderers have the right to have their lawyer present while they're questioned by the Examining Magistrate, we won't enjoy such privileges. Vichy has decided that the proceedings will be closed; Ribet won't be able to attend.

Grumbach,[51] Moch,[52] and either Auriol[53] or Dormoy[54] are being formally held in that little hotel in the Indre that Courrier had gone to fix up.

---

49. Following the defeat at Waterloo, the Royalists returned to power and began exacting revenge by instituting a court-martial for Napoleon's principal military leaders. In southeastern France, this *terreur blanche* assumed the form of mob violence and was at times reminiscent of the sixteenth-century religious wars, as in Nîmes, where Protestants were slaughtered by Catholic Royalists led by a street porter calling himself Trestaillons.

50. Maurice Ribet, World War I veteran and former President of the Bar Association. He was Daladier's lawyer during the trial in Riom. He was a republican and a man of great courage. He participated in Daladier's various plans to escape and became a close personal friend.

51. Salomon Grumbach, Socialist Deputy who left for North Africa on the *Massilia* in June 1940.

52. Jules Moch, Socialist politician and member of the Resistance. Between 1945 and 1958, he held several positions as Minister: Public Works, Defense, Interior.

53. Vincent Auriol, a Socialist who became Finance Minister under Léon Blum in 1936. In Vichy, he voted against giving plenary powers to Marshal Pétain and eventually made his way to London in 1943. He headed the Foreign Affairs Committee in Algiers and later served as President of France, from 1947 to 1954.

As M. de Carbuccia[55] would say (the same M. de Carbuccia who had received a medal for a wound in his heel that he got twenty days into the last war, after which he carefully spent the next four years waiting the war out), the weeding out continues.

September 28, 1940

The Examining Magistrate from Riom's Cour Suprême has come to Chazeron with a court recorder.

He questioned me about the causes of the war, our military preparations, and the delays in arms manufacturing resulting from the nationalization of certain industries and from the laws guaranteeing a forty-hour workweek, paid time off, and so on and so forth. The defeated Generals, and above all those who were most responsible for our defeat, have written up statements said to be terribly damning. Why didn't they write them up before the war, instead of assuring me that they were prepared and confident of victory? The person who seems to have gone furthest is the one and only General Georges, who was Commander in Chief of the front lines in the Northeast, where the Germans broke through. If there were weak spots in the front lines between Sedan and Mézières, if they weren't shored up in time with reinforcements, if there wasn't adequate matériel there, who is to be held responsible for that, if not the General in command of the area and the entire northeast region?

I asked to see a copy of those statements so that I could look them over and respond to them. The Examining Magistrate explained to me that it wouldn't be possible, for reasons of national security. I told him that it was a disgrace that he and the court would have to live with forever. He

54. Marx Dormoy, a Socialist who became Junior Minister under Léon Blum in 1936, and subsequently Interior Minister in 1937–1938. He voted against giving plenary powers to Pétain. On orders from the Vichy government, he was assassinated while under house arrest, apparently by terrorist elements of the Cagoule, an organization he had actively pursued while Minister of the Interior (see diary entries for July 24 and 31, 1941).

55. Horace de Carbuccia, Editor in Chief of the far-right weekly, *Gringoire*. He supported Marshal Pétain and the politics of collaboration.

started equivocating and said that those were the government's orders. I told him that in that case I wouldn't answer any more of his questions.

This is even better than the Dreyfus affair.

September 29, 1940

I waited for Ribet, but he didn't appear, probably because automobiles are not allowed on the roads on Sundays. Reread *Les Mémoires d'outre-tombe* again, the volume with the lovely narration of Chateaubriand's meeting with Charles X in Prague.

I heard that Reynaud expects to be released on his own recognizance.

September 30, 1940

A lovely day. Jean and Mazé stepped out of the mist that has settled over this crow's nest. We spent a good three hours together and, inexplicably, without any policemen lurking around. We just left the door to the room open. It's a small miracle.

Ribet arrived. He had met with the presiding judges in the Riom court. Some of them are feeling a kind of shame at having to sit in judgment at this trial, but they'll of course do as they're ordered. We sketched out a plan for my defense. I agreed with him that the verdict really doesn't matter. The government will dictate the verdict and might even have drafted it already. What counts is that we state the truth, that we let it be known and make it a part of the record. That is how we can best serve our country.

October 1, 1940

It rained all night. There were a few snowflakes in the morning. It rained throughout the day.

October 8, 1940

I haven't kept up with this diary for a week. Afternoons have been almost entirely taken up by meetings with Ribet or whatever reading I have been able to get done in the presence of the court recorder taking down the depositions of the military leaders here. What a pathetic lot they are. How could I ever have trusted such men? Yet they all conducted themselves honorably in 1914, although they were at considerably lower ranks then. On my brief official visits to the front, each of them had expressed the utmost confidence. Now they claim that they didn't have any weapons to fight with and that the battle was lost before the first shot was fired. They alternate between whining and bellowing.

The measure that Weygand pushed through to roll back the retirement age from sixty-two to sixty-five for members of the Supreme War Council was of disastrous consequence. I tried to get it repealed in November 1936 but ran into the opposition of the President of the Republic and General Gamelin, who had been named wartime Commander in Chief and who had absolute confidence in his fellow commanders. I should have held out. Of course, at the time, our military leaders were worried, or at least pretended to be worried, about certain incidents instigated by the Communists that I in fact decisively put down. I was told that if I named a new Supreme War Council at that point I would be sowing confusion in an already unstable structure. It was a major error not to have wiped that slate clean. What an amazing accumulation of incompetent individuals! What a bunch of weepers, whiners, and tremblers! They're armchair reactionaries made for political intrigue, each of them more a warmonger than a war maker, and all of them primarily interested in growing old and collecting their sizable pensions, not to mention the handsome income they receive from the various boards of directors they sit on. Weygand once launched a brilliant offensive against the Board of Directors of the Suez Canal and came away with some 400,000 francs a year to add to what was already a comfortable pension.

Others like them have lent their skills to the war industry or more or less directly to national defense. Some have gone into optics, some into oil. Once Weygand and others had taken that route, why wouldn't those who succeeded them? How could I not have gotten rid of pathetic old officers like Dufieux,[56] Prételat, Requin, and so many others of their kind? Poor old Gamelin pleaded their case with me from 1936 to 1939. Now that he is

56. General Julien Dufieux, Inspector General of Infantry and Tanks.

in Chazeron, they have shown their thanks by attacking him more contemptibly than anyone else testifying against him, whereas, when he was Supreme Commander, they used to drip all over him with their flattery and servility.

Dufieux was always moaning because he had not been given a medal. Georges kept bowing and scraping, even though he was furious inside. Prételat came and pleaded with me to name him Military Governor of Paris (after Gouraud, a real hero, had vacated the position), swearing to me with his hand on his heart that he was a republican and a friend of Paul-Boncour[57] and Camille Chautemps. If I had pushed a little, I probably could have gotten him to swear that he was a Freemason. These men were born defeated, by virtue of their limited abilities, and they're the ones now parading through the courthouse in Riom. Each of them shows up with his list of charges, his little scraps of paper, and his big pile of crap. What a difference there is between them and the men who went into battle, like the admirable General Frère and General Touchon; what a difference between them and real fighting men like Colonel Perré, the Commander of the Second Armored Division, whose testimony, even if not entirely above reproach, is still the word of a true soldier.

To lighten things up, we turn to *L'Action française*, where I see that our favorite comedian, Charles Maurras,[58] has outdone himself—vilifying de Gaulle, the British, and Churchill. The only people he hasn't worked over are the Krauts. Then this hateful old man has the nerve to ask for contributions. He's also the only person encouraging people to turn informer. Here too, he has had his comeuppance on occasion, but what does it matter to him if he has to retract what he writes from one issue to the next—his slanderous comments have made their mark.

57. Joseph Paul-Boncour, leftist politician and former Prime Minister, who voted against the establishment of Pétain's government in 1940.

58. Writer, political theorist, member of the Académie Française, who was a strong supporter of Pétain. Maurras, a monarchist, was one of the founders of the nationalistic review *L'Action française*.

November 7, 1940[59]

On September 16, Mme Guyon, who is a close personal friend of Laval's, suggested to my secretary of many years, Mlle Mollet, that she go to see me in Chazeron; Pierre Laval would be pleased to supply her with the necessary authorizations. Mlle Mollet accepted the offer immediately; but instead of calling her back the next day, as had been agreed, Mme Guyon didn't get in touch with her again until October 2. Mme Guyon told her that she was dining with Laval that very evening and that she would call back the following day to let her know when she could make the trip. In fact, Mme Guyon didn't phone again until October 4, and then only to tell her that Laval could no longer procure the necessary authorizations. Mme Guyon carries a card with her, written in German, instructing German officials to consider her a German officer and treat her that way.

On September 20, M. Achenbach, who is with the German Embassy in Paris and whom Mlle Mollet had met, with my consent, several times before the war, called to say that he absolutely had to discuss with her certain matters of great urgency and importance.

They left together for Trouville on Saturday, September 21, at 9 A.M., accompanied by M. Jardin,[60] from the SNCF (French National Railroad). Their conversation lasted from 10 A.M. Saturday through Sunday evening. It dealt with the causes of the war, peace terms, the political climate in France, and the possibility of reuniting the country under the banner of the Radical Party! They asked about me and told her she could meet with me, after first meeting with M. Abetz, Germany's Ambassador to Paris. This is the very same Abetz that I had expelled from France as a spy before the war; now he is trying to enlist my support!

59. This is the story of the attempt by Abetz, Ribbentrop, Laval, Huntziger, Jardin, and Pétain to get Daladier to sign a document they had prepared showing Roosevelt to be a warmonger who had violated the laws of neutrality.

60. Jean Jardin, Laval's Chief of Staff in Vichy from 1941 to 1943. He was an associate of Raoul Dautry (see "1941," n. 25).

The following day, Mlle Mollet met with General Bineau[61] to apprise him of these conversations. He told her to keep him posted and, on arriving in Vichy, to inform General Huntziger, the only person with direct access to Marshal Pétain.

For several days, Achenbach, whom Mlle Mollet had advised of Mme Guyon's proposition, called to find out if she had in fact obtained the necessary papers. He had himself provided her with a Vichy pass valid for the week of October 13–20. When she spoke with him at noon on October 21 to ask him to extend it, he requested that she meet him at the Embassy immediately. There she would lunch with him and Ambassador Abetz.

Abetz had met with Laval and Alibert a day earlier. For the authorizations, he told Mlle Mollet to arrange for an appointment with Alibert as soon as she got to Vichy. Abetz and Achenbach were openly optimistic about the coming negotiations between the French and the Germans. They went back over the points they had raised in Trouville. They repeatedly asked her if there were any documents in Daladier's file proving that France had not wished to go to war, that it had done so only to fulfill a commitment, that Daladier would not have declared war had it not been for pressure from the British, who pledged complete cooperation, and had he not received the promise of American war matériel.

They said they had to have those documents by 10 A.M. the following day, October 22. Abetz knew that at 10 A.M., on the Ambassador's invitation, Laval would be leaving for a destination unknown to him and would end up face to face with Hitler in the latter's private train, somewhere in the countryside around Tours. Mlle Mollet told them that she would not be able to supply the documents in the allotted time. They pressed her to leave for Vichy and Chazeron at once. Achenbach gave her his word that Ribet's living quarters would not be searched before her return, although he knew that Ribet kept Daladier's file at his home, after having earlier entrusted it to the American Embassy in Paris.

61. General Henri Bineau was a Major General in September 1939. He was transferred to the War Minister's staff in January 1940 and subsequently became Pétain's Chief of Staff.

Mlle Mollet arrived in Vichy on October 23 but did not get to see General Huntziger until the 25th. She informed him of her conversations with the Germans. She also met with Alibert to request authorization to see me in Chazeron, but he put off giving her an answer. Then she heard that Laval wanted to see her. She went directly to his Ministry, where she was made to wait for a while before being informed that Laval had left and that she would be contacted by phone. It was not until Monday, October 28, that she learned from M. Anglade, Laval's Chief of Staff, and then from the Ministers of the Interior and of Justice, that she could meet with me in Chazeron without police inspectors present.

She got to Vichy at 5:30 that afternoon. M. Anglade told her that Brinon[62] had phoned from Paris several times in the course of the day to ask her to return there immediately, regardless of whether she had seen Prime Minister Daladier.

Nonetheless, she came to Chazeron on Tuesday morning at 8:45. I had been notified of her visit by M. Perrin, the warden of this bucolic Bastille, at 9 o'clock the previous evening. After relating all the conversations she had had, she told me pointedly that Abetz and Achenbach were in agreement with Laval and Pétain. All of them wanted a signed statement from me to be carried in the press and broadcast on the radio. I was to say that I hadn't wanted to go to war, that I had yielded under pressure from England and from the American Ambassador to Paris, who had promised to provide us with great quantities of matériel, but that now I was forced to acknowledge that England's aid had been seriously wanting just when we needed it most, and that the advice I had received from Mr. Bullitt was disastrous. Mlle Mollet showed me a typed draft of a statement drawn up along these lines, several paragraphs long. She added that Abetz and Achenbach thought the trial in Riom was absurd and that Laval and Brinon agreed. They were of a mind to let it drag on for a long time, perhaps until it was forgotten entirely. In the meantime, they could make my

62. Fernand de Brinon, newspaperman in charge of the Foreign Affairs desk at *L'Information*. He founded the Comité France-Allemagne in 1935. During the Occupation years, he was Vichy's representative to the German authorities in Paris. He was executed by firing squad in 1947.

stay at Chazeron far more enjoyable, starting right now, and allow someone close to me to keep me company, and so on. After thanking Mlle Mollet for her trouble, I explained to her that if I ever signed a statement of that sort, I might perhaps regain my freedom, but I would surely lose my honor.

What do they expect to get out of this statement? First, it would breathe new life into the violently anti-British campaign being waged in French and German-Italian newspapers. Second, it would seriously implicate Bullitt, who is Roosevelt's personal friend, and present them both as having insidiously played a role in our declaration of war and as presently trying to bring the United States into it.

Wilkie is running on a strict isolationist platform. He is also apparently from a family of German immigrants, which has probably given Ribbentrop the wrong idea.

Would such a statement from me mean better peace terms for France? The German diplomatic corps might actually be working at cross-purposes with the Reich's High Command, as was the case after Sadowa in 1866 and after Paris surrendered in 1871. It's perfectly conceivable that they would prefer a policy of "collaboration," to use the term in vogue in the French press, which has not yet figured out that this would guarantee Germany control over our principal industries—metallurgy, mechanical engineering, chemical engineering—and reduce France to the state of a colony or a protectorate. As an approach, it is far less spectacular for the victor and far less painful for the defeated nation than territorial annexation, but it is far more effective. It undermines virtually all the material and moral reasons for revenge. In any event, even if I am wrong about the "better peace terms" that Abetz and Achenbach are dangling in front of us, a statement signed by me and issued from my prison cell in Chazeron would have no sway with public or foreign opinion, in fact, no real impact whatsoever. Besides which, isn't the policy of collaboration already a fait accompli, given the meetings between Laval and Hitler and Pétain and Hitler? Isn't our entire press urging us to collaborate? Hasn't Marshal Pétain, with his last two public statements, already incriminated the government that was in office in September 1939 and condemned the pressure that was supposedly brought to bear on us by England and international

Jewry? On the other hand, it is true that he has yet to implicate Bullitt and Roosevelt.

I told Mlle Mollet that I could certainly be mistaken and that if a statement from me could have a positive effect on the terms of the peace treaty, then in the sole interest of France, I was prepared to sign it unconditionally, but the French government would have to make that request of me. I was under the impression that Pétain was aware of these dealings, and Mlle Mollet confirmed that he was.

She left on Tuesday October 29 at around 10:30 in the morning and headed back to Paris in the Vice Premier's car, the same one that had brought her down to Chazeron. She was driven directly to the German Embassy and arrived there at 8 P.M. Achenbach apologized for having hastened her return to Paris, a decision with which he claimed Laval had concurred. Had she brought back any documents? Had she obtained a statement from me about the pressure exerted by England and the war supplies promised by the United States? They were needed to justify the lenient peace terms that were being negotiated. Mlle Mollet replied that she had not had the time to address issues of such moment. Achenbach caustically shot back that the other matter was no longer of interest to him, adding that counselor Ribet had come to see him on October 28 to request an extension for his pass to Vichy, and that in the course of their conversation, he asked Ribet whether there were any documents in the file relative to Britain's pressure and America's promise. Ribet had assured him there weren't. When Achenbach insisted that he return immediately to Chazeron to obtain the statement he wanted from me, Ribet had categorically refused.

At midnight on October 29, four German police officers showed up at Ribet's door with a search warrant. Having expected it, he had asked the head of the bar association to be present during the search. After poring over the file until 4 in the morning, the German officers left, taking with them a considerable number of documents. They came back for the remainder of the file the following morning around 10:30.

Mlle Mollet was to meet with either Laval or Brinon that same day, October 30. She saw Brinon and asked him to accompany her to the German Embassy. Achenbach told her that the search had been ordered only after she had failed to bring back a signed statement. The search had turned up a significant number of diplomatic memoranda and provided evidence proving that Bullitt had frequently met with Prime Minister Daladier in the days preceding the war. Abetz was present for part of the discussion. He claimed that Laval shared their views on all of this. Then he asked Mlle Mollet to head back down to Chazeron and emphasize to me how important this statement would be for France.

Mlle Mollet thus returned to Vichy on October 31. Laval had twice called his Chief of Staff Anglade from Paris to verify that the formalities for her meeting with me had been arranged. He had also called Peyrouton and requested that Mlle Mollet be allowed to see me without delay. Peyrouton admitted her and provided her with the necessary papers.

I met with Mlle Mollet at 10:30 on the morning of November 1, without having been told she was coming. She left me as dusk was falling, to keep an appointment with Laval in Vichy. She recounted the events of her last few days, adding that Laval had asked her to insist that I prepare a statement dealing with the causes of the war and assigning responsibility for it. She said that he would have it published immediately and that it would be in the best interests of the nation. It would be the first act of Franco-German collaboration and in the eyes of the Germans would justify more generous peace terms.

I thanked her and dictated a few comments, which she took down in shorthand, to be typed up when she got back. I noted first that at the same time as negotiations were being carried out with me, unannounced searches were being carried out at my lawyer's residence; second, that while Laval was imploring me to write that statement, his personal friends were submitting affidavits against me in Riom, in utter bad faith and with a hatred that spoke volumes. To be sure, this would in no way prevent me from performing any act whatsoever that might bring France more favorable peace terms, but I did not believe that the statement I had been asked to prepare would produce such a result.

I felt they should once and for all back up what they were saying with specifics. Until I was shown otherwise, I wouldn't believe that there was any more to it than what had been said in Marshal Pétain's speech and Laval's communiqué. Besides, I intended to present my account of what brought on the war in the courthouse in Riom. I added, moreover, that I could not submit a statement of that kind without first having it reviewed by my lawyer, and that it seemed reasonable to conclude that if Mlle Mollet had been asked to make a second trip to Chazeron, documents implicating Bullitt, the United States, and England had not been found among my papers. I said to her, "If you should see Laval this evening, who you said is expecting you, tell him to call counselor Ribet so that he can head back down here."

I was surprised to see Mlle Mollet again at 6 P.M. on November 2. She had not met with Laval but had managed to see General Huntziger. It was the latter's opinion that although the statement might conceivably be used against me at the Riom trial, it could improve chances for better peace terms for France. Mlle Mollet departed at 7:30. I have since learned that she and Mme Guyon were driven in an official limousine to Moulins, where a German officer and a car had been waiting for them since that morning. Because they arrived so late, they spent the night in a hotel before leaving on the following morning, Sunday, November 3.

On November 5, a Paris correspondent for the *Moniteur*, Laval's newspaper, submitted an interview Brinon had given to a "representative from the American press" with insinuations about the role played by "an unidentified high-ranking American official" and emphasizing France's position, etc., etc. It was a pathetic, ineffectual article. Anyway, it came too late; Roosevelt was reelected on November 5.[63]

I have not had to wait long to find out what all this means for me. The head warden has begun the paperwork for my incarceration.[64]

63. In this way, acting in secret, Daladier was able to buy a little time by misleading both the Germans and Vichy. Roosevelt would be grateful to him for this throughout the war.

64. In the middle of November, Daladier, together with Blum, Gamelin, and La Chambre (see "1941," n. 16), were transferred to a country estate at Bourassol, a few miles south of Riom. The dilapidated old house served as their new prison.

December 15, 1940

Yesterday morning, the head prison guard, looking furtive, came to me and said: "I heard that there was a sensational arrest in Vichy. And Mussolini has been assassinated and the Prince of Piedmont is marching on Rome." The Italians are intelligent and well informed, but I found it hard to believe that piece of "news."

As for the "sensational arrest," I had absolutely no doubt that the story was true and bet him that it was Laval, an opinion shared by Master Sergeant Passemard, an old, intelligent, kindly veteran of the Moroccan campaign, who is always trying to be helpful. He had been telling me these last few days that Laval's popularity had plummeted, even in the Puy-de-Dôme, where he is from, and that virtually everyone, from the upper middle class to the workers, was accusing him of corrupting officials, taking payoffs, and misappropriating public funds. British radio announcers keep labeling him a traitor, and British broadcasts are given considerable credit in Unoccupied France, just as they are in the Occupied Zone. I had also heard that Flandin had come down and set up residence in Vichy a few days ago. In the desert, when you see a jackal leave his lair, you know he's smelled the sweet scent of a carcass ... or a Minister's portfolio.

One of the young guards, Guichard, brought in the newspapers and left without saying a word. There were blaring headlines: "Pierre Laval No Longer a Member of the Government." "Laval Replaced as Foreign Affairs Minister by Pierre-Etienne Flandin." Marshal Pétain had given an eight-sentence speech on the radio that was reprinted in the newspapers: "I have just made a decision that I believe to be in the best interests of the nation. M. Pierre Laval is no longer a member of my Cabinet. M. Pierre-Etienne Flandin is now in charge of Foreign Affairs. Constitutional Act Number 4, naming my successor, is hereby rescinded. I have resolved to make this decision for compelling political reasons. It in no way alters our relationship with Germany. I remain at the helm. The National Revolution will continue to move forward." And as every drama has its light moment, a philosophy professor named Chevalier, with a particular gift for looking ridiculous, who has wooed and worn down every Cabinet for the last twenty years with his tedious flattery and platitudes, has been named Minister of Education.

So once again we find ourselves in the midst of a ministerial crisis. Ever since the creation of the New Order, whose continuity and administrative stability were to be its cornerstones, not a month has gone by without some palace revolution to purge a few Ministers and replace them with others. But today's is the most significant crisis of all. It is not just Vice Premier Laval who has been unseated, it's the heir apparent, the man Pétain had designated to succeed him when he leaves us for that paradise that awaits cautious warriors such as he. Laval had surrounded himself with men of action, all of them, like himself, thoroughly devoid of scruples, and they proved to be of tremendous help to him in Bordeaux, in anesthetizing Albert Lebrun and putting a stranglehold on Paul Reynaud and then, after they joined forces with the general staffs of Pétain and Weygand, in handing France over to the Germans. He spent more time in Paris than in Vichy, the better to play up to the victors, but in doing so—a fatal slip—he left the field open for his enemies, Alibert and Peyrouton. Laval was the man behind Déat's articles and similar pieces in other papers attacking his adversaries and the Royalist- and church-dominated government in Vichy. All of this he did as the German Ambassador, whom he had managed to win over, looked on indulgently. His frequent stays in Paris led to his downfall. How could he not have understood that? And when that little rat Montigny,[65] with his menacing mouth and his twisted nose, abandoned the Laval ship a few days earlier, how could the sly lord of Châteldon have failed to see the ominous meaning of that?

Peyrouton and Alibert would never have been able to accomplish this without the help of the coterie of officers in civilian clothes who surround and manipulate Pétain. Laval had threatened both of these Ministers, without ever translating talk into action, which is the ultimate act of imprudence. None of these people liked him. They found him insolent, vulgar, and underhanded. They were bruised by his appointment as heir apparent, and black and blue from the blows delivered by Déat and the pro-Laval press in Paris. But who would have guessed that the Marshal

65. Jean Montigny, unaffiliated member of the Left and close associate of President Caillaux. In Vichy, he voted to give Pétain plenary powers and was later named to the Conseil National, Vichy's pseudo-parliament.

himself, who ever since Doumergue's death had been young Laval's trump card, his associate and accomplice through all the twists and turns of French politics, who would ever have guessed that he would desert the cunning Auvergnard and throw him to the wolves, when he owed him so much? No one would have believed it possible. Apparently Pétain and his entourage finally made up their minds to do something about the domestic political situation.

Laval was toppled because he worked exclusively to promote his own interests. He saw himself as a führer, like Hitler or Mussolini, at the head of a one-party system, a French National Socialist Party, with Déat as a sort of party ideologist. National socialism or socialist nationalism, the name reads the same backwards and forwards—like Laval's.

"Compelling political reasons," Marshal Pétain is supposed to have said. I can't imagine any other kind. He specifically denied any departure from the policy of collaboration with Germany. Bringing in Flandin adds respectability. He was already pro-Hitler before the war, whereas Laval first adopted that line in Bordeaux. Besides, Hitler was consulted by Pétain about Flandin and approved the appointment. Our great patriot Pétain actually solicited the approval of the conquering enemy before naming his Foreign Minister. No French government in history ever stooped so low. Last of all, the Constitution that the National Revolution has been assembling piece by piece since July of this year is now the subject of an operation aimed at "arresting the spread." They've disposed not only of the heir apparent but of the very idea of having one. Should M. Pétain return to tending his olive trees or be called by the Lord, his successor will be chosen directly from among the members of the Cabinet. That's one fine conclave we can look forward to. In the meantime, they'll continue to be at each other's throats.

I never really got to know Pierre Laval until 1926, when we were both members of Briand's Cabinet.[66] In 1914, although he was barely thirty-one years old, he stayed riveted to his seat in the Chamber of Deputies. He re-

66. Aristide Briand, Socialist statesman, twenty-three times a Minister, Prime Minister eleven times.

mained there throughout the war, without ever once displaying a desire to breathe in the air of the trenches. At least he never gave a patriotic speech.

In truth, he quickly became a proponent of peace at any cost and, without involving himself directly, supported the Socialist Deputies and other Socialist Party members who went to Kienthal at the height of the war to confer with elected representatives from Germany. A little later, faced with the prospect of a long, drawn-out war, in a speech on the floor of Parliament that is painful to read today, he lent his support to a peace conference in Stockholm with Germany, sponsored by Socialists from a number of countries. This poor revolutionary Socialist, who could barely pay for the clothes on his back, suddenly became fabulously wealthy at the end of the war, at a time when many war profiteers were seeing their fortunes reduced to the subsistence level or going bankrupt. Their estates had been placed, as it were, in Laval's personal receivership.

He had had dealings with Stavisky,[67] who once presented him with a magnificent painting that hung in Villa Saïd, Laval's beautiful house on the Avenue du Bois, in appreciation for either his arbitrating some matter or his offering legal counsel. By intervening with Assistant Prosecutor Albert Prince, he had obtained a long series of postponements that amounted to a virtual dismissal of the case against Stavisky, which was of considerable benefit to the Foncière, headed by his friend Hudelot, a former Prefect. It later surfaced that these postponements had benefited Stavisky as much as they had Hudelot, and that disclosure led directly to Prince's suicide, which the Royalist clique naturally represented as a murder perpetrated by either the Freemasons or the police.

Laval was able to involve himself in these various machinations, once he had shed his Socialist garb, as Minister of Justice in the Briand-Painlevé government. Before the war, he was the capitalists' choice to defend their interests from within the government.

When he became Prime Minister, he held on to power for a time by buying off some of the more mediocre and compliant Deputies in Parliament. His associate Stora was specifically assigned to transact this dirty

67. Serge Alexandre, alias Sacha Stavisky, the man responsible for the financial scandal that served as a pretext for the riots of February 6, 1934.

business, and he did so masterfully. Laval used his position to enrich the people who backed him and, of course, himself, as in 1935 when he instituted the so-called deflationary policy, which consisted of lowering the wages and retirement benefits for people of modest means, thus carrying us out of an economic crisis on the backs of the neediest. With his hatred both for French democracy, which had never forgiven him for the values he had renounced, and for England and the United States, which had always viewed him with suspicion, he was also a voice within the government for international fascism. He acted as if he were Mussolini's friend; during the war in Ethiopia, he kept up a personal correspondence with him, which I had occasion to read while at the Quai d'Orsay, all of which placed him in a highly compromising situation. Officially, he upheld the League of Nations vote to impose economic sanctions on Italy, but in practice he did all he could to render the sanctions meaningless. After 1936, he became a constant table companion of, first, the Italian Ambassador, then, the Spanish Ambassador, and defended the interests of both of these countries against those of his own. In 1939, he voted in favor of war allocations but sided with Montigny, Brinon, Tixier-Vignancour, and the other defeatists on the Comité France-Allemagne, although he did so far more adroitly than any of the others.

France's defeat in July finally brought Laval his revenge and his triumph. In Bordeaux, he was able to achieve in the political arena what Pétain and Weygand had managed with the military: getting France to capitulate. He stormed into the Cabinet room with a group of defeatist Senators and Deputies behind him and put on a show of intimidation that he had been working up since May 19. Then, once a shattered Paul Reynaud had stepped aside, Laval set his sights on the seat of power, and as a result of the cowardice of the leaders of the Republic, instead of being thrown into jail with his accomplices, he became the virtual head of the government overseeing the capitulation. In a cynical book entitled, as one might imagine, *Toute La Vérité* (The whole truth), Montigny extols the victory of Laval and his gang. These days, he must be having it pulled off the shelves.

Was Laval actually arrested, as rumor has had it for the last two days? It wouldn't surprise me. Our conquering enemies have no reason at all to show him special consideration. They might be intimidated by his capacity for intrigue, although with Parliament having fallen into disgrace, he has become an infinitely less dangerous man. When there is no bargaining to be done, when there are no men to be bought and sold, there is little room for Laval to display his great talents, which are essentially those of a horse trader. He doesn't need a speaker's platform to be effective; in fact, he is generally ill at ease there, especially when launching extemporaneously into a heated debate. He prefers the back corridors of power and those parliamentary sessions that go on for hours, where he can flatter and corrupt and promise whomever he meets a few thousand francs, or civil service jobs, or a few positions as court reporter, or a Minister's portfolio or two. If Pétain has decided to bring down the man to whom he owes so much, clearly that man is no longer to be feared.

It might be a mistake for Flandin to start celebrating his newfound success. His career might turn out to be shorter than he expects, even if he did send congratulatory telegrams to Hitler and Mussolini two years ago.

December 17, 1940

Otto Abetz, Germany's Ambassador to France, arrived in Vichy on Monday evening, December 16. He was received the following morning at 10 o'clock by Marshal Pétain, in the Sévigné Pavilion. An infantry guard gave him military honors.

"The Chief of State invited him to an official luncheon in his honor, attended by Admiral Darlan, Minister of the Navy; General Huntziger, War Minister; and M. Baudouin, Special Counsel to the Executive." The Germans have remained loyal to their servants and their accomplices, the kind of loyalty common among thieves. Abetz stepped off the train in Vichy and was immediately surrounded by more than a dozen machine gun-toting German soldiers and policemen, who escorted him everywhere. I doubt very much that Abetz beat around the bush with Pétain. He must have demanded from him what Laval had already conceded: unobstructed passage across French territory for 300,000 German soldiers headed for Italy.

I have learned from one of the people who came to see me that Abetz met with Pierre Laval during the afternoon following yesterday's luncheon.

December 18, 1940

Today's newspapers are carrying the following item: "Marshal Pétain has met with Pierre Laval to discuss the general state of the nation." What a farce! They have put together a board of directors chaired by Darlan, with Huntziger and Flandin as vice chairs.

Darlan met with Hitler in his private train, near Beauvais. The skillfully worded terms of the Armistice worked out in June 1940 are long forgotten. The Germans keep piling on the demands, and Darlan and Pétain are their willing servants.

1941

January 2, 1941

As I reflect on the American elections and Roosevelt's new term, I am reminded of what Bullitt once told me, that Roosevelt would really be in a position to intervene in the war only if he were returned to office a third time.

There is no denying that the Americans harbored ill feelings about France's refusal to settle her debts from 1914–1918, or that they campaigned against us strenuously. In a phone conversation with Roosevelt in 1939, I went as far as to tell him that I wanted to pay them back what we owed. He laughed and said: "What for? I'd just put your check in the safe and never cash it."

January 7, 1941

Yesterday, having been elected President of the great American republic for a third time, Roosevelt went up to Capitol Hill and spoke to the Congress.

At a time when heroic England has refused Hitler's offers of peace and is alone in waging a debilitating war in the air and at sea, at a time when so many statesmen elsewhere have resigned themselves to the situation or become accomplices in it, Roosevelt hurled defiance at the world's dictators. He has been untiring in his skillful efforts to bring American public opinion to support his views. He has come an incredible way since his first term.

This marks the definitive break of the United States with the arrogant, isolationist policy that brought about the downfall of the League of Nations and was one of the essential causes of the second world war.

January 10, 1941

Why haven't Herriot[1] and Jeanneney[2] convened parliamentary sessions? What are they afraid of? It was their duty to do so.

January 21, 1941

The German-Soviet Pact has been reinforced. The "alliance cemented in blood" during the war against Poland is being further strengthened by significantly increased shipments of oil and wheat. The USSR has become vital to the Third Reich's interests and its principal supplier. These shipments have effectively neutralized the Allied blockade.

February 1, 1941

9:30 A.M. Ribet and Mazé. Once again we discussed the causes of the war and compared Bonnet's phone calls, which have been doctored, with the telegrams included in the blue book.

The Germans deliberately sought war; they made it inevitable. They were convinced, moreover, that they would be able to break the ties between France and England. I now believe that that was the point of the Italian proposal calling for a conference similar to the one held in Munich.

What really transpired between Ribbentrop and Bonnet in Paris in 1938? Which one of them is lying? From December to August, Bonnet acted as if Ribbentrop were the liar. It seems to me the opposite is true. I should review the facts to see if Bonnet didn't actually encourage Ribbentrop's Eastern European ventures.

For years now, I have thought that only America's industrial capacity could match Germany's. America's isolationism represented the greatest danger facing Western democracies. I was the first to order planes, convinced as I was that American industry, once its productive machinery had been set into motion, could match Germany's aviation production within two or three years.

1. Edouard Herriot, President of the Chamber of Deputies

2. Jules Jeanneney, President of the Senate.

Thanks to my friendship with Ambassador Bullitt, who is as much a Frenchman as the most patriotic Frenchman among us, I was able to get Roosevelt to intervene personally on several occasions. In particular, in May and October 1938, he helped us overcome a great many obstacles that confronted us when we tried to place orders with American factories. I can still hear that kindly voice of his, when I called him from Ambassador Bullitt's office, expressing his affection for France and offering me encouragement in my efforts on behalf of an Army fighting for freedom.

At the beginning of the summer of 1939, I was sufficiently worried about the worsening international situation to wonder whether the time had not come for America to step in on the side of Great Britain and France. In carefully worded terms, Bullitt put the question to Roosevelt and brought back his answer. Roosevelt felt that the majority of Americans still believed that the United States could, and should, stay out of European affairs.

Needless to say, the President said he would work through diplomatic channels to defend peace and the freedom of nations. If the situation were to worsen in Europe, he said, he would be able to intervene only after being reelected, and that could come to pass only if his health allowed him to run for a third term. That time is now at hand. On July 1, 1939, there were only 174,000 men in military service in America, all of them volunteers, spread out over 130 bases. There were few officers, and their equipment dated almost entirely from the last war. Beginning in May 1940, after Roosevelt's messages to Congress on May 16 and 31, the Army received appropriations of $2 billion, and that amount was subsequently increased in congressional committees. On September 16, the draft was put into effect, with the result that the number of men in service jumped almost instantly to more than 1.5 million. The training of officers was organized on a broad scale, and America's industry, with its enormous war potential, took on the task of equipping its Army, under the leadership of General Marshall, the Commander in Chief.

America's aviation industry had excellent prototypes to work with. They had been mass produced in 1938, thanks largely to orders placed first by France, then Britain, and finally France and Britain jointly.

By June 1940, French orders for American-built planes had risen to more than $500 million worth. So why did the French Air Force receive no more than 500 planes—all of them in fact excellent—during the war? In compliance with American laws, we had to wait three months before the embargo prohibiting the export of war supplies could be lifted, but the resulting delay could easily have been made up for by shipping parts, under the protection of our Navy. They could have shipped them to Caen and Bordeaux, where we had set up heavily protected assembly plants. Unfortunately, the French Air Force's High Command—without consulting me, but probably with the approval of the War Ministry—had them routed instead to Casablanca, where no such assembly plants existed, where everything had to be improvised. That is the principal reason—which I didn't know until it was too late—why France received only 500 planes. We could have been supplied with 1,000 warplanes to fight alongside our 2,000 modern French aircraft in May and June 1940. That is, if the Air Force High Command had wanted us to.

On June 16, 1940, Colonel Jacquin, the head of the French Air Force's mission in the United States, learned that the new government in Bordeaux was going to ask for an armistice. Pétain had the power to revoke Jacquin's authority or invalidate previously made agreements at any time. He could even have issued an order for the planes to remain in the United States. Colonel Jacquin courageously moved to transfer all the French contracts to the British purchasing commission that Purvis headed, thus allowing the war matériel intended for France to go to England, at a time that was critical for her salvation, in fact for all of Europe's salvation.

Prior to July 1, 1940, France and Britain, having been threatened and then attacked by Hitler, ordered a total of 10,000 aircraft. In the two and a half years from January 1, 1938, to June 30, 1940, the U.S. Army and Navy ordered a mere 5,400. In July 1940, the monthly output moved up to 550, and it continued increasing thereafter.[3]

In his admirable inaugural address, Roosevelt announced America's departure from her isolationist policies, her desire to become the arsenal of

3. In a speech given after the war, Edward R. Stettinius, Roosevelt's Secretary of State, noted that it was as a result of French orders first placed in 1938 that American industry had been able to supply the Allied forces beginning in 1942.

democratic nations, increase her military strength, and guarantee freedom of the high seas. This will surely draw America into war with Germany.

February 7, 1941

Meanwhile, Mazé went to Clermont Ferrand to meet with the brilliant young commander Jacquot,[4] who told him: "Everything I have learned has confirmed my belief that enormous blunders were committed by our military commanders. In fact, by the third day of the attack, there were no military commanders. There were neither orders nor chains of command. Large amounts of equipment were stupidly left sitting in hangars. The will to lead was totally absent.

"There was a complete collapse in French military thinking. The men who were responsible for the defeat are the men now reorganizing the French Army of the Armistice. General Huntziger, who bears greater responsibility than anyone, is absolutely loathed by everyone in the military."

They have been hounding Jacquot, but he is determined either to go on thinking his own thoughts or leave the Army.

Ribet and Mazé returned the same day, accompanied by Croquez, a young lawyer and veteran of the fighting in Belgium. He came to tell me that at 12:30 P.M. British radio had announced the capture of Benghazi.

What joy, what brightness filled this prison.

I spread the news, which everyone welcomed enthusiastically. The prisoners and the guards share similar feelings. In fact, the guards would much prefer to have other inmates, and they would be happy to handpick them from among the members of the Cabinet, or even better, from among those traitors in Paris who have been playing the role of Germany's valets for several years now. We have been following the British advance

4. Pierre-Elie Jacquot, a captain in the Third Bureau (Operations), who was in constant contact with Edouard Daladier's staff. He commanded a battalion from April to June 1940, then joined the Army's Resistance Forces (L'Organisation de la Résistance de l'Armée) in 1942. After having served as a colonel in the *maquis* and then in the Alsace-Lorraine brigade, he joined the First French Army. By the end of his career, he was an Army General and Commander of NATO forces at Fontainebleau.

together on maps. Their progress is continuing, through Eritrea, Somalia, and Abyssinia.

After my guests had left, I asked to see the prison guard, that is, the kindly prison guard, Passemard, who had been away that afternoon. I gave him the news. He gushed with emotion and shook my hand. We raised a glass to the capture of Benghazi.

February 25, 1941

Darlan has been handed the reins of power.

Mazé, who knew Darlan well, met with him for an hour in Vichy, at 11:30 in the morning. "I have seen Hitler; he agrees that I should be Prime Minister," Darlan said. "We have to defeat our enemy, England."

He was undoubtedly a less than scrupulous broker in the negotiations. The Germans have been pressuring Pétain, but then so have the Americans, for opposite reasons. Pétain had told Chauvel,[5] with whom he's very close, that he was afraid of the Germans.

Flandin has resigned. In an exchange of letters, the Marshal told him that "he had nobly sacrificed himself for France." That was followed by an item from the Havas News Agency exalting Flandin's sacrifice. It's a kind of hedge against the future, not unlike the waiting game almost everyone was playing before the war. By 1936, Flandin had been prepared to surrender anything he had.

Since then, we have been deluged with constitutional decrees. Darlan has been appointed Minister of Foreign Affairs, Minister of the Radio and the Press, and Minister of the Navy; he has even been named France's heir apparent, just as they use to do in the days of Hugh Capet.

In the meantime, all sorts of laudatory statements have been issued about his career and his person: "The grandson and great-grandson of sailors." Who were the parents?

5. Henry Chauvel, Edouard Daladier's second lawyer.

March 18, 1941

Saw Blum when he came back from his walk. He showed me the text of Roosevelt's speech, the speech of a nation at war: "The Vital Bridge Across the Ocean."

I find Blum's optimism frightening.

The British government will move to Canada if it has to, and the naval battle will continue.

The Krauts have opposed the release of Reynaud and Mandel. As for the Vichy government, they are annoyed with themselves for having demanded that we be put on trial, but they won't take any new initiatives. In Paris, they have freed Langeron.[6] He had been forced into retirement while he was being held prisoner!

March 20, 1941

Was absolutely delighted to see Roger Génébrier, a fine and faithful friend, the finest of them all. He recounted Peyrouton's ignominious attempts to have him demoted just because he is a friend of mine. Peyrouton had tried the same thing with his brother-in-law, Monnier, who is also a Prefect and one of my friends.

March 21, 1941

Ribet came by again at 10:30 A.M. He had met with Lagarde, who confirmed that the government was in the process of rewriting Constitutional Act Number 7, granting itself the authority to postpone ongoing trials whenever the interests of the nation so dictate. A fine example of new French law!

The truth is that neither Pétain, Darlan, nor Barthélemy[7] wants anything to do with this trial, even though they are the ones who initiated it. They are afraid there will be unavoidable incidents and a public indictment of military Generals. This is what Ribet thinks, and he so informed Le Trocquer, Blum's attorney.

6. Roger Langeron, former Prefect of Police.

7. Joseph Barthélemy, Minister of Justice.

Génébrier related the admissions and platitudes that constituted his talk with Chavin, better known as "tricky Chavin." Like so many others, Chavin and Peyrouton, who were once at my feet, have been unrelenting in their efforts to destroy the people close to me, who were once their friends.

March 23, 1941

Had lunch with Génébrier. He was in Paris the day after the government headed south. He found the city mournful, completely deserted. He had a difficult time finding an open restaurant. At the War Ministry, where it had been decided that an officer would remain in charge, he saw only one NCO, two antiriot policemen at the door, and, in place of the guard inside, Maury, the chauffeur!

He also told me about a conversation Ribet had had with Bonnet at the Hotel Pailleret. Bonnet was scared and spent two hours trying to defend his position. He protested that he had remained absolutely faithful to me, and so on and so forth. He added that the government was doing everything it could to save Gamelin. Some of my friends have joined up with the Vichy government.

Daridan[8] came to see me this evening. We went for a stroll in the courtyard. He is a good man. He spoke to me about the new Europe and the plans the English supposedly have for the future.

March 24, 1941

It has been rainy and bitter cold, but this afternoon, while he was out for his walk, Blum managed to find some sunlight. Sitting there with his beret,

8. Jean Daridan, career diplomat who prior to the war held positions on the staffs of Herriot and Paul-Boncour. After having worked with the French Committee of National Liberation in Algiers, he served in numerous government capacities, among them Ambassador to Japan and India. He was a close associate of Daladier's and provided the footnotes for the French edition of this diary. The English-language annotations are substantially based on his.

his long skinny body and walrus mustache, which is almost entirely white, he looked very much the prophet of Israel.

3 P.M. Théry and I discussed our reasons for being hopeful. He brought me copies of the depositions given by Happish and General Corap. The latter was not questioned once about the defeat at the Meuse. I continued reading Gamelin's memoirs and found his loyalty wanting on more than one occasion.

Then my former associate, Léonard,[9] arrived. He too had met with Commander Jacquot, who felt that Germany versus an England backed by the United States would be an even match. Jacquot stated that everyone in the Army was hostile to the High Command. It is his hope that if Germany should falter, the new French Army could play some role. There is enough equipment to arm 300,000 men. Young men have been sneaking illegally into the Unoccupied Zone to enlist.

Léonard said that in the winter of 1939, Pétain had told him that he didn't think Gamelin was fit to command the French Army. Léonard said that he then asked : "Have you informed Prime Minister Daladier of this?" Pétain answered, "No, let him handle it."

March 27, 1941

Mazé has been held up by the Germans, who have refused to give him a pass. The orders they have placed with French factories are for immediate delivery only, for the war will have been won by year's end, or so they claim.

Received a strange letter from a woman in Brittany telling me that the Germans had laid waste to the woods near her home and hidden camouflaged cannons and trucks there. Is this just one part of a more extensive operation in preparation for an impending invasion of England?

Chauvel confirmed that a new law has been enacted, modifying Constitutional Act Number 7 and allowing for the postponement of trials.

9. Roger Léonard, member of Edouard Daladier's staff from 1938 to 1940.

"That should be a good thing both for France and for you," he added. That is not my opinion.

Read a thoroughly disgraceful interview with de Brinon.

March 28, 1941

When the guard left his post momentarily, Spanien, one of Blum's lawyers, took advantage of the situation and stopped off to see me, after leaving his client. Blum wanted him to inform me of the coup d'état in Belgrade. Peter II is setting up a new government that will include every political party. Is this merely a matter of internal politics, or will it undermine their pact with Hitler and Mussolini? Whatever the case, it is a magnificent example of a popular uprising.

Blum, however, went even further, with his prophetic imagination conjuring images of a "German Army threatened on its right flank by the Greeks and on the left by the Turks." He gives me the shivers.

The British took Keran and Harrar at the very time Italian communiqués were claiming that all attacks there had been repelled.

March 28, 1941, afternoon

At 3 P.M. Théry came to see me at the prosecutor's request. He was flushed and visibly ill at ease. A few smoked sardines and a glass of the cognac Génébrier had brought me helped him find the nerve to show me an important document, one that they refuse to give me a copy of, on grounds of national security! "But," he said, "you can make your own copy."

It was the deposition of Colonel Rivet, a good man whom I knew well. He stated that the number of German tanks actually engaged in the Battle of France on May 10 was at most 3,600.[10] Well, on that same date, we had 3,000 tanks, with superior armor plating and superior weaponry. This is a vital document. The first part of it includes a rather hypocritical letter from Picquendar. Had our commanders done their duty, there is no reason why we should have been defeated.

10. In Vichy and even in London, the figure generally cited was 8,000. There were actually fewer than 3,000.

April 1, 1941

The Italian Navy has suffered another defeat in the Mediterranean. The Italian squadron was spotted by the RAF off the southwest coast of Crete. The *Littorio* was hit by a bomb and fled. The English squadron gave chase and sank three cruisers and two torpedo boats.

What overblown ideas we had about Italian naval power before the war. The Franco-British plan to secure the Mediterranean called for the entire French fleet and 200,000 tons of British shipping. This proves once again that we should have continued fighting in North Africa. We could have knocked out the Italians in a matter of weeks.

In 1939, I drew up a plan for the occupation of Salonika ... but the British were against it. They held certain illusions about Italy and wanted at all costs to appease her with concessions, French concessions, naturally.

3 P.M. Théry returned. He lives in Douai and has four kids. He was a prisoner in Germany in 1914. His father was mistreated by the Germans and eventually died from the abuse. He brought me greetings from the President and Vice President of the Army's National Federation of Volunteers.

April 6, 1941

Jean came. He has been a little discouraged by life in his high school in Marseilles. He kept coming back to this idea he has about going to England to enlist.

2 P.M. One of the guards, Lelauze, told me that Germany had attacked Yugoslavia. Belgrade is being bombed. Greece is at war; Thrace is occupied. Those are two great peoples.

Blum told me through his window that Hitler was going to run into the same kind of quagmire there that defeated Napoleon in Russia. I pointed out to him that this was a Russia with a network of roads and railroads and with aircraft flying overhead.

April 7, 1941

French newspapers have confirmed the German invasion of Greece and Yugoslavia.

Hitler claims, naturally, that Germany is merely defending herself against the Greek ogre and the Serbian bear that have attacked her. Anyone who doesn't revere slavery is an enemy of peace.

Russia had signed a nonaggression pact with Yugoslavia on the very day the Germans invaded.

The English have taken Addis Ababa. The Duke of Aosta and his Army have fled the city and taken refuge in the mountains. There are strikes and factory sit-ins in America, just as there were in France in 1936, and they are just as unconscionable.

In reading the newspapers, I learned that my apartment in Paris had been ransacked.

April 14, 1941

In spite of Blum's prophecies, the Yugoslav Army has been routed; they were taken by surprise in the middle of their mobilization efforts. There was a severe shortage of modern equipment. Just as in France and Poland, those Yugoslavs who either believed in Hitler or were on his payroll had a major hand in it. Bulgaria and Hungary are rushing in to get a share of the spoils.

Stalin and Matsuoka[11] have signed a treaty of friendship and nonaggression, leaving Japan free to take on the Americans.

I saw Blum with his daughter from my window. He remains optimistic. He thinks that the Sino-Russian pact has no real meaning. He also said that Yugoslavia and Greece could hold out for a month. He believes what he wants to believe.

April 15, 1941

The saddest day of all. According to a dispatch reprinted in *La Montagne*, the British are evacuating their troops from Greece.

I sent the following note to Blum: "Now Crete has fallen.

"Did you notice that the English neglected to destroy their airfields in the Northwest of the island prior to the German invasion?

---

11. Matsuoka Yosuke, Japanese Minister.

"I have a bad feeling about this.

"I fear that if American warships don't start protecting British convoys, the British government will have to retreat to Canada this summer.

"How could the 40,000 British soldiers stationed on Crete not successfully defend it?

"As for Admiral Darlan's speech, I think it is the work of a jackal. What about you?"

Blum sent back the following reply: "I saw in *La Montagne* that the criticism leveled against the English commanders, although by no means groundless, came from the Air and Sea Editor of the *Sunday Times*. Generals are the same everywhere.

"My feelings about the situation are not negative. Iraq was won back without a shot fired, which is a vital point; Hitler has got a lot riding on the Iraqi card. It took the Germans twelve full days of uninterrupted fighting to take Crete, with the English struggling under the worst conditions imaginable.

"With regard to the protection of convoys, Roosevelt made his position absolutely clear in the copy of the speech I gave you. It will be a good many weeks, in fact probably months, before they'll be able to attack England again.

"As for Admiral Darlan's speech, that is another matter entirely. I found it even more reprehensible than the previous one, but I interpret it differently from the way you do. First of all, it seems to me that his main idea is to put the Marshal in an untenable position. The Admiral believes that his time has come and he is growing impatient. Moreover, Germany's repeated attempts to provoke a split between England and France and between the United States and France are not signs of strength, quite the opposite. ... They show just how much the Germans need us.

"We now find Germany more and more deeply involved in a peripheral action in the Mediterranean, one that she would have given anything to avoid; it is costing her in troops, in troop carriers, in oil, and most of all, in time. She has had to postpone indefinitely launching a single, decisive strike, which has become increasingly risky. Months have gone by already. Read Roosevelt's speech again and take heart, the way he has."

In the April 13 issue of the *Journal de Genève*, René Payot offers a defense of Pétain in the following terms: "We must rally round our leader. ... The Armistice was the least harmful solution for the nation. ... The French psyche had been so perverted that it would have been impossible for us to follow the Queen of Holland's example and refuse to capitulate. ... The Marshal has opted for a reasonable approach, instead of a jingoistic one."

He went on to say that the actions de Gaulle was engaged in were dangerous for France and that peace alone could allow us to rebuild ourselves morally and materially, etc., etc.[12]

April 22, 1941

Jacomet,[13] the former Inspector General, has arrived. He too is to be interned here with us. He is accused of having failed to fulfill his professional obligations. I had heard that he was coming and so informed the guards, with the idea of offering him some small consolation.

I spotted him near the entrance. His back was hunched, his face pale, and his eyes looked hollow with fatigue. He seemed to be in a profound state of depression. The shock has apparently had serious consequences, or so I fear.

I asked my lawyers, Ribet and Chauvel, to go and give him my regards. Jacomet insisted on seeing me. I had them tell him that I would try to talk with him from my window tomorrow, when he went out for his walk. He assured me profusely of his undying loyalty. It all makes me very sad.

Word has it that the Germans have been exerting pressure to bring Laval back to head the government, which would carry with it the return of some 500,000 French prisoners, easier passage at the line separating Occupied France from the Unoccupied Zone, and probably the opportu-

12. In 1944 and 1945, the same Payot would be writing in the same newspaper as a fervent advocate of de Gaulle (see diary entry for January 6, 1945).

13. Robert Jacomet, Army Inspector General and Secretary-General at the National Defense Ministry until June 1940. He is one of the principal figures responsible for France's rearmament.

nity for the opening of preliminary peace talks. There might even be a secret clause in the deal calling for France's active participation in the fight against England, our former ally.

In fact, it appears that the German divisions in Cyrenaica moved across Bizerte and Tunisia.

This time, Laval will make himself out to be the adversary of the military establishment and a democrat seeking to bring Parliament together to govern with him in a cooperative effort.

He requested that Daridan come and see him, and Chauvel, too, in other words, my friends. He would like to have the support of the Radical Party. Laval is probably behind the party's convention in Nîmes, which he has organized to pull the wool over their eyes.

April 27, 1941

Swastikas are flying over the Acropolis!

Génébrier told me about the Radical Party convention in Nîmes. Few of my friends have remained faithful to me. Even Fabre, who owes me everything, wanted to attend. Maurice Sarraut[14] boldly wrote an article condemning the event. It had been organized behind the scenes by Vichy, to hoodwink the Radicals.

Mazé came; he had been in Brest. The English bombed the port and then the docks, inflicting serious damage to the *Scharnhorst* and the *Gneisenau* and various German installations in the city.

May 6, 1941

Blum called to me in the course of his walk in the courtyard. I opened my window and we chatted through the bars.

"Did you know that Iraq has been at war with England for the last two days?"

I said to him, "In my opinion, that is a serious blow." Then I added, "Mosul and the oil pipeline there are of major importance to the British fleet and their forces in Egypt. There is no doubt in my mind that these

14. Maurice Sarraut, owner and Editor in Chief of *La Dépêche de Toulouse*.

operations have been carried out by German and Italian troops. They have succeeded in bypassing Turkey. British reinforcements will have to be drawn from their troops in Egypt, who are already dangerously thin, and precisely at a time when Rommel's Army is being built up."

I told him that to my mind, American industry was not moving fast enough; they were turning out a mere 500 bombers a month and only 300 for England. As I saw it, that made for a very bad situation indeed. Blum would have none of it. He found support for his views in the fact that Hitler was no longer predicting victory by the end of the year.

"But Hitler never said that," I said to him. "That was Goebbels!" No matter. Nothing could shake the great prophet. He believed that the Iraqi business would be resolved in two days' time.

We spoke about the way Chavin, the Director of the *Sûreté*, had been denying us the right to have visitors. Chavin is avenging himself for all the kind things I did for him while he was under me.

Then we got around to talking about Vuillemin[15] and Guy La Chambre.[16] Blum has nothing but contempt for my former Minister, because of the perfidious comments about me that run through his deposition. He too was saddened to see Jacomet laid so low. I told Blum that he was doing much better and that he seemed to have gotten over the initial shock of being interned.

I watched Blum as he walked away in his handsome dark blue jacket and his gray hat. He looked incredibly youthful. If you want to grow old and do it right, you either have to remain optimistic like him, or egotistical like Pétain, or maybe both.

May 8, 1941

I managed to have a word with Blum and said to him: "The news from Vichy is not good. They have relaxed restrictions governing the movement

15. General Joseph Vuillemin, Air Force Chief of Staff and Commander in Chief of the Air Force 1938–1940.

16. Guy La Chambre, Radical-Socialist Member of Parliament. He was Air Force Minister in Daladier's third government (1938–1940). He voted in favor of granting Marshal Pétain plenary powers. He was imprisoned by Pétain in 1941.

of merchandise and currency across the line separating the two zones. From now on they'll allow regular postcards to go through. And the war debt will be reduced by 100 million francs per day. Hallelujah! In exchange, France will simply have to turn over Bizerte, Dakar, and Syria to the Germans."

Our sense of honor should prohibit us from doing anything whatsoever against our allies. We have become a nation of cutthroats. England is surrounded in the eastern Mediterranean and the Middle East. Gibraltar is threatened, and the route to the Cape has been cut off.

May 9, 1941

An item from the Havas News Agency sings the praises of Darlan and hails the greatest victory won since June 1940. After Montoire, our efforts at collaboration had produced nothing really positive. Fortunately, Darlan appeared on the scene. *Fiat lux*—how incredibly despicable!

In America, someone finally demonstrated a clear perception of the situation: Stimson, in a speech. As for Roosevelt, he has made progress. Let's just hope it is not too late and that they will finally start supplying England in significant quantities.

Jacomet has fallen prey to an idée fixe. I explained to him the real reasons for his incarceration. Every member of the Joint Chiefs is out to get him. He hasn't even had a chance to see Picquendar's new depositions attacking him.

May 10, 1941

I took great pleasure in reading Amédée Thierry's wonderful essays about the beginnings of monasticism in 1866 issues of *La Revue des deux mondes*. Read about Saint Jerome and the heresies in Early Christianity.

Was taken with Saint Jerome's admirable talent. He was a magnificent writer, capable of a dense, clear, and vigorous dialectic. Read his polemic with Augustine over the "Jewish bent" of Saint Peter's and Saint Paul's views and his exchanges with Rufin about Origen. Read about the life and impassioned movements of Early Christianity, about the breakup and the subversion of the Roman Empire, which dropped into the hands of the barbarians like rotten fruit falling from a tree, all of it recounted with the capture and pillaging of Rome merely as backdrop.

For the monks and the clerics, the City of God was far more important.

It made me think about my studies. After getting the *agrégation* in history, I began working on a thesis on Carolingian abbeys. Where has all that work gone? Why did I ever give it up? It could have brought me considerable pleasure. I could have been a historian instead of the eternal Sisyphus that every statesman is. I should have listened to Martonne.

Read some wonderful essays on the wars between the German states. The parallels between Bismarck and Hitler are obvious: their common desire to gain control over all of Europe progressively, and France's and England's blindness to it.

May 11, 1941

Paul Reynaud's birthday. It is also Joan of Arc day. The last celebration took place on May 11, 1939, with a military parade. *L'Action française*,[17] La Roque, Doriot[18] and some warmed over Catholics cheered their hearts out. I wonder why democratic parties have always eschewed this great celebration?

May 12, 1941

Passemard, the kindly guard, told me about the Joan of Arc festivities in Riom. A lot of people turned out. The school children all went to mass and to the stadium. There were a great many priests, too. Passemard saw people singing the *Marseillaise* who not that long before had been singing the Communist *Internationale* with their fists raised in the air. This is exactly what the Veterans' Legion does; it is the single-party-system party Déat

17. A Royalist newspaper, violently racist, supportive of Vichy and collaboration.

18. Jacques Doriot, who, before founding the French People's Party (the Parti Populaire Français, the PPF) in 1936, had been a union organizer and a Communist. During the war, he launched the Legion of French Volunteers (the Légion des Volontaires Francais, the LVF) to fight Russia alongside Germany. He wore the German uniform and took refuge in Germany in 1945, where he died under circumstances that remain unclear.

would like to have, but run by Doriotists and Royalists. And it's a lot shrewder than setting up an overtly Nazi party.

Fascism has surreptitiously settled in under the colors of the war veterans by virtue of their monopoly over certain privileges (ration cards, pensions, etc.). That is why the Royalists and other groups are fighting to get control over Déat.

May 15, 1941

Clapier[19] came to see me for the first time since I was arrested. Finding the moral courage for a mere visit apparently required months of prolonged reflection. From just after the last war, he followed me throughout my career as Director of my Cabinet. I made him what he is. He didn't even answer my telegram from Morocco in June 1940, sent via Hutin and the Navy, asking him to keep me informed about what was going on in France. He hid out at his place in La Bastide, then went back to Paris, knowing full well that my situation was critical and that we had to go on fighting in North Africa. He is a gullible man of bovine dullness, but a diligent worker with solid common sense and a man very easy to get along with, in spite of his conceit. My wife was right in her judgment of him.

He was very close to Darlan, who courted and flattered him to get into my good graces. In fact, it was Darlan who got him the pass that allowed him to come and see me.

May 16, 1941

Clapier came back at 11:30. He had seen Lagarde, who at first refused to allow him to see me again. He finally relented, although not without taking some measure of revenge—he had Lesueur and Baraveau question him. He will have to come back at 3 P.M. and give a deposition, after which he won't be able to return anymore. Prior to this trial, I knew very little about the legal world. I certainly know how it works now.

19. Marcel Clapier, who was associated with Edouard Daladier from 1920 on, was Daladier's Chief of Staff in 1940.

Chauvel came by at 5 P.M., but he had not seen Jean. He and Herriot were in the same train compartment, but they couldn't talk because they weren't alone. Herriot was wearing an old cap and looked fatter and older.

He had also met Wilhem, who before the war had obtained franchise rights for Krupp's all-terrain vehicle. They were magnificent machines. From 1935 to 1937, Colonel Lefèvre, who was at Vincennes, while claiming he was delighted with the vehicles, kept insisting on so many changes that after having complied with a few of his demands, Krupp and Wilhem finally gave up the idea of producing them in France.

Around midnight, I heard loud noises coming from bus and truck engines and saw armed, helmeted gendarmes in battle gear.

May 18, 1941

I have been in bed. Read Henri Bidou's *Paris.* It is a huge catalogue, with neither unity nor life to it, a massive, failed effort. It relates the history of the growth of Paris and the opening of new thoroughfares, but without any sense of the grandeur of the subject matter.

Worth remembering are the strikes that took place under Napoleon. There were some seventy to ninety thousand apolitical workers in Paris then. In the middle of a crisis, Napoleon is supposed to have said to Chaptal: "A man who can't find work is prey to any subversive who comes along. He can be led to revolt. I am more afraid of insurrections that come about because people don't have enough to eat than I am of a battle against two hundred thousand men."

Construction workers struck in 1806. In 1809, they struck at the Arc de Triomphe to get two additional paid hours of work, which they subsequently lost.

There was a strike during the coronation and, later, on the construction site at Notre-Dame. They ended up getting raises.

May 19, 1941

Things are happening in Bourassol. There were more gendarmes on motorcycles and in trucks, and fighter planes flying overhead, all apparently because the Cagoulards have been bragging that they are going to kidnap us and administer their own brand of justice. I have my doubts. I rather suspect that the government wants to get out from under the accusation that they are being too kind toward us. The government is afraid of *Gringoire*, *L'Œuvre*, and *Le Matin*.

May 20, 1941

German planes have landed in Syria, provoking a sharp reaction from England and the United States, where Roosevelt issued a statement that was a lot tougher than the one that appeared in the French press.

I think that Darlan and Pétain have made their decision and have effectively excluded Laval for the moment. They are pursuing his policies with perhaps even greater servility toward Hitler than Laval showed.

Blum explained to me the reason for all the gendarmes bustling about. It seems that stores of weapons hidden by the Cagoulards at the home of a certain Dr. Martin[20] have been discovered. Martin and Filhol, the killer of the Rosselli brothers, had bragged about pulling something off in Bourassol. Filhol is being actively sought everywhere, whereas Martin is in Vichy, as everyone knows. He is being kept there as bait.

In Syria, General Dentz[21] says that France will retain its control. … Ribet and Croquez came around 3 P.M. *Le Pilori* and *Le Matin* are trying to mold public opinion by publishing articles against the Jews and the Freemasons, who, according to them, are more and more entrenched in Vichy's Ministries. The politicians who were responsible for France's defeat will not even be brought to justice, etc., etc. These are the same blackmailers who have been on Hitler's payroll for a long time.

May 24, 1941

A speech of Darlan's was broadcast on the radio.

Back when Blum was the head of the government, Darlan tried every approach he could think of with Blum, Gasnier-Duparc, and me to get himself appointed head of the General Staff of the Navy. He would have

20. Dr. Henri Martin, one of the leaders of the Cagoule.

21. General Henri Dentz, Vichy's Commander of French forces in Syria.

liked to be named to the position before the departure of Admiral Durand-Viel, who was the target of his unrelenting sarcasm.

He also schemed to get himself named Admiral of the Fleet and even Head of the Joint Chiefs, which was absurd.

During my trip to Tunisia, he was constantly licking my boots. On August 26, 1939, he uttered not one word against our policy of support for Poland. In June of 1940, he cabled Noguès to have a personal command post set up in North Africa. The man's ambition knows no bounds. He outwitted Laval by fawning before Hitler even more than Laval himself.

I heard that Lagarde, one of the judges at the court of Riom, found Darlan's speech admirable.

May 26, 1941

The *Hood* has been sunk by the *Bismarck*. The British Navy suffered heavy losses. The Germans have widened their beachhead in Crete.

May 27, 1941

Wonderful article by Montégut in *La Revue des deux mondes* about Laurence Sterne, "the most ordinary man of genius ever." His *Sentimental Journey* is a true masterpiece. It gives you everything about the France of Louis XV: the good life in Paris and London, Diderot, Crébillon …

At 9 P.M. Passemard came to tell me that the British had sunk the *Bismarck*. From my room I could hear Blum shouting, " Hip, hip hurrah!"

May 28, 1941

Roosevelt made a speech on May 27. Blum showed me an unabridged version of it. His resolve is firmer than ever. He laid out what a world dominated by the Nazis would look like and skillfully showed how the standard of living of Americans would decline, how there would be a loss of independence and an end to the American way of life.

May 31, 1941

Pierre and Marie won't get here before 11 P.M. I'll have to ask Lagarde for permission for Pierre to speak with his own father. The last time they came, he informed them that a four-day visit was too long. He pretended to be consulting my file, which he had laid out on his desk, probably for the effect it would have on my young son.

The police here have been relieved. They assembled at noon but didn't leave until 3 P.M.; the Army hasn't changed. I went for my walk in the cesspool the courtyard has become. I was closely watched by a policeman and a guard. Hard to tell which of the two of them is the less polite. The guard is impolite in a more direct and insolent way. All week long, there have been more planes flying over Bourassol than there were over Sedan during the battle of the Meuse. They are rehearsing for Pétain's upcoming review of the military at Aulnat.

Read a fascinating article by Renan in *La Revue des deux mondes* (1866) about Joachim de Flore and the "Eternal Gospel": the rule of the Holy Spirit versus the simony and the lifestyles of the clergy.

He talks about the reasons for the Reformation that existed three centuries before Luther, about the eleventh- and thirteenth-century Renaissance movements and how colossal an error it is to reduce the Middle Ages to a monolithic period. He points out that the passion of the time was a burning one, but one limited in scope, and speaks of the Greek influences on Joachim de Flore and his disciples. "The Lord will raise his sword against the German empire, for it has been hard and cruel toward us." The monks Gérard and Léonard were sentenced to life in an underground prison, where Gérard died. His body was buried in the corner of the garden they used as a garbage dump.

June 1, 1941

Gamelin has taken communion for a second time, the first having been this past Easter.

A handicapped priest arrived by car at 8 A.M. with a portable altar, like the ones we had at the front. It would all be rather moving if Gamelin were actually sincere. Before the war, he was not a practicing Catholic and often mentioned his friendship with Sarraut. He added that if he had been a civilian he would have been a Radical. He converted in Chazeron. Legueu related the following exchange with the priest: "Father, can you teach me a short prayer that I could recite in the evenings while meditating." Somewhat embarrassed, the priest answered: "There is the 'Our Father. ... ' Let's recite it together," but Gamelin had forgotten it.

When he got to "Forgive us our trespasses as we forgive those who have trespassed against us," Gamelin said, "I'll never forgive Daladier." "You will have to," the priest told him. "Otherwise the prayer makes no sense." So Gamelin recited the sentence he had balked at.

I wondered what I had done to Gamelin, whom I had always supported, often at a cost to myself, and even when he was in the wrong. In reading his memoirs and the testimony he has given, I came to understand that what he holds against me are the official minutes of the meeting that took place on August 23, 1939, which indicate that all the people present voted in favor of our going to war.

His religious conversion has been followed by a political one. Gamelin now has the nerve to write that he merely went along with the government's decision to go to war and that he personally had been opposed to it. In truth, he advocated declaring war in September 1938; he even advised me not to divulge the actual state of our Air Force to the British. If I wanted to, I could have his letter included in the Examining Magistrate's dossier. With regard to Poland, he told me that it would be a great dishonor for France to refuse to come to its aid. Such is the measure of the man. I can't say that the rest of them are any better, but can they possibly be as hypocritical? I had always been struck by Gamelin's flabby handshake.

June 9, 1941

Sensational news: British and Gaullist forces have crossed the border into Syria.

June 10, 1941

Not a peep out of Pétain or Darlan. It is hard to understand.

June 11, 1941

Today is Saint Barnaby's day. Barnaby was the nickname we gave Pitous, my orderly during the War of 1914–1918. At 10 A.M. Jean brought me news that Blum later confirmed in a note: It would appear that the British and the Gaullist forces have encountered no resistance in Syria.

Darlan's latest speech made no mention of the Gaullist attack in Syria. He simply offered a sniveling justification of France's collaboration, with the Marshal portrayed as its leading proponent, naturally. He came up with this sordid turn of phrase: "Presiding over our defeat."

Jean said good-bye to me at 7 P.M. He'll get back to Marseilles at about 4 in the morning.

June 13, 1941

There has been fighting in Syria. And they said there weren't any Germans there.

June 15, 1941

Mazé came here from Brest, where he said that young men are being executed frequently. Mayor Gorjeu and a priest are forced to witness the executions, as are the mothers, fathers, brothers, and sisters of the condemned men. The priest tries to get them to keep their spirits up by telling them they are dying as good Christians and Frenchmen. They are dying as heroes.

June 20, 1941

Chauvel thinks that there will be war between the Russians and the Germans. This was the information he picked up from Ostrorog and a number of officers.

June 21, 1941

I passed on to Blum the news that Chauvel had brought me. He answered with a note and by giving me a copy of today's *Journal de Genève*. Is war between Russia and Germany imminent?

Blum's note, as handed to me by the guard, follows: "Thank you. I am sending you a copy of today's issue of the *Journal de Genève*. Take a look at the last page, with Vichy's correspondence relative to the conflict between Germany and Russia.

"British radio broadcast an ultimatum issued by Germany this morning. I have the feeling that Hitler wants to bring the situation to a head, whereas Stalin wants to drag it out.

"As for the events in Syria, I still have the impression that the operation will soon be brought to a close. There is a lot of bluffing going on.

"With regard to the trial, have you read, included in what Gamelin's come up with most recently, the copy of the letter Admiral Darlan sent him on September 17, 1938? It makes absolutely devastating reading now. If Admiral Herr gets to see it, it will not make him change his opinion of Darlan.

"The heat is killing me. My 'apartment' is absolutely unbearable.

"Best wishes, fraternal wishes. L.B."

June 22, 1941

I was coming back half naked from lying out in the sun, which I do during the time I am allotted for a walk, when a white dove came and landed on my head!

4 P.M. Mazé came here by bike. He had gone and waited for Lagarde after mass to ask him for a pass to see me, which Lagarde graciously gave him. With Germany having declared war on Russia, life at Bourassol will improve during the next few days.

Mazé traveled in trains bursting with "legionnaires," "fellows," and "youth group members." They were going to rally in Limoges, Aubusson, and all the other cities Pétain plans to visit. These are the military extras who do the cheering.

In Orange and Carpentras, Mazé saw our friends again, not all of whom have remained faithful.

He left for Paris at 2 A.M. to work on the plan from within the Occupied Zone.[22]

Alone in my cell this evening, I reflected at leisure on the events of the day.

22. The reference is to a plan to escape to England.

At 10 o'clock this morning, Renée Blum[23] informed us of the declaration of war Hitler had sent to Stalin. The guards and the gendarmes in Bourassol were as enthusiastic about it as the prisoners.

If Stalin had been allied with us in September 1939, as I repeatedly proposed to him, we wouldn't be caught in the Nazi nightmare today.

I spotted Gamelin from my window—unnoteworthy.

Once again the French Communists are going to be forced to "follow the Party line." They are going to be forced to become patriots again. Hitler has said that "Russia will be beaten, Russia will be crushed." Of course, Napoleon made it to Moscow and what did it get him? Most important is that England will benefit from a respite. In a release to the Havas News Agency, Vichy expressed its approval of the actions taken by Hitler, the man defending order against the evils of Bolshevism.

June 26, 1941

According to British radio, the fighting in Russia is fierce. It will be a number of days before we can get a clear idea of any kind.

June 29, 1941

I had one last lunch with Roger Génébrier. He left me at 4:30 to meet with Léonard at the *Café des Voyageurs* but came back at 6:30. I was surprised to see him again. He brought me two important pieces of information: Colonel Rivet, who has debunked the myth of the 7,000 tanks used in the German offensive, is prepared to testify and produce precise figures. Secondly, Jacquot has finished his interviews with two hundred heads of military units in which he inquired about the orders they had received from their superiors. The results are devastating. We didn't lose the war because of a lack of matériel; we lost it because of the mind-boggling incompetence of military leaders mired in the past.

23. Léon Blum's daughter-in-law.

July 1, 1941

2 P.M. I was visited by Guichard, a Deputy from the Vaucluse. He brought me cherries, a pipe, a pouch of tobacco, a pack of Boyard cigarettes, a box of matches, and a flask of brandy. He let me know how valuable it all was by telling me how much trouble he had had getting them. He thought my setup wasn't bad at all. Did he just come out of sympathy, or more likely curiosity, or was it out of a desire to be able to tell everyone about it back in the Vaucluse?

July 2, 1941

Pierre arrived unexpectedly at 11 A.M. while I was waiting for Ribet. He has grown thin and pale. He is a good-natured boy, so much like his mother. We talked about his studies and what he has been reading and working on, and for a few minutes I became a professor again. He seemed to like me in that role. We talked about Russia, England, and America. He remains a rabid Gaullist.

Ribet came around four that afternoon. We discussed the trial. People in Paris are beginning to see through it. The fellow in the cloakroom at the courthouse asked him, "How's Edouard doing?" and added, "I used to be a Communist, but now I'm all for him."

July 3, 1941

People have nothing but scorn for the French newspapers run by the Germans, especially for Déat. The French Hitlerites—Camelots du Roi, Doriotists, Cagoulards, revolutionaries in uniform, and mindless fanatics supporting totalitarian regimes—are all at one another's throats.

Ribet brought with him several different newspapers of this ilk, written by the visionary cranks working with Châteaubriand at *La Gerbe*, the scum at *Pilori*, who had already sold out before the war, Luchaire[24] and his

24. Jean Luchaire, Radical journalist. He launched the weekly *Notre Temps*, for which Otto Abetz wrote and which the German government subsidized from 1936 to 1939, then founded *Les Nouveaux Temps*. After 1940, he became the behind-the-scenes liaison between Laval and Abetz. He took refuge in Germany in 1944 and was executed in 1946.

cronies at the *Nouveaux Temps*, who have been taking payoffs forever, and of course the lily-livered Déat, who wanted peace right away, along with a few other little turds. That Déat is furious with the Veterans' Legion, which has become the only recognized political party, is comical, as every instance of a cuckold's fury is comical.

At around 3 P.M. the Ribets came to see me. We drew up a request for my provisional release and a letter to Pétain. I have no illusions about the outcome, but I'll wait and see. I had drafted a forceful, aggressive letter, but Ribet thought I should tone it down, which is the way the final version came out. I am not too happy about it.

Ribet met with Lagarde, who is considerably put out now at having to sit in judgment of this case. "We are in a terrible predicament," he told Ribet. "We have to act both as examining magistrate and judge. The situation is filled with pitfalls." Then he proceeded to rattle off all the practical difficulties without ever once elevating the discussion to matters of principle. He suggested that Barthélemy include in the Constitution he is drafting a High Court composed of magistrates elected by the High Court of Appeals, the Conseil d'Etat, and the Veterans' Legion. The court in Riom would function as an investigative commission. Not a word of these exchanges was reported to Allard this morning.

They absolutely loathe Darlan in Paris. He would like to use Hitler's methods to do what Hitler did, that is, bring all of France to march in step. But Hitler won majority support in Germany in free elections, by appealing to nationalist feelings and denouncing the Treaty of Versailles, and by decrying unemployment and calling for economic expansion. Darlan, in contrast, comes across like a servile partisan of surrender, a traitor, the man who is organizing France so that the Krauts can squeeze the most out of her. It is the very difference that sets the Restoration of 1814–1815 apart from the one that took place under Louis-Napoléon in 1852.

From here on in, the German thrust into Russia will advance very quickly to Petrograd, Moscow, and Kiev, with the Stuka dive-bombers undoubtedly playing a major role. Vuillemin wouldn't believe me when I told him of the panic the Stukas could create. What's worse, this is an aircraft that was invented by a Frenchman.

July 4, 1941

5 P.M. I saw Jacomet in the courtyard with his wife. As soon as he noticed me at the window, he came over and started talking about the trial, which is the only subject of conversation he is capable of. He has undertaken a huge project that could turn out to have considerable impact. What was the reason for the delays between the time the decision to order equipment was made and the signing of those contracts? Jacomet places responsibility squarely at the feet of Castelnau, who was in charge of that department. Castelnau was the engineer General who had Deloncle (a Cagoulard) freed at the time of the mobilization and got him a position in an armory under Dautry's jurisdiction.[25] Dautry felt uncomfortable enough to have him transferred to a Naval armory.

July 5, 1941

Darlan has dismissed Gasnier-Duparc, the Mayor of Saint-Malo, and made a number of harsh comments about his opposition to the great work of the National Revolution. They were old friends and neighbors, too. Gasnier had even pushed through Darlan's appointment as head of the General Staff of the Navy six months early.

Stalin is reported to have said that if necessary, he'll set up the command position of the Russian front in the Urals.

July 6, 1941

Vichy. Various War Tribunals have been sentencing people to three-year prison terms for possession of Communist tracts. Similar sentences were handed down for people who had maligned the Head of State.

Read excerpts from Stalin's speech in the July 5 *Journal de Genève*, which we received today. What a sorry explanation he offers for the German-Soviet Pact of August 23, 1939. Absolutely shameful! It is all so inept, with the exception of those moments when he falls back on Kutuzov.

25. Raoul Dautry, Arms Minister under Daladier. He was a former executive officer of the SNCF, the French National Railroad.

Jacomet thinks the Russians will draw the Germans all the way back to the Urals, but he is mainly thinking about the trial and all the bribing Brandt did. From what he says, Reibel,[26] a Senator, was Brandt's attorney, as was Bénazet,[27] who received some 50,000 francs from the Lorraine Corporation by bragging to them that he was the one who had got their tractors chosen. There was also the story General Sthelé told about a letter Bénazet had stolen.

Vichy's War Minister has reduced Jacomet's status to that of an "imprisoned officer," with a salary of 2,500 francs a month. And he has got his wife, his daughter, and his two grandchildren in Riom!

Monday, July 7, 1941

Ribet came back from Vals. He is defending Bretty's[28] and Mandel's interests. The latter's apartment has been taken over by an Anti-Jewry Board. Mandel has his own lawyer, who doesn't have the nerve to defend his client. He is not the only one.

Saw a photograph of Chautemps with his two- or three-year-old son in his arms. He got the pose just right. What a self-satisfied look. The country can fall apart ...

Tuesday, July 8, 1941

Spent a wonderful afternoon with Jeanne Boucoiran.[29] Offie[30] keeps sending me American-made products, with the best wishes of Bullitt. Got a whole shipload via diplomatic pouch. I am touched by their undying consideration.

26. Claude Reibel, Deputy, then Senator and a member of the Senate's Defense Committee. In Vichy, in 1940, he voted in favor of the Marshal.

27. Paul Bénazet, Deputy, Senator, friend of Briand, and member of the Socialist Party. In July 1940, he voted in favor of granting Marshal Pétain plenary powers.

28. Georges Mandel's female companion.

29. She and Daladier married after the war.

30. Carmel Offie, one of Bullitt's associates in Paris.

From her vantage point in the park, Jeanne has formulated her opinion of the people working for the National Revolution: a bunch of greedy, incompetent, piggish informers.

I find the *Gazette de Lausanne* nauseating. In the name of anti-Bolshevism, they have stooped to fawning over Hitler and carrying "Vichy's realistic approach" even further. Poor old Switzerland. Just as in France, only the common folk are noble and brave. All those bourgeois politicians and businessmen make me sick.

At 4 A.M. I was awakened by the chirping of a nightingale, a kind of robin. I tried to lure it over with lemon peels and peach pits. When I was a child in Provence, I used to listen to the rhythmic singing of quail in the quiet of the fields. Over the plains of Limagne, the roosters are surely calling to each other right now. Here, there have been a few horse-drawn carts on the road to Riom, the voices of the guards behind the trees, and an invasion of fleas.

Recent communiqués from the Krauts reveal the ferocity with which the Russian Army is fighting. Western German cities have been bombed, and there have been considerable civilian casualties. Italian Generals have surrendered in Abyssinia.

Benoist-Méchin,[31] one of Vichy's Ministers, was in Ankara, soliciting Turkish assistance in Syria. He heard the Turks tell him, "You don't really expect us to grant a weak French nation what we have already refused a powerful Germany."

July 10, 1941

General Dentz in Syria has been ordered to request a truce.

Daridan came at 12:30 this afternoon. He told me that our losses in Syria were high, mostly among the officers. Ismet Inonu refused to grant passage to our reinforcements. What has all this gotten us? Could not this painful conflict have been avoided? Had the airfields in Syria been made

31. Jacques Benoist-Méchin, historian, Minister under Marshal Pétain, advocate of close ties, including military ties, with Hitler.

available to the Germans? Was this the opportunity that certain people had been waiting for?

The Russians continue to put up considerable resistance. I am surprised by the quantity of matériel that the Russian Army has as well as by the bravery of their fighting men. They have demonstrated heroism and genuine patriotism, just as they did in 1812.

They are still at one another's throats in Vichy, where a new ministerial crisis is looming, involving Huntziger, Achard, Bouthillier,[32] and so on.

Had an interesting talk with Daridan about possible peace terms: the reestablishing of legitimate democracies in Europe (for France, meaning the Republic), which is to say, governments that have the consent of the governed. As for territorial matters, there would be a much modified version of the Europe framed by the Treaty of Versailles. I fear that there is a little too much Congress of Vienna in Daridan's thinking. In any event, even if Hitler is eventually defeated, there will still be issues to be resolved between France and Germany. But then, can we really expect anyone to take our views into account given the way we withdrew to Bordeaux after the battle of the Somme?

Baudouin had met with Pétain and Weygand on May 29. The three agreed to push Reynaud out at the very first setback. They planned to move the government out of Paris, naturally, to avoid another Commune. Bouthillier and Chautemps were in on it.

Chautemps is in the United States in an unofficial capacity. They say he is getting paid $1,200 a month (40,000 francs). Pétain is rewarding him for his help.

July 12, 1941

4 P.M. Chauvel stopped by. His brother, a delightful fellow I very much liked, is gravely ill. His mother has come to Vichy and is supposed to dine with Marshal Pétain this evening. Chauvel is optimistic about the outcome

32. Yves Bouthillier, Finance Inspector and an associate of Paul Reynaud. He worked to bring Pétain to power and was named Vichy's Minister of Finance and National Economy in 1940.

of the war. Mme Chauvel witnessed a scene between Pétain and Darlan, and thinks that it won't be long before Darlan is gone.

The Germans have made a real killing: They got all of Polish industry cheap. They are preparing a military parade in Paris to celebrate the fall of Moscow, which is imminent. Reports have it that there remain no more than 200,000 German troops in France.

July 14, 1941

A radio broadcast from last night was reprinted this morning: "Once again July 14 will be celebrated this year." The first we had heard of it was in a communiqué from the Labor Ministry three or four days ago.

Of course, to listen to Pétain, France has been perpetuating a mistake for the last 150 years, which is what Maurras has been saying for the last 30. Maurras has at last discovered his finest disciple and scored his greatest triumph.

I couldn't find a French blue, white, and red flag to hang out of my window. Blum had better luck and came up with some tricolor ribbons. Brings back memories of July 14, 1939.

July 15, 1941

I saw Chauvel at 5 P.M. Sunday evening. He had dined with Pétain in his villa two miles from Vichy, in the company of his mother, Mme Chauvel; Ménétrel[33] and his son, Benoist-Méchin; and a naval officer from Pétain's staff and his wife. It turned out to be a wearisome dinner, because of Benoist's lecturing and the clowning around of Ménétrel, whom Pétain nearly had leave the table. Pétain is partially deaf, which meant that there could be no general conversation involving everyone. He had some very harsh words for Ménétrel, although none of this prevented him from displaying a hearty appetite and downing half a bottle of white wine. After dinner, he went for a walk in the park with Mme Chauvel, who is an intimate of his, and spoke to her of his loneliness. He said he hoped he

33. Bernard Ménétrel, Pétain's adviser and physician.

wouldn't die before signing the peace treaty, lest France be thrown into frightful chaos.

Weygand, whom Pétain can't stand, would like to succeed him. Darlan, whom Pétain doesn't like, is working at it harder and harder, and scheming more and more. Laval hasn't completely given up either. And in addition to these people, he said, there were a number of highly suspect and dangerous groups in Paris.

Pétain also talked to her about Catroux and de Gaulle. They might have been motivated by patriotism in the beginning, but now it is all a matter of pride on their part. Their actions in Syria were ignominious. Pétain refused to discuss their claims.

"From a purely military point of view, the British were pathetic in Syria. If 200,000 Germans were ever to land in England, it would be all over for them.

"The Russians are very good soldiers and what is more, they are considerably better armed than had been thought. Nonetheless, the Germans will take Leningrad, Moscow, Kiev, and the Caucasus. By occupying the 'exploitable' part of Russia, they will be able to make use of her mineral and oil resources, her grain, her oils and dairy products, and her industrial machinery. Russia will probably break up as the result of civil wars. Moreover, Japan will very likely enter the war by the end of the month. All of this should come to pass by the end of August, after which Hitler will launch his invasion of England, primarily by air. All of Europe's industrial capacity is now geared to replenishing and upgrading the German war machine.

"There is no doubt that British and American aviation has made great progress, both qualitatively and quantitatively. Nonetheless:

"1. In the end, the outcome of the war will be decided on land, and the British foot soldier, just like his commanding officers, isn't worth much.

"2. Roosevelt has encountered stiff resistance and in any event, the American soldier is even more inept than his British counterpart.

"3. Even if Hitler does not attempt to invade England, he could unify Europe and then wait it out, however long it takes. Closing the Eu-

> ropean market to England and America would be even more effective than the naval blockade."

Tuesday morning, in spite of Ménétrel, Pétain conferred individually with Mme Chauvel's son, my lawyer.

Chauvel told him that I had decided to seek a trial or, failing that, my temporary release. Pétain agreed that the situation was deplorable. He added that the trial was making him ill and said that it was the work of Marquet, which, he claimed, was one of the principal reasons why he forced him out of his government. He added, however, that he could not "under the present circumstances, authorize my release, because the government has learned of plots to kidnap the prisoners in Bourassol. To release them would be to jeopardize their safety, especially Blum's." He went on to say that "another solution to the problem will have to be found, such as an island, like Corsica." But he said he needed a few days to think about it and discuss it with Barthélemy. He asked Chauvel to take back both my letter and Ribet's, and to wait two weeks or so.

He said he himself would get back in touch with Chauvel. He asked him about M.L.[34] and was happy to learn that she had remained faithful and devoted to me.

July 19, 1941

Renée Blum informed me that a decision has been made to transfer us to the island of Porquerolles, where we are to be housed in reconditioned barracks. This was revealed two or three days ago, during a press conference. Blum thinks that the situation will be worse there. I am not so sure, but I'd like to ask Chauvel about it. It was from Porquerolles that I left on August 15, 1938, before the Munich crisis.

July 21, 1941

There has apparently been a counterorder; we will not be going to Porquerolles.

34. Edouard Daladier's female companion.

July 22, 1941

According to Jeanne, Radio Paris, which is to say the Krauts, has announced plans for our transfer to Porquerolles, with this added comment, "Undoubtedly so that they can be more easily kidnapped by a British vessel." American radio carried the same item. Judge Lagarde, however, told Jeanne that they had never seriously considered that option, which is the real truth. The rest is just so much hot air.

July 24, 1941

Talking with Blum through the window, I mentioned the tenacious resistance put up by the Russians. For the last few days, the names of the same cities keep reappearing in the communiqués, which is an indication of the ferocity of the fighting. It is now a matter of whether the Russian Army will be able to regroup its forces and continue fighting east of Moscow. If it can do that, victory is a real possibility.

At 4:30 P.M. Susset and his lovely wife came to see me, loaded down with presents. Spent two joyful hours in the company of friends. Susset was told by a German officer that the invasion of England was planned for August 20 and that all coastal ports would have to be cleared by that date.

Communiqué from the Havas Agency: We have agreed to meet Japan's ultimatum. The government acts as if it were proud to have been able to capitulate once again. They asked for an armistice supposedly to save the Empire. Is there anything left of our Empire?

Pétain went to Aix, where he went all out about Darlan and had something bad to say about every one of his Ministers. The demagoguery of a slick politician.

Passemard just informed me that Dormoy was assassinated in Montélimar.

July 31, 1941

Pierre's birthday.

At 11 A.M. Mme Reichenbach[35] came back from Montélimar where she had attended funeral services for Dormoy. They were held on Monday at 7 A.M. and carried out as if it had been the burial of a guillotined criminal whose unclaimed body gets carted to the cemetery from the basket into which it's dropped.

At first, the Secretary-General from the Prefecture and the Police Commissioner were deferential toward Jeanne Dormoy,[36] but after a phone call to Vichy, the only thing they were interested in, as they themselves said, was "getting it over with."

Dormoy's killer is a woman. She had a room in the same hotel and placed a bomb in his bed, between the mattress and the box spring. The bomb went off at two in the morning. He was torn to shreds. Blum feels that Vichy's attitude is as much a product of their fear as of their hatred. Such is the way the Nazis operate.

August 2, 1941

The Russians are still holding out. If we had continued fighting in North Africa, the war between Russia and Germany would have offered France a second opportunity to regain her freedom, the first being the Italian defeat in Cyrenaica.

Jean returned from Vichy, where he saw Brinon in the park, a fat man bearing his fat with pride.

What new German demands has Brinon joyfully brought back to the men of Vichy? The occupation of Casablanca? Dakar? Bizerte? All, naturally, for the salvation of our Empire.

35. Léon Blum's female companion. They married in 1943.

36. Marx Dormoy's sister.

August 5, 1941

I learned from Jeanne that Dommange has been arrested. His closest associate had informed on him; he had two grenades in his house.

It reminds me of Gaston Boissier's writings on informers in the days of Tiberius. Mutatis mutandis—we have improved on it since.

5:30 in the afternoon. Mazé came, talked about the heroism of the Bretons. They have put up a veritable "united front" in the cities and villages. The anticlerical Mazé is even on the same side as his parish priest. There are always fresh flowers on the graves of the fallen British pilots. Groups are being organized in the Occupied Zone. Then, at the other end of the spectrum, there are Landry and his Cagoulards.

With the packages I had received from my American friends, I was able to invite Mazé to stay for dinner.

August 7, 1941

Saw both Jean and Mazé. The latter showed me a copy of Sumner Welles's[37] speech denouncing Vichy's policies, which go well beyond the conditions agreed to in the Armistice, and threatening a break in the traditionally amicable Franco-American relations.

The Parisian press is aflame. Read some absolutely vile articles by Déat, Brinon, and Marion,[38] Chief of Information.

August 8, 1941

From my window, I tried to offer Jacomet some measure of comfort. A report filed by that wretch Cunin had left him beside himself. He had broken down in a fit of crying that drove his daughter to despair and was even a cause of concern for the guards. I spoke to him through the bars, while he was on the pathway in the courtyard, in front of the primitive toilets

37. Welles was Roosevelt's Under Secretary of State.

38. Paul Marion, first a Communist, then a Socialist, then a member of Doriot's Fascist Party, the PPF, with which he broke after Munich. He sided with the Vichy government and was appointed head of Propaganda and Junior Minister in the Information Ministry. He was imprisoned at the end of the war.

there. What could make for a more appropriate setting for a discussion about the trial? I joked with him and made fun of Cunin. I threw in a few new touches about Lagarde, the judge who has just had one of the witnesses done away with. I showed him who was really on trial here and appealed to his energy. When he left, he moved with determination and at a brisk pace.

August 9, 1941

Jean saw Chauvel in Vichy. Dampierre, a Minister, cabled from Budapest to say that the Germans had hit a snag in Russia. It's the beginning of the end. They will end up being defeated.

The cable was shown to Pétain, Weygand, and then Darlan, with the latter snorting, "It's just a bunch of crap."

Chauvel did not get to see Pétain. The issue of the moment is whether France will allow the Krauts to occupy Dakar, Bizerte, and Marseilles. The last Cabinet meeting was suspended until Monday, at which time a decision will be made. I am convinced that the matter had already been decided at the time of Brinon's trip. They are simply trying to figure out how to package it. Rumor has it that Weygand has opposed the move, but I don't believe a word of that.

Pétain and Weygand made a public appearance at the Grand Prix de Vichy. They were hailed by the crowd at the weigh-in.

August 11, 1941

An old friend of mine from Carpentras, Albert Josselme, came all the way up here but couldn't get permission to visit with me. Jean told him to stand behind the gates where he could see me when I went out for my walk. We waved to each other from afar. He gave Jean two packs of Boyards for me. Jean had to console him; he was crying and calling to me.

August 13, 1941

Renée Blum filled me in on the broad outlines of Pétain's radio address: total adherence to the doctrine and the practices of the Nazis. I read a printed version of it shortly thereafter in *La Montagne.*

1. Pétain's admission of his miserable failure.
2. Responsibility for the failure placed on the republicans and the Freemasons. The *Journal officiel* published a list of the supposed opposition leaders: Juvanon, Fabien de Champoille, and Paul Perrin, all of them poor souls who never had any influence whatsoever.
3. Adherence to Nazi principles and a condemnation of trusts à la Bergery.[39]
4. Submission to Germany in the name of collaboration.
5. Pétain's decision to pass sentence himself on those responsible for our defeat, which is his way of avoiding a trial with its public debates and comparisons. He claims he is "saving the honor of the Army," by which he means those incompetent leaders whose failings were revealed in the pretrial investigation.

2 P.M. Blum characterizes the speech as an explosion of furor and impotence. He interprets it as a sign that Germany is having serious problems. I think just the opposite. If there were a risk that Germany was about to lose the war, Pétain would never have burned his bridges. He still believes in a German victory, as he told his friend Mme Chauvel, only he doesn't say so outright, as opposed to Laval, who expresses his feelings publicly. Besides, Pétain has displayed considerable tact in his handling of the United States.

August 20, 1941

Desgranges[40] came to see me. He is a canon and an old war buddy, a magnificent human being. He refused to dine with Pétain and told Romier[41] and Moysset what he thought of their articles. He has been vigorously critical of the government's policies, especially their religious policies. He

39. Gaston Bergery, Centrist Deputy. He launched a weekly, *La Flèche*, and founded the Fascist "Frontist" Party in collaboration, most notably, with several former Communists. He was successively Vichy's Ambassador to Moscow and Ankara.

40. Canon Desgranges (1874–1958), militant priest in the Sillon movement as well as Deputy and republican. He fought brilliantly in World War I.

41. Lucien Romier, prewar journalist and right-wing author, Minister in the Vichy government.

has been praying for the victory of the democratic forces of the world and believes they will win. I find his courage and his boldness admirable. While we were together in this prison of mine, we enjoyed the memories of our camaraderie at Verdun.

6 P.M. Mazé has returned from the South. He met with Herriot, who hasn't changed. He is still upset at not having been arrested, although in his heart he hopes he won't be.

August 22, 1941

Génébrier has seen the high holy office manager of the high holy Minister of Justice, and Lagarde as well. They claim that there will indeed be a trial, but after the war!

August 30, 1941

Anniversary celebration of the Veterans' Legion, otherwise known as an exercise in how to create rifts among the veterans of the Great War.

Blum cleverly slipped me the following note: "In a recent speech, Cordell Hull claimed that France had misled the United States. America's aviation and naval production is now equal to that of Germany's; it will triple in a year's time.

"For a year, the French government took advantage of their Consul in Salonika by using him to spy on the British and the Greeks for the Germans. He found out about it when the Germans arrived in Salonika, whereupon he left to join the Gaullist movement in London. He has just made a statement to that effect on the radio."

September 1, 1941

I am suffering so from a painful abscess that I asked the Cour Suprême for permission to be seen by Dr. Bernard, who comes to take care of Blum. I was told that I would have to submit my request in writing, and that it could not be sent out before tomorrow. Not only will I get to keep my abscess for another twenty-four hours, but I'll also have the pleasure of hearing Dr. Bernard call upon Blum and leave without looking in on me. Oh, National Revolution!

September 9, 1941

Mazé has had a talk of vital importance with a friend of M. Nouvelle's; a meeting has been set for 6 P.M. If this isn't mere romantic fancy, it's terrific.[42]

September 21, 1941

Saw my son Pierre; he is more and more like Madeleine.

September 22, 1941

Spent the day with Pierre.

September 23, 1941

Saw Pierre and Marie and then Jean, who provided a picturesque description of his life in Marseilles. He is living with longshoremen.

Having been named Mayor of Annecy, General Cartier made the following obscene statement: "This is the first time since 1860 that the Savoie region has been united with the fatherland."

September 26, 1941

Jean left Thursday, Pierre and Marie Friday.

September 29, 1941

Judge Bruzin didn't even wait to have a look at Jacomet's excellent notes on the rearmament before submitting the completed indictment!

September 30, 1941

Claudius was even more responsible than Caligula for the debasement of power. In the most hideous way possible, he demonstrated to the Romans what favoring one race over all others can bring. Whither zealous obedience and the fervid desire to act the slave?

---

42. The reference is to Daladier's escape plans. A British plane would land in a nearby field and Daladier would escape with the head guard, Passemard, a member of the Resistance who was eventually caught, tortured, and killed by the Germans.

October 1, 1941

The government employee who has just read aloud to me the definitive version of my pretrial examination and the list of charges against me admitted himself that it was all a farce.

October 14, 1941

Perretti della Rocca, a former Ambassador, president of a life insurance company, a shady one at that, and head of the Political Justice Committee, presented his committee's report to the Marshal. I wonder whether they were able to look at each other without cracking a smile.

October 16, 1941

At 11 A.M. the head guard came and asked me to countersign a letter from Judge Lagarde. The indictment was to be presented to us at 5 P.M. today, after which we would have five days in which to respond. Then at noon, Pétain, in a statement broadcast on the radio, indicated that his decision regarding the actions to be taken against us would be announced at 7 P.M. At 6 P.M. we still had not received a copy of the indictment, which we were in fact never to receive. I will have been convicted without ever having had a chance to defend myself, as I have known I would be for a long time, ever since it became clear that France had not actually been defeated; she had been handed over to the enemy by a bunch of incompetent fools and traitors.

My thoughts are for my sons. They'll not lose courage, I know.

Having heard Pétain's address, Chauvel came to relay it to me. In a decision rendered publicly, Pétain has sentenced us to be imprisoned in the fortress of Le Portalet. He requested, moreover, that an even stiffer sentence be handed down by the Riom tribunal at the time of our trial.[43]

43. This is a long way both from the regrets Pétain expressed to Chauvel and the plan to send the defendants to the island of Porquerolles. It is highly unusual for a head of state to issue instructions to a tribunal publicly.

Our attorneys, Chauvel and Spanien, can't understand these contradictions. They have no idea of Pétain's hatred for republican regimes and for Poincaré and Clemenceau, who were so unerring in their opinion of him. He will never forgive them for not having named him Commander in Chief instead of Foch.

I heard that on October 13, Funck, one of Hitler's Ministers, gave a speech in Berlin: "Pétain will punish those who were responsible for the war as proof of his sincere desire to collaborate with victorious Germany."

Perretti della Rocca submitted the Political Justice Committee's report to Pétain on Tuesday, October 14. Every single member of that committee is a notorious reactionary. Some of them are particularly vicious, like Jassa, the epitome of the venomous cretin, and Vallin, a Deputy and member of the Croix de feu. Since Cassagneau had still not signed the indictment, one can only imagine the kind of fabricated and rigged dossier they based their judgment on. They have made a mockery of justice. The indictment was eventually signed on October 15, which just happened to be the day Pétain pronounced sentence.

October 17, 1941

Pétain's speech has been reprinted in the newspapers, and all of them ran the same headline. Will anyone ever have the courage to say that we were convicted before we even had a chance to read and respond to the indictment? Pétain actually invoked the principle of the separation of powers on the very day he violated it. Stranger still, he dropped the charge he has been making against me on the radio since August 13, 1940, namely that I had thrown France into war in violation of the Constitution. I was supposed to have gulled the entire Parliament. He was joined in this accusation by all the French Nazis, like Benoist-Méchin, Bergery, Déat, Montigny, and so on. The Parisian press, under German orders, has been accusing me of this unmercifully, as had Pétain, through the Legion and the newspapers it controls. In fact, Judge Lagarde never questioned me about anything else. All of a sudden, Pétain has abandoned this approach. Hitler is not going to like it.

Whether I am detained in a fortress in the Pyrenees or deported to a work camp somewhere, I shall not suffer as a result of that. I know that my sons and my sister, however much it grieves them, will be able to endure the ordeal. As for me, only the outcome of the war is of real concern. If Germany should be victorious, what would dying in the depths of some fortress matter? I would just as soon not survive, just as soon not have to witness the moral decline and the decay that would result. What meaning could life have, what would be the point of living then, even if I were free and no longer a prisoner? All that really matters is the ultimate victory or defeat of Nazi Germany.

Ribet came at 6 P.M. We drafted a protest to the "man sent by Providence," as His Eminence Cardinal Gerlier calls him.

October 18, 1941

My courageous friend Génébrier set out to see me as soon as he heard Pétain's announcement. We were speaking together about prewar politics, men, and ideas, when we were suddenly informed that Watteau, who is a General in the Reserves and a member of the Cour Suprême, had resigned. Other judges would appear to be on the verge of resigning. The government has let them know that if they do, they'll be sent to prison.

As for Charles Maurras, he is exultant. He continues to strike out against England and claims that this is Pétain's worthiest political act.

October 26, 1941

Laval: Moved from the cafe in Châteldon to a job as a school monitor and then a position as lawyer for revolutionary trade unions. Elected Deputy in 1914, he spent the entire war in the Chamber, even though he was only thirty-one. He spoke out against the expulsion of Trotsky in 1916. He was a defeatist, in favor of peace even back then (speech of July 1, 1917). According to Torrès, he was Mandel's contact with extremist groups. He became rich in the very midst of the war; defended a pathetic Malvy before the Board of Inquiry. During the Stavisky affair, he intervened with Mouton, the Director of Criminal Affairs at the Ministry of Justice, in favor of Hudelot's Foncière and Stavisky. Mouton lied to the Board of Inquiry, Mandel kept silent, and Loucheur died opportunely. In September 1939, again according to Torrès, it was Laval who staged the whole affair with

Portmann, Malvy, Monzie, et al., and sent Mistler[44] to Spain to meet with Pétain.

November 7, 1941

Pétain has issued a statement: I have been sentenced to life imprisonment.

November 11, 1941

It's the anniversary of our victory in 1918. M. Belin has informed us that there will be no official holiday this year, but we shall have the good fortune to see Marshal Pétain go to mass and have flowers placed at the memorial to the dead in Vichy. The Germans were probably afraid there would be demonstrations. Once again, Unoccupied France will offer us an abject example of servility, and once again their example won't be followed in the Occupied Zone, where our victory will be celebrated as a day of hope. The Republic has never known how to commemorate this great victory her fighting men won. Even the battle of the Marne, the greatest victory of them all, is only celebrated in some hole in the wall somewhere. The commemoration of the Armistice was never more than a funereal rite, with no mention whatsoever of the fact that it was signed at Germany's request. The Arc de Triomphe, which was dedicated to the magnificent victories of the nation, has become little more than a glorified sepulcher ever since the Tomb of the Unknown Soldier was placed at its base. That somber official parade on November 11, those huge wreaths they place on tombs, and those lugubrious trumpet calls to the dead are just so many burial rituals performed before a crowd huddled in meditation, as if at graveside.

As I was sitting here thinking of the last war, of a time when the French Army had real leaders, I was notified that there were to be no further visits after 6 P.M. At 7:30, the head guard came into my cell accompa-

44. Jean Mistler, writer, Radical-Socialist Member of Parliament and Minister in Daladier's Cabinet in 1934. In Vichy, in 1940, he voted to give plenary powers to Pétain. He was a member of the Conseil National.

nied by a handsome government commissioner in a spanking new suit. Looking as smug as Mistler himself, he solemnly informed me that at 6 A.M. the following morning we would be leaving for the fortress of Le Portalet and that we would be served a cold meal at noon. Whereupon, in his little priest's voice, he read aloud to me, punctuated by appropriate reverences, a statement from Pétain countersigned by Barthélemy. Then he bowed one final time and disappeared. How does the National Revolution manage to produce so many of these simpletons?

November 12, 1941

At 10 A.M., as a ribbon of light over the Clermont road fought to break through the torrential rain, a long procession filed into the prison: a police official, policemen, etc. There was a feeling in the air of an execution. After a good deal of time wasted in floundering, prattling, and formalities, we finally headed out. A lead car was followed by guards with machine guns and policemen, and then by our cars, in which we were each "protected" by a guard and a police official. Blum was ahead of me, Gamelin behind, and behind us were more police cars, more machine guns, and even an ambulance. All of these precautions had been taken for fear that some of the government's supporters had taken too seriously the Marshal's speeches and the campaign against us.

"My" police official was one of a well-known kind: a society man, who knew all the best people in those wealthy bourgeois circles where Hitler is revered. Their admiration for Hitler, which had long been kept under wraps, burst into the open the day he attacked Russia. Some of those people are actually indignant that the Pope has not given his blessing to this crusade and are absolutely convinced he will be unseated by council decree in Berlin after Germany's victory. Fortunately for us, we have the Marshal, who addressed the two thousand volunteer mercenaries of the anti-Bolshevik Legion. As they marched off in their German uniforms to fight the Russians, he praised them for saving France's honor.

My "traveling companion" had something to say about everything and everyone: the Count of Paris and his continuing claims to the throne, Weygand, et al. He finally came around to talking about the trial in Riom. He was clearly playing the game the way it is supposed to be played, frankly offering information in exchange for some he wanted to get from me. I obliged him. I told him that the Riom trial was no longer a matter of concern, since Pétain had already issued instructions to the judges. I told him I planned to spend my time in prison waiting for Hitler's defeat to be played out in a blast of Wagnerian horns and trumpets. As for Göring, Mussolini, Himmler, and Farinacci,[45] they would all end up escaping to Franco's Spain where they would join Pétain, Darlan, Laval, and Barthélemy in a reunion that would be nothing like the dethroned kings' dinner at the Carnival in Venice, which is recounted in *Candide*. Thus would the war end precisely where it had begun, in Spain. And the renascent Republic, taking a page from the Bourbons, would launch its own Spanish expedition and bring them all back to France. That is what I offered my friendly companion: more than enough for him to file his report with the Director of the *Sûreté!*

A lovely road crossing autumn-colored forests took us from Clermont to Cahors, Gambetta's birthplace, where Monzie was later to settle. We then went through Souillac, the home of that wretched fellow Malvy, who after having been saved by the Republic, went on to betray it. A gambling addiction tripped him into venality, and he became an agent on the payroll of the Spanish Ambassador, Lequerica, as soon as diplomatic relations were restored with Spain. We passed through Auch, Mirande, Tarbes, Pau, and Oloron and were stared at everywhere we went by large numbers of curious onlookers and members of the Veterans' Legion, the French Nazi Party. I was surprised to hear so few jeers, although as we went through Barthou's territory, I heard one resounding "Bastards, Crooks" shouted by a well-dressed woman. That night, we drove down a winding road that ran along the Aspe stream, at the bottom of a hollow walled in by boulders rising straight up, and then moved on to the Fontaines d'Escot and the valley where Queen Margot, in the company of various lords and damsels, gamboled and prattled about love and the pleasures of life. We came to a gorge with a hellish bridge and saw a few stars twinkling over the

45. Roberto Farinacci began committing acts of violence for the Italian Fascist Party as early as 1922. He subsequently became the party's Secretary-General (1925–1926). He served as permanent liaison between Hitler and Mussolini during the war.

ridge across the way: the fortress of Le Portalet. The procession came to a halt.

Leaving our escorts behind, Blum, Gamelin, and I entered the fortress. In the glow from the headlights, I was pleasantly surprised to discover the presence of Bartalet, the same considerate and fearless fellow who had overseen my living arrangements in Chazeron, which was the worst period of my captivity. He had since then been appointed Commissioner of Police in Nancy, but the Germans had had him quickly removed from the position. This superb pilot from the Great War, who has remained undaunted and unyielding, was then named to a position in Pau, which is why he was there to take care of me at Le Portalet, making the hardship of my captivity easier to bear. I thanked him and we shook hands, as all those distinguished gentlemen from the police looked on.

Before leaving me, a Lieutenant in the guards told me that he too was from the Vaucluse. As it happens, I knew his father, who was a highly respected physician. They are friends of Lally-Nevière, who was the most generous of men, a man adored by all the peasants in the Aygues Valley, which was once a refuge for Calvinists. When I would go to visit him in Saint-Martin-de-la-Brasque, his servant, Némorin Pourpre, used to rush to get his drum, which he had bought in Avignon to while away his loneliness, and greet me with furious drum rolls, after which he would wipe his brow and shout out in Provençal: " I really got a kick out of that!"

I walked across the drawbridge and was greeted by the warden of the fortress, Commander Vidala, a disabled veteran from the Great War. He is a fine officer whom I had awarded an instructorship at the Saint-Cyr Military Academy in 1936. I tried to keep our encounter as short as I could, for I could feel all the warmth he still felt for me, which seemed even greater, given the ordeal I was going through and my shameful conviction. Vichy had unknowingly appointed an officer who was both a patriot and a republican.

As I was leaving, I ran into the dwarf who used to be the warden at the prison in Riom. He is Clémentel's protégé, a man who became a reactionary overnight just to keep his job. He let some sixty prisoners die of hunger this winter. He should roast in hell.

I went down the stairs to the fourth level of the basement, where we stopped in front of a massive door held by five bolts and a huge lock. There is a gendarme stationed in front of it night and day. I walked into a small, narrow room with a barred window that looked out onto a mountain stream with a monotonous gurgle and, beyond it, a sheer mountain face blocking the horizon. As General Laure once wrote, Marshal Pétain knows how to do things right. In this desert deprived of light and far removed from everything and everyone, I will receive no visitors, not even my sons, except over vacations, and I won't be able to offer them any comfort or take care of them when they do come. Pétain knows well that nothing could be more painful to me than that. He is hoping that by isolating me in this pit he will eventually drive me into some kind of depression.

In his October 16 diktat, he told the judges what their duties were in this trial. He thinks that by having us incarcerated far from our families and our lawyers he will be able to hamper us in the preparation of our defense and break down our resistance. I can do nothing about his judges, but I can do everything about myself.

As I do every year, I recalled, as the evening came to a close, a night in 1932, when in our little house in Garches my wife accepted death with a simplicity that was probably more heartrending for me than the anguish or horror of dying would have been. I relive that night every year on this date and hear her once again uttering her last wishes with a smile and a farewell.

November 13, 1941

I have been reading and working. I rest by putting my personal effects in order. Around 11 A.M. I went out for a little air on a windswept terrace of sorts. Seeing no point in turning around in circles in that narrow cage, hemmed in on all sides, I went back down to my cell. Vidala, the warden, was genuinely concerned about me. I tried to reassure him, but he later had a real promenade installed on the roof of the fortress.

During the afternoon, in an extraordinary display of baseness and childishness, the dwarf came to inform me of the regulations governing prison life. He claimed that this grotesque hodgepodge of rules was the work of Barthélemy, over in the Justice Department. I asked him for a copy of them, but he refused. Too bad—I would have loved to have sent them to the United States. Fate will apparently never reward Barthélemy with the glory he deserves.

November 16, 1941

Sunday. Chauvel was able to get in to see me at 2 P.M. Russia is still holding out. The United States has effectively repealed the laws imposing neutrality. He told me that Gamelin was ill and had been taken to a hospital in Pau. We looked out at the Aspe. A small group of children accompanied by their schoolteacher walked by. They stopped across from my window and shouted and waved a joyful hello to me.

November 18, 1941

Jeanne sent me a bouquet of violets and two packs of cigarettes. Got a letter of encouragement from my friend Gence d'Aubagne.

November 19, 1941

A gendarme and a cook who are both from Villeneuve met in my room to rail against the policy of collaboration and Nazism within France. They still think that Pétain is playing both ends against the middle, and that once the Germans show signs of faltering, he'll kick them out. I explained to them just who Pétain is—a vicious old man—and told them of the rancor he bears against Foch, Poincaré, and Joffre. I told them that in his preface to Chauvineau's book, Pétain spoke out against modernizing the Army, against armored divisions, against changes in the Army and in its officer corps. He even claimed that there was no way to get through the Ardennes, which was precisely where the Germans broke through, adding that if they ever tried, they would suffer terrible defeat. We all know what happened. On one point they agreed with me: that all our hopes lie with the United States.

November 22, 1941

The young gendarme from Villeneuve informed me that Weygand has been pushed into retirement (although they have made it look like an honor). The November 21 newspapers report that after a glorious career and fifty-six years of public service, General Weygand has decided to step down. He has been awarded a special commendation for meritorious service! He has not left Pétain's side since he got to Vichy, which coincided with an earlier visit from Abetz and Brinon. The news item from the Havas agency is a sparkling example of malaise, hypocrisy, and loutishness.

It reminds me of what the society-type police official who brought me here said about there being three problems:

1. Weygand, who does not want us to give up our bases
2. The Legion, which is modeled after the Nazi Party
3. The Count of Paris

Looks as if the Weygand problem has been resolved. One curious note was sounded here: In his retirement, Weygand will continue writing his memoirs. Which Weygand? The strict reactionary? The soldier? He is clear-sighted and has a gift for expressing himself, but his military knowledge is terribly outdated. He played a major role in ousting Reynaud and pushing through the decision to surrender in Bordeaux, in collaboration with Pétain, Baudouin, and Bouthillier. Consider the depositions he supplied for Riom—and his own ambitions. Pétain hates him, but he did not relieve him of his command gratuitously. Weygand was probably sacrificed to counterbalance the departure of Marquet and other pro-German types. He is at bottom just an African proconsul who succeeded in making a good name for himself with the Americans and the British, and in creating illusions about himself in the minds of French patriots; in sum, he's a Prefect masquerading as a General. Someday I'll have to put down in writing the nature of my relations with him in 1933, and his with Paul-Boncour and Pétain, and include reports from the Supreme War Councils of 1934 and 1935 and his letter to Reibel. He has also written a book about Turenne, which is mediocre. And then there is the speech he gave in Lille: "I was privy to Marshal Foch's secrets ..." A marvelous example of political, military, and moral chicanery.

November 24, 1941

Blum managed to get word to me that the Germans have taken Rostov and that the British have gained ground in Libya. He added that Radio Paris has announced that Pétain is about to resign and be replaced by a General. I don't believe a word of it.

November 27, 1941

I am suddenly overcome with fatigue. I have been shivering and feeling nauseous.

December 7, 1941

The gendarme on duty came and told me: "Bad news. Japan is at war with the United States." I know nothing more.

December 16, 1941

Some of the fine gendarmes here came to say good-bye. They have been relieved of their duty at Le Portalet and will be moving on to Pau. They have been replaced by young, rather vulgar types.

The British are evacuating Malaysia. I always felt that if Japan were to enter the war, it would weigh heavily on the British. How will the United States be able to continue supplying them? Or China? or Russia?

December 22, 1941

Jean has come here from Grenoble, via Lyons, Avignon, Toulouse, and Pau. He is a wonderful lad, bursting with indignation and cheer. Grenoble is a veritable hotbed of patriotism and rebelliousness.

December 23, 1941

Hitler has appointed himself Supreme Commander in Chief, or rather, since he was already that, Supreme Commander with a direct and personal hand on things. This says a lot more about the failure of the German offensive in Russia than did his October 9 statement, in which he claimed success. Just as it was in ancient Germania, Hitler is trying to cultivate confidence in and devotion to his person.

December 24, 1941

At 7 P.M. Ernest, the young cook here, walked into my cell with a huge soup tureen. Since I never eat soup, I looked at him quizzically. He put a finger to his lips and left with his gendarme escort. When I lifted the cover, I found a magnificent Yule log![46]

Although Jean had lunched with me earlier, he managed to come back in the evening. I had saved a large slice of Ernest's Yule log for him.

December 25, 1941

Mazé[47] came, faithful as always.

46. A cake in the shape of a log, traditional Christmas fare.

47. The escape plan was dropped following Daladier's transfer to Le Portalet.

1942

[The prisoners are once again in Bourassol prison. They were brought back to stand trial in the courthouse in Riom, just a few miles away.]

January 2, 1942

The press has reprinted Marshal Pétain's New Year's Day address—an avowal of impotence. We have come a long way since the bravado that followed the signing of the Armistice. How sweet the National Revolution was … while there was still a Republic.

January 5, 1942

At 11 o'clock this morning, I spotted Blum standing at his window. He looked relaxed and rested. He had hated being in Le Portalet, because of the hordes of guards who would come into our cells ten times a day and shadow us whenever we went out on the terraces. This, of course, is what prison life is all about. He smiled and reminded me of Bazaine's captivity on Sainte-Marguérite Island, where he enjoyed the company of his wife, his children, and his orderlies. I told him that the difference between that fellow's treatment and ours is proof that we are not traitors; if we were, the French-speaking Nazis who are running our country—after having handed it over to the Germans—would have afforded us the same pleasant lifestyle that comrades in treason always reserve for each other.

We also spoke about the trial. In spite of our having been brought back to Bourassol to be made available for Vichy justice, Blum doesn't believe we'll ever see the inside of a courtroom. He asked, "Can you really expect the government to be so stupid as to hand us the stick to beat them with?"

I replied: "The government is probably a lot stupider than you think; in fact, if Napoleon is to be believed, it's the stupidest form of government of all, since it is a military government. Remember what he told Roederer about military regimes? The French will not stand for them. Moreover, after the resounding speech Pétain gave on October 16, when he sentenced us before our trial, he couldn't go back on his word even if he wanted to. How could anyone think otherwise?"

Still, Blum felt that in view of the crisscross appointments that sent that sorry creature Lagarde to the High Court of Appeals as head prosecutor and brought Caous from there to preside over the Cour Suprême, there was reason to think that the case would be deferred. Caous is a man who likes to wield authority, and Blum feels he'll wield enough of it to have the case postponed indefinitely, "pending a more complete investigation," which is what the government really wants. I told Blum that I didn't believe any of that. Caous was brought in because during the last war he was the man who demanded the death penalty for those poor firing squad victims that history refers to as the Vingré Martyrs, which was a horrible tragedy. It is true, however, that after having demanded the death penalty, Caous voluntarily joined a fighting unit.

We then turned to the most recent depositions and the evidence that had been compiled to date. At the outbreak of the war, Blum had been critical of my record at the War Ministry. He told me now that he had not fully appreciated what I had done during that three-year period. If he had not himself seen the Examining Magistrate's file, he could never have even guessed that arms manufacturing had received so sizable a stimulus. He thought that we should have instituted currency controls after Munich. I had to remind him that the Senate had brought down the government in his second term as Prime Minister precisely over that issue. Moreover, currency controls would have created problems not only within France but above all in our relations with the United States and England, with which we had signed a monetary agreement in 1936. At any rate, could we possibly have used more than the 65 billion francs that had been earmarked for arms manufacturing?

It was a bright, sunny January morning, so conducive to outdoor conversation that we went right on chatting, with me in the courtyard and Blum standing behind the bars of his cell.

I asked him what he knew about the conditions under which Reynaud had resigned in Bordeaux. Blum asserted that Reynaud had not lost his majority in the Cabinet. The discussion there had already gone on for a long time, as I recalled it, when they recessed for three hours, with the debate over Chautemps's proposal resuming at 10 P.M. That is when it was agreed that Lebrun; Herriot, the President of the Chamber of Deputies; Jeanneney, the President of the Senate; and all the Ministers would board ship at Port-Vendres and leave for Algeria. Pomaret, the Minister of the Interior, even offered to give me a ride in his car, an offer I declined, preferring to leave with the Members of Parliament traveling on the *Massilia.* Blum confirmed these facts, but with one correction. Jeanneney had departed earlier and was already in Toulouse when he was called back to Bordeaux. Of course, while Parliament and the Cabinet were being led down this garden path, while people were assuring us with their hands over their hearts of their heroic resolve to continue the war from North Africa, telling us that our powerful Navy was still intact and how we had more than a thousand modern aircraft, the Armistice was secretly being negotiated with Germany through Franco's Ambassador, Lequerica.

I went back to my "apartment." The newspapers were carrying a Reuters dispatch, dateline Washington, January 3: "Twenty-six nations have issued a joint statement, pledging not to negotiate a separate armistice or peace with the enemies and to commit their full resources to the defeat of the members of the Tripartite Pact." These governments in exile are far more loyal and reliable representatives of their temporarily enslaved countrymen than the traitors the Nazis have installed in their place. That France alone did not join in signing that statement makes Pétain's grim New Year's address all the more appalling.

January 9, 1942

"The ocean liner *Lamoricière,* victim of a violent storm, has sunk off the coast of the Balearic Islands, as it was making its crossing from Algiers to Marseilles." That is the boat on which I was brought back to France from Morocco. I had left Casablanca by train and been warmly greeted by railroad workers and soldiers, in spite of Prouvost's[1] and Baudouin's slanderous remarks about me and their attempts to incite political assassination.

1. Jean Prouvost, founder of *Paris-Soir* and supporter of Marshal Pétain.

I was accompanied on the trip by Forneret, the Moroccan Chief of Police. Forneret was one of the first to come to Blum's aid after the Royalist attack on his life during the funeral services for Bainville. In 1936, he became associated with Salengro.[2] He is a devoted follower of Noguès and in all likelihood a Freemason. When Pétain took over, Forneret hoped to hold on to the excellent job he'd been awarded under the Popular Front. I had occasion to visit his magnificent police station in Rabat, which is more lavishly outfitted than any police headquarters in France. I would be very surprised if he were kept in the position. He always acted kindly toward me in Morocco and has always been restrained in his efforts to stay in the good graces of those now in power, efforts that have probably been unsuccessful. We parted company in Rabat, where I was met by policemen from the Algiers division of the *Sûreté*, there to assure my "protection." As it happened, they were both republicans and patriots. The heat was oppressive. Soot from the engine showered onto every compartment of the train, where the crowds of passengers massed together were dripping with sweat.

In Bel-Abbes, I was greeted by the Subprefect, come to share with me briefly his contempt for our having surrendered in Bordeaux and for the men who had handed over France in order to destroy the Republic. The train stopped in Maison-Carrée, where the gentlemen from the *Sûreté* decided that we would get off, on the grounds that in Algiers there might be demonstrations or incidents. Guillermet, former Subprefect in Carpentras and the man who started me in my career in politics, received me in the middle of the night. He was dressed in white. They put me up in a hotel on the top of a hill. The following morning, I was awakened by military bands, the regimental marching of soldiers, and the roar of crowds setting off to welcome Admiral Abrial, as the newly appointed Governor of Algeria made his grand entrance into the city. I knew what it was like to be welcomed by the French and Islamic populations in Algiers, having been received there in 1939, but today, I was a prisoner in a second-class hotel, not allowed to leave, day or night, as per the orders of Chevalier, the local

2. Roger Salengro, Socialist politician and Minister of the Interior. His suicide came in the aftermath of a campaign to defame him orchestrated by right-wing and far-right-wing newspapers, among them *L'Action française* and the weekly *Gringoire*.

Prefect, with whom I used to have considerable dealings. I objected so strenuously to those outrageous conditions that Chevalier eventually grew ashamed of himself, at which point I simply went off to dine at the seaside home of a kindly employee from the Prefecture.

At noon the following day, I boarded the *Lamoricière* with my son Jean. We traveled under destroyer escort, with the ship avoiding its normal course and hugging the West African and then the Spanish coastlines on its way to Marseilles. These precautions had been taken because the British had plans to intercept the ship and take me to London.

On our arrival, my son Jean set down the following account: "When our ship reached port in Marseilles, there was a welcoming committee on hand—workers, longshoremen, and agitators screaming and shouting threats, 'Cowards, deserters, traitors.' My father pointed to a fat character screaming his lungs out and laughed as he rolled himself a cigarette. Just as we were pulling alongside the dock, I heaved a sigh of relief when I saw Mazé coming on board to get us. We managed to get out safely through an office and fled in Giaccobi's truck before the mob could catch us. Giaccobi is a good and well-meaning fellow; he had taken care to load iron bars in the back so that we could defend ourselves, but hadn't bothered about the damaged rear wheel that forced us to stop every mile or so. It was a hairy experience, but our friends at the dock hadn't thought to follow us. We made it to Orange, where Diard had the courage to put us up, and where we learned rather quickly who our real friends were. Those first few days, there was no need to set additional places at the dinner table."

January 10, 1942

At 4 P.M. Dr. Mazé arrived, visibly upset, from Châtelguyon, where Jeanneney had asked to meet with him at 11 in the morning. In a discussion they had had four or five days earlier, Mazé found Jeanneney well disposed both toward him and toward me. Today, on arriving, Mazé was informed that he would not be received before 2 in the afternoon. Jeanneney probably needed all that time to prepare the "audience" he was about to grant him, in which, after criticizing Pétain, the Vichy government, and the Riom trial, he complained bitterly that I had never actually ordered an offensive in September 1939, that I had not issued Italy an ultimatum, that

I had come to Gamelin's defense, and so on. In sum, the President of the Senate leveled a scathing indictment against me, which he concluded by expressing his regret that Reynaud had not taken over from me as head of the government a lot earlier. Mazé was so infuriated that he snapped back violently. He probably should have just let it pass, but who ever heard of an infuriated Breton who could control his temper? Mazé was absolutely fuming, and to be fair to everyone, he laid it on Reynaud too, criticizing him for having brought Pétain into the government and having appointed Weygand Supreme Commander, in other words, for having chosen the hangmen who put the cord around his own neck after all those sleazy dealings in Bordeaux that brought about his downfall. He also criticized Reynaud for having surrounded himself with notorious defeatists, like the pro-Fascist Baudouin and the Cagoulard Bouthillier, whom he appointed Minister. Those two started betraying him from their very first day on the job. Gamelin at least would have remained a good soldier and executed the order calling for the organization of resistance forces in North Africa.

Mazé, who was still out of control when he related all of this to me, said that Jeanneney was so flustered that he couldn't find anything to say. I did my best to calm him down, but it wasn't easy. He added that, on the other hand, he had been very warmly received by the staff employees of the Chamber of Deputies and the Senate, whose offices had been moved from Vichy to Châtelguyon. They told him to offer me their respects and to ask me if there were anything that they could get for me to make my detention less unpleasant. Once again, the "little people" were giving a lesson in magnanimity to those who were supposedly their superiors.

Jeanneney is a mediocre sort whose surface severity impressed the high livers that more often than not Senators are. I was on good terms with him until the winter of 1939, when he actually did want us to launch an attack against the Italians, a point on which we were in total disagreement. I explained my position on numerous occasions before parliamentary committees and the War Committee. On the basis of all the intelligence coming out of Italy that September, it was clear that under the influence of the Crown, the Catholic church and various working-class organizations, the Italian people were opposed to going to war on the side of Germany. In fact, it was precisely because Hitler couldn't draw Italy into the war against Poland that he ended up turning to Stalin. Count Ciano was clear in his talks with François-Poncet,[3] our Ambassador to Rome, that it was his desire to work with us in maintaining Italy's neutrality. We had also signed an attractive trade agreement with them in October and ordered large amounts of equipment through their Air Force Ministry, which we had begun receiving at the end of 1939.

To be sure, we knew that if France were ever to suffer defeat or be dealt a truly debilitating blow, Mussolini would very likely make the political choice, as any jackal would. But no one in the military doubted the strength of the French Army or the solidity of France's fortified and well-organized defenses. Wasn't it enough to have to fight the powerful German Army? Did we have to go looking deliberately for a second enemy, one whose Air Force and above all whose Navy could inflict serious damage and sever our communications with North Africa?

However, if we assumed a purely defensive posture, four or five divisions plus the troops manning our fortresses would have been enough to defend the border in the Alps, and another five or six divisions would have sufficed to hold the coast and the lines that I had had fortified in southern Tunisia. The troops thus spared from duty in the Alps and North Africa could have been concentrated in northeastern France, which would have been our wisest course of action.

For all these reasons, launching an offensive against Italy appeared to me inappropriate, however weakened their forces were after the conquest of Abyssinia and their participation in the civil war in Spain. It also struck me as an unjust and gratuitous act, considering that the Italians had kept out of the war despite their alliance with Germany. I felt that the war would go on for a long time and that what had begun as a limited conflict would expand into a war between large coalitions of forces, eventually boiling down to a war of attrition. My idea was to hold the line in the North and the Northeast and to go on the offensive if the Poles managed to hold out against the German attack that winter and the following spring, as our military leaders believed they would. That would have been

3. André François-Poncet, French Ambassador to Berlin until 1938, then Ambassador to Rome.

the time to go on the offensive, in close cooperation with the British Army and above all, the British Air Force; that was my idea of how the war should be conducted. I should add as well that I was privy to the telegrams the British government was receiving from Sir Percy Lorraine, their Ambassador to Rome, and that they echoed those being sent to us by François-Poncet. Lorraine, too, was firmly opposed to any action being taken against Italy. Moreover, no one at any time, either on the War Committee or during Cabinet meetings, had ever proposed or even alluded to such an attack, with the exception of Jeanneney—during Parisian dinner parties. Whenever positions involving real responsibility were offered to this "man of iron," he always turned them down.

All of this was so futile, anyway. Couldn't Jeanneney have directed his outrage at matters closer to hand, like the dissolution of certain institutions guaranteeing freedom, which has now been officially ratified by the National Assembly in Vichy?

According to a British broadcast picked up in Châtelguyon, the Russians are just thirty miles outside of Smolensk. It seemed to me that that was far more important than Jeanneney's warmed-over rancor, and Mazé agreed.

February 4, 1942

5 P.M. Ribet met with Minister of Justice Barthélemy in Paris to discuss the possibility of bringing his file and various other documents with him to Riom for the trial. He was told that the Germans had been insisting that lawyers' files be submitted to their Embassy for a quick and "obviously superficial" review, in the presence of the lawyers themselves. Ribet strongly protested. He suggested to Barthélemy that he simply pass a law eliminating lawyers' rights to privileged communication altogether. When he refused, as we had agreed, to hand the file over to the German Embassy, Barthélemy sputtered and whined. He claimed he was doing everything in his power and that he was opposed to there being a trial at this time, but said that Romier had forced it on them. Whatever the truth, if the Germans insist on reviewing our file, we'll drop our defense rather than comply.

February 5, 1942

Ribet ran into Monzie at a lawyers' meeting about some case. The author of *Ci-devant* has switched sides once again. He no longer believes the Germans will win the war. Marshal Pétain's failure to find a place for him equal to his talents has made him an embittered man. If I have understood correctly, he would like to write another *Ci-devant*, this time with the Marshal as the prime target. Ribet filled me in on some of the juicier parts of Monzie's youth. More recently, he testified against Chaumié, who had given him a medal when he was Education Minister. As he was waiting for his turn to testify, Jouvenel[4] went over to Monzie and pointed to the *Légion d'honneur* ribbon he had pinned to his lapel. Monzie immediately removed it and then went in to testify against the very man who had given it to him. He also testified against me last year. Of course, I merely appointed him Minister.

February 6, 1942

Mazé, Ribet, and his wife came around 11:30. Mme Ribet repeated a conversation she had had with Bénazet the night before at the Hotel Pailleret, near Riom. To get away from his wife, Bénazet had told her he was going there to testify. He had been merciless when he testified against me at the Riom tribunal in the summer of 1941, the main thrust of his testimony being an attempt to prove that if he had been appointed War Minister or Air Force Minister, or better yet both, France would have repelled the German attack and been victorious. Since that time, after having expected to be named, at the very least, special counsel to Marshal Pétain, he has been removed from both his mayoralty and from his seat on a regional council. Furthermore, he has been denounced as a Freemason, which is why he is now a Gaullist. He showed Mme Ribet his latest deposition, in which he states that our military leaders alone, by virtue of their incompetence, were responsible for France's defeat; that we had 2,500 modern aircraft and 4,000 tanks, which they proved incapable of putting into operation; that there were all those traitors who wanted France to be defeated so that

4. Bertrand de Jouvenel, economist, philosopher, and essayist.

the Republic could be destroyed. He said he knew at least one of them personally, a classmate from the Saint-Cyr Military Academy. Pétain's police keep him informed. If Pétain doesn't personally apologize, Bénazet will pronounce so stinging an indictment of him that the very walls of the Riom courthouse will shake from it.

Today is the anniversary of the Fascist demonstrations of 1934, the first significant attack on the Republic. The mob included the curious and the stupid. Good people, driven to anger by the press's blown-up accounts of the Stavisky affair, had taken to the streets to demonstrate alongside French-style Fascists, all of them straining to force their way into the Senate and the Chamber of Deputies. Among the working classes, it is now thought that the men of February 6 took their revenge by surrendering in Bordeaux, and that they handed France over to the Germans so as to finish off the Republic. Laval was the man behind the Stavisky affair, as Torrès has ably demonstrated.

February 8, 1942

Had lunch with Jean, who talked about his life in Grenoble. We spoke of Hitler and the coming spring offensives, probably into the Caucasus and Egypt. Like Napoleon long before him, Hitler will be forced to recruit auxiliary troops: Romanians, Hungarians, Slovaks, and Poles, a veritable international army under the orders of the German High Command. This is why Göring and Ribbentrop went to Budapest. If Germany should fail to defeat Russia, the breakup of that international army will herald Europe's revolt.

February 9, 1942

At around ten this morning I opened my window to take in a little cold air and Guy La Chambre interrupted his walk in the courtyard to come over and chat with me. He is pleased about the upcoming trial in Riom, which will offer him not only a chance to defend himself in front of the nation, but also a pleasant diversion from his present life. Unfortunately the cells that have been set aside for us and that Marshal Pétain's government has been so kind as to furnish with a wooden table and a cane armchair are infested with lice and fleas.

La Chambre claimed that the heads of the Air Force lied. At the time of the battle of the Meuse, 2,000 fighters were available to them, but Corap's forces had only 2. Our military commanders didn't recognize the seriousness of the battle until it was virtually lost. We still had 2,500 modern aircraft left when the Armistice was signed.

February 10, 1942

American and British airplanes have dropped some 3 million extremely well-written propaganda tracts over Occupied France. They were probably well received. They do justice to the efforts made by the French.

A news item from Alsace relates in moving terms the Alsatians' resistance to nazification there, in spite of German brutality. There were demonstrations in Mulhouse and Colmar on November 11, even though laying wreaths on the graves of soldiers was officially prohibited. Boys eighteen and older are being sent to German camps and subjected to intensive military training, in preparation for being shipped out to the Russian front. Girls are being sent to Germany and Norway. All able-bodied men are being given roles in civil defense. They have set up concentration camps bursting with Alsatians; they have persecuted nuns in Ribeauvillé and they are demanding sworn allegiance to Hitler. Nonetheless, a great many young Alsatians continue to make their way into Unoccupied France at night.

February 17, 1942

The trial was supposed to open in Riom today, but when Ribet pointed out that this was Mardi Gras, the judges decided not to put on their costumes until the day after tomorrow.

February 19, 1942

We left Bourassol for the prison in Riom. It made for an imposing procession, with motorcycles at the lead, five cars, one for each of us plus the inspectors from the *Sûreté* at our sides, and a vanload of helmeted and armed guards from the new state police force, Pétain's SS.

The streets were dotted with curious souls, looking on the whole sympathetic toward us. When we reached the prison, we were met by the warden, a gentlemanly sort, who deep down disapproves of the trial. We were escorted to our cells by Dumas, the head guard, whose southern accent resonated against the vaulting of the long, dark, and humid corridor. We passed the exercise yard, the sleeping quarters, the workshop, and a thick oak door with massive locks. At the end of the corridor, we took a long staircase down to our cells. Mine is spacious, dark, and, in spite of the iron stove that Dumas had had lit for me, ice cold. The walls have been recently whitewashed. I suppose the straw mattress wrapped in gray cloth and set onto a wooden frame could pass for a couch, but there are vermin running all through it. The rest of the furnishings include a wooden table, three zinc tubs, an old armchair and two straight-back chairs, one of which wobbles. Fortunately, there is a little electric lamp I can read and work by.

February 25, 1942

I awakened in a state of such extreme fatigue that I was incapable of going to the courthouse. I so informed the Head Magistrate, who had the medical examiner from Riom sent to my cell at 12:30. No sooner had the jailer closed the door behind him than the doctor began shaking both my hands and clasped his arms about my neck to hug me. I had to pinch myself when I realized it was Renard, an old classmate of mine. We used to have our meals together at old lady Bisoud's place down on Marseilles Street in Lyons. I had nicknamed him Montesquieu because they have the same profile. After listening to my lungs and heart with his stethoscope and taking my blood pressure, Montesquieu told me I needed a full week's bed rest. I blew up at him, just as I used to in the days of our youth. He finally gave in. We reminisced for a while about that distant past. He wanted to get me cigarettes, coffee, God knows what else, and absolutely insisted that I be given a week's rest. He headed back to the Cour Suprême, where the judges were awaiting the results of his examination before rendering their decision. What a pleasure it was to see him. If this were ancient Rome, I'd take his coming for an omen.

February 26, 1942

I've got a fever, a pounding headache, and a hacking cough that's going to rip my lungs apart.

February 27, 1942

Spent the day dozing in bed, feverish and fatigued.

February 28, 1942

The Riom trial opened, and I was cross-examined for the first time. I was still running a fever and was nervous, but as soon as they started asking me questions, I lashed back at them. Over and over, I battered away at all those contemptible traitors who had handed France over to the Germans just so they could bring down the Republic.

When court reconvened for the second session, I struck even harder, stopping only when I was too exhausted to go on. I could sense panic in the balcony, where the New Order's inspectors were observing the scene, and could hear the frightened rustling of judicial robes. The presiding judge took this all in with a calm demeanor, which resulted in his being attacked by the Nazi-controlled press. As far as he was concerned, an accused man who had already been sentenced by Pétain was obviously a guilty man, but in spite of that, he seemed to have maintained some honorable ideas about his profession. Every now and then, the judge sitting next to him would lean over and whisper something. I would have liked to have known what they were saying, but I went on pummeling away with increasing vehemence.

Then it was all over and the lawyers began congratulating me. The gendarmes saluted me as I walked out past them, as if I were reviewing troops. There is no mistaking the meaning of a gesture like that. Back at the prison, the guards shook hands with me and seemed delighted. They are good Frenchmen, good republicans. They had fired the iron stove in my cell, where Génébrier and Mazé were waiting for me, both of them bursting with enthusiasm. I was so terribly sleepy.

February 29, 1942

Off again to the courthouse for another session. In the prison's outer office, I ran into a war veteran under police escort, wearing his medals and stars from 1914. He had been working in Vichy when he suffered some sort of humiliation that led him to speak disparagingly of the government and Pétain. A policeman informed on him and he was given a three-month prison sentence and prohibited from residing in Vichy, where he had built a house. His children cried their hearts out. Oyez! Oyez! Make way for the Marshal's justice!

Back in the courtroom, I continued my attack, as Vichy's grim-faced bureaucrats, overseeing the judges, went about their voluminous note taking. Afterwards, I was returned first to the Riom prison, where the good folk there congratulated me, then to Bourassol, where I hoped to get some sleep. When I got there, Marie was waiting for me, smiling and bright-eyed and very happy about the way things had gone. I chatted with her and the Alsatian guard Ancel, who is a good man. Ancel told me that he had filled out the prison register, which he claimed was the only place where you could still find the words, "in the name of the people of France."

March 1, 1942

The sun was up and the sky once again a soft, subdued blue, but high up in a pine tree, my friend the Bourassol owl went right on with his nocturnal song, even well after the break of day. I went down to the courtyard and set off on my walk. From his window, Blum kindly asked me how I was feeling, and his daughter-in-law Renée read the text of British radio broadcasts to me. Then I spotted Mme La Chambre heading toward me. She shook my hand and asked to have a word with me. She had been ignoring me for the past two years. She is superstitious, the way theater people are, and probably thinks luck has turned my way. I went back up to my cell. She had brought me a nice chicken leg. I gave her a can of apricot jam in return. My two faithful companions, Roger and the doctor, who have been so courageous and patient, were in excellent spirits, as they have been everyday.

March 2, 1942

Another beautiful sunny day. After all the dreadful snow we had been having, it is as if the earth has come back to life. Bourassol's pigeons are once again sailing across the sky. In the cafes in Riom, people are drinking to the Fourth Republic, one freed of the fetters, the rust, and the parliamentary demagoguery that eventually made the Third Republic unrecognizable.

My lawyer, Ribet, dropped by to see me at 5 P.M. Listening to me talk for two whole days has apparently worn him out.

March 3, 1942

For an entire afternoon, I laid out for those finely robed fellows on the bench all the problems associated with harnessing our industrial resources and the various solutions I had painstakingly sought to implement. At the start, I had absolutely nothing to work with because in 1934, Pétain, as War Minister, had cut back the military budget that I had managed to get passed by Parliament when I was Prime Minister in 1933. Neither the judges nor the prosecutors knew anything about these matters, and they prudently refrained from intervening. If I failed in the industrial sector, how is it that the output of war matériel tripled over the winter months? It is a real stickler of a subject, but because I was completely absorbed by my desire to make everything perfectly clear for the stenographers, the journalists, the policemen, and the gendarmes, who were the true representatives of the French people in that courtroom, it appeared to the judges to be no more than a pleasant and interesting issue; I made no mention of the contemptible traitors in Vichy.

Gamelin was supposed to be cross-examined after me. He stated at the outset that he would answer no questions whatsoever. The presiding judge struggled for an hour to get him to talk, but to no avail. It was distressing and painful to watch, enough to make you sick.

March 4, 1942

Guy La Chambre was on the stand for the whole afternoon. For two hours, starting at 1:30, he went over his handling of the Air Force Ministry. The people on our side must not have been too pleased. Why didn't he go on the attack? The second half was better. At the time of the signing of the Armistice, there were 2,500 modern warplanes that had never seen action; they had been left sitting in hangars while our soldiers, pounded by bombs and strafed by Stukas, were begging for air support.

The accusations contained in the depositions given by Massenet, d'Harcourt, and other Air Force Generals like Le Chatelet were terribly damaging for La Chambre. He answered them point by point, graciously excusing the Air Force Chiefs of Staff for having spent their time reflecting on the future while the battle for the life or death of France raged on outside. His final statements were better still, as much in what he said as in the way he said it, and his concluding comments were excellent. I congratulated him and his lawyer, Cresteil, as well.

When I got back to the prison, the head guard came to chat with me. He is a generous and brave fellow, and the epitome of a Marseillais. Quite unexpectedly, he handed me a flask of pastis, out of friendship for me and probably also as a result of the defamation campaign they have been running in *Gringoire* for years, in which they portray me as an alcoholic. Afterwards, this very good fellow began raving about his two daughters, one of whom is a gifted stenographer and the other a law school student. I waved hello to them just a while ago when I saw them at the window of their quarters.

Thursday, March 5, 1942

I just learned today that on March 3, British planes bombed the Renault, Rosengard, and Salmson factories in Billancourt, where they have been manufacturing tanks and airplane engines for the Germans ever since the signing of the Armistice. The death of hundreds of innocent victims is deplorable, but why didn't the sirens sound the alert so that the people could take cover in the excellent shelters that had been provided for them? The German military command in Paris wanted them to be massacred, that's why.

La Chambre took the stand for the last time. He did all right from a purely oratorical point of view, but he praised Vuillemin and the Air Force Chiefs of Staff, and that was a little bit much. He also made a few treacherous comments about me and above all, Blum. As Mme Ribet observed, he was trying to find some loophole to sneak through to save his skin.

March 6, 1942

Young Commander Jacquot came in uniform to see me at the prison and, right in front of all the policemen, boldly handed me a present. Nothing touches me as much as thoughtful gestures of this kind that come from a real soldier.

The court had ruled that the minutes of the meeting of August 23, 1939, would be taken up in closed session. As soon as the presiding judge began his examination, I told him that I was prepared to discuss behind closed doors the diplomatic matters raised at that meeting, but not the military matters. When he insisted that we proceed, I calmly began discussing the diplomatic issues and had absolutely no trouble demonstrating that France had taken all steps necessary to maintain peace.

As early as May 16, 1939, we notified Poland that we would not go to war over Danzig, which the Germans knew well. They wanted war, wanted to destroy Poland and take one more step toward the total domination of Europe. Whoever wrote the article about Danzig under the name Bruère is a traitor. On August 23, 1939, I added, British air power compensated in part for the weakness of our own Air Force. I made reference to a speech Hitler gave on October 12, 1941, which shows that he chose not to invade England in the summer of 1940 because it would have meant committing and very likely sacrificing the entire German Air Force, which is proof of the size and effectiveness of the British Air Force. The meeting that was held on August 23, 1939, was above all given to bringing everyone up to date on events; in no way did it prevent us from subsequently devoting all our energies to saving the peace. To have cowardly resigned ourselves to let the attack on Poland stand would have brought dishonor on the nation. It was, moreover, an attack on France as well, for the only way to remain secure in the face of Germany's might was to defend the bridges over the Rhine or maintain the presence of a counterbalancing force in the East. I concluded by publicly stating that I was convinced that Germany would ultimately suffer defeat.[5]

5. Daladier turned his back to the judges and, speaking directly to the people in the courthouse, declared: "Germany suffered its first defeat with England and its second with Russia. There is no doubt that Germany will be defeated; it is inevitable. We must not let our confidence waver."

April 12, 1942

Rules governing the coverage of the trial in Riom as issued by the French National News Bureau:[6] "Wire services are not to carry any discussion of a political nature, any opinion bearing on the ongoing events of the war, any criticism of the government, any reference to actions taken by Pétain or even to statements he has made about the Army. Tendentious statements that can be construed as Gaullist propaganda will be subject to the severest penalties. Any person failing to comply with these rules will be immediately dismissed and turned over to the appropriate legal authorities."

April 14, 1942

Preparations were being made for our being moved to the prison in Riom, but my intuition told me that it wouldn't happen. At around 9:30 this morning, Commissioner Morel arrived with the latest issue of the *Journal officiel.* It included a legal decree adjourning the trial, pending completion of certain aspects of the investigation. All of Bourassol—prisoners, guards, and policemen alike—rang with laughter. At the time, the judges still hadn't heard about it; they were busy going about their preparations for the coming court sessions with all requisite seriousness.

At the main police station in Riom, Ribet's request for a gasoline coupon was genially turned down. He was told, "There is no need for it, counselor, now that the trial has been put off," and shown a copy of the *Journal officiel,* after which he raced over to the courthouse to inform the judges, who were totally in the dark. No one could find a copy of the *Journal.* Bruzin phoned the Police Commissioner but learned that he had given his copy to Morel, who had already left for Bourassol. So Bruzin, the Solicitor-General arguing the case, ended up calling the Bourassol jailhouse so that they would send him the *Journal officiel,* which was being shared with all the prisoners. Ever since, lawyers have been in and out of this place,

6. At the close of each courtroom session, the French National News Bureau issued similar orders accompanied by similar threats. See Appendix B: The Riom Trial, and Frédéric Pottecher, *Le Procès de la défaite* (Paris: Fayard, 1990).

some asking me to autograph their courthouse passes for them. Thus has come to an end Vichy's attempt, as orchestrated by Pétain and his Ministers, to place responsibility for France's defeat on the Republic. I have gone from accused to accuser. Since they had no way to respond to my accusations, they simply canceled the trial, but without setting us free, naturally.

Received a note from Jacomet: "Pétain has once again called for an armistice."

May 1, 1942

Tixier, a fine man and the owner of the Hotel des Voyageurs, sent me a small bottle of champagne to celebrate May 1. Jean sent me some lines from Walt Whitman's "O Star of France" (1870–1871):

> Like some proud ship that led the fleet so long,
> Be-seems to-day a wreck driven by the gale, a mastless hulk
> And 'mid its teeming madden'd half-drown'd crowds,
> Nor helm nor helmsman.
> Star crucified—by traitors sold,
> Star panting o'er a land of death, heroic land,
> Strange, passionate, mocking, frivolous land.
> O star! O ship of France,
> Sure as the ship of all, the Earth itself.

May 3, 1942

The Japanese have taken Mandalay. Supply routes have been cut off and the invasion of India is imminent. Nehru has been preaching passive resistance and nonviolence. Cripps's mission was a total failure. After the war, the British Empire will survive only at the cost of far-reaching changes, and even then its survival is open to question. This is the final chapter of a splendid story.

May 4, 1942

For two hours starting at 9:00 this morning, a lawyer named Baraveau and a court reporter named Paulin were at Bourassol questioning me about the progress made in our military buildup between 1936 and the end of 1938, and the fact that by the spring of 1939 we were six months ahead of schedule. That matériel, however, never made it out of the warehouse. I answered their questions, then read a statement I had prepared refusing to continue to be a part of this farce of theirs. Has the trial been suspended, or hasn't it?

There have been reactions to the Riom trial. The Italians are indignant over the testimony given about the battle in the Alps. They would like to lay claim to Nice, Corsica, and Tunisia. As for the Russians, they have been enjoying themselves at both Blum's expense and mine: the bull of the Vaucluse at Munich, they call me. And just what were *they* prepared to do for Czechoslovakia? They did nothing but equivocate, as is evidenced by the diplomatic cables of the period. The Americans, via radio, have been emphasizing the courage of the men who stood accused in the Riom courthouse and who effectively put Hitler and Pétain on trial. All of France knows what went on there. Our actions haven't gone unnoticed by the international community either.

Hostages are being executed in Norway, Belgium, Yugoslavia, and France. Just before he died, a Communist named Semard wrote a remarkable letter. He had informed the British of the plans of commando groups and collaborators.

But what had really been missing until now was the kind of contribution Chautemps has just made in the *Nacion de Buenos Aires:* a testimonial to Pétain, whom he helped bring to power, followed, naturally, by a violent diatribe against Laval. He's got two irons in the fire.

I believe that the Allies have a very good chance of winning this war.

May 5, 1942

Roosevelt gave a remarkable speech on April 28. I read both the English version and the French translation. He spoke of the struggle to maintain a humanitarian form of democracy. After Canada voted heavily in favor of joining the conflict, Vichy issued a despicable commentary on Quebec's supposed dissidence. Their interpretation of the facts is pure falsification. The majority of the people in Canada and an overwhelming majority of Canada's men in the military are in favor of sending combat troops overseas. The Anglo-Saxons are the only people to have understood what democracy is and to have practiced it. They have clearly been influenced by religious principles, most notably by those of the Frotestants. Can there be true democracy, and the idealism and the necessary sacrifice it demands, if people do not hold to some sort of religious conviction? Prior to the war, I worked with Cardinal Verdier, Monsignor Beaussart, and Canon Desgranges to bring about a reconciliation between republicanism and Christianity, without which we could never become a great nation. There were, to be sure, numerous obstacles to overcome, but Nazism and Bolshevism did their part to help us. Basically, we tried to move in the same direction as the early Renaissance had, by seeking a purified religion, more focused on human concerns. The Humanists effectively helped destroy that movement by forcing the Catholic church to harden its position into what became the Counter-Reformation, which eventually led to the creation of the order of the Jesuits. The way the Cardinals acted after the Armistice and made Pétain into "the man sent by Providence" is sure to revive anticlerical sentiment, which will be extremely difficult to quell.

May 6, 1942

At around 12:30 at night, a lovely, clear night, British aircraft flew over Bourassol. I could hear the sound of their engines flying low in the sky. Was it a reconnaissance flight over the Michelin factories? A raid on Genoa and on into an Italy protected by the well-defended Rhone Valley? Or better still, could it be ... ? In all events, the ack-ack started pounding away, probably from Clermont and Aulnat. Everyone in Bourassol was looking out the window, as were the people in all the surrounding villages. Whatever was the mission of those mysterious aircraft, the people of France were at their side as they streaked across the sky.

May 7, 1942

Had several long conversations with Léon Blum, who has been suffering from sciatica for a month now. We spoke about the future. He outlined what he felt the political and social consequences of the war would be. He believes that the work we began in 1936 will be continued, work that, sadly, fell victim to demagoguery. After the agreements signed at Matignon, we were frustrated by the rhetoric of the unions, just as we had been constantly undermined by the rhetoric of Members of Parliament, which started as far back as 1910 and reached its peak in the years just before the war. Sooner or later, it was bound to undo the Republic. Consequently, in creating the new institutions of the Fourth Republic, we must focus specifically on erecting insurmountable barriers to demagoguery, by basing those institutions on the American Constitution and British practices. The majority of people in France think that once the British and the Americans win this war, we will be back to the good life they knew in 1936. We cannot afford to tolerate facile solutions.

May 8, 1942

In Clermont-Ferrand, at a meeting conducted by General Lenclud, Colonel Perré,[7] former Commander of the Second Armored Division, which he made into an excellent fighting unit during the war, lectured officers from the area on the role played by his armored division. Then he moved on to address the Riom trial, which, fortunately, he said, focused primarily on the lack of matériel. That left the Army looking just great! But, he added, it is important for you to know, just between us, that matériel was not lacking. We were defeated because we were not mentally prepared for war. In sum, his analysis was no different from Colonel Allerme's. His talk, which was given with General Lenclud's approval, caused quite a stir among the young officers there. Doctor B. was present to see it. He told Blum that he would take the stand should ever the trial in Riom be reconvened.

May 9, 1942

On Monday, Japanese admirals were in Vichy negotiating their plans to occupy Madagascar, just as they had done before occupying Indochina. For once, the British were on time. On the very same day, their fleet positioned itself just off Diego-Suarez.

7. During the trial in Riom, however, Colonel Perré stated that his tanks had given him complete satisfaction.

At a luncheon given for the regional press, Laval made a speech that the French National News Bureau characterized as moving. He believes in Germany's ultimate victory. "If we believed differently, we might as well have handed over power to the men being tried in Riom." If there is a negotiated peace settlement, it will cost us just Alsace and Lorraine. If the Germans dictate peace terms, it will be a lot worse.

May 11, 1942

The most horrible catastrophes can occur, war can spread to every continent on the planet, millions of people can be dying of hunger, and Réal Del Sarte will go on, unchecked, dotting the land with the garbage he calls sculpture. The war has made him richer and richer. Most recently, Chambéry and Limoges have each been graced with a Joan of Arc, fully as unattractive as the ones that came before them. The only thing missing in all this was for Pétain to glorify the artist. Now even that has been done. When will we ever be able to rid our town squares of these grotesque statues—Joan of Arc, Joffre, Alexander—and replace them with real works of art? I read an excellent article by Thierry Maulnier in *Le Figaro* on the ravages wrought by academicism over the last half century. Pétain is the Réal Del Sarte of politics.

May 12, 1942

Laval has been in power for a month now, brought back by the German Embassy in Paris and the French newspapermen on their payroll. Actually, from the time the rough going in the Russian campaign began, there have been two clans vying for Hitler's favors: Ribbentrop and the moderates on one side, and the hard-liners—the Gestapo and the High Command—on the other. The heavy German losses in Russia have led Hitler and the hard-liners to adopt a more aggressive approach and force France to join them in an anti-Bolshevik alliance and, by so doing, assume a more overtly hostile position toward the British and the Americans. With the war becoming more and more difficult for the Germans, the French fleet has taken on increasing value. Ribbentrop and Abetz would like to see a French government that still has some influence over public opinion, a government headed by Laval. The Gestapo and the Army would prefer an authentic French version of Norway's Quisling. A month ago, Pétain was forced to surrender as a result of the campaign orchestrated by the German Embassy in Paris, Brinon's efforts, and the threats that appeared in the Parisian press. Of course, he had had practice at it. See that these matters are attended to, gentlemen, the hard-liners said, and let's hope your M. Laval's actions are not limited to words.

Laval and Abetz have taken a common stand, proposing that in exchange for further material advantages, Germany release French prisoners of war and ease the formalities restricting movement between the Occupied and the Unoccupied Zones. They would present France's pro-German approach as the profound desire of the people, by reestablishing regional councils and bringing into the government noted pro-German Members of Parliament, such as Monzie, Bergery, Marquet, and Lamoureux. It took Laval forty-eight hours, almost as long as it used to take before the war, to put together, or rather to fail to put together, his government. Pétain remains basically hostile to Laval, and the people in his entourage have done what they can to destroy Laval's career. Pétain insisted that he keep Barthélemy and Romier. As for the Germans, they have demanded posts for Bonnard[8] and Marion. In Parliament, people were so convinced that this great new government would not last long that they all made themselves scarce. But there was no way for Laval to retreat from his position, and now that a month has gone by, his situation would seem to be highly compromised. There are several groups against him: the Marshal and his clique, the Royalists, the clergy, and, of course, the Army. People in France have generally become either defiant or irritated with him. His pal Mussolini, troubled by the manifest loss of the support of the Italian people, is laying claim to Tunisia and Corsica. The Gestapo and the German High Command are asking Hitler exactly what he thinks he can gain from backing a man as wasted and out of step as Laval. Abetz is starting to worry. Doriot and Déat are watching him closely, getting ready to take his place as soon as the first occasion presents itself.

8. Abel Bonnard, writer and supporter of Marshal Pétain, who named him Minister of Education.

May 14, 1942

As a side story to last month's ministerial crisis, Senator Reibel made his play, the same Reibel about whom Mme Poincaré would squeeze her nose and say, "Pooh, Reibel" every time his name was mentioned. He is a kind of Charles Humbert, but less colorful, less intelligent, and decidedly more corrupt. He had the backing of Brandt, the man whose name is stamped on mortars he didn't really invent. Having brought discredit on himself in the Senate, Reibel got the bright idea of going to Vichy a few weeks ago and huddling with Du Moulin de Labarthète, one of the birdbrains close to Pétain. His brilliant scheme was to eliminate both Laval and Darlan and replace them with the team of Barthélemy and Reibel. Outside of these two conspirators, there was only one person capable of taking this business seriously: the aviator Fonck,[9] Göring's friend. Fonck headed off for Paris, absolutely delighted to be playing a role in this affair, and went about congratulating himself in front of everyone he met. He was arrested and had his papers confiscated, whereupon the master plan was uncovered. Abetz became frightened and sent Brinon to Vichy to deliver an ultimatum to Pétain: either Laval or a Quisling-like Doriot. Pétain, panic-stricken, agreed to meet with Laval in Randan Forest. We all know what happened after that.

May 18, 1942

Mussolini returned to Rome after having spent six days in Sardinia. Before leaving, he went to kneel at Garibaldi's tomb!

June 6, 1942

Chauvel was consulted by one of his Jewish clients, a war orphan who lost her father in 1914 and her husband in 1940. She has two children and wears a yellow star of David, which is considered a sign of infamy by the people who made wearing it mandatory.

There was an announcement in today's newspapers from the Legion of French Volunteers Against Bolshevism: "The maximum age for enlist-

9. René Fonck, pilot and hero in World War I.

ment has been moved up to forty and the minimum age is now eighteen," *Dépêche de Toulouse* (June 6).

June 7, 1942

Midway. At 9 A.M. Mme Reichenbach brought word of a British radio broadcast announcing a major American naval victory. Three Japanese aircraft carriers were sunk, along with three submarines and fourteen other warships and transports. The Midway Islands are the outposts of the Hawaiian Islands, more or less equidistant from Japan and California, 2,200 to 2,400 miles away. We'll have to wait for more complete reports; we can't forget what happened at the Coral Sea battle. But if these facts are true, they will give an enormous boost to America's war production, which is already substantial. It will boost morale in England and Russia as well. Still, the consequences of an American victory would be felt most deeply in Germany, where Japan's triumphs, which have been stunning indeed, have been repeatedly exploited by Germany's propaganda agencies to offset the grimness of the war in Russia and the appalling losses the Germans have suffered there.

America's decision to intervene in the war was hard on the German people, for whom the ghosts of 1918 are still quite alive. Goebbels ridiculed it, telling his fellow Germans that this time, thanks to the Führer's genius, America's intervention would go for naught. "The Japanese will take care of those Yankees from New England and hog merchants from Chicago. Those people have all sold their souls for dollar bills, refrigerators, and mass-produced automobiles. Every Babbitt they send off to war will end up as food for the fish at the bottom of the Pacific." It made for a great story in the Kraut press and on their radio. Too bad. Now they'll have to find something else.

British radio also hailed the Libyan exploits of a Frenchman, Colonel Kœnig.[10] French people can take great comfort in what he has done,

10. General Pierre Kœnig, commander of the heroic Free French Resistance Forces fighting Rommel.

which will be of considerable importance in the peace negotiations. Kœnig and a few others like him will counterbalance the Georgeses, Requins, Bessons, and Weygands. He has brought glory back to our flag. I saw Jacomet from my window. He told me how overjoyed he was with the news—a sign of the times. "It's all over for Germany," he said and then added, "Midway, Libya, and the statements I have been submitting to the judges ... they're finished!"

June 9, 1942

Mme Reichenbach told us that British broadcasts, last night and again this morning, have been alerting the French people in the Occupied Zone to an impending Allied landing. They've been told to withdraw from combat areas and not to participate in any way, and that subsequent broadcasts will announce the time for them to take action. The news spread throughout Bourassol and drew considerable attention from every quarter. Blum takes this to mean that aerial bombings are imminent. I think it will be another few days yet. Could this signal at long last the liberation of France? Are there leaders anywhere in the ranks of our young Army capable of throwing themselves into the fray and bringing freedom back to their country and honor back to their flag? J.B. confirmed this evening that German soldiers have been notifying people living in restricted areas, which is to say along the coast, to be prepared to leave their homes.

June 12, 1942

The newspapers have reported that Molotov[11] has returned from a trip to London and Washington, where agreement was reached over plans for the continuation of the war and postwar peace terms. According to Russian, American, and British radio, ten points were agreed to, among them: not to sign separate peace treaties; to supply each other with material support; to establish a second front; not to seek territorial gains; to form a twenty-

11. Vyacheslav Molotov, the Soviet Union's Commissar of Foreign Affairs.

year alliance (barring the creation of an effective international peace organization); not to intervene in the internal affairs of other nations.

As Blum went down the list of these various points, he stopped to express his pleasure over the last one. That matter had been of particular concern to him, and he was now relieved. He exclaimed, "Now we'll be able to rebuild the world." In his joy, he must have forgotten that there was a similar clause in the agreement signed by Stalin and Laval.

Sumner Welles gave a Memorial Day speech in Arlington Cemetery. It was an impassioned and moving expression of the guilt Americans feel for the position they took in 1919 when peace terms were being negotiated, for their isolationism, and the frightful consequences it had for Europeans.

June 17, 1942

"Marshal Bazaine on trial, the Monarchy or the Republic on trial—in their differing forms, these all reduce to one and the same phenomenon: France questioning herself, peering into the confusion to define her role in what happened in the past and her perspectives for the future," *La Revue des deux mondes* (1873).

The Riom trial was in no way a 1940 remake of Bazaine's trial. Pétain was careful to exclude any inquiry into the functioning of the military. In the minds of the people who engineered this—Pétain, Laval, and their valets—the Republic and the Republic alone was to be put on trial, but from the very first day on, I made a point of putting Pétain on trial. Unfortunately, I didn't get the chance to go as far as I would have liked. Pétain panicked again and called for another armistice.

Thursday, June 18, 1942

Pétain gave a speech yesterday that was broadcast over the radio several times throughout the day. It was supposed to commemorate his coming to "power," a word that has been so weakened that it is no longer really applicable. Anyone wishing to find out exactly what the conditions were surrounding his rise to power has only to consult the proceedings of the Riom trial, Elie Bois's[12] account of the crisis in Bordeaux and how Reynaud took flight, and, let us not forget, Montigny's book *Toute La Vérité!*

It is now manifestly clear that there was a criminal plot to hand France over to the enemy and that it succeeded because there were enough cowards to go along with the plotters. The idea was to deal a death blow to the Republic and replace it with some form of fascism or Salazarism. An agreement with the Germans had been reached probably as early as May 25 and in all events no later than June 15, but Pétain and his accomplices went about preparing the government's transfer to North Africa, under the pretense of organizing French resistance there. Lebrun, Jeanneney, and Herriot were to go by land, the loyal Members of Parliament by sea. The latter group were all later to be accused of having fled; that's the now well known story of the *Massilia.* As for Darlan's role in this business, at first he was taken in as well, as is clear in the cables he sent General Noguès: "Set up a command post for me in Rabat, next to yours."

June 19, 1942

Pétain's speech seemed curious at first. The flourish we had come to expect was replaced by the muffled trill of a Magic-less Flute. The man who gave France "the gift of his person" has begun to fear that the gift hasn't worn well, which is why he blamed the bureaucrats for the poor results of his two years of absolute power. Our national Tartuffe declared that the Jews and the Freemasons were responsible for things having gone so poorly. The speech must have been either prompted by Laval or reworked by him, and it didn't want for shrewdness. Laval, after having been arrested on Pétain's orders on December 13, 1940, and released only after Hitler's direct intervention in the matter, managed to get the Marshal to acknowledge a long list of failures brought on by his predecessor, Admiral Darlan, and the Ministers who became the underlings of that brainless head of state. It's a nice piece of work; add to that the fact that the French are good people, born naïve. Oh, the Marshal is such a fine man! He tells us the truth. He is

12. Elie Bois, Editor in Chief of the *Petit Parisien* prior to the war.

so honest, so good. He has been as much a victim as we are of that gang of administrators, Prefects, distributors, and swindlers, etc. Another case of Orgon feeling sorry for Tartuffe after the latter has confessed to having tried to seduce the former's wife.

June 20, 1942

My friend the owl was flying about at daybreak from the pine tree to his nest and back. I heard the familiar call I used to hear at nightfall when I would come back from the Riom courthouse.

June 22, 1942

Tobruk has fallen. Just this past winter, Blum assured me that the Germans would run out of gasoline by May! In spite of all the communiqués from the front and the reports in the British press, he's still reserving comment, on the grounds that we couldn't pick up British radio yesterday.

June 23, 1942

Laval's latest speech is couched in terms of the inevitable. Had he already foreseen a few days ago Mussolini's ultimatum and Hitler's threats? The man is so extraordinarily soulless. I can't think of any words to describe what moves him other than the Italian *vilta*. Jacomet, who is absolutely indignant, thinks the speech is proof that Laval was already a traitor both before and during the war. He spoke mainly of Bolshevism, in an attempt to incite fear and appeal to the bourgeoisie. Yet it was Laval who negotiated the 1935 pact with Stalin that allowed for the creation of the Popular Front. It's quite a way from Kienthal (or Stockholm) to Vichy; just look at the speeches he gave in 1916 and 1917. Everyone in Vichy is up in arms. According to the orderly of General Bridoux, the War Minister, the part where Laval decried General Giraud's escape was received especially badly in the Ministry and throughout the Army.

Chauvel ran into Flandin, who thinks the Germans will be defeated and that they and the British will be the war's principal losers. He anticipates several months of Communist agitation following the war, but feels that it will be quashed rather easily when the country as a whole rises up against it. Communism will fall into disrepute, along with neofascism and the neo-Nazism of the collaborators, after which we'll witness a return to a Republic freed of extremists. In other words, Flandin will live to see the dream of a Democratic Alliance—his party—come true!

Flandin believes that in his district, the Riom trial seriously cut into the government's popularity. What could have been more absurd than having politicians tried in the courts? The judges were obviously going to be overwhelmed by the people they were judging. Since the high court had been dissolved, they should simply have carried out the Marshal's sentence and left these men to rot in Le Portalet. Flandin concluded by saying that if an election were to be held today in his circumscription, Daladier would carry it easily.

In *Les Nouveaux Temps*, that traitor Luchaire and someone named Guy Crouzet are demanding a people's court for us, so we can be sentenced without judicial proceedings. It's all perfectly logical, given that he believes that Germany's victory will bring good to both the world as a whole and France individually. Luchaire, Crouzet, and Mallet basically run the paper, along with Lassguiwer. Du Moulin de Labarthète gave a speech about the Frenchmen working in Germany, praising them for the quality of the work they have been doing for the Germans.

Sunday, June 28, 1942

I have a very low opinion of Stafford Cripps and the Australian Minister whose fears led to the breakup of the forces in Libya. The Japanese have given further proof of their cleverness by feigning an attack on Australia and India while marching into Chiang Kai-shek's China, gaining a foothold on the Aleutian Islands, and preparing to intervene in Siberia.

Blumel[13] came to spend the day with Blum. The Portuguese police had turned him over to the Spanish, whose uniformed brutes beat him when he refused to answer their questions. He was imprisoned in Spain before being handed over to Vichy, then sent to an internment camp in southeastern France, and finally released.

13. André Blumel, Daladier's Chief of Staff.

The picture he drew of Spanish prisons, where three years after Franco's victory there are still almost a million political prisoners, was in marked contrast to what has generally been presented to the world as the retribution taken against a handful of terrorists and Bolsheviks by a victorious, broad-based, national movement. He said that executions were being carried out daily and that the prison halls rang with the *Marseillaise* and the Communist *Internationale.*

In the Pyrénées-Orientales and the Hérault, the people (among them, Badie) have been putting up admirable resistance, above all among the lower-level civil servants. Laval's speech was met with indignation. Large numbers of farmers are reportedly refusing to deliver their produce to the official redistribution centers; they are convinced that most of it ends up in Germany. In Nîmes, they are selling *Combat*[14] in the streets. Several people have been arrested.

June 30, 1942

German and Italian forces have taken Mersa Matruh and another 6,000 prisoners. Air raids are being carried out over Alexandria. Will the Egyptians go to war against England? And what about the Turks? Papen is undoubtedly trying to lure them with visions of Armenia, Syria, and Palestine. What is the explanation for Britain's collapse?

Australia's Labor Party Prime Minister, who took over from Menzies, has been bluffed by Japan into pulling his troops out. In any event, England is on the verge of being run out of the Mediterranean. The Italian fleet will be able to operate in the Atlantic, and their bombers, which have already gone into action there, will be given the means to do even more damage.

The Russians have put up heroic resistance in Sebastopol. Timoshenko has been counterattacking.

In France "All Parisian high society was at Longchamp. ... Attendance records were broken. ... The prize at the weigh-in was raised ... women had on absolutely ravishing outfits." All this while workers, forced

14. A Resistance newspaper.

onto the unemployment rolls as a result of the closing of 1,500 factories and the shipping of raw materials to Germany, have to sign up to work for the victory of the Third Reich.

July 1, 1942

Met with Reverend Father Dillard,[15] from the Society of Jesus, who has taken over for Candan in giving Gamelin confession. He expressed the desire to see me also, if I was so inclined. I was happy to receive him and was quickly won over by his directness, his candor, and the loftiness of his heart and mind. He has traveled a great deal; knows the United States, Italy, and Germany well; and is an admirer of the youthfulness and the idealism basic to Americans and so often misunderstood by Europeans. He holds Roosevelt in great esteem, on perfectly legitimate grounds. Talked about what he had done during the war as commander of an artillery unit on the Meuse (a support group for Etcheberrigaray's 102nd Division). He is unforgiving in his judgment of the High Command and the leaders who lost their heads—and never found them again—as soon as Germany attacked. Thinks that the Germans will ultimately go down to defeat, that they will take one tumble after another before the final catastrophe. Also thinks that the British Empire is doomed and does not share Candan's enthusiasm for Japan.

He said the Vatican is hostile to Hitler and to Mussolini (which I knew) and that the overfed and overpraised farmers in France had fallen victim to material values. He finds the workers to be the most attractive part of the population. He spoke of the heroic death of Communists at the hands of German torturers: "They died like true Christians." He feels that this war marks the failure of the bourgeois values incarnated in tax inspectors, capitalists, engineers from L'Ecole Polytechnique and politicians from Sciences-Politiques, etc. He fears that there will be bloody incidents once it's over, and that, as a result of the current government's stupidity and the church's naïveté, there will be a resurgence of anticlerical sentiment.

15. The Reverend Father Dillard, a Jesuit who volunteered to work in Germany. Informed on, he was deported to a concentration camp, where he died.

July 13, 1942

Le Roy Ladurie[16] issued a vehement statement, reprinted in *Le Temps*, about the manner in which vegetables have been brought to market: "At the beginning of July, at the very height of the vegetable season and after the splendid work done by our farmers, the public markets are bare, store shelves are empty, and goods are being sold at outrageous prices; the only people profiting from this situation are those with special privileges and the idle rich. Given the hardships people are facing, this is scandalous."

Every man is his own best judge. Le Roy Ladurie, one of the principal prewar demagogues in matters of agrarianism, is in perfect position to draw up an indictment of his bankrupt policies. He can go right on rattling his cardboard saber and rereading his *Philippics*.[17] One after the other, he castigated the farmers, the distributors, the storekeepers, and the consumers. He spared no one except himself. He should come here and look out my window onto the farm worked by Poles. He'd witness the continuous procession of barterers who, under the eyes of the garrison that surrounds Bourassol, come to exchange tobacco, shoes, or, if they have to, money for ham, eggs, poultry, milk, butter, and so on. It is the perfect illustration of what has resulted from the economy as structured by these "National Revolutionaries," a bunch as corrupt as any group of smugglers.

Last night, I reread Herriot's excellent books on the Lyons revolution. "For their revolution to succeed, the lower classes must be led by a core of incorruptible men." You're not going to find any of those at the Bank of Worms or among those well-heeled demagogues of the Agrarian Party. Farmers are starting to take seriously all the theories that the Mathés, the Le Roy Laduries,[18] the Achards, and the Dorgèreses went on ranting about before the war, in what was a pure attempt to use the farmers

16. Jacques Le Roy Ladurie, farmer and Marshal Pétain's Agriculture Minister.

17. Demosthenes' exhortations to the people of Athens, in which he accused them of apathy and of failing to live up to their glorious past.

18. Gabriel Le Roy Ladurie, financier and member of the Worms conglomerate. He had close ties with Paul Reynaud (1940), then with Admiral Darlan. Edouard Daladier considered him to be the kingpin in the plot against the Republic. He was affiliated with the Synarchie, a secret organization working to seize power.

as a political stepping stone. To date, there hasn't been a word out of Caziot, even though he is second in command at the Ministry of Agriculture and sticks closer to Le Roy Ladurie than his shadow.

Le Temps ran a four-column spread on the ceremonial oath-taking of the Rhône chapter of the SOL,[19] France's version of the SS, so to speak. The speeches that were given there, the oath they took on bended knee (not even Hitler came up with that), the remarks made about the kindness and generosity the German people would show the French, using Poland as an example of it—it was all enough to make you sick. We must really have sunk awfully low for so abject a performance to be possible, even in the wake of our defeat, on Terreaux Square in Lyons.

July 14, 1942

The Riom trial will not be reconvened, neither to assign blame for our having gone to war (the court effectively dropped that charge for lack of evidence), nor to assign blame for our defeat; on that score, the most recent documents demonstrate the overwhelming responsibility of our Generals. Laval's idea is to put La Chambre and possibly Jacomet under house arrest and either have Reynaud and Mandel brought to Bourassol or find a house for all five of us. Pétain, in contrast, wants to ship us off to Le Portalet. For two years now, they have been dragging me through the mud without giving me a chance to defend myself. The traitors have been taking shots at me to their hearts' content, Pétain most of all, followed by the Doriots, Déats, Carbuccias, and Fontinis, not to mention the Marquets, Aliberts, Baudouins, and company. In the early court sessions, I demolished the testimony of their phony experts and their phony witnesses, but that didn't faze them. They simply gagged us, starting last April. Since then, the admissions made by those who were truly responsible for our defeat and piles of staggering documentary evidence have continued to pour in. Even the judges appointed by Pétain and Alibert to conduct the pretrial investigation had to conclude that France was not defeated; France was

19. The Service d'Ordre de la Légion, an organization of shock troops created by Pétain and his Ministers.

handed over to the enemy. That truth will have to be buried in the moats around Le Portalet.

Bousquet[20] asked Génébrier, "How do you know Laval doesn't think that Germany will ultimately be defeated?" Thoughts like that are sure to provide him with terrific evenings galore.

They say that the Count of Paris[21] is a man with nothing to recommend him. He has a few stirred-up Generals in his entourage, all as mediocre as he. He came to see Pétain to express his astonishment at not having been made King of France. "I have been waiting for eight years," he told him. Nothing could be more unpleasant for that conceited old man, Pétain. As is his wont, he didn't let it show and sent the Count to see Laval.

July 15, 1942

American radio was absolutely magnificent yesterday. Roosevelt delivered a short, powerful address and the Senate adopted a resolution glorifying France and France's fight for freedom and pledging to restore France to its former greatness and wipe tyranny from the face of the earth. It had all the resonance of the best pieces written in the days of the *Convention*. I received a telegram Bullitt sent me from abroad. "The day will come when we'll be singing the *Marseillaise* in a France once again free and strong." They also read on the air a long excerpt from a *New York Times* article.

There have been large patriotic demonstrations in the major cities in Unoccupied France. Thousands of people sang the *Marseillaise* in the streets of Lyons, Grenoble, Marseilles, Toulouse, Montpellier, Nîmes, and Avignon. Shooting out of windows in Marseilles, SOL members killed four people and wounded several others.

---

20. René Bousquet, a former Prefect named Superintendent of Police in Vichy. At the end of the war, he took a position with the Bank of Indochina. Tried by the High Court, he got off with a token sentence and was immediately granted amnesty. Many years later, he was charged with crimes against humanity. He was awaiting trial when he was gunned down in his apartment in Paris in June 1993.

21. The Pretender to the French crown, in exile until then.

July 18, 1942

Jean showed up unexpectedly at 5 P.M. He told me about the July 14 demonstration in Grenoble, where five to six thousand people turned out, among them Abbot Desgranges. They shouted, "Down with the Krauts, long live France, long live de Gaulle, long live the Republic," and held off the SOL.

They call this version of the country legal? With a bunch of people in charge who were traitors before and during the war and again in Bordeaux? With the fraud they perpetrated in the National Assembly? With Generals who turned and ran or turned traitor and came back dishonored from Germany? With the capitalist concentration of wealth in the hands of trusts and the Bank of Worms, all of it now legalized and sanctified by a government order shutting down 1,200 businesses? The result has been that great numbers of workers have been forced to go to Germany to find work. And all this rottenness sits there under the banner of a collaboration effort undertaken for Europe's salvation.

July 19, 1942

They say that Pétain is just about senile in the afternoon. He remains lucid for two to three hours a day. He is surrounded by a bunch of nonentities, with General Campet at the top of the list. His whole entourage—and Pétain at times, too—is hostile to Laval. Behind this clique at the Sévigné Pavilion there is another one gravitating around Weygand and especially around Giraud, who is motivated by his dual hatred for Germany and democracy. Half of these people envision a military dictatorship à la Franco, the others a *Consulat*, lacking only a Napoleon to head it. Laval would have liked to pursue his servile policies toward Germany by putting up as many working-class front men as he could come up with: a union leader brought back to power; Lagardelle, brought in to replace Belin; parliamentarians in the style of Bonnet, Monzie, Mistler, Chichery, but the boys refused to go for it; they preferred to promote their own interests. He had to fall back on Bergery, Belmont, Reibel, and that bunch. Paul Faure[22] has written a book proving that everything that has been done since the National Assembly convened in Vichy was illegal. He had Susset give me his best regards.

Laval has been trying to broaden the role of the regional administrative councils. He has gotten nowhere with the Germans, who have in fact split into two clans: Ribbentrop, Abetz, and those who would pick France clean little by little, and the Army officers, who would simply slit her throat. The latter have Hitler's ear. Anyway, Hitler hates France. The Army officers have made a mockery of everything Laval has tried. So how does one get into their good graces? By mobilizing against the British and the Americans if they attempt a landing in France? By sending troops to Syria to support the Germans if they decide to invade? The question was put to General Frère, who responded that the French Army would never agree to dishonor itself in that way. They almost dismissed him for making those comments, but eventually backed down. He has been firmly opposed to the creation of the Tricolor Legion[23] and spoken against it openly on his rounds of military inspections. It is obvious that the German Army officers favor Doriot over Laval, although it is probably just a game. Outside of the groups in Marseilles and Nice, the PPF doesn't have that many members—two to three thousand adventurers all told, according to the Prefect of Police, who also said that it would not take much to wipe them all out.

Vichy was clearly upset and worried about the July 14 demonstrations, especially those held in Lyons, Marseilles, Grenoble, Clermont, Montpellier, and Nîmes, where waves of human beings flooded the streets. Popular demonstrations of this sort could only have been made possible at the present time by deep-seated feelings of rebellion and the growing sense of a veritable and profound national unity that extends from Communist workers to Catholics. It is our duty to see to it that the true great-

22. Paul Faure became Secretary-General of the Socialist Party after the break with the Communists in 1920. He held ministerial positions under Blum and Chautemps. Prior to the war, he was a pacifist. He did not participate in the vote of July 10, 1940, in Vichy but later became a member of Marshal Pétain's Conseil National.

23. A French Legion created to fight alongside the Germans, against the Allies.

ness of this national sentiment is preserved. I stand prepared to risk my life to oppose the manipulations and rhetoric of partisan politicians and stave off any attempt to thwart what is in effect the greatest national movement in all of French history. Perhaps our defeat was a necessary step for us, but not at all in the way that it is presented by Pétain and his cliques of hypocrites and traitors.

Laval would like to have the Riom trial suppressed. He has had Vals closed and disbanded. Every little fluctuation of contemporary history has had its repercussions on this trial, which has proven to be an event of major importance.

July 21, 1942

Last night in Riom, Génébrier ran into Commander Jacquot, who is a member of General Frère's staff and who has kept the General apprised of his meetings with my associates from the very outset. Frère is politically right-wing, but he is a fine and patriotic soldier. Jacquot still believes that Germany will ultimately be defeated, but not because of a shortage of raw materials, equipment, or workers. He thinks they will lose because they are going to run short of men and sacrifice their youth. By drawing recruits from among the able-bodied male population aged seventeen to fifty, they can raise 15 to 16 million men. If the Russian Army isn't surrounded and destroyed—and it seems clear that Timoshenko has understood the need to retreat—Germany will be facing yet another winter campaign that will inflict more frightening losses, at the very time that America is completing its preparations.

Jacquot is opposed, quite correctly, to the creation of a second front before next fall. He would prefer to wait until the following spring. I totally agree with him. He thinks that the French Army will join up with the Americans and bring with them twenty or so divisions outfitted with infantry gear but without airplanes and tanks, which the Americans will have to supply. I fear that the French Army's role in the liberation of France is little more than a lovely dream in the minds of our young officers.

July 24, 1942

Génébrier spent the day in Vichy, where they are still at one another's throats, but they keep on fighting without ever delivering any death blows. If they did, the species would have become extinct long ago. Pétain's entourage is now led by his doctor, Ménétrel, a high-society Royalist who is being stroked nowadays by Bonnet and the Count of Paris.

His court includes a few Jesuits and, every now and then, Du Moulin de Labarthète, a wait-and-see reactionary. Then there is General Laure,[24] alias Calamity Jane; Laval; and the Doriotists grouped under Darnand's[25] aegis, where the rifts have become serious ever since Valentin's departure. Génébrier also saw Jael, who believes that Vuillemin and Georges will be indicted once the new investigation is completed. He is a young fellow, still naïve.

On his way back to see me, Génébrier stopped off at the courthouse to get passes. Bruzin has become quite kindly and cordial. When Génébrier thanked Caous for having been so gracious during the trial, Caous was moved to tears. He said he would never have agreed to preside over it if he had known it was going to be suspended.

Jacques Kayser[26] came to see me. He has moved to the area around Villeneuve-sur-Lot. He told of the reawakening of public conscience that has followed the Riom trial and Laval's rise to power.

Young Raphaël-Leygues has put my photo on the desk in his law office ... next to Darlan's!

August 2, 1942

The trial is the only thing Jacomet can think of, and it will never be reconvened. There is no point in trying to discuss England or the events in Russia with him. Within a few seconds, he is back talking about the trial and the scandalous way the trusts, the capitalists, the High Command,

24. General Emile Laure, Commander of the Ninth Army Corps in September 1939, then, temporarily, in May 1940, of the French Eighth Army. He was Pétain's Chief Administrative Officer. In 1943, he was imprisoned in Germany.

25. Joseph Darnand, Chief of Vichy's Militia. He was executed after the war.

26. Jacques Kayser, attaché in Daladier's Cabinet from 1938 to 1940.

Weygand, and a few other ogres treated him. The truth is that I have known very few men in my lifetime who were genuinely concerned with anything other than themselves. Nowadays, Jacomet spends every minute of his time at Blum's window, whereas he used to consider him a visionary and a danger to the people around him. But our resident prophet has complimented and flattered him and above all praised his wife. His bereft wife is doing her best too, by piling on the chocolates, the potatoes, and the apricots ... the most recent props for the most recent dance form of the most recent Salome.

August 3, 1942

Ribet, who has come down here to spend his vacation at the Hotel Pailleret, came to see me at 4:30 P.M., bringing news from Paris. The Germans arrested 8,000 Jews, who were to be deported to Cracow. The women were hauled to the Vélodrome d'Hiver after having been brutally separated from their children, who looked absolutely dazed and frightened to death as they were piled onto trucks and herded to detention centers. It was unbearable to watch. Some mothers went mad. An employee at the Prefecture of Police told Ribet that when two police inspectors arrived to arrest a Jewish woman and her two children, she threw them out of the window and jumped out to her death after them. Marshal Pétain offered the services of his police force and the National Guard to help carry out this ignominious act, and it's just one more in a whole series of outrages. He personally handed over Communist hostages to be executed by the Germans. Barthélemy, the Minister of Justice, placed their heads right onto the chopping block. The National Revolution has planted its roots in blood and infamy.

The renowned lawyer Pierre Masse, a Senator and, if I am not mistaken, a former Junior Minister under Clemenceau, was interned in the camp in Drancy for several months. He held up admirably. He was supposed to be deported to Cracow, but because he'd been keeping the records of the personal effects removed from Jews at the time of their arrest—watches, pens, money, etc.—and recording as well the formal requests made so that objects of value could revert to family or friends, a high-ranking Nazi policeman accused him of fraud. This turned out to be a godsend. He was sent to La Santé prison to be tried by French authorities. Ribet has been untiring in his attempts to help him. With the aid of a state prosecutor named Gabolde, who is incidentally a collaborator and a supporter of Pétain, he managed to extend Masse's imprisonment in La Santé beyond the date on which he was to be deported to Cracow. Ribet went to see him before leaving for Lyons and found him as courageous and steadfast as ever.

Before the trial, I insisted that Perretti della Rocca, the former Ambassador who headed the notorious Council of Political Justice that met in Vichy in October 1941, be made to testify. After having read the table of contents of the prosecutor's lengthy indictment, in which a good two-thirds of the figures cited are false, Perretti proposed, in agreement with Pétain, that we be sentenced to life imprisonment within the thick-walled medieval fortress at Le Portalet. When Perretti retired, he got himself appointed Chairman of the Board of Française Capitalisation, which is a finance company on the order of Séquanaise and which has had a considerable number of run-ins with the legal authorities over the last few years. He was named to head the Council of Political Justice through the good graces of Pétain and appointed thereafter Vice President of the State Tribunal in Paris by Barthélemy. Now he is under the threat of an indictment for fraud. Ribet had a look at the investigators' report, which is brutal. He said he would send me a copy of it. Moreover, he will be assisting Lemaire, counsel for the liquidators. This should get him a seat right up front to admire Barthélemy's efforts to rescue Perretti. The testimony to be given at the Riom trial by the head of the Council of Political Justice and the Chairman of Française Capitalisation is looking juicier and juicier.

Georges Bonnet has been working with the Nazis. He recently had dinner with a few high holy German lordships, each of them incidentally in the charming company of a woman from French high society. For the moment, the Germans are preoccupied with getting their hands on Portuguese coal mines whose stock is jointly held by the French, the English, the Portuguese, and so on. The British would like to get control of these mines too. Bonnet is doing whatever he can to help the Germans, which is just more of the same. I made a similar judgment about him when I read his latest deposition, which is in effect a confession.

Chichery is going around telling everyone that Laval won't do anything without consulting him first.

Ribet heard from one of his friends who had recently dined with Maillefaud, Deputy Chief Judge of the Cour Suprême, that I had torn the prosecutor's indictment to shreds and totally dominated the proceedings.

August 6, 1942

Admiral Abrial has been taking his traveling circus from city to city, giving crude, vehement anti-British propaganda talks. The heads of the Legion take these occasions to spew forth their hatred for the Republic, the Jews, the Freemasons, and Churchill. I can't say whether Abrial made a hero of himself at Dunkerque, but he has certainly made a jackass of himself with the violence of his verbal attacks. It is sad to see so highly decorated a naval officer stooping to the role of German propagandist.

August 7, 1942

Ribet and his wife were out for a walk with Bénazet in the gardens of the Hotel Pailleret when all of a sudden a limousine drove up and Laval stepped out. Policemen piled out of a second car and surrounded him. Ribet knows Laval well; they're on a first-name basis. He went up to him, followed by Bénazet.

Laval: So this is where you are. Come to see your client.

Ribet: Right, and to get some rest, too. Did you know that the Count of Paris was here yesterday?

Laval: Yes I know. He came by plane from Morocco to see Pétain, who sent him on to see me. I am going to have dinner with him, then I'll put him back on a plane to Morocco.

Then Laval spoke of the Riom trial, which he claimed hadn't dealt with the right issues.

Laval: They should have tried the people responsible for the war. France was the instigator, as I have been saying everywhere I go. And I could have prevented it from ever happening, if only they had let me take the floor in the Senate on September 2. The responsible parties should be put on trial along with the defendants in Riom.

Ribet: So bring the case to court. I don't think there is a judge in France who would agree to dishonor himself in that way.

Laval: We'll see about that soon enough. In any event, we're in the midst of a worldwide revolution. There is a choice to be made between fascism and Bolshevism. And when I say Bolshevism, I mean democracy as well.

At that point another car pulled up, with the Count of Paris, Ménétrel, and an Air Force Colonel from Pétain's Cabinet, followed by a swarm of policemen. Laval and his guests went into the dining room, where a table had been set for them. It was 8 P.M. and beautiful outside, but for fear of an attempt on their lives, the policemen closed the shutters and the windows and they dined by lamplight.

August 12, 1942

"A sacred relief effort has begun." "An intense, emotional moment was lived yesterday morning at the train station in Compiègne." An unknown number of repatriated prisoners and volunteers who had offered to work for Hitler embraced each other. The *Marseillaise* and a speech by Laval were right on cue in celebrating this act of treason under the mocking or disdainful eye of Von Ritter, the leader of the German workers' front. In a speech dripping with hate, Laval offered a defense of his treason. He termed those pitiful deals a triumph of his genius. A total of 50,000 farmers will be released from Prussian prisoner-of-war camps in exchange for 150,000 French workers who will go to Germany to promote their war effort.

When Laval came to power, he was what Voltaire used to call "everyone's daddy." He opened his arms to friends and enemies alike and hugged them warmly. Then, as soon as the first problem arose, the real Laval would rise to the surface: vicious and, wherever possible, insolent. It's mind-boggling to hear that in speaking with Ribet in the gardens of the Hotel Pailleret this past Friday, August 7, at 8 P.M., while waiting for the Count of Paris, Laval once again spoke of me in the same terms reported by Dignac and again by Bousquet in his talks with Génébrier: He claimed that he holds me in high esteem and is concerned about my safety.[27]

August 19, 1942

The Germans have now reached the Don and positioned themselves all along its banks. The ferocious fighting around Stalingrad rages on, but everywhere else the Germans have assumed a defensive posture. They have set up a base of operations with superior numbers of men and supplies between the Caucasus, the Don, and the Volga. The Soviets have launched diversionary counterattacks in Rzhev, Vyazma, and Voronezh, which have resulted in bloody battles but no appreciable strategic gains. We have clearly reached the critical point of the war. If there is still a Russian Army at the end of the summer and if the industrial centers in the Urals and Siberia are really what Butler said they were, 1943 could be the year of our victory. The future of the world is being decided at this very moment. If Germany should triumph, I will arrange for my two sons to leave for the United States, and rather than live in an enslaved France, whether I am free or imprisoned, I will have no choice but to put an end to my life.

The heat has been unbearable. To let in a little breathable air, Blum has propped his door open. I have done the same with mine and with the windows that face north, to give him a little bit of a breeze. Then I went over to chat with him. Once again the discussion centered on Germany and what would happen after the war. He went back over his feelings from 1919. We made two major errors then, he said. The first was in being so ungenerous toward the German people; the second, in allowing Germany's military, administrative, industrial, and capitalist structures either to remain functional or to be recreated, and thereafter in recognizing and dealing with them out of our fear of Karl Liebknecht, Rosa Luxemburg, and the inroads the Communists might make.

27. At the end of 1942, Laval told Jean Daridan that he would never let Daladier be deported to Germany. "If Blum and Daladier are forced to leave Bourassol, there's only one place for them to go, my place, Châteldon." In truth, Laval shipped them off to Germany in 1943.

Our first Ambassador to Berlin was Laurent, of the foundry owners' group, and the most highly respected German then was Hugo Stinner, a steel magnate from the Ruhr Valley. We can't afford to repeat those mistakes after this war. It would be good for Germany to be dominated by the working classes for a few years, under a regime analogous to the one created under the Russian Revolution. And we should demonstrate generosity toward that new Germany and not seek to destroy its unity.

I don't agree with Blum. There can be no lasting peace in Europe so long as Germany is dominated by the Prussians; if that state of affairs continues, a new war will break out twenty years from now.

Has Germany really changed that much in all this time? Isn't the essence of the Nazi doctrine already present in Fichte? I am afraid that Blum's ideas, which are attractive, to be sure, are just so many pipe dreams. He is right: We have to destroy the structures, but we also have to see to it that they are not rebuilt. Ancel, the prison guard from Alsace, knows the Germans a lot better than either Blum or I. I put the question to him. He didn't hesitate a second in answering: If we don't put an end to the Prussian domination of Germany, which we should have done in 1918, there is no possibility of a lasting peace.

Reverend Father Dillard came to Bourassol this morning. Gamelin, La Chambre, and Jacomet attended mass, while I lay outside, nude, on a blanket, taking in the hot sun.[28] Father Dillard came to see me after the church services and we chatted about the present state of the French Army's officer corps, which appears to him to be terribly mediocre. I heard that Blum took a snapshot of this dialogue in the sun.

August 20, 1942

Daridan, France's delegate at the Armistice Commission in Turin, dropped in out of the blue. He said that the Italians in Piedmont and Lombardy are absolutely exasperated with Germany's dictatorial attitudes. Their greatest wish is for the war to come to an end. Antifascist groups

28. During his hour's outing, Daladier would sometimes take sunbaths "top to bottom." The guards would remain off at a distance, which allowed him to speak without being overheard.

have been gaining ground, especially in Piedmont. Rationing has been imposed, just as in France. When word of the capture of Tobruk came, Mussolini took off to North Africa with fifty cameramen in tow to film his entrance into Alexandria. He grew indignant over Rommel's sluggishness and went and complained to Hitler. In any case, Daridan believes the Germans will be defeated by late 1943.

While in Vichy, Daridan met with Jardin, who admitted that his boss, Laval, had failed in every way. He would like to see Laval backed by a centrist party, which people have been dreaming about since the time of Louis XVIII and which I almost managed to create in early 1939, after the collapse of the general strikes. Anyway, the Germans take no notice whatsoever of the government in Vichy. Daridan said that the corruption that has taken hold in that town is absolutely appalling, and that goes for Pétain's staff as well, where every request for an interview is met with the question: "What's he offering?" The same holds true for the Ministries. Daridan brought me the kind respects of Revers, an anti-German French General, whose dream it is to be part of an "Armistice Army" expelling the Germans.

August 21, 1942

The press has reported a British sneak attack at Dieppe. *La Dépêche de Neuchâtel* carried dispatches from both London and Berlin. It was a large-scale raid, no comparison with the one carried out earlier at Saint-Nazaire, but it wasn't an attempted landing, as the Germans are claiming, which is perhaps regrettable. If the landing of a large force, protected by air power, had been attempted at several points on the coast, it is very likely that they could have gained a foothold. The conclusion to be drawn from comparing communiqués from the two different sources is that the Germans were taken by surprise and that Dieppe remained in British hands until almost four in the afternoon, when a division of German reinforcements arrived. A French officer from the Air Force base in Aulnat who witnessed the battle said that almost 200 German warplanes were shot down and that they had to bring in planes from as far away as Belgium and Holland. The people of Dieppe sided with the British, but they refrained from participating in the fighting, having been alerted by British radio that this was a reconnaissance mission and that they should take shelter and not intervene. Vichy and Berlin have been congratulating the local population so insistently that it's become a joke. General Stulpnagel has had 10 million francs run off for them on his presses. We'll see where they stand when the Americans and British attempt a real landing.

Americans victorious in the Solomon Islands. Riots in China. Heroic Russian soldiers and, two months from now, winter.

August 23, 1942

America's industrial war output. Fact: In June 1939, the United States manufactured only 224 aircraft, commercial planes included; in June 1940, 600; in May 1941, 4,000. Fact: In May 1942, more than 1,500 tanks rolled off the assembly lines. These figures demonstrate once again that it took between a year and a half and two years to bring the world's greatest industrial power to function at capacity. In France, the indolence of the different War Ministers in 1934 put our rearmament program a year behind the Germans'. If I had not demanded that the Finance Minister[29] order 4,500 airplanes from the United States before the war and at its outbreak, America would never have been able to turn out 4,000 planes in May 1941. This is all further proof that we could have and should have continued the fight from North Africa.

August 26, 1942

A recent law "eliminates the regulating agencies of the Chamber of Deputies and the Senate." Henceforth, civil servants and a commissioner appointed by the government will oversee the financial and administrative affairs of the two chambers. Legally, the powers of the legislative presidents and administrative officers expired on January 10, 1941. I never understood why Jeanneney didn't convene a session of the National Assem-

29. At the time, Paul Reynaud was Finance Minister. He considered the orders that Daladier had placed with the United States excessive. Daladier answered his criticism as follows: "If I can't get those planes, you'll have to find another Prime Minister, one who will make peace with Germany."

bly on that date to state for the record that Pétain had violated decisions made by the Assembly in Vichy.

I also ran across a particularly grotesque edict approving the rules governing the equally grotesque Francisque.[30] Members of this new order will now have to recite the following pledge: "I offer my life to Marshal Pétain, as he has offered his to France," etc.

August 29, 1942

At around 4 P.M. a truckload of SOL, the Legion's security forces, in other words, the Marshal's SS, passed by on the Clermont road. When they were in front of Bourassol, they started shouting, "Death to all cops." The cops in Bourassol did nothing. Probably just a whiskey-driven rivalry among thugs.

August 30, 1942

A parade of automobiles has been driving by here since eight this morning, official cars racing to get to the show they are putting on in Gergovie. Pétain wants to be both Joan of Arc and Vercingetorix.[31]

September 9, 1942

Génébrier spent yesterday, Tuesday, in Vichy with a number of his friends, some of whom are well informed. Deshuses's[32] loyalty to me has been magnificent. He told Génébrier of his plans in the event of a putsch by the German-backed Doriotists.

The real head of the Militia is Darnand, a brave and energetic hatchet man. Men have been dropping out of the Legion in large numbers. Those who have stayed are either Doriotists or Lavalists, like their leaders. And like those in the SOL, they were recruited from the ranks of Doriot's PPF.

30. A fraternal order instituted by Marshal Pétain.

31. The leader of the Gauls who in 52 B.C. held out against Caesar's troops during the siege of Gergovie, a site just a few miles from Clermont-Ferrand.

32. Deshuses, a young Subprefect and one of Bousquet's advisers. He was one of Daladier's faithful and courageous friends and assisted him in his attempts to escape in 1942. He helped members of the Resistance make their way into Switzerland.

Bombs have been thrown into Legion headquarters in Nice and Saint-Etienne. That explains why antiriot police are here at Bourassol: They think the Doriotists might try to exact revenge.

Saw Spanien, as well informed and friendly as ever. It seems that Laval is being simultaneously attacked by two opposing groups, not counting the republicans. On one side, there are Doriot and his party, backed by the Gestapo and the Nazi Party. In his recent talks with Laval, Doriot hadn't backed off from any of his demands: a military alliance with Germany, participation in the war under the leadership of the Germans, and the total and immediate institution by force of a Nazi regime in France. Doriot doesn't have many people behind him, just a bunch of adventurers, murderers, and hoods, but if the Germans should ever choose to, they could very easily set him up as *Gauleiter* in Paris.

Laval is also opposed by the Count of Paris and some Army Generals, who are doubtless spurred on by Pétain and his entourage, with Ménétrel right behind them. Far from taking the plane straight back to Morocco, the Count spent several days at the Bourbon-Busset château, where he met with Ménétrel, Alibert, General Laure, General Giraud, General Frère, General Bridoux, the War Minister, and others. Their plans are as vague and paradoxical as they are grandiose, and the inherent contradictions have not slowed them down any. The Army officers have shown no more genius around a table than they did on the battlefield. Their idea is to rise up against the Germans while remaining hostile toward the British, and they take pride in being in agreement on this with the Prince of Piedmont.

France would become a monarchy, ruled by military men, mostly mediocre sorts who have been discredited. Conceived under the hot Moroccan sun, the plan has received the stamp of each of these drawing-room heroes in succession, which raises anew a question that has until now defied answering: How is it that French military thinking has been mired in such mindlessness over the last twenty years?

Laval is forced to maneuver his way through all of this intrigue while fighting off a patriotic, republican movement that continues to grow as the war goes on. He also needs to win Hitler's support, lest the latter unleash Doriot. He knows perfectly well, and he admitted it at a luncheon for schoolteachers, that Hitler hates France, adding that for proof one has only to read *Mein Kampf*. At the most recent Cabinet meeting, in addressing the problem of the limited number of volunteers leaving to work in Germany, he proposed invoking the July 11, 1888, law relative to the organization of the nation in time of war, which allows for the requisitioning of the population. Workers would be drafted by the government and sent to Germany. Three Ministers rose to protest: Bichelonne, Le Roy Ladurie, and Lagardelle. There was even a rumor going around Vichy that they had resigned, but for the moment, anyway, Laval has not forced the issue.

An edict dated August 25 decrees the annexation of Alsace-Lorraine by the Third Reich, which is a direct violation of the Armistice Commission's agreement to address this matter at the time of the peace settlement. The French government addressed a letter of protest to the Germans and showed copies of it to Deputies from the region. Laval is reported to have thought of having it published, but he didn't go through with it.

French Cardinals, Archbishops, and Bishops have condemned the barbaric anti-Semitic acts that are being committed. Their pastorals were read aloud either inside churches, in spite of the law forbidding them to do so, or on the steps in front of them. The Nuncio also issued a protest in the name of the Pope. This is all to the Catholic church's honor, but it hasn't stopped the government from going even further. A missionary priest from Lyons, whose name I unfortunately don't know, refused to turn over to Angély, the Prefect in Lyons, Jewish children he had taken in. He was imprisoned but escaped. History shows that for a French government, no act is fraught with greater peril than arresting priests, but here again history has obviously taught us nothing.

September 10, 1942

5 P.M. Roger Génébrier has come back from Vichy, where he saw Bousquet. The Krauts have dropped Doriot. They had it in for him, first of all, because of the wild nightlife he's been enjoying, notably at the Lido, where he spends his evenings drinking in the company of jewel-bedecked whores; secondly, because after giving innumerable speeches about the so-called Bolshevik Legion and putting on the German uniform, he never dared venture near the front lines when he finally went out there.

September 13, 1942

Chauvel dropped by for a quick visit around 5 P.M. We were supposed to meet on September 8, but when he got to the train station, he saw machine guns on the platform and a General on the roof, and when he walked over to the post office to phone, he spotted more machine guns and soldiers on the sidewalks. The people in Vichy, who have seen it all, offered as an explanation the threat of an attack by Doriot and his buddies. But it would also appear that bombs have been thrown into the Lyons and Saint-Etienne headquarters of Doriot's party and of the Legion—which more often than not are one and the same—and that there is the fear that there will be other, similar acts.

This evening, Bourassol had the honor of being visited by a Brigadier General named Delmotte who inspected the guardroom with all the skill and method of a Battalion Sergeant. He pointed out that the walls weren't high enough and the locks not strong enough. He asked whether visitors were searched and whether their identification papers were scrupulously checked. The guard Passemard, who is a former Army Sergeant, told him that he followed the orders given to him by his superior, the warden of the Riom Penitentiary, and that he wasn't interested in hearing about any others. The General quickly beat a retreat, which was apparently nothing new to him. Gendarmes have arrived to reinforce the policemen here, but now we'll never know whether it's Doriot they are afraid of, or our escaping.

September 14, 1942

Three men showed up late this afternoon and introduced themselves as associates of that ninny Barthélemy. Members of his personal staff or prison officials of his? From the looks of them, as seen through the bars on my window, I would have sworn that they were real-life copies of Javert, the notorious police inspector from *Les Misérables*. But these are precisely the cruel martinets that Barthélemy has been recruiting as leaders and advisers ever since he started guillotining people who had been sentenced to a few months in prison for some minor political offense. Fear must be rippling through every ounce of that fattened prig's flab. The three Javerts started asking questions and making comments. They, too, talked about the walls and the locks, and they were coarse, if not quite vulgar. Then they said that reinforcements would be sent, which turned out to be so; two new guards came to bolster the forces in Bourassol. They said hello to me, and we chatted for a while. They are both loyal patriots. Let's face it, you just can't find a nicer bunch of people than prison guards.

September 15, 1942

I found Blum visibly preoccupied. His son Robert, who was captured while commanding an artillery battery and cited by the Army for his bravery, has been moved to a camp near Lübeck where conditions are reputed to be particularly harsh. He lives by himself at one end of the barracks, with Stalin's son alone at the other end and a guardroom between them. The Germans have grouped together the Socialists, the Gaullists, and the Communists. For two hours a day, Robert Blum can be visited by his friends in the camp, providing that they sign up the day before. He has the use of a piano and is allowed to go for walks, as long as there are guards right behind him. What does this brutal isolation augur for the future? I can sense that Blum fears that at some point the Germans will persecute the son to get at the father. Or could it be that the Germans are anxious about a possible uprising, now that there are so many prisoners and that they are in contact with the Socialist and Communist workers who went to Germany as part of the infamous "relief effort"? That would explain Robert Blum and Stalin's son being held in isolation. That's what I told Blum, without much conviction, unfortunately.

September 16, 1942

Bousquet came to see me. He had first stopped by to tell La Chambre that he would soon be released on his own recognizance, which, for form's sake, would be announced as being put under house arrest at a site of his choosing. I was happy to hear that they had made this decision, which, among other things, makes it obvious that our Air Force wasn't responsible for our defeat. I regretted, however, as I told Bousquet in no uncertain terms, that similar measures were not taken for Jacomet, but I could see that the possibility hadn't even been considered.

Bousquet spent almost two hours with me. I have known him for a long time. He is intelligent and kind and highly devoted to Maurice Sarraut. He was the Prefect in the Marne before the Armistice and acquitted himself very well. To his mind, our Generals were not up to their duties. They abandoned their troops and never understood the first thing about German tactics. General Thierry, for example, and others like Giraud and his staff officers went around trumpeting their contempt for democracy and insulting republicans, Mayors, and regional councilmen, all of which had a deplorable effect on the local populations. The RAF stationed in Reims took off as soon as the first bombs hit; the French command groups took off a day after the very first battles, leaving their troops with neither orders nor lines of communication. The French Air Force took no action whatsoever against German bombers. Waves of ragamuffin, unarmed French soldiers could be seen retreating everywhere, looting villages along the way. Then came the German Army: orderly, disciplined, powerful, and proper, which explains why they were welcomed by the locals. According to Bousquet, at that point, France was primed for a policy of collaboration with Germany.

The line France had taken at Montoire, the line promoted by Laval, became inoperative when he was arrested on December 13, which was the work of Peyrouton, Alibert, and, Bousquet said, the British as well. Laval had gotten the Germans to accept the presence of a French Army in North Africa that would fight off the English and win back the territory that had been lost. Laval was arrested by Peyrouton's surrogate police force, which planned to kill him, claiming he had tried to escape. He was saved by the police and the Germans.

Bousquet had more to say. He felt that any attempt to go back to the line taken at Montoire would meet with the worst kinds of difficulties. The country is divided. People don't understand. Some are pursuing hard-line, reactionary policies without even looking at the reality of the situation, whereas others think that although we are weaponless, we should tell the Germans to go to hell. As for the masses, they are not interested in anything other than putting food on their plates. The government is caught between the Germans, who are demanding and contemptuous at the same time, and public opinion, which is feeding on fantasy and chasing mirages.

At least he, Bousquet, was able to halt the execution of hostages, or so he claimed.

He thinks the Germans are in a position of great strength. They have organized the conquered Russian territories and harvested huge wheat crops there. With the Germans having reached the Volga and the Caucasus, their front lines are now even better structured for the Russian winter. After that they will invade Iraq, Syria, and Palestine, while Rommel attacks Egypt from the West. England will once and for all be driven out of the Mediterranean. Germany will then unify Europe according to the plans drawn up by Hitler's brain trust and say to the United States: "Do you want peace? You don't? All right then, come and fight."

Right, right. I had gotten Bousquet to talk. I answered by saying simply that in spite of their power, the Germans would be defeated in the end, probably after a long, drawn-out war. Bousquet then spoke of the trial. I reminded him that among its consequences, it had brought down Darlan's government and in so doing greatly benefited Laval, even though it was Laval who had determined in August 1940 that there would actually be a trial.

Saturday, September 19, 1942

Along the wall at 3 P.M. the hot sun was beating down on the nettles and the droppings of the livestock they keep at Bourassol. I went to sunbathe, nude, in the exercise yard. Croquez, a lawyer in Ribet's office who pleads at the High Court of Appeals, showed up unexpectedly, in his spiffy gray jacket, starched collar, and white shirt with cufflinks. Too bad for counselor Croquez. I didn't get up. I had him pull over a chair into the burning sunlight. It wasn't long before his head started to turn red. He tried to shade himself as best he could with an elegant little handkerchief but wasn't too successful. Tapping two Gauloises out of a pack, he offered me one. I put it away for later. One of these days, though, he is going to bring me Belgian tobacco. He said he had just arrived from Belgium and Holland and was taking a few days' rest at the Hotel Pailleret. He had met with Devèze, Carton de Viard, and others. All of them are convinced that they'll be free of the Germans as of next spring. The King still considers himself a prisoner in his castle and all Belgium is behind him. Pierlot, their

Prime Minister, in an address from London, let it be known that he did not recognize the legitimacy of any of the acts performed by the occupying powers. With the exception of Degrelle and the 50,000 Walloons and 50,000 Flemish traitors he has with him, the Belgians are unanimous in their resistance. Croquez also had a chance to visit Ostende, which he found very poorly defended. The Dutch are even more savagely hostile, and the Krauts are repeatedly confronted by gestures of contempt, even in the most ordinary aspects of daily life. The Dutch aren't about to forget that the Germans destroyed Rotterdam without declaring war.

Croquez dined with Bouffet, a Prefect from Normandy, who told him about the attack on Dieppe. Violent hand-to-hand fighting went on in the city streets while British planes, dominating the skies, knocked out the antiaircraft guns and the artillery along the coast. British tanks rolled several miles inland. The Germans had to call in air support from planes stationed in Belgium, Holland, and France and send in a division of reinforcements. The British pulled out around 5 P.M. What was the point of this half-hearted attack that was more than a commando raid but still far short of a full-fledged landing? To set up a bridgehead? With Russia fighting so heroically, if there isn't a serious landing attempt after the coming equinox, then something fundamental has broken down in the British High Command.

Croquez saw his friend Barthélemy, who is so full of himself he is going to burst. He brought back a perfect definition for the National Revolution: blue-blooded terror, black market, and rose-colored glasses. I asked Croquez if Barthélemy realized that he would probably be guillotined after the war, just like all those poor souls he has been sending up to the State Tribunal with orders to have them sentenced to death that same day, while the executioner and his helpers go about sharpening the blades. Croquez looked at me utterly flabbergasted. I repeated the question: Is he aware of the consequences that this royal reign of terror will have for those administering it? He said that Barthélemy told him that the Germans had summoned him to Paris and told him, with all due courtesy, that he would be held personally responsible for bringing in ten death sentences a day, to be handed down by the State Tribunal and carried out immediately, failing which they themselves would handle matters and execute a hundred people a day, among them Barthélemy's friends. "He should have resisted; he should have protested and done everything possible," I said. Croquez answered that Barthélemy's wife would rather he *didn't* do everything possible. She had been dreaming her whole life of being a Minister's wife, and now that she was, she planned to keep it that way.

Croquez is no longer a collaborator. Now he is a member of the Resistance. In the winter of 1940, he was singing the praises of Laval and a few unscrupulous Radicals like Lamoureux and Chichery, who is beneath contempt. He explained how theirs was the only viable political approach. Everything is different now. Now he sides with the Resistance; he's a Gaullist and an Anglophile. When he goes to have dinner at Olivier Jallu's, one of his Germanophile colleagues, and Mme Jallu raises her glass to honor the Marshal, Croquez puts in loudly, "Timoshenko." Our friend Croquez has changed clients; he has gone over to the other side. Congratulations, counselor.

But I was set on making him pay for his past mistakes. While he went on talking, I moved to the side of my blanket, bringing him directly under the sun's rays. He stretched his handkerchief and tried to use it as a parasol. His head was quickly turning fire-engine red. I asked him if he would care for a tub of delightfully iced Bourassol water, but he preferred to return immediately to his hotel.

September 24, 1942

René Besse, my former Pensions Minister, came at 2 P.M. and spent three hours with me. His right arm had been amputated at the shoulder as the result of wounds he received in the war. He was dripping with sweat, having come on a bicycle one of his colleagues in Riom lent him. After we hugged each other, he took his sleeve in his teeth to remove his jacket.

I have never met a more loyal or more proudly patriotic man in my entire life. What a pleasure it was to look into his face, open and candid, and hear once again his distinct, clear voice. The day will come, he said, when France will be proud to have gone to war and to have been the first to have risen up against those who tried to rule the world. Unfortunately, our armies were led by commanding officers from the preceding war, not by real leaders. They were bureaucrats, more concerned with their typewriters than with the enemy.

In the Lot, in the midst of the rout, he observed a number of Generals, including General Lenclud, who was calling himself "Commander of the Dordogne front"! It was, Besse said, a pathetic performance. The man was without will or energy and was incapable of inspiring his men.[33] I told Besse that this same General was pitifully ill at ease in testifying against me at the Riom trial, obviously wanting nothing better than to get out of there as quickly as possible. They have probably retired him since then. If they had wanted to get real leaders, they would have had to promote Battalion Commanders and Lieutenant Colonels to the rank of General. Before the war, that was unthinkable, and they refused to do it during the eight-month standoff from September 1939 on. Besse also spoke to me about the National Assembly and about Vichy, where no one had the courage to object to anything.

Besse is struck by the amount of ground the Communists have gained, especially in the Occupied Zone. He fears that there will be very serious incidents once the Germans evacuate Paris. Monzie is now living in the Lot. He is still just as flighty and capricious as ever and seems to have been discredited as a result of the visit he paid Ambassador Abetz. Monzie had his wife appointed City Councilwoman in Souillac, while he divides his time between Cannes and Paris in the company of Edmonde Guy.

September 26, 1942

Received a large crop of cable messages from J.B. They will all have to be burned, unfortunately. Russian radio has published excerpts from letters that German soldiers killed in Russia never got to mail. They refer to the living hell they were going through at the Battle of Stalingrad, which has been going on for a month. Many of the letters from Germany relate the destruction wrought by the Allied bombing of German cities.

33. Besse did not know that General Lenclud's son had been killed at the front just a few days earlier. Moreover, it has since then been established that General Lenclud played an important role in the Resistance.

Radio Free France broadcast the speech of a Socialist, Brossolette,[34] who left for London with Vallin,[35] a Deputy from the Croix de Feu Party. Vallin was one of the most rabid members of Vichy's Council of Political Justice. Without having looked at the file or hearing the accused men defend themselves, he suggested to Pétain that we be imprisoned for life in some dungeon. Either de Gaulle is not very well informed or he is not too choosy about the company he keeps.

September 28, 1942

Benoist-Méchin has been dismissed by Laval. He left, but not without threatening Laval before going. He was pro-German before the war, then became a supporter of Nazism during it, as Commander Ragaine, a witness at the Riom trial, pointed out in the wonderful letter he submitted.

Trouble is brewing at Bourassol. There are only three guards in all and they can't get along. Try and get a league of nations to work!

It appears that Vallin broadcast a talk over British radio. He felt the need to address a message to Herriot, under house arrest at his home in the Isère, and greetings to all prisoners. He won't get any greetings back from me. I find it obscene for de Gaulle to have given him this role. It has the foul smell of political maneuvering.

October 9, 1942

7 P.M. Le Trocquer came and spoke with me on the bench at the foot of Bourassol's linden tree. He confirmed what sweet little Simone had told me this morning: The court had denied the request that La Chambre be released on his own recognizance. Le Trocquer met this morning with the most important, or rather the two most important, judges. They told him that French judges had a sense of dignity and found the government's attempt to pressure them into releasing La Chambre totally unacceptable. Caous, the presiding judge, asked Le Trocquer: "Who is this fellow

34. Pierre Brossolette, journalist who joined the Resistance in 1940. Upon his arrest in February 1944, he committed suicide rather than risk informing on his comrades.

35. Prior to his decision to leave for London, Charles Vallin had been faithful to Marshal Pétain and a fervent supporter of the National Revolution and the Armistice.

Bousquet? He can't possibly be a lawyer." Bursting with pride, his face blown up like a balloon, Le Trocquer started pouring it on. This was a historic occasion; it signaled the awakening of France's magistrates. I have rarely had so good a laugh.

8 P.M. After taking his constitutional, Blum knocked at my door and came in, which was highly unusual. Right off, he informed me that de Gaulle hadn't been in London when Vallin arrived and had nothing to do with the obscene radio greetings that Vallin had had the nerve to send prisoncrs in France. He added that as soon as he got back to London, de Gaulle sent Vallin on a mission to Equatorial Africa with the rank of Captain. This confirmed my suspicions that Blum is in close contact with de Gaulle, probably through the news sources in Clermont (*La M.*, V., Fabre),[36] where his lawyer Spanien has an in.

Guy La Chambre, whom I have nicknamed the Bourgeois Gentilhomme, has been walking up and down the paths in Bourassol. Three days ago, he ordered Passemard to bring down a heavy trunk and his foot locker, where he had stowed his Commanding Officer's uniform—that makes two wars he has spent safely away from the action.

October 11, 1942

At 9 A.M. the Reverend Father Dillard drove up in a fancy Delahaye powered by a wood-burning engine. Highly symbolic: The slick body represents Catholicism, the wood-burning engine, the internal workings of the Church. Dillard came to console La Chambre, whose request to be released had been turned down.

October 13, 1942

Jean came around 10:30 in the morning and recounted the foolishness of the Youth Camps.[37] People are trying to get him to enroll. He had interesting stories to tell about his travels.

36. Probably *La Montagne*, central France's principal newspaper, and the two men who ran it: Alexandre Varenne and Francisque Fabre.

37. The Youth Camps, with Pétainism as the moving spirit, replaced military service.

Blum gave me the typewritten text of the speech Churchill gave in Edinburgh. I found it elegant in its form, sober, and moving. We have survived the first year. A new chapter is opening before us. The grandeur of these islands and of our Empire is to have held out alone and to have given ourselves the time to arm and organize and patiently assemble the invincible forces of the civilized world.

There are massacres throughout Russia and Yugoslavia. In Kiev 54,000 people were executed the day after Hitler marched in.

We have reached a turning point in the war; there can be no doubt about that now. The Vatican has just issued a statement reminding Catholics that although the Church, eternal and universal, does not concern itself with political regimes, it does not condone regimes that limit freedom of thought and engage in persecution.

There have been strikes in cities all over France: Villeurbanne, Grenoble, and Clermont.

The Germans battled Mihailović's forces for several days in southern Bosnia and had to bring in armored divisions. Germany was furious over Vichy's wait-and-see attitude when the British and Americans were threatening Dakar. They're fighting in Croatia; there are fires and incidents of sabotage in Belgium and executions in Norway and Poland.

A new assault will be made on Stalingrad to preserve Hitler's prestige.

A grotesque communiqué has been issued about the resistance shown in Madagascar.

8:30 P.M. Spoke with Blum about the speech Laval made to a Senate committee meeting in closed session on March 15, 1938. In an attempt to seize power, he presented himself as an enemy of the Germans and the only person capable of getting Russia and Italy to stand up to them. That was the same argument he made to Deputy Laroche during their train ride from Châtelguyon to Paris.

We raised the issue of our relations with Italy. Baudouin told Blum of his meeting with us, Mussolini's request, and his own trip to Rome, when he met with Ciano. He told Blum that although I was highly circumspect, I had not completely severed our ties. It was agreed that I would give a speech and that Mussolini would respond to it favorably. I did make that speech and Mussolini did prepare his, but then the Prince of Hesse, the

King of Italy's son-in-law, suddenly showed up in Rome, probably carrying demands from Hitler. Mussolini never gave his speech.

October 20, 1942

Pétain was in Avignon, speaking to the farmers' union. He told them: "My friends, don't let yourselves be fooled into thinking that I can do what I want. I feel like this ... " whereupon he crossed his forearms on his chest, like a man in chains. Then he went on to tell his astonished audience: "Above all, don't repeat to anyone what I just said. If they ever heard about it in Vichy, I would be whipped when I got back there." He got a cold reception, except from the mercenaries from neighboring regions who had been ordered to attend.

Legueu, a former associate of mine, came to see me. His parents were close friends of Pétain's, who used to lunch at their house once a month. Legueu was a member of Pétain's staffs in Bordeaux, Clermont, and Vichy. He quit at the same time as General Bineau, disgusted with the people in Pétain's entourage. He made a point of mentioning General Laure's stupidity.

Legueu fought brilliantly in the war at Jacquot's side, after having spent time with him at Command Headquarters, which Major General Bineau once referred to as "a paradise for madmen." Legueu also pointed out the extraordinary difference between the bravery our soldiers displayed every time they had real leaders and the failings of the High Command. On the Seine, near Senlis, they would be given orders to fight and told not even to consider the possibility of a retreat. Then in the evening, they would be told to pull back.

Legueu has doubts about an Anglo-American victory. He thinks the British are not intelligent enough and that the Americans are not willing to make the effort necessary to win.

Finally, he spoke about how extremely serious the financial situation had become and the inflationary spiral we were in. Vichy hasn't the slightest clue; Cathala, the Minister of the Economy, is optimistic. It is basically a continuation of the moral collapse we witnessed in the bourgeoisie between 1914 and 1939.

3 P.M. Claude Perchot stopped by. He is in the Resistance and confident. He confirmed the information I had received. He thinks the war will soon be over. I am not so sure.

November 1, 1942

Spent the morning disappointed and conjecturing as to why Pierre hadn't come.

Gamelin told Jacomet that prior to the trial, Darlan had sent General Revers to see him, to ask him to incriminate me by putting responsibility for our defeat on the civilian government and the republican regime. That is supposedly when Gamelin decided not to answer any questions.

I am tempted to check whether General Revers actually visited him, and when. In any event, Gamelin's attitude shortly before the trial was quite different. His defense rested on the claim that he had not been supplied with what he had requested. So much for me. As for his subordinates, and in particular General Georges, they simply had not carried out his orders. Later, though, he must have reflected on the testimony given by the production managers and engineers, which stood as proof of the quantity and quality of our weapons. Three days of court hearings and my violent attacks during those opening sessions did the rest. In contrast, in the time since the trial was suspended, he has submitted excellent responses to written depositions and direct testimony given against him by various Generals. He also told Jacomet that, back when all this started, a Senator from the Ariège who was present with him at Gaboriau's told him that Pétain did not intend to target him, so as to avoid a Gamelin versus Georges slugfest and spare the Army.

Jean came at around 11:15 A.M. with a radio built by Abel Farnoux, who lives in Carpentras. He sneaked it past the guards in a large sack filled with foul-smelling vegetables, which was enough to evade a search. I put on the headset, wrapped myself in a huge greatcoat to muffle even further the noises around me and tried to bring in every station I could. Thus did I reestablish contact with the outside world, from which I had been separated for two years. No gift could have been finer.

November 2, 1942

All Souls' Day.

November 5, 1942

This morning, Ancel[38] brought me impressive news. At midnight, Sottens broadcast a communiqué from Cairo. The British appear to have defeated Rommel's Army, which is now in retreat, and taken some 9,000 prisoners. German ships bringing reinforcements and supplies were sunk off Tobruk. Will there be a second half to this brilliant offensive, launched from Chad into the oases of southern Tunisia? Large numbers of men and warplanes have been brought in through Liberia and over the new African highway. Large numbers of American troops have landed as well. A second front would appear to have been opened in Africa.

Stalingrad is still holding out. Timoshenko has made successful thrusts both south and north. The feeling I have been getting for a month has thus been confirmed: The Germans have begun their descent down the road to defeat and ruin, bringing with them the traitors here in France. Vichy is in a funk. The press has been barred from publishing the Cairo communiqué and was almost prohibited from publishing one from the DNB[39] announcing the capture of a German General commanding an armored division. If Laval's idea of negotiating a compromise peace settlement at Russia's expense was ever a real possibility—and I don't think it was and never did—it is much less a possibility now.

Pierre came by at 2:30. His eyes have been hurting him terribly. In spite of that, he performed brilliantly on the oral part of the *baccalauréat.* All of a sudden, in the middle of the questioning, Jardillier, who was examining him, asked, "How is Edouard doing?"

November 11, 1942

It has been bleak and gray. I was given to think back on the Armistice and what happened when my division's regiment, stationed around Origny-

38. A guard at the prison, hostile to Vichy.

39. Deutsches Nachrichtenbüro, German News Bureau.

Sainte-Benoite, heard the news. Beneath the surface joy at no longer having to risk one's life and at being able to go back home, free of apprehension, you could sense a certain disappointment. Some of the men were actually open about it. A young schoolteacher stated proudly that under the First Republic, France had said that it would never enter into negotiations so long as the enemy remained on our territory. He was accused of being a die-hard extremist. That was also Pétain's feeling at the time. At the Elysée Palace, at the end of the traditional meal that would follow the July 14 celebrations, Pétain would often tell us how much he regretted that the Armistice had prevented General de Castelnau from launching an all-out offensive that would have driven the German armies back across the Rhine. He used to criticize Foch for having too quickly aligned himself with Wilson's position. I wonder what he thinks about that now. During this past night, he got a letter from Hitler informing him that the German Army would cross into Unoccupied France today and occupy coastal zones along the Mediterranean. Hitler is convinced that the Allies are preparing a landing. Of course, he will continue to respect the sovereignty and independence of the French nation. Pétain and his government will be free to set up in Versailles, as they have long desired to do. Shades of Grippeminaud.[40]

This morning, Marshal Von Rundstedt, escorted by armed soldiers, went to see Pétain to reaffirm Hitler's decision. The Marshal vehemently protested against this violation of the Armistice and at around 11 A.M. Vichy radio broadcast his emphatic response. The two years in which we had been violently criticizing his collaboration with the enemy were seemingly swept away. What would he do? Take a plane to Algiers?[41] Call all Frenchmen to unite and resist? Call on the world at large to bear witness to the Nazi dictator's new breach of faith? Was that too much to ask of his

40. In one of La Fontaine's fables, a weasel and a rabbit call on the cat, Grippeminaud, to settle a dispute between them. The cat puts an end to the dispute by eating them both.

41. After the Allied landing in North Africa, people in the Marshal's entourage suggested that he fly to Algiers. Pétain told them that his doctor had advised him against flying. They then suggested that he step down, but he refused. See General de Serigny's memoirs.

advanced years? And that being the case, why not declare himself a prisoner of the Germans and relinquish a power that was just for show, anyway? Hours went by. Vichy radio remained silent. The solemn statement of protest was not repeated. The telephone rang here. It was the Riom Penitentiary on the line, dictating orders: All visits by relatives and lawyers were to be suspended; no newspapers were to be allowed in the prison; surveillance was to be doubled. Its meaning was clear. Our moment of elation was crushed by the brutally painful news of yet another capitulation. After digesting his lunch, Pétain changed his mind and decided to shame himself anew.

Remaining Chief of State is the only thing that really matters to this selfish and conceited old man. There was an admirable stand to be taken. He could have declared himself a prisoner of the Germans or left for Algiers by plane and broadcast an appeal to all Frenchmen to take heart and unite; he could have called for the world to take note that Hitler was once again violating his word. Instead, he thought about it, and in the end, this prisoner of his own self-image preferred to remain the "merry old King" under German protection. And that's not the last such act he'll favor us with. Clemenceau and Joffre were absolutely right in their judgment of France's "victor at Verdun."

Bourassol is all astir. Mme La Chambre came at the usual time, highly agitated. I asked the Lieutenant in command of the garrison what orders he would issue if the Germans were to march through the prison gates. He replied that his operating procedures did not cover that contingency and that he would phone for instructions. The prisoners began discussing the idea of leaving, of conspicuously walking out through the gates. One thought that the guards would just let us go. I didn't believe that at all. That was pure fantasy. The guards despise Vichy, but they are old-fashioned soldiers for whom an order is an order. So the choice was between making our way through the barbed wire and racing to Riom on foot, which at 11 o'clock in the morning would have been a futile exercise, or calmly and bravely awaiting the arrival of the Germans, which was what I resolved to do. Having reached that decision, we went back to our rooms. I burned some papers and asked to have my cigarettes, tea, coffee, and the other precious possessions that my good friend Hippolyte[42] had sent me from America, as well as the excellent liqueurs that my brave friends from Toulouse had brought me, stored away in an obscure attic that young Simone told me about. I had the other hired help, Marcelle, take this diary to a neighboring farm, along with other documents that I didn't want to destroy.

Then someone started shouting, "The Krauts are here!" I went down to see, but it turned out to be just the power of suggestion having its way with Mme La Chambre. She and Mme Reichenbach were in fact asked to leave the premises. The guards at the gate were turning away my son Pierre. I raced over to talk to him. He was calm, as I would have wanted him to be. I urged him to return to Riom and make note of the bearing, the physical state, and the equipment of the German soldiers who would soon be making their way through the city.

Time passed. It was 2 P.M. before the first German column appeared, heading down the Clermont road, with armored vehicles at the lead, automobiles with officers, and then Citroën trucks packed with armed soldiers standing in the rear. They were followed by a large detachment of men on bikes, Czechs and Poles, word had it, who had been drafted to fight under the Nazi flag. They moved slowly, fifteen miles an hour at most, sometimes at an even slower pace. A few trucks had broken down while climbing the hill. It was an impressive showing, but this was not the German Army of 1940. The troops heading south to the Spanish border would take three days and three nights to get there.

November 12, 1942

The procession of German troops has gone on. I watched them from the center walkway in the prison as they headed down the road. A lot of them looked very young; others were apparently recruits from German territories overseas. Could it be that Germania was already feeling the shortage of men? The local population in Riom reacted with absolute dignity. They

42. Daladier's pseudonym for William Bullitt.

too had sensed the difference between this Army and the one that had marched through their city in June 1940.

Then I noticed a car with a chauffeur and two impeccably dressed civilians standing in front of the entrance to the Bourassol jailhouse, looking sinister with their hats jammed tight on their heads: the Subprefect and the Superintendent of Police. I had to walk right past them to get back into the "castle," as they were gesturing broadly toward the barbed wire, the farmyard, and the screened gate, which they subsequently had padlocked. They also claimed that we were not watched closely enough during our daily walks. New guards and soldiers were brought in to tighten security.

La Chambre and I wrote to Bousquet to complain about these restrictive measures, which were totally gratuitous. Blum complained strenuously in a letter to Barthélemy. Le Trocquer and Spanien, who were the only lawyers present, went off to object to our being harassed in this way, but Barthélemy, groveling and gutless as usual, just raised his arms in the air and asked them to understand that there was nothing he could do about it. Meanwhile, Contencin, who managed the penitentiary system and was somewhat concerned about managing his future too, declared that the measures prohibiting visits did not apply to the prisoners' families and legal counsel.

November 13, 1942

Had lunch with Pierre and J.B., who told us about what had gone on in Vichy on November 11. Marshal Von Rundstedt showed up at Pétain's door with an armed escort and dismissed the French guards on duty; they didn't return until the Germans had left. In the course of the first exchange between the two Marshals, Pétain protested against the violation of the terms of the Armistice. Had he finally been aroused? No. That afternoon, he backed down. Did he do so because of pressure from Laval, who had just returned from Munich? I think these two cronies are still in cahoots, only Pétain would have liked to have made some gesture for the loyal patriots in France. After that, he made another great sacrifice and once again gave the gift of his person to France.

At 4 P.M. Le Trocquer met with Laval, who rejected the possibility of our being released from Bourassol, claiming that it would result in new hardships for France. Nevertheless, he accepted full responsibility for our safety.

Meanwhile, in Algeria, Darlan ordered soldiers, sailors, and airplane pilots to join up with the Anglo-American forces, in accordance with the Marshal's true desire, which he alone was capable of interpreting. There is some of the Artful Dodger in everything this Gascon does.

November 14, 1942

I picked up a radio broadcast from Moscow and heard London radio in Italian. As for Vichy's broadcasts, they are hailing the Anglo-American landing in Algeria as the beginning of a true military collaboration, a real alliance between France and Germany. Together they will defend Africa and the French coast against the British and the Americans.

Received good news about the way the French troops in Africa were being trained and how they performed in combat, a fact that will have great bearing on the future. Victories will mean more to France than all the speeches in the world.

November 17, 1942

According to the terms of the June 1940 Armistice, the Vichy government was to be allowed to maintain an Army of 100,000 men to preserve law and order. When the Germans marched into the Unoccupied Zone, General Huntziger commanded all men to remain within their garrisons. The Germans burst into barracks, gruffly ordered the soldiers to disperse, and seized their weapons, their equipment, and the war matériel that had been concealed. French officers, above all General Frère, who had anticipated leading these men into action when the time came, watched their hopes evaporate before their eyes.

Weygand has been arrested, after having refused the American High Command's offer to join forces with them. Pétain has accused Giraud of disloyalty and duplicity. In Algiers, Darlan has stated that at the request of General Noguès and in compliance with the Marshal's true wishes, he was taking command. There is no way I can make my way through this labyrinth of contradictions. We lost lives; men were wounded; we lost our best ship, the *Jean Bart,* which I had had such a difficult time getting funds to build. This was our ungallant last stand.

November 19, 1942

Pétain has renewed his order to the French troops in Africa to repel the Anglo-American invasion!!

Friday, November 27, 1942

Jean came by around 9:30 this morning, spirited as always. He was able to catch the train in Lyons because a girlfriend drove him to the station. Unfortunately, it was already too late when he got word by telegram; he was supposed to have been phoned Wednesday evening. It cost us a whole day and effectively compromised the plan that had been worked out Wednesday. Maybe that is just as well, since P. had been discussing Le Trocquer and Spanien's plan at the National Café in Clermont with just about everyone who came along. Guy La Chambre's wife told me herself that it was the subject of conversation in cafes all over Riom. Still, if Jean had been able to get here Thursday, we might have been able to manage, although somewhat differently.

I was looking out my window around eleven when I spotted a group of German soldiers standing at the foot of an electric-power pylon a few yards from the Bourassol outer wall, and others stationed all around the castle. Suddenly, the door flew open and a tall German Captain with a revolver on his belt appeared on the threshold, followed by a soldier with a rifle and a submachine gun. "This German officer," the prison guard explained, "has come to verify that you are here." The Captain bowed, looked closely at me and withdrew.

Had lunch with Jean, who left me to catch the train for Vichy, where he was to meet with P. After he had gone, I got another visit from the inescapable Subprefect, his Superintendent of Police, and an officer from the gendarmerie. They huddled in the north yard, gesticulating broadly. In the end they decided to bar all visits and limit our daily walks. Imagination is obviously not their strong point.

I learned that Bousquet ordered that everything possible be done to prevent the Germans from setting up inside of Bourassol, everything short of using force. Will the young Police Superintendent's arguments carry the day? At 5 P.M. I went jogging in the farmyard. I spent the evening reading a book by Gignoux and listening to the radio. Impossible to pick up New York and London. Heard a broadcast of Hitler's letter to Pétain.

Saturday, November 28, 1942

The news coming out of Russia is good; they are still driving forward. In Tunisia, Anderson's First Army, which includes sizable numbers of French troops, is just ten miles outside of Tunis, according to Sottens. Yesterday, at three in the morning, after having opened fire on the German and Italian troops invading Toulon, the French scuttled their own fleet. I imagine we are supposed to take this as an act of heroism commanding our respect, but didn't our Navy deserve a better fate? Darlan's responsibility in all of this is appalling.

November 29, 1942

At 7 P.M. I was visited by three other officers from the gendarmerie, including a Commander. I couldn't figure out what they wanted, probably because they didn't know what they wanted either. Jean called. He had met with Bousquet.[43]

December 4, 1942

Darlan has set up a government in Africa and declared himself Head of State, on behalf of the Marshal, of course. He has got a kind of Colonial Executive Council with him: Noguès, Boisson,[44] and Giraud, along with a pseudo-ministry of three or four members. I had no idea that this little sailor had so much guile in him. De Gaulle and the National Committee in London have protested to the British government and several Members of the House of Commons have raised a hue and cry. Eden has responded by saying that Darlan's power is only temporary. Eisenhower, however,

43. Bousquet told Jean Daladier that the police would protect the prisoners in Bourassol from the German troops.

44. Pierre Boisson, Governor-General of French West Africa.

made an announcement to say how pleased he was to have Darlan's support.

Roosevelt referred to his previous statement in which he said, basically, that the Americans would use all the means at their disposal and accept help from anyone ready to provide it. It would be up to the people of France alone to choose the form of government under which they would live. Strange that Moroccan radio hasn't been jammed.

Confirmation has come in from everywhere that the Germans had no trouble at all getting their hands on considerable amounts of equipment, clothing, shoes, etc., stored in our barracks and supply depots. Nothing had been secreted away. Eyewitnesses claim that there was enough to clothe and equip 100,000 men.

December 6, 1942

Spent a lovely day with Jean, who is a lot more mature than I thought. He is a fine young man, somewhat of a swashbuckler. The desire to go off and fight is still burning inside him. He'll have plenty of time for that.

December 7, 1942

Spent the day with Jean, who got a tube for my radio, which I have been hiding with greater and greater care. I wouldn't have known how to get one.

Sottens confirmed that the Americans had suffered defeat in Tunisia, apparently as a result of the superior training of the German troops and their superior air power. Sicily has become a veritable aircraft carrier, with squadrons of fighters and Stukas brought in from the Russian front, where the winter has left them free to be used as reinforcements in North Africa. There are only 125 miles separating Sicily and Bizerte.

It has become painful to listen to the verbal fencing between the Moroccan radio and the Gaullist broadcasts. Can you imagine what it would have been like if Homer's heroes had had access to the airwaves? De Gaulle wrote a long article for *La Marseillaise* that was broadcast on every station. The controversy is sure to have a nefarious effect on the French living in Africa and the Moslems. All those Christians seem to have forgotten the parable about the return of the prodigal son, and the scripture about the sinner who repents and the eleventh-hour laborer in the vineyard. I have no respect whatsoever for Darlan; I find him thoroughly despicable. Nonetheless, I am given to wonder what de Gaulle would have done if he had been commanding a division in France at the time of the June 1940 invasion, instead of on a mission to London.

December 8, 1942

At 3:30 P.M. a German captain came in, with an officer from the gendarmerie behind him and another lower-ranking gendarme in front. He was in Bourassol again to verify that we were actually there. Short in stature, his hair cropped close, he ceremoniously entered each of our cells, read our name off a paper he was holding, turned, and left.

A young Lieutenant of Alsatian descent told me that he had been summoned to the German Commandant's office this morning, following incidents between French and German guards. The Captain notified him that he himself, on orders from his Commanding General, would come to inspect Bourassol between 3 and 4 P.M. The Lieutenant replied that unless otherwise ordered by Vichy, he would meet force with force, after which he left to inform the Subprefect and the Captain at the Gendarmerie, sowing panic everywhere he went. In the end, they decided to let the Germans have their way and accompany them on their rounds. The procession reached Bourassol at 3:30 P.M., at which time the prison fell under German control. So now we know exactly what Laval's word was worth when he told Le Trocquer that he would guarantee our protection.

December 12, 1942

Churchill gave a wonderful speech, with a passage devoted to the immortal grandeur of the Commonwealth, reaffirmed in its having withstood adversity while France lay prostrate. He evaded the matter of British air support in France during the battles on the German and Belgian borders. Look at Vuillemin's testimony and the orders he was issuing at a time when the replies coming out of the British Air Ministry were totally at odds with what Chamberlain had pledged; or look at the exchanges with Paul

Reynaud in his office at the Quai d'Orsay, while we were busy burning documents. The answer the British gave Reynaud at his home in the middle of the night was practically insulting.

Churchill said he was delighted that the Germans are now occupying all of France. He claims it will serve to unite the French, after which he praised de Gaulle. The truth is that the British were saved by the United States, and of course also by their own Air Force, during the most spectacular period of the war. Why Hitler didn't attack England in the summer of 1940 is something I still haven't figured out.

We have been informed that Léon Blum, Paul Reynaud, and I are to be taken to Germany. In truth, I have been expecting this since November 11.

December 14, 1942

Pétain has written a letter to Hitler to express his gratitude for the new disgraces inflicted on France. He said he is now prepared to forge a military and political alliance with the victors and has put Laval in charge of working out the details. At no time throughout the trip from Paris to Bordeaux in June 1940, at no point on the way to Brittany and across the Touraine, Charente, and Gironde regions, when he often mingled with the crowds and was greeted as we drove down country roads and through cities, did I ever hear Pétain call for peace. The only time he did that was when he was conspiring with the other traitors. There is an analogy here with what happened in 1815 following Waterloo, a similar split between the people and their leaders.

December 15, 1942

It has been one dreary day after another. This morning, I had the pleasure of receiving Daridan. His subtle and witty irony has given way to an uncustomary vehemence. He found the presence of German police around the château sickening, and the attitude of the Cour Suprême despicable. He felt that once the Germans had violated the separation between the Occupied and Unoccupied Zones, the court should have met, released us provisionally, and dissolved itself as a body, instead of waiting for Laval to dissolve it. The French have offered no resistance whatsoever, and the

Germans have responded to their servility with increased scorn. Daridan has decided to take a leave of absence.

"Come on, Daridan. Tell me about your Italian friends."

His eyes lit up behind his glasses as he began unleashing his irony on the Fascist militia, the King—who can't go into the bombed-out cities of Turin and Genoa without hearing crowds shouting, "Pace, pace!"—and Mussolini, who has been stiffed until now and is still waiting for his tip. He painted a whole series of such portraits; he has become a master at it. What light and joy filled this room of mine, where the sun rarely shines.

Then he read Lord Gort's report on the British Expeditionary Force during the campaign in France. I copied down several excerpts; I'll want to comment on them later.

I was really sorry to see him go. He left me a clipping from *Le Moniteur*, Laval's newspaper, with the transcription of the press conference Laval gave yesterday, stating: "I *want* Germany to be victorious. ... The people who are counting on an American victory refuse to see that Roosevelt is bringing with him the triumph of the Jews and the Communists. People are free to wish for whatever they want, but I intend to crush them, whatever it takes." He referred to the way our two nations had been faithful to the spirit of collaboration, when in fact Germany has been violating the terms of the Armistice from the very beginning. Yet Laval has read what Goebbels wrote just as I have: "If the French knew what our peace terms included, they would have nothing left but their eyes to cry over it." France would shrink back to its 1450 borders. We'll never be able to collaborate with the Germans without first having rooted out Nazism. Laval is in so far now that he'll go through right to the end.

Received greetings from Louis Marin,[45] a proud patriot from Lorraine.

45. Louis Marin, President of the Republican Federation from 1925 to 1940 and several times a Minister. He refused to be a part of the Vichy government. He made it to London in 1944 and was a member of the Provisional Consultative Assembly in Algiers.

December 18, 1942

Catroux was interviewed in London by the Anglo-American press. A certain conceit came out of it, that of a man wounded in his pride and threatened in his ambitions. He pounded away at Darlan's presence in Africa, which he said jeopardized communications within the Anglo-American Expeditionary Force. In other words, if there were anything in it for him, Darlan would betray the Allies. Wrangling of this kind is not likely to encourage the French people of North Africa to join in the fight alongside the Anglo-Saxons.

De Gaulle's merits are beyond question, but this bickering shouldn't be tolerated. As for Darlan, he proved to be far more skilled when he was interviewed by the Anglo-Americans in Algiers. He claimed that the political approach he had adopted in France had been forced on him by events. He said that once the war is over, he will return to civilian life and let the people of France decide what form of government they want and who they want running it.

There is good news about the training our French troops received in Africa and the way they acquitted themselves in combat, a fact likely to have considerable importance later on.

December 19, 1942

Roger Génébrier had lunch with me on his way back from Vichy, bringing me good wishes from Louis Marin. He had met at length with Bousquet, who informed him that Laval had left for Paris and was thereafter to head for Munich to see Hitler, apparently to discuss the creation of a military draft to bolster the German forces, either by protecting maritime zones against a possible Anglo-Saxon landing or by relieving German troops occupying territories that now stretch from the Balkans to Norway. The French government would move its offices to Paris and the line separating the two zones would disappear. This would make Laval's plan a reality and would effectively result in an earnest collaboration, with Germany playing the beneficent suzerain and France the vassal at long last brought under control. Déat would be given a Ministry, but certainly not Interior, with control over the police force; trust is not the strong point of this group. All political parties, which is to say the only party that exists, Doriot's party, would be dissolved. Differences still remain between Pétain's entourage and Laval's. "We should move cautiously on this," Bonnefoy said. "After all, the old man could issue a new constitutional decree and chuck it all out the window."

December 20, 1942

At 7:15 A.M. Sottens announced that according to a late-night communiqué from Moscow, the Russians have won a major victory at Voronezh and broken through the German lines at two points. They have advanced an average of about forty miles along a front fifty-five miles long. There are some 10,000 German dead and as many prisoners, and the Russians have also destroyed a great deal of matériel. The strategic importance of this victory is obvious: Now they will fix their sights on Kharkov. But to date, after initial successes, every Russian attack has been beaten back by German counterattacks. We are still in the picador stage; we have got a long way to go before the matador makes his entry into the arena.

Radio message from Pope Pius XII.

Gaullist radio has announced that the Germans have been routed, but they have been announcing this every time the Russians attack. Their propaganda is clearly ill conceived. They must think the French are all simpletons. Fortunately, the American War Secretary Stimson has made a more objective assessment and clarified the situation without attempting, and rightly so, to obscure the difficulties. *That* is sound propaganda. The British do it similarly. Italian radio, in contrast, is as grandiloquent as ever. According to their announcer, just about everything in the United States is Italian. Nothing would ever have been built in New York without the Italians—bridges, railroads—they did everything. The very conquest of America might have been the work of Italians.

Finally, we were graced with a message from Marshal Pétain, in which he summarized in his quavering voice the results of his bankrupt policies.

December 25, 1942

I just learned that on December 24, at 3 P.M., Admiral Darlan was assassinated in Algiers by a twenty-year-old Frenchman. Six bullets from a handgun, fired point-blank.

I spent a lot of time with Darlan in 1933, when he was an adviser to Georges Leygues, my Minister of the Navy. He was a man consumed by vaulting ambition. Darlan came to see me when Leygues died following a long and painful illness. I had gone to see Leygues several times in his villa in Saint-Cloud and found him steadfast and courageous in facing death and abounding in the affectionate civility with which he had always favored me. When Leygues died, Darlan called me from my office and informed me of his passing with a flippancy that he was forced to curb when he sensed my sorrow.

In 1936, with Gasnier-Duparc's consent, Darlan pushed out Admiral Durand-Viel, getting him to retire early in exchange for who knows what. Darlan was lavish in assuring Blum of his devotion to him, but after we had reviewed troops somewhere, on May 11, if I am not mistaken, he told me how Pétain had snickeringly said to him, "So Darlan, I see you got yourself appointed Admiral of the Popular Front." In those days, Darlan was merciless in his sarcastic remarks about "the senile old man."

He didn't get along with Campinchi, the Minister above him, and worked on both General Bourret, who was very close to me, and above all Clapier, my Chief of Staff, dropping in on them, lunching, and dining with them. Darlan wanted to become head of the Joint Chiefs of Staff for National Defense, which was absolutely absurd.

I ran into him during maneuvers in Normandy. He was a doer, quite intelligent, and closely supervised our naval construction there. His hatred for Campinchi was ever increasing, and he tried to go over his head through the friendly contacts he had made with Clapier. However, the loss of his aide, Tavera, who had a lot more horse sense than he did, left him severely handicapped. In 1939, during the famous August 23 meeting at which we discussed the possibility of France's entering the war, he stated that the Navy was ready and that their Italian plans—for Genoa, Rome, and Naples—had been finalized. He hadn't understood any more about the role air power was to play than the Army Generals. Our two aircraft carriers, the *Béarn* and the *Teste*, were outdated; still there is no doubt in my mind that we outclassed the Italians. In 1939, he set himself up as a minor potentate in Maintenon, with a private train.

As soon as Reynaud took over, Darlan began playing the sycophant again, criticizing Gamelin. On May 19, having been disappointed at not having been named to replace Gamelin, he turned on Reynaud, but cautiously. He was simultaneously working both ends: resistance and capitulation. On the resistance end, he agreed with and ended up organizing plans for the Members of Parliament to leave for Morocco on the *Massilia;* he even cabled Noguès, the Governor-General in Morocco, to set up a command post next to his from which he would lead the resistance in North Africa. At that very same time, Vuillemin was issuing an order to have 2,000 planes flown to North Africa. Then Darlan turned traitor, refused to bring the fleet to Noguès, and became a collaborator.

After the palace revolution of December 13, 1940, he went to see Hitler. Once Laval was back in power, Darlan was relegated to the simple role of Commander in Chief of the Armed Forces. Since he was anti-British, he decided to try out the Americans. I still remember what he said about the British Admiralty and Admiral Pound. During the Supreme Council meetings in London and even more so in Paris, he couldn't keep his sarcasm in check.

Did he actually urge Marshal Pétain to resist on November 8, as he kept on claiming? In all events, that the French fleet chose to oppose the American landing during the first few days is totally incomprehensible. If Darlan and Noguès were in agreement, how could they have sent hundreds of officers, soldiers, and sailors to a useless death? If they weren't in agreement, how does one explain the sudden turnaround? The key to the puzzle lies in Pétain's November 11 address, in which he protested the movement of German troops into Unoccupied France. Marion intervened to stop that address from being broadcast, and Laval, who returned from Munich in the early afternoon, approved his decision. He declared in that statement that France was no longer bound by the conditions of the Armistice, which explains the turnaround in Africa. Laval managed to have Darlan, Giraud, Boisson, and Bireau stripped of their French nationality and handed them over to Vichy's "newspapermen," without either a trial or a sentencing. What is more, neither Noguès, Chatel, nor Bergeret[46] lost his citizenship.

De Gaulle was furious. They were absolutely out of control on the radio every night. The British press got into it. There was a great stir in the House of Commons. The realistic Americans, in contrast, remained unruffled. It was clear that Darlan served the French and Allied cause in North Africa. If the Anglo-Saxons had continued to encounter resistance, they would have lost at least a month, and the entire undertaking could have been compromised, for the Germans would have had the time to regroup.

A war council in Algiers has decided to execute the assassin. They have refused to disclose his name "for reasons of military security." His father is French and his mother Italian. Is he a Fascist? A Doriotist? One of the boys from the Youth Camps? A Gaullist? There have been all sorts of conjectures, especially in light of what Darlan is supposed to have said to the officers who rushed to his side: "It is useless. The British have attained their objective." Of course, that information came through the Stéfani Press Agency. Reuters offered bizarre comments, basically expressing pleasure at the assassination, which would pave the way for a centrist agreement between de Gaulle and Giraud, with the latter taking charge of the French fighting forces and de Gaulle assuming control over political and diplomatic matters. On the other side, Roosevelt condemned the assassination.

December 26, 1942

On her way out, Mme Reichenbach stopped off to tell me that she had decided to sew marks into the shoulder pads in Blum's overcoat and offered to do the same for me.

46. General Jean Bergeret, Air Force Brigadier General, member of the French delegation at the signing of the Armistice and Air Force Junior Minister in the Vichy government from 1940 to 1942. He left for Algiers at the end of 1942 and was appointed Commander in Chief of the French West African Air Force. He was dismissed by de Gaulle, arrested at the end of 1943, and eventually spent several years in prison.

December 30, 1942

Léon Blum told me that his lawyer, Le Trocquer, had gone to Vichy to see Bousquet, which was a mistake. First of all, because both Laval and Bousquet despise him and suspect him of belonging to a Gaullist organization in Clermont; second and most important, because there is no point in just going through the motions; the government in Vichy decides what to do on the basis of what it thinks will please the Germans most. Le Trocquer asked for permission to meet with Blum in his capacity as lawyer. Bousquet denied his request, saying that when Laval returns from Paris he will inform the Cour Suprême that it has been dissolved. The court would have done better to dissolve itself when the Germans moved in to occupy Riom.

What will become of us? Jacomet and La Chambre will doubtless be placed under house arrest. But what of the three of us, the men sentenced by Pétain: Blum, Gamelin, and myself? There is no way to send us back to Le Portalet, so we'll be shipped out to Germany. I have no doubt about that now, in spite of everything that's been promised by Laval and his cronies. Blum, however, thinks that we'll remain in Bourassol, which will be made into a fortified compound. I remain skeptical.

It doesn't really matter much anyway. The end of this year has been wonderful. The Allies have taken the initiative. The Russians are relentlessly hammering away at the front, taking a page from Marshal Foch. In the time since the beginning of the offensive, German losses have reached 300,000 men. The threat of an attack on Rostov has increased, and Rommel has been forced to draw back even further west. Moreover, just as I had predicted, the rate at which ships and planes are being built in the United States has continued to accelerate.

The word on Herriot is not at all good. He is thoroughly depressed. They have imposed restrictions that are simply loathsome. He has the right to have one three-hour visit per week, with a policeman present, and two letters a week.

December 31, 1942

Today is the last day of a year that witnessed the opening, then the suspension sine die, of the Riom trial, as ordered by a government in panic and frightened by its own stupidity. All they have left are Maurras and Déat. All France is now under the enemy's heel, all our colonies occupied. This is precisely the catastrophe that Pétain claimed that he had been sparing us ever since the betrayal in Bordeaux. We are no longer dealing with the "disinherited King" or the "merry old King of nowhere." Pétain definitively dishonored himself on November 11, 1942.

The Germans have gone into a slow downhill slide. After having achieved almost total domination of the world in 1941, they are now irreversibly heading into the abyss. It will of course not take place without terrible convulsions, but defeat and the invasion of Germany are inevitable. The initiative lies with the Allies on every front, which is why yesterday's traitors and cowards can be seen popping up here and there. North Africa appears to them to be a particularly propitious setting in which to shift allegiances. In Africa, they are even expecting the arrival of Peyrouton and Chautemps.

LEFT: *Daladier at age twenty-eight, when he was a history teacher(1912)*

BELOW: *Daladier as a soldier in the French Infantry (1914)*

Daladier (above the X) in the Foreign Legion during World War I

Prime Minister Daladier (right) and General Bourret, during an inspection of the front lines (1939)

Minister of War Daladier visits the front (1939)

Mayor Daladier greets a constituent in Avignon

ABOVE: *Birthplace and early childhood home of Daladier in Carpentras*

LEFT: *Daladier, in the garden at his home, overlooking the Rhone River*

Parliamentary Deputy Daladier at his desk (1955)

Daladier in later years

1943

January 15, 1943

Vichy radio has announced that the "relief corps" is making great headway. The number of volunteers leaving to work in Germany is increasing daily!

This morning, Mme L.C. related a story told by her "carriageman," M. Gilbert. He had taken the train to Clermont to buy a horse for butchering. Antiriot police and German soldiers herded him and all the other passengers into the waiting room. Forty yards away, on the public squares and the streets leading to the station, women and children were screaming and crying. Every so often, when the crowd would regroup and march on the station, the police would disperse them with the butts of their rifles, as the amused German soldiers looked on. The police were under orders to stop the protesters from overrunning the station and lying down on the tracks to prevent the trains from leaving, as they had done in Montluçon. On the platform, workers were lined up in rows of twos, with guards and German soldiers on either side. As each train pulled out, people would start singing the Communist *Internationale* and shouting, "Down with Pétain" and "Death to Laval."

January 22, 1943

At around 3 P.M. Bourassol was rattled with bursts from automatic weapons and exploding hand grenades. I got the feeling, though, that they were firing blanks. I saw Lieutenant Niepven prancing about on his handsome horse, his gold bars shining in the sunlight. I later learned that these were maneuvers to ward off possible aggressors from the North … but the Germans had already invaded Bourassol last November!

Last night, a broadcast from Algiers announced the appointment of Peyrouton, Vichy's fascist ex-Minister of the Interior, to a position in the government in Algeria. The Gaullists have protested, and their outrage is perfectly legitimate. It was Peyrouton who organized Pétain's personal police force and masterminded the plot that ended with Laval's arrest. In Algiers, he will be up to his neck again in personal intrigue, unless Giraud manages to bring him into the Count of Paris's camp. It is unfortunate that Roosevelt wasn't informed of just how deplorable a choice he is.

January 28, 1943

Two thousand local assemblies have been dissolved; 800 Mayors and Deputy Mayors have been removed from office: These figures are an indication not only of what the men in Vichy have done, but of their very reason for seizing power in the first place. The words "National Revolution" are hardly devoid of meaning; nor are the piles of decrees, laws, and various measures that have been enacted.

January 29, 1943

At the Riom trial, our Generals testified that the French Army had not been provided with shooting ranges. Right here, in Riom, the Germans have been taking rifle and antiaircraft target practice, using live ammunition.

January 30, 1943

Pierre came. He is brave and involved. He told me that the Italians had pulled out of Carpentras.

It's the tenth anniversary of Hitler's rise to power, the day he was named Chancellor by Marshal Hindenburg. At 11 A.M. it was announced that Göring would address the nation; at 11:15, that he would address the nation in a few minutes. It was about noon when he actually spoke, the British having decided to mark this anniversary by bombing Berlin in broad daylight. This is what they call British humor: making Göring wait until the end of the air raid. The people of Berlin must have had no trouble measuring the difference between January 1943 and January 1942 or 1941. Now they can reflect on Göring's famous challenge to the British Air Force.

The lines taken by Briand and Stresemann, England's blindness, and America's isolationism all made it easier for the clauses of the Treaty of Versailles to be broken. Inflation and the destruction of Germany's middle class created a favorable climate.

There is something permanently and specifically German in Nazism. One has only to read Fichte's *Addresses to the German Nation.*

Hitler's paramount error was to have attacked Russia instead of invading England.

February 2, 1943

On January 30, Hitler, Göring, and Goebbels were already eulogizing the dead at Stalingrad, hours before their actual capture or death. The Russians continue to push forward along a vast front. Stalingrad is this war's Verdun, but more decisive and even crueler. The German Army is retreating along the entire front, and they are retreating slowly, perhaps more slowly than they'd like. Maybe mechanized armies have a harder time withdrawing than their earlier counterparts. How do you stealthily pull out all that huge machinery?

It is "victory or death," the Nazi leaders are now saying, borrowing a phrase from the French Revolution; earlier they had compared themselves to Napoleon for military genius. In any event, they have hidden nothing from the German people, although they may have exaggerated somewhat the gravity of the situation to trigger a burst of popular energy. Now that a compromise peace settlement is no longer a possibility, the Nazi leaders will be asking their people to make an enormous effort. The only thing that can save Hitler would be for the Russians to pull out of the war, once they have liberated their own territory and strengthened their influence over Poland, the Baltic States, Bulgaria, and Romania. In the eighteenth century, Berlin and Frederick II were spared when Czar Paul pulled out, but I tend to think that Stalin's vision stretches further than old man Kutuzov's.

While the world tragedy is hastening toward a climax, the phantoms of Vichy have kept right on with their ridiculous pantomime: Pétain has stripped Bergeret and everyone else who went to Africa of their *francisque gallique* decorations, a medal he made up himself. He has given his blessing to France's SS. Joffre, Foch, and Clemenceau were right in their judgment of the man twenty years ago.

Ever since the Americans set up Giraud in Algiers, the same Giraud that Reynaud wanted to name Supreme Commander, the English and Eden have found themselves in a very uncomfortable position.

It is obvious that the Americans' realistic approach has led them to endorse Giraud and Peyrouton in order to gain the support of officers like Noguès and Boisson, who are conservative but nonetheless favor democracy. And the Americans are the ones running operations in Africa.

February 9, 1943

Mazé showed up unexpectedly. He spoke of his odyssey, the American High Command, and new plans.[1] I'm worried about my sons.

Around noon, the presiding judge, Caous, called Bourassol to announce that Jacomet and La Chambre were to be released on their own recognizance. Then a car drove up with the warden of the Riom Penitentiary. Mme La Chambre was deeply moved, absolutely overjoyed, but the rest of the afternoon was spent on the phone with Bousquet, the Superintendent of Police. Apparently Laval had not yet submitted the court's decision to the Germans. Bousquet feared there might be incidents. So, instead of spending the night in a hotel, Jacomet and La Chambre had to spend it here.

Around 8:30 P.M. they came into my room. They were joyous, exultant. Neither one of them had a word or a thought for me, even though I was going to remain a prisoner. They said that their release was proof that the charge of their having ill-prepared us with arms and equipment had been dropped. On that score, they were right.

1. After having opposed plans to escape as long as the Riom trial was in progress, Daladier was now prepared to go to London, as Churchill, Eden, and de Gaulle had been urging him to do. Pierre de Vomécourt, who was later arrested and deported, served as liaison. Because a plane could land no closer than the area around Châteauroux, the principal difficulty lay in covering the distance between Riom and Châteauroux at night, without being caught.

February 10, 1943

The day went by without our "releasees" making it out of here, and yet they had donned their finest clothes for the occasion. Both of them were getting increasingly edgy, especially when their wives couldn't keep from showing how concerned they were and started asking preposterous questions. A guard named Fouilland chose to express ironically his doubts about their ever leaving, which didn't help matters. I found out this evening that the court recorder, Théry, had come with an order for their release, but that Brun, the Prefect, notified them that Laval would be going to Paris tomorrow to inform the Germans and request their authorization. Back to prison they went. Another guard, Young, who goes by the book, even bolted their doors shut, despite their vehement protests.

Neither one of them has had a considerate word for us these last two days, yet they should feel at least partially indebted to me for their release. Didn't I praise them at the trial? Wasn't I the one who tore apart the charges that we were not properly prepared to go to war?

Is man fundamentally evil, as the Church teaches us, and as is the contention of my old friend Dr. Renard, who came and spent the rest of the day with me?

After dinner, sweet little Simone, who was waiting on us, told me that Jacomet was becoming demanding and La Chambre even more condescending than before, and that it was making her sick.

February 11, 1943

I think Giraud and Peyrouton see things as Pétain does and that at the end of the war they'll head for Vichy and sing, "Maréchal, nous voilà."[2]

Why wasn't de Gaulle with the British and American troops when they landed in Algiers? I can't figure it out.

2. Literally, "Marshall, here we are," with "ready to serve you" implied. This was the song that all French schoolchildren sang in honor of Pétain and that became a kind of national anthem. The allegiance to and reverence for an individual leader was one of the typically Fascist aspects of the Vichy regime.

February 13, 1943

Had a final important talk with Mazé at 2 P.M. He left at 5. I pray that he'll succeed.

February 15, 1943

The Archbishop of New York is being received by the Primate of Spain, a meeting not without importance.

The *Richelieu*, a powerful 35,000-ton cruiser, whose construction was finished at my insistence, has just reached New York after first being damaged at Dakar and then crossing the Atlantic through a horrifying storm. The cruiser *Montcalm* and other ships made a similar journey, thus, along with the ships that had already gone back into combat, saving the honor of the French Navy.

The Russians have advanced to within five miles of Kharkov. Berlin claims that its forces have simply withdrawn from positions that had become useless and that were not actually threatened, and that they have inflicted terrible losses on the Reds. Try and figure it out.

The Bourassol owl is back.

February 17, 1943

3:30 P.M. Suddenly, Bourassol was all astir as a car with two magnificent chauffeurs pulled in. Out of it, in all his majesty, stepped the honorable Superintendent of Police. I assumed that he had finally come for the two men who had been freed, but I could hear people yelling and women's voices squealing above the men's vociferous protests. Doors opened and slammed shut; then the halls rang anew with the noise of shouting. Fouilland, an old veteran from North African campaigns, filled me in on what was going on. After Jacomet and La Chambre had gotten all of their personal effects together this morning, in anticipation of their definitive release, the Superintendent of Police came and read them a new order from the Minister of the Interior. Instead of being released on their own recognizance, they were placed under house arrest and, worse, here in Bourassol. They both refused to sign the order, fumed at the Superintendent of Police, and began railing against poor old Young, accusing him of being responsible for everything. They must have forgotten that this poor old head guard had been threatened with losing his job for having failed to bolt our doors shut these last few days.

Fouilland came up to see me later to express his indignation and his fear that Bourassol would be transformed into a site for prisoners placed under house arrest, in which case Blum, Gamelin, and I would be handed over to the Germans. In other words, as Horace wrote, "Quieta non movere."

February 20, 1943

Goebbels gave a speech that was highly structured and forceful, which is in fact characteristic of all his speeches. He emphasized the extreme danger that the unexpected strength of the USSR represented for the Reich. He said that stopping them would require the total mobilization of Germany and the neighboring countries. "Let the people rise up," he said. "Let the storm loose its fury." Of course Goebbels, no more than any other orator, was not about to lift the veil covering the cordial relations between Russia and Japan.

I'll have to reread Spengler.

Jean came at 2 P.M. We discussed Mazé's plan.

February 22, 1943

There's been a new episode in the soap opera about our "releasees." This time, Jacomet and La Chambre were actually expecting to leave sometime today. People were running all over the place, with no one minding especially about us. The Germans have had their attention focused too sharply on Bourassol. They could end up moving in here or taking their guests to Germany, without so much as a nod to the decisions of Vichy's Cour Suprême.

Jean left at 1:30 P.M.

February 23, 1943

Daridan related his meeting with Monsignor Suhard[3] and Monsignor Chapoulié,[4] in which they distanced themselves from Pétain with all due ecclesiastical unction. They are worried about what will happen after the war. Will the Church be able to hold on to the gains it has made? Wouldn't it be in the Church's best interests to relinquish certain overly spectacular favors it has received? According to Daridan, the Church is leaning toward the idea of relying on the Socialists as protection from the Communists. At the Vatican, they no longer believe that Germany can win, but they are concerned about a Soviet victory.

February 25, 1943

This General Giraud of ours is either a Royalist or a Fascist, depending on circumstances, but in every instance he is antirepublican. That is his meeting ground with Pétain, Maurras's boy, the "Monck" whom the Action Française group couldn't find on February 6, 1934.

Following the assassination of Darlan, who had promoted himself as anti-Fascist and anti-Nazi in Africa, Giraud sided for a time with the Count of Paris, the Pretender to the French throne. The latter made a visit to Algiers, but in the face of the vehement protests from the Gaullists in Algeria, the British, the Americans, and the democratic factions in Algiers and other cities, he was forced to turn back to Spanish Morocco. Thereafter, Peyrouton and Flandin freed the Gaullists, Communists, and Spanish Republicans imprisoned in Algiers. Stay tuned for more.

Stalin has stated that the Red Army has no mission beyond that of liberating its national territory. This reassured the moderate elements, who had been clearly shaken by Vichy's constant talk of the Red peril—Europe submerged under a flood of Bolsheviks. They have been relentless in milking Laval's pet themes: the German as civilization's soldier; Hitler as the knight of Teutonic order, etc., etc. Stalin's speech obviously comes in response to this propaganda. He was also highly ironic with regard to the

3. Cardinal Suhard, Archbishop of Paris.

4. Chapoulié was a Bishop and the Episcopate's liaison with the government.

Anglo-Saxons, above all the British, calling for them once again to launch an offensive in the West. The sword of honor that King George had cast for Stalingrad is not enough to satisfy him. The insolence with which it was accepted by Kalinin, the "little father" of Soviet peoples, was magnificent.

March 2, 1943

Senator Maroselli[5] has arrived in London. He made a statement, which I couldn't hear very clearly, about the military reasons for our defeat, which he ascribed to the inferiority of our Air Force, in spite of the tenacious efforts that he, Maroselli, had made. One more example of someone who thinks he's the center of the universe.

March 3, 1943

Gamelin came to see me at 9 A.M. He had had a visit from his lawyer Arnal, a former classmate of the prosecutor, Cassagneau. At a gathering with Cassagneau, Barthélemy, and Caous, the presiding judge, Arnal learned how furious the Germans were when they found out about the court decision releasing the two prisoners. It took a full two weeks of negotiations between Hitler and Laval just to get the two of them placed under house arrest.

Caous and Cassagneau are relieved that we too didn't ask to be released on our own recognizance, for if we had, the court would have found itself in the position of having to order us freed and, in so doing, of handing us over to the German authorities. They're nonetheless reserving the right to release us when the Anglo-Saxons land in France.

As for me, I never even dreamed of asking to be released on my own recognizance, which serves no purpose in practical terms and represents a feeble, contrived compromise in terms of justice.

Sooner or later, the world of French jurisprudence will have to recognize that from 1919 to 1939 no Minister of War did what I did for our national defense. In September 1939, no French statesman could have left

5. André Maroselli, Radical-Socialist Senator.

France open to an accusation of breach of promise without inflicting on the nation a dishonor greater even than defeat. In 1939, there was nothing for us to do other than become involved in a war that Hitler wanted.

March 4, 1943

Jacomet and La Chambre came by to see me at 6 P.M. They had been notified by the Regional Prefect that the German military authorities have refused to authorize their release.

That was inevitable. The only thing that will come out of this business will be the sterner conditions the Germans will impose in Bourassol. How could anyone have believed for as much as a second that at a time when the war in Russia has taken an irreversible turn, the Germans would allow the French government to free two men who are standing trial? It just goes to show how much sway even the most childish illusions can have over intelligent men.

The actual consequences weren't long in coming. At nightfall, the Gestapo arrived to relieve the German soldiers stationed here. There are now twice as many guards, all of them Gestapo.

It is their intention to keep Mme Fouilland, the cleaning lady, from leaving Bourassol every evening to go home. The German captain demanded that the head guard bring him the visitors' register, which he examined in detail and put his mark on.

Ever since the court's decision releasing the two of them, I have been expecting us to be sent to Germany. "Quieta non movere."

March 5, 1943

There have been more incidents at the barriers set up at the entrance. The Gestapo tried to keep one of the guards, Ancel, from returning to his job. Mme Reichenbach and people who have been coming here regularly received a thorough going-over. All of this is highly significant.

March 10, 1943

Vichy has been mobilizing French youth to serve the German cause. They're handing out travel papers for Silesia, Poland, and Sebastopol. Soon they'll be handing out German uniforms. It's reported that thousands of young men have sought refuge in the Alps. Pétain is paving the way for the Communists.

March 31, 1943

Around 10 A.M. Bousquet, the Superintendent of Police, and a thoroughly dejected-looking Génébrier came into my room. I knew right away that Vichy had backed down. Bousquet confirmed as much, saying that Laval had held out for as long as he could, but that the Gestapo was convinced that the British and Americans were plotting to kidnap us. Bousquet explained that we would be lodged in perfectly suitable quarters and that we could correspond with the outside world through him and even take someone along with us to Germany. I thanked him, but that wasn't the issue. I had nothing to say about the decision the Germans had made. However, I had plenty to say about the attitude of the government in Vichy, which was the sole responsible party in all this. A German Colonel with the Gestapo walked in and quite courteously repeated what Bousquet had said. Génébrier, my friend in need, agreed to carry out my last wishes if that became necessary. Jacomet stopped by briefly.

Our departure was set for 12:30 P.M. I went down to the outer office where a number of French officers saluted me. I answered back with the refrain, "Maréchal, nous voilà." The three prison guards reacted with dignity. This time, I found myself sharing a car with Blum.

On the road to Aulnat, I spotted Génébrier. He waved a final goodbye in my direction. When we arrived, they put us in a room where we spent the whole day. There were gendarmes, sentries, and searchlights all around. We met up with Léon Jouhaux,[6] whom they had brought in from Evaux-les-Bains; he would be traveling with us. Got news of Herriot, who had been taken with his wife to the Seine-et-Marne. There was some improvement though—we had our meals together.

6. Léon Jouhaux, union organizer and leader of the CGT union.

April 2, 1943

Left Aulnat. Five cars. Jouhaux didn't come with us. Went through Montferrand, Bourassol, Riom, Moulins, Nevers, La Charité. Saw well-equipped German soldiers. Went on to Montargis.

There seemed to be no men anywhere in the region. Shops were closed. Drove on to Fontainebleau and Paris. I was overcome with a feeling of anguish; the city seemed to have been chloroformed. Drove up the Avenue d'Italie—empty—to the Gobelins, onto the Boulevard Saint Michel, where there was some activity. Rode by Vilmorin's plant shop on the quay.

Reached the Place de la Concorde. Went down the Champs Elysées, passing in front of number 32, where I had lived with my father-in-law for several years after the Great War.

Sent a salute that carried all our hopes to the Unknown Soldier.

In Maisons-Lafitte, I was recognized by a few civilians, which didn't sit well with our German guard.

Came to a house surrounded by guards and sentries, who had orders to shoot if we got close to the garden gates. Dinner at 8 P.M.

April 3, 1943

Left Maisons-Lafitte at 8 A.M. Went by car, with two armed soldiers.

Reached Le Bourget at 9 A.M., where several civilians recognized me. A little human warmth.

Arrived in Mannheim at 11:20 A.M., but we were kept locked on the plane until 7 P.M. Took off, with orders to land in Frankfurt. Had dinner at the Air Force base, where we were courteously received by the officers. Had sausages and tasteless coffee.

Left for the Weimar region by highway at 10:30 P.M. Got there before dawn.

Around 6 A.M. we were welcomed by a Gestapo Commandant, tall, well built, and cordial. He reminded me of a British officer. "Horresco referens." He assigned us rooms; I settled into mine.

Day was breaking on the plateau, over the forest of pines. From my window I could see a sentry with a police dog and beyond them fences, barbed wire, and more sentries and dogs. There were bars on my windows but done in better taste than those at Bourassol. We were cut off from the world and life in France, but no more so than a million other French prisoners and the French youths that had been taken to Germany.

France will rise again. That is the only thing that matters.

April 7, 1943

Snowed all day. At 11 A.M. I went for a walk outside the house, stepping over the roots of the pine trees. The sentry was right behind me with his police dog.

Had lunch at 1 P.M. We could only bring in two stations on the radio. What are the Germans getting out of keeping us sequestered here?

Jouhaux talked to me about workers' lives and the strikes in the old days over sardine nets and the rotating nets in Concarneau. He also sketched a few portraits of some working-class activists: Rivelle, Vignaud, and Gautier.

Won't this war herald Asia's entry onto the international stage?

Will Europe be able to go on living by and for itself without lowering its standard of living?

Got two 20-gram packs of Croatian tobacco.

April 9, 1943

There was a storm last night. Soldiers were shouting and dogs were barking. The pine trees are covered with snow.

April 10, 1943

The camp Commandant came to see us at 4:30 P.M. He was as helpful as he could be within the limits of his prerogatives. It's a huge camp, with 20,000 SS, all of them volunteers. Before the war, it held three divisions; today it holds twenty. The men undergo training for seventy-five days and then leave for the front. There's a lesson in that for the French High Command.

A lot of the men are sick, even though the authorities go to great lengths to see to the well-being of their soldiers.

The food, which is the same for officers and enlisted men alike, is healthy and plentiful, and the diet well balanced. The pay and the child benefits are high. Many of the soldiers come back from Russia having saved up a considerable amount of money. They try to do more or less the same for the workers, with certain advantages clearly favoring the soldiers. There's a lesson in that for the French working class.

The Commandant told us that there were now a million French workers, men and women, at work in Germany, and that they had proven to be productive and conscientious once they got used to the factories.

He mentioned productivity records that French workers had broken.

April 15, 1943

Jouhaux is relatively realistic. He fears that through overcapitalization, the United States will eventually dominate Europe economically and thereby politically. He is opposed to granting independence to the colonies, although he believes that we should maintain an open-door policy.

Jouhaux is a proponent of international treaties and a multinational defense; he foresees American capitalism leading the world under a new banner. Blum actually waxes lyrical. He's very much taken by Wallace's[7] views. He thinks some compromise will be reached between communism and a modified version of private ownership. Like Jouhaux and myself, he believes that there will have to be a genuine federation of European nations. I am of the belief that it will take time to rebuild France and that the political system of the future will have to be different from the last one. We'll have to choose between a British-style parliamentary system and a presidential system.

April 18, 1943

Palm Sunday. This was a major day of celebration in Provence, with olive trees and boxwoods. Part of the greatness of Christianity. In the current war, however, the Catholic and Protestant churches have once again fallen short of their mission. The political parties of the Left erred significantly

7. Henry Wallace, successively Secretary of Agriculture and Commerce under Roosevelt.

in ignoring the religious problem and the place it holds in France. There was a tendency to confuse secularity with secularism, which is a caricature, or rather a denial, of secularity.

April 21, 1943

De Gaulle made a formal statement on the radio, a typical Minister's declaration from the old school, in which you do your utmost to reconcile all interests and satisfy all concerned parties. It contained a mix of Communist and conservative catch phrases: the exploitation of our common wealth, a renewed and reformed Republic, protection for large families, etc.

Blum was enthusiastic about it: "He has never spoken so clearly." He probably put in some of those phrases himself, with the help of his friends in Algiers. In all events, he has given up the idea of calling back Members of Parliament and reconvening the National Assembly for a few days.

De Gaulle has appointed himself Head of the Provisional Government in all free territories of France. He has named Ministers and Junior Ministers to assure himself of support from all parts of the population. This will be followed by a Constituent Assembly, to be ratified through elections, and finally by a definitive government. I am in agreement on all points except the re-creation of a Popular Front, to which I am violently opposed because of the duplicity of the Communists. I am also opposed to a return to political parties, which, given the present international situation, would favor the Communists.

Blum doesn't believe that a British-style parliamentary system is suited to France. He sees no drawbacks in reestablishing political parties so long as we opt for a presidential system. He says it would be impossible to govern in association with a party tied to a foreign power, but he believes that Stalin has given up the idea of leading a world revolution and is now interested in becoming a great national leader. I remained highly skeptical as I listened to his prophesies. I believe precisely the opposite.

According to Jouhaux, the Communists have assured de Gaulle, "We are with you heart and soul." That is exactly what they told Blum in 1936.

April 22, 1943

The regional newspapers are filled with obituaries every day: "Fallen for the German Fatherland." "Died for the Fatherland, the German people, and the Führer." "Gave his young life for the Fatherland." There are lists of the dead from March and April and statements of appreciation from families who have received condolences. The stoicism of the German people during this third year of the war is undeniable. The fall of Stalingrad was met with an officially decreed period of mourning. Foreign countries have grossly underestimated the extraordinary degree to which Nazism has been instilled in the German people and their youth.

April 24, 1943

Had a sumptuous dinner: meatballs, potatoes, lettuce, and two eggs. I have been trying to get the new radio to work.

A massive attack on Tunisia would appear to be imminent. In Russia, there has been heavy fighting on the Donets. On the other hand, there has been no further word on Timoshenko's offensive. The tragedy has now spread to the entire world. As for Gamelin, he continues telling tales of his days in the Middle East and his memories of Brazil. He is writing his memoirs. According to him, we lost the war for lack of resolve. Facing the dynamism of the Germans, public opinion in France was divided, the middle classes had forgotten their mission, and political intrigues were raging among Pétain, Weygand, and Georges. He noted the failings of our fighting men and above all their leaders. Patriotism had become a matter of circumstance. The only thing he neglected to mention was the crisis in military thinking.

April 25, 1943

Easter Sunday. It's bitter cold out and foggy. Read some newspapers: *Je suis partout*, *La Gerbe*, *L'Echo de Nancy*, *Le Nouveau Journal de Bruxelles*. In the latter, there was a piece on the funeral ceremonies for Paul Collin, the Belgian Déat, and the speech given by Degrelle. This was already a Nazi movement well before the war began.

The Belgian newspaper went back over the abominable Katyn Forest massacre, where 10,000 imprisoned Polish officers died.[8] Their bodies, with their hands tied behind their backs, were piled up in long, deep trenches. The officers had knelt at the edge of the ditch and been shot in the neck.

April 29, 1943

Had a medical examination, with a curt, distant doctor, a General by rank, who seemed to have swallowed a sword, and another younger one, who was only slightly less arrogant, plus an interpreter who didn't know any French. There were measuring instruments laid out all over the table; you would have thought it was a scene from *Doctor Knock*. They listened to my lungs, took measurements, and urine samples—the whole business. It was far more comical than anything else.

Dr. Hauffmann, however, has been courteous and kind. He brought me a package and letters from Jean, Pierre, and M.L. I was quite moved by the letter from Jean, delighted to see what a brave lad he is. The Commandant told us that Mandel would be brought here, close to Blum. Blum quipped that "they were going to turn the place into a ghetto," but he took comfort in the news and on the whole everyone was pleased. As for us, we are going to be taken into the Tirol, not far from Innsbruck.

April 30, 1943

We said our good-byes this morning at the forest lodge of the camp. We chatted with the two men who waited on us, one of whom was from the area, the other a Croatian who told us about his seven children and showed us their photos. He is a Croatian volunteer SS.

At around 6 P.M. we got a call from the Assistant Commandant; our departure had been postponed again. Instantly, everyone started speculating, as if to see who could come up with the most imaginative explanation. I had fun claiming that under threats from Pétain and Laval to resign, the

8. The Polish officers were killed by the Soviets, who have only recently admitted responsibility.

Germans had agreed to send us back to France; either that or they had discovered an Anglo-American plot in Innsbruck. My first suggestion spawned others, and Gamelin began gleefully pulling ideas out of his brain like a magician pulling omelets, bottles, and rabbits out of a hat.

May 2, 1943

Awakened at 4 A.M. for a departure at 6; waited uselessly until 8. There had apparently been some misunderstanding in the transmission of orders. Dr. Hauffmann came by; he had just returned from the Tirol. Finally, we were on the highway. In the suburbs of Munich, we spotted a detachment of French prisoners looking proud and determined. We drove on very quickly along the quays.

All the SS NCOs were on hand for our arrival at the "castle" in Itter.[9] Went through a first gate with bars and locks, then a second one identical to the first, but with armed sentries. Beyond a small, triangular courtyard lay a raised inner yard 150 feet long and 100 feet wide, dotted with shacks and sheds. I was deeply moved when I saw two rows of prisoners go by, forty men or so with their heads shaved, wearing gray shirts with large brown stripes, similar to what prison laborers used to wear. Each had a number stamped on the left side of his chest. There were men of all ages, some of them just kids, others quite old. Some of them were political prisoners; their faces brightened a bit when they saw me. Received a few friendly smiles from some who obviously recognized me. They were quickly dispersed by SS NCOs who came running up from the chapel that had been transformed into dormitories and refectories. The sight of these men is powerful. It's part of the same chain of suffering, torture, and infamy that links the centuries. I went up to my room on the fourth floor, number 19. It reminded me of the Portalet fortress where Pétain had had us imprisoned, but with fresh air and a view of the mountains.

9. Near the Tirol and the Dachau concentration camp.

May 11, 1943

It has been reported that Franco offered to serve as a mediator to end the war and that the British and the Americans rejected his offer. Some of the guards who have been keeping us informed told us that "two gentlemen would be arriving tomorrow." I told my companions that it would likely be Reynaud and possibly Herriot and that Hitler would then tell them—or us: "I am holding you hostage. You, Reynaud, you're to work on Churchill and get a compromise peace settlement with him; you, Herriot, you work on Stalin and Roosevelt; you, Daladier, on the Radical Party; and you, Jouhaux, on the unions. I'll give you a week, after which you'll be shot."

Jouhaux was sulking. Gamelin was beside himself: How could I have omitted him in so important a matter!

May 12, 1943

At around 3 P.M. Reynaud and Borotra[10] arrived from Berlin, after having spent two days in Weimar, where they had left Mandel with Blum.[11] That Borotra has remained loyal to Pétain prompted violent attacks from Reynaud, which allowed him to overlook the fact that it was he, Reynaud, who had brought Pétain to power.

May 13, 1943

Our discussions at meal times carry over into the evening. Borotra is full of life, impassioned, and open-handed. We have been relentless in teasing him about his collaboration with Pétain, to whom he remains devoted. In his eyes, France was fortunate to have come upon Pétain in 1940. "What would have happened without him?" We answered that what would have happened was exactly what happened in Norway, Holland, and Belgium and even in Greece and Serbia. Borotra goes running and does strenuous

10. Jean Borotra, industrialist and tennis champion prior to the war, served as Vichy's Youth and Sports Minister. He was arrested by the Germans and liberated in 1945.

11. Blum and Mandel were both deported to Buchenwald. Blum spent two years there, receiving special treatment. In 1944 Mandel was transferred to Paris and eventually handed over to the French Militia and executed.

physical exercises every morning at seven. The German SS watch him admiringly.

Hitler sent a message to Von Arnim's Army. The undeniable bravery of the Afrikakorps was not enough to prevent bitter defeat.

May 14, 1943

Churchill made an important speech before the American Congress. He has sent General Giraud an eloquent and noble telegram. As I said in June 1940 in Bordeaux, and then again in Morocco, it is in Africa that France will reclaim its greatness. The shame of Sedan will be drowned in the Mediterranean.

This morning Reynaud was set on explaining to me how Pétain had begun conspiring as early as May 29, 1940, by trying to lure away Mandel over a few lunches at the Café de Paris. Reynaud told me that he had resigned in the hopes that Lebrun would call him back, but that he hadn't received the backing of either Jeanneney or Herriot. He added that Weygand had told them, "In three month's time, Germany will have wrung England's neck like a chicken's." He talked about the *commune blanche* in Bordeaux, adding that Marquet and Monzie had done everything they could to prevent the government from going to North Africa. He also mentioned Belin's role. He emphasized that it was a vast operation, a real conspiracy. Reynaud also accused Bouthillier, but for some reason left out Baudouin, and yet he had brought both of them into the government.

May 17, 1943

Once again, Reynaud spoke to me about Pétain's maneuvering. Pétain had told Monzie in April, "They'll soon have need of me." Once he got a government post, he began trying to draw certain Ministers into his corner, among them Mandel. Reynaud repeated to me one more time that Pétain had taken Mandel to lunch at the Café de Paris, even before the Germans launched their offensive. After the German attack, he asked Reynaud to get rid of me, invoking the Army's feelings about me. Paul Reynaud, along with everyone else in his entourage, was absolutely delighted with what this so-called maneuvering augured for me. He hadn't noticed the shadow on the wall, that of the noose they were preparing to use on him once I had been pushed out.

In the May 13 edition of *L'Echo de Nancy*, I came across the citation General Bridoux, Minister of War, read to the Legion of French Volunteers in Tunisia for having fought against the Allies: "For having engaged the enemy in combat on the 14, 16, 17, 23, and 25 of April 1943 alongside German troops; for having offered staunch resistance to a powerful assault led by tank-supported infantry; and for having counterattacked in hand-to-hand combat with grenades and bayonets. Although two-thirds of their men were lost, they carried out their orders, gaining the respect of yesterday's foes and today's comrades in arms," in other words, the Krauts.

I also read the short speech Admiral Esteva gave on Vichy radio on April 20, in which he reminded everyone that he had set up his command post in Bizerte in May 1940 and that he had remained in Tunisia for three years, loyal to the Marshal.

Pétain replied to him, which I also saw in the papers: "You have placed the principle of loyalty above all others. As fearless and above reproach as the knight Bayard himself, you have been faithful and true. There lies within your inner nature that spiritual strength without which no man can display heroism and selflessness."

Ribbentrop wrote Esteva, too: "Your work has allowed for the cooperation between the various parts of the Tunisian population and the German and Italian garrisons to proceed smoothly. In so doing, you have aided the powers of the Third Reich in the performance of military operations. I offer you the thanks and the gratitude of the representatives of the German nation."

At least Admiral Esteva felt somewhat uncomfortable when it came to returning their thanks. He pointed out that he had merely followed his government's orders: "In the present instance, I did nothing more than serve my country, as I have done throughout my life."

May 18, 1943

At 3 P.M. I took a bath in a kind of fountain where the water was around 50 or 55 degrees. A young German officer took one right after me. We agreed that the water was just too cold.

May 20, 1943

Took another bath in the fountain at 4 P.M. The Germans would have liked to follow my example, but the cold water was too much for them.

May 21, 1943

At 10 o'clock last night, the guards tried out their new searchlights. My whole room was illuminated by beams coming in from the South and the West. They will probably soon be trying out their new barbed wire, followed by their new police dogs.

May 22, 1943

I just heard an important piece of news: The voluntary dissolution of the Communist International has been decided by a meeting of representatives held in Moscow. It's a shrewd move, designed to reassure public opinion in the countries bordering on Russia as well as in Algeria, England, and throughout the world. In some countries, like France, it may lead to the fusion of the Socialist and Communist parties, which is Blum's old dream. It seems to me we would do better to question their ulterior motives. Jouhaux is delighted with the decision. He sees only good things coming out of this, both in the long term and the short.

May 23, 1943

In the time since Giraud has been in Africa, de Gaulle has been engaged in a veritable campaign to round up support in France from every political party. The last to join him is Queuille,[12] who while in Bordeaux, according to Reynaud, was in favor of signing an armistice ...

Jacquinot,[13] Maroselli, and Gouin[14] are among those who had hopped on the bandwagon earlier. De Gaulle is trying to impress Giraud by handing all these men microphones and sending them up to the front lines

12. Henri Queuille, Radical who initially supported the Vichy regime.

13. Louis Jacquinot, conservative Deputy from the Meuse from 1932 to 1940. He was Under Secretary on the French Committee of National Liberation in Algiers. From 1944 to 1946, he was Minister of the Navy, then Junior Minister.

of his London radio broadcasts. But Giraud now has with him an Army of some 100,000 men, many officers, and the prestige of the victory in Tunisia, which, although it clearly doesn't efface our shame, offers nonetheless bright hopes for a fresh start. Why should he yield to de Gaulle? The Allies will align themselves with one or the other of these two men, on the basis of their own plans.

June 1, 1943

Chatted again with Reynaud last night. I reminded him of the proposition Churchill communicated to Bordeaux through de Gaulle on June 16, 1940. Reynaud was surprised; he didn't know I was aware of it. Their phone call had been picked up in Bordeaux and a transcription was included as evidence at the Riom trial. Churchill wanted to bind the two countries together and make them inseparable. Reynaud said that he noted down everything Churchill dictated to him and read it aloud before the Cabinet. Pétain, Weygand, Chautemps, Frossard, and the rest accused him of wanting to reduce France to a part of the Commonwealth. That is when, instead of having the other Ministers resign, as was both the rule and the custom, Reynaud himself resigned. How could he have turned power over to these people without so much as putting up a fight? Now he says he expected Lebrun to call him back, but that when the time came, Jeanneney and Herriot didn't support him. Whereupon Lebrun, unsettled, called in Pétain, and the rest, as they say, is history!

The following day, June 17, de Gaulle left for London and embarked upon his career as a politician. Reynaud added that de Gaulle is an intelligent and highly ambitious man, whereas Giraud is a soldier.

At this point, Gamelin launched into new scathing attacks on General Georges. In March 1936, at a time when the French government seemed inclined to oppose Germany's reoccupation of the Rhineland, Georges, or so said Gamelin, was sending emissaries to various newspapers to have them write that it would be absurd to get involved in a war. This is sup-

14. Félix Gouin, Socialist Deputy from 1924 to 1940. He served as President of the Constituent Assemblies in Algiers and Paris in 1944–1945.

posed to be the explanation for Henri de Kérillis's article that appeared in *L'Echo de Paris* in which he opposed any form of armed intervention. Georges was both Pétain's and Weygand's protégé. The sole reason behind all that business about creating a National Defense Ministry separate from the War Ministry, and consequently creating two distinct military commands, was to promote Georges to a command position in the Army's Ground Forces and keep him in active rank beyond the retirement age of sixty-five and even until sixty-eight. Their machinations got nowhere in the Chamber of Deputies. However, their schemes were played out by Weygand's and Georges's boys in the Senate, most prominently by the renowned M. Fabry, former War Minister, and "honest" Claude Reibel. They eventually won over the Senate's Armed Forces Committee and the joint session of the Senate's three military committees.

But all of that is past now, as is Gamelin's criticism of Georges's serious mistakes and failings during the war. It is enough to read the evidence accumulated at the Riom trial to be convinced of Georges's shortcomings and of just how disastrous a choice Pétain and Weygand had made.

It is equally undeniable, though, that in leaving for Algiers, Georges, this eleventh-hour resistance fighter, has taken a step of major consequence:

1. It has dealt a serious blow to the Vichy government and to Laval's policies, which bear Pétain's stamp of approval. (Nonetheless, I personally don't exclude the possibility that Georges and Pétain see eye to eye on this.) It has had considerable effect on parts of the reactionary bourgeoisie and on a great many officers who until now have loyally supported Pétain's official policies.

2. It is sure to infuriate Hitler, who will think that he has been duped and won't accept Vichy's failure to have had Georges placed under tight police surveillance in Chambéry.

3. The Americans and the British were undoubtedly aware of Georges's decision to leave. Jean Monnet must have played an important part in this affair. For France's bourgeoisie, even if not, obviously, for the democratic elements in France, the fact that Georges has joined the Algiers Committee will have considerable impact. He has also strengthened Giraud's position in relation to de Gaulle's.

All of this makes me think back on my relations with Monnet. I appointed him to head the Joint Purchasing Committee during the war. He was at first very much an admirer of Paul Reynaud but grew hostile toward him when Reynaud became Prime Minister. He had close ties with Roosevelt and Bullitt. Then there is the story of his commercial enterprise in Shanghai. Much to his credit, he gave up an important post at the League of Nations to revive the business his father had founded, which was going through very difficult times.

June 5, 1943

De Gaulle's speech at 9:30 P.M. was pompous. Giraud's, although five minutes too long, was excellent: simple, moving, and very much to the point. Must have been written by Jean Monnet. He mentioned Metz and Strasbourg and the prisoners of war. He alluded to the heavy losses in Russia, probably inspired by his meeting with Litvinov. The Committee's 11:30 A.M. meeting ran more than two and a half hours. It was similar to those morning Cabinet meetings that used to run on beyond 1 in the afternoon, after which a statement would be issued hailing our unanimity.

Now that de Gaulle has arrived in Algiers, a huge battle for power is being waged, even though an agreement in principle was reached under pressure from Churchill and Roosevelt. De Gaulle wants to be head of the executive branch of a provisional government to be instituted in France by him, after the Allied landing. He seems to have drawn recruits from the National Committee in London. The plan had the backing of Blum, Jouhaux, and Grenier, a Communist who declared, "We are with you body and soul." Awakening to the fact that there were also Radicals in France, they rounded up Queuille and Maroselli, then people like Jacquinot, Vallin, Viénot,[15] and so on. Noguès has resigned and been replaced by Puaux.

15. Pierre Viénot, Socialist Deputy. He was Under Secretary for Foreign Affairs in Léon Blum's government in 1936. He voted in favor of the Munich Agreement in 1938 and joined the Free French forces in 1942.

June 11, 1943

The city of Pantelleria surrendered at noon. All day long we have been deluged with speeches on the radio, pouring in like the Tirolean rains: "the first piece of Italian soil," "the Italian Navy was nowhere to be seen." The Gaullist radio announcers are clearly right out of the Homeric hero school, with this minor difference: They do their fighting with microphones, on the air.

At 8 P.M. Henri Bénazet, a former announcer from Paris, was back on the air in Algiers. He is another one of those who first supported Pétain and even testified against his employer to placate Vichy. Everyone of us found him grotesque. In his excitement, he gave himself away and attacked the former Republican system in the typical style of Pétain or Laval: "a Republic of comrades and profiteers." Knowing what kind of a man he is didn't diminish our stupefaction at hearing his insults coming over Free French radio.

June 16, 1943

An SS General showed up; his visit had been announced yesterday. At around 11:30 A.M. he went to the room that Reynaud and Borotra have dubbed their office. He was received by Reynaud, Borotra, Jouhaux, and Gamelin, the latter acting as if it were a military school inspection from his days as a cadet at Saint-Cyr. Paul Reynaud had put on a sparkling, long-tipped white collar. I had hoped to avoid this ridiculous ceremony, but they sent Jouhaux to get me in my room, where I was reading Forster.

I went in, received greetings, listened to the conversation already in progress. "Living conditions are just fine here," Paul Reynaud was saying, but then he asked for three packages that had been mailed from Bordeaux but hadn't been given to him and for the jewelry box that had been stolen. They didn't spare us the standard gestures of shocked surprise. Borotra filled me in on what had been discussed earlier. The Germans have agreed to allow Jouhaux to bring his secretary here, and we had word of Blum and Mandel, who are doing well. Borotra went on to say that since the Germans want the conditions in Itter to duplicate those in Bourassol, we should be allowed to have visitors here, as we did in France. I told him that as far as I was concerned, I would absolutely refuse to add anyone at all to the number of prisoners already housed in this "castle."

The General and his escort went off to lunch; I went off for a walk. I watched them as they went into the dining room. All the NCOs in the garrison were invited to lunch with them. There isn't another Army in the world whose practices are so democratic. Gamelin felt the need to say that the situation was the same in the French Army: "Whenever a noncommissioned officer in my brigade carried out a mission or performed some act of heroism, I would invite him to dine at my table."

June 18, 1943

8:35 P.M. To our absolute astonishment, the announcer on Algiers radio unleashed a diatribe against the French Committee of National Liberation, lambasting the divisiveness that is paralyzing the committee and the jealousies and the ambitions of the Generals on it, and expressing regret over the disrepute into which France has fallen in the eyes of the nations of the world. The announcer's vocabulary seemed to be that of the Communist Party. We had the impression that he was transmitting the violent criticism of the Communist deputies currently in Algiers, who have to be upset at having none of their members represented on the committee.

Thereafter, the announcer launched into an epithet-filled tirade, reminiscent of political rallies of the past, to explain the reasons we had been defeated, apparently for an audience of the ignorant. Without naming him specifically, he attacked General Giraud and, above him in rank, General Georges, as the representative of a High Command hostile to engines, tanks, and airplanes, a High Command that had carried the doctrines of defensive strength and fixed fortifications to the point of superstition. Without intending to and without knowing he was doing it, he also attacked de Gaulle, who is a strong supporter of a professional army, by criticizing our Generals for not having had enough faith in the people to create a people's army.

It would not take much to tear all this grandiloquence to shreds and impeach the Communists and denounce their traitorous acts. But what is important here is the simple existence of the criticism and the conditions under which the announcer voiced it. If Laval were clever enough, if he had a competent and reliable Information Minister, there is no telling how much he could capitalize on all this sorry infighting!

June 19, 1943

In France, they have been making much of the announcement of Léon Blum's coming marriage. People are convinced the Allies are using us to draw the French closer to the Germans and bring them to sue for a compromise peace settlement, which is what Vichy thinks as well. Vichy, meanwhile, is falling apart. Word has it that Platon has been arrested. Ménétrel has left. Many of the Chiefs and Deputy Chiefs of Staff have been getting themselves appointed Subprefect or even better, when they can manage it. Gangrene has set in. Vichy is dying a death like Louis XVIII's: Every day, one of Louis's bones would break or one of his fingers drop off onto his deathbed. Throughout it all, Pétain has gone right on receiving delegations and looking over his gifts.

June 23, 1943

Our two Generals here have sent Stalin a telegram congratulating him on the anniversary of Russia's entry into the war. It seems to me that they, and along with them Churchill, Roosevelt, Benes,[16] Sikorski, and so on, should also have sent one to Hitler, who is really the man responsible for Russia's entering the war. There is just no justice in this world.

June 27, 1943

Fog shrouded the mountain tops until noon. In one of his speeches from Tunis, de Gaulle said something that was quite accurate: "In 1940, France succumbed in isolation." The greater part of that speech was excellent.

16. Edward Benes, President of Czechoslovakia until June 1938. He subsequently took refuge in London.

July 2, 1943

Christiane Mabire, Paul Reynaud's secretary, arrived at noon along with Marcel Granger, the brother of Giraud's son-in-law. Mlle Mabire had been imprisoned in Berlin since December 1942, living in a cell, in isolation, with no light but daylight and no news from her family. All she heard were the cries of a woman being tortured. She was gaunt.

Granger had been living in Tunisia. He was arrested in April by the PPF, Doriot's party, while he was planting chickpeas. The Germans took him in a Junker plane to Naples and from there to Dachau, near Munich. At first they had him in a prison laborer's uniform and in a cell; then they transferred him to another building. They sent him to work in the fields where there were 800 Poles, 200 Germans, and quite a few priests, several of whom had once been Alsatian separatists. The Germans have named a Canon and sent him to replace the Bishop in Metz.

There were also two British officers in the camp, one of whom was chained in his cell. After having first subjected him to brutal conditions, they suddenly eased up. There are large numbers of Communists in Dachau; they know we are here. The mix of people of all nationalities and from all walks of life is incredible. The new Europe, in prisoner-of-war camps.

Granger left us dumbfounded when he told us of the existence of crematoriums and the experiments with various gasses they perform on prisoners. When prisoners arrive at the camp, their entire bodies are shaven. They are read a list of possible punishments and forced to go twenty-four hours without food. The SS threaten to hang them by their wrists for an hour and to flog their kidneys between five and twenty-five times. No one can withstand twenty-five blows; they die before. He said there were SS who would grab a prisoner's cap, toss it in the air, and then shoot at it, and the prisoner as well, as he ran to retrieve it. They live piled together in barracks, with beds one on top of the other, wooden bowls, wretched soup and food that is hardly edible, and barely enough of it to survive. He told horrifying stories about the Polish block and the Russian prisoners they had brought back from the front, locked in boxcars for five days, without food or fresh air or sanitary facilities.

Granger had spent much of his life in Tunisia. He spoke highly of Peyrouton, who had been Governor-General there, and regretted his decision to resign, which he claimed de Gaulle and Giraud had unsuccessfully tried to refuse. After the defeat in 1940, Granger accepted a position as head of the Legion. He had been present during my trip to Tunisia in 1939 and told me that no other Prime Minister had ever received so warm a welcome. Before the war, he had been a member of the PSF, Colonel de La Roque's party.

I saw Granger again this afternoon. He spoke to me of his life in Tunisia. He frequented a club where a hundred or so naval officers used to gather, most of them Anglophobes. They broke out the champagne when the *Bismarck* sank the *Hood.* The majority of them felt that Giraud was a turncoat, devoid of honor, who had betrayed the Marshal. They were all devoted to Darlan and Pétain, in that order. When the Germans arrived, they welcomed them with open arms. According to Granger, they were all pure products of the Naval Academy, every last one of them antirepublican. In contrast, the engineer officers were almost all republicans, and there was sharp antagonism between the two groups.

July 11, 1943

At 8:30 this morning, I heard the news about the American-British-Canadian landing in Sicily yesterday. The terrain is difficult, rugged, with inland plateaus rising high up to the mountaintops in tiers. The coastline is rocky and the coastal plains don't extend very far inland. The Italians have been heavily reinforcing their fortifications for the last several months. There are said to be about 150,000 Germans and 350,000 Italians on the island. The antiaircraft weapons, attack planes, and one armored division are apparently German as well. I would have thought the Allies would sooner attempt a landing in Greece or even in Flanders.

On the Russian front, the battle rages on with increasing intensity. So many people are dying these days in Russia, in the Mediterranean, and in the Pacific, just to mention these few areas. At day's end, I reread the Polish blue book's account of diplomatic events as they accelerated after March 15, 1939, with the destruction of the Czechoslovakian state. That is really the date that marks the start of the world war.

Today, I received a great many books and presents of all kinds. My friends have been generous.

Some of the prisoners left this morning and Russians have arrived. The Russians look emaciated. One of them is very ill, many of them are very young. Their faces are closed and hardened.

July 12, 1943

According to a communiqué, the landing on Sicily is proceeding successfully with the taking of Syracuse and ten other localities. The Anglo-Saxons have advanced twenty miles inland, but the real counterattack is yet to come.

In Gamelin's view, the Allies have gone the difficult route and taken the bull by the horns. They might have been counting on the fact that they would be facing principally Italian soldiers, but it is possible that the Germans will blunt the Russian offensive and send enormous air support to Sicily. We shouldn't let our imaginations run wild.

July 14, 1943

To remind us that today is Bastille Day, the German authorities have ordered the Commandant of the castle to close off the western terrace, to which we previously had access, with doors with iron bars and padlocks. There we were, corralled in between the walls and the fountain, when Dr. Hauffmann arrived, all smiles. Needless to say, he had nothing to do with it ... he knew nothing about it ... I think it's just as well that way.

July 18, 1943

A speech by Sforza, the new Secretary-General of the Italian Fascist Party, was broadcast on every Italian radio station this evening. I have a good command of Italian and I have rarely heard so poor a speech. It was a deplorably long mix of whining and blustering.

His leitmotif: We must resist, resist. He must have used the word once a minute. It's worth noting that he said that the Fascist Party proudly claimed responsibility for the war. Also worth noting was his desperate appeal to all those who had profited from the Fascist regime. The speech makes me more and more convinced that Italian morale is very low. The only question is whether the Germans can still put the pieces back together. The explanation for the success of the Allied landing and the advances they have made in Sicily lies in their overwhelming air superiority.

The Russians are apparently ten miles outside of Orel and moving on the railroad lines at Briansk. I doubt that they can continue to push forward without stopping sometime in the next few days to catch their breath.

July 23, 1943

At 9 P.M. I was visited by the officer-dentist who had already made a good impression on me a month ago. He immediately examined the area causing me pain and proposed to take care of it right away. He takes the train to Dachau and said he wanted to leave at 6 A.M. the following morning because he had a lot of work. We went downstairs three flights to find the sergeant in charge of the sanitary corps. He led us across a courtyard into a remarkably well equipped medical unit. The dentist submitted me to a second examination and was especially careful not to jar me, to spare me any pain. He then explained clearly and precisely what he planned to do. I put myself in his hands, with total confidence. A few seconds later he had already pulled out two teeth and the bridge they supported. He is an outstanding technician and a man of charm and politeness. Thanks to him, I'll be able to get some sleep tonight.

July 25, 1943

At 8:30 P.M. Paul Reynaud and Borotra came into my room while I was reading Falloux's *Memoirs*. They told me that they had just heard on the radio that Mussolini had resigned. He is supposed to have tendered his resignation to the Emperor-King on July 23 and been immediately replaced by Badoglio[17] (a well-known anti-Fascist who is very close to Gamelin). Guariglia, the Italian Ambassador to Paris, has been appointed Minister of

17. Marshal Pietro Badoglio, anti-Fascist leader of the Italian High Command and Governor-General of Abyssinia. He was the head of state throughout the final days of Fascist Italy.

Foreign Affairs. Italy is in a state of siege. The people, which means the Fascists as well, have been prohibited from bearing arms. Secretary-General Sforza is reported to have organized an insurgent movement, which was quickly put down. For the Italian people, these events offer the promise of impending peace. There are apparently huge crowds gathered on Saint Peter's Square and around the Vatican.

Mussolini's downfall awakens memories of Munich: theatrical speeches and the Corsican knife business. He resented my trip to Corsica, claiming that I had brandished a knife at Italy in a threatening way. What utter nonsense! I also remember what Laval and Baudouin undertook to do, none of which succeeded. Traditionally, there are two approaches to Italy's relations with France: that of Mazzini, Crespi, and Mussolini, on the one hand, and that of the Piedmontese and the Garibaldians, on the other.

The current turn of events finds Italy renewing its friendship with the British and perhaps developing cordial relations with France, the latter possibility being contingent on their renouncing all claims to Tunisia.

I am also reminded of my meeting with the British in Abbeville in 1939: the Salonika affair, Chamberlain's and Percy Lorraine's illusions about Italy, and their attempts to get me to yield. Naturally, it was up to France to make sacrifices, in the hopes that Mussolini, once sated, would be able to calm Hitler down. They tried for months to get me to give ground, but on that occasion, I was able to hold them off.

July 27, 1943

Before he resigned, Mussolini is said to have convened a meeting of the Fascist executive council last Saturday with Grandi, de Bono, Sforza, and all the other leaders who were there when it all began. After twenty years of effort and domination, it had all come to this. Is there an analogy here with the abdication of Napoleon, abandoned by all his Marshals? I never thought the end would be so pathetic. I thought Mussolini would either offer ferocious resistance or choose to die. Maybe events didn't exactly happen as they have been reported.

July 30, 1943

I am wondering whether Italy won't be drawn into a Communist movement. Heard another version of events in Italy related on London and Brazzaville radios.

There was a meeting of the Fascist executive council last Sunday. Mussolini presented the military plans for defending northern Italy that had been worked out in the Führer's headquarters. That triggered sharp opposition and scenes of great violence. Mussolini left for the countryside, to reflect on the situation and develop a new plan. The King had him brought back. Their talk lasted an hour, after which the King had him arrested.

The King then brought in Badoglio, who dissolved the Fascist Party and all its various offshoots and had the members of the Fascist executive council incarcerated. Suddenly that evening, waves of people began pouring into Rome, which had been virtually deserted until then, to demonstrate against Mussolini. These are, needless to say, the very same people who acclaimed him twenty years ago.

Badoglio isn't suing for an armistice. On the contrary, he asked the Germans to send in forty divisions to defend all of Italy, but it isn't possible to drain that many troops from the Russian front and the Balkans.

Italian political parties have called on Badoglio to convene a duly elected legislative body. The red flag is flying over Milan. The Germans occupy Trieste, Fiume, and the Istrian peninsula, as well as the principal communication routes.

August 7, 1943

So many events have transpired this past week! What serious playwright, from Aeschylus to Shakespeare, could have imagined such a drama, or rather such a tragedy? The masses are no longer playing the role of Greek choruses: They have been directly drawn into the action, with their misery, their despair, and their suffering.

Mussolini has abdicated; thousands of Italian soldiers have thrown down their arms and deserted. The Russians have recaptured cities the Germans abandoned after long and bloody battles. Airplanes are raining death onto huge metropolises like Hamburg, as local populations flee in terror. Berlin is being partially evacuated while Guariglia and Ribbentrop are meeting in Verona. It has been reported that Hitler met in Berchtesgaden with the top leaders of the party and the Army. It brings back memories of the sermon the Bishop of New York gave at Easter in 1939.

And throughout these dramatic days, the serenity of the Alps endures. Peace dwells on the mountaintops. The sun is shining down on the vast tiered plateaus; peasants are bringing in the hay.

August 8, 1943

Six Germans showed up wearing red armbands. They asked to take the place of political prisoners, all of this under the watchful eye of an SS woman dressed halfway like a man, with a gigantic butt and a hard and unsightly face.

Talked with Gamelin tonight. He repeated to me that Georges had made one error in not bringing his reserve troops into action as early as May 10, and another in assigning command for the entire front, including even the Second Army, to an incompetent General. He swore once again that if the French government had refused to allow us to come to the aid of Belgium, he would have resigned. It was a matter of honor, he said, and of the commitment he had made to the Belgian King. He also said that from a military point of view, the area between Wavre and Namur offered the best terrain for stopping tanks, far better than our northern border. Moreover, with the addition of Belgian, Dutch, and British troops, we would have been an even match for Germany. And we could have held on to our industrial basin, too. Marshal Ironside had told him, in one of their conversations, that with England itself directly threatened, the British would no longer send troops or airplanes into France.

August 12, 1943

There was a magnificent storm last night. The mountaintops would suddenly be illuminated by lightning, the thunder would echo back and forth between the narrow mountain valleys, then blasts of rain would pelt the walls and windows of the castle. The searchlights on the watchtowers made a pitiful contrast, making me think of a line from Vergil, "And suddenly there appeared a sign from the heavens."

August 17, 1943

According to Brazzaville radio, the Germans have launched a powerful counterattack on Kharkov, where they have brought in considerable reinforcements, and the Russian advance has been halted. Are we now witnessing, with this latest Russian offensive, what we have seen with all those that preceded it? After marking great initial successes, will it peter out just as they reach the heart of the German position?

After the first months of the war, it became obvious that armored divisions were ineffective as they had been used in Poland and France. Tanks, in coordination with infantry troops and attack planes, have to be supported by artillery fire, both before and during an assault. Artillery has to be moved forward in coordination with every advance. Isn't Germany's air inferiority, which we observed in the Allied offensive in Tunisia, a result of the Germans' having moved their factories into forests and quarries; and the result of their vast effort to decentralize, which has still not been completed? Or is it a result of the priority they gave last year to the construction of locomotives and submarines?

Once they no longer have women and children to worry about, won't the civilian populations in Germany find a way to cope with the bombings, just as people coped with artillery fire in 1914–1918 in Reims, Arras, Revigny, etc.?

What is the situation in Russia really like after two years of war? And what would Stalin do if, in the absence of a real second front, Hitler were to propose to withdraw from all of Russia, from the Baltic States and parts of Poland, and to accept the propositions made earlier by Molotov, turning the Balkans into a Russian sphere of influence? …

The Allies have made a serious mistake in pushing the King and Badoglio back into Germany's embrace, with their demands for an unconditional surrender and their condescending words, "Let Italy fry in its own fat for a while."

It took 3,000 ships to transport 300,000 men from Africa to Sicily. How many will it take, and how long will it take, to transport 600,000 to the Italian mainland? They must be counting on the material effects of their bombing of the major Italian cities and its effect on the morale of the population.

Brazzaville radio has announced a forthcoming meeting between the leaders of the Axis powers and stated that Badoglio has offered his apologies to the German government for the violent incidents against German citizens in Italy. He promised to compensate all those who suffered material loss. The Germans are fortifying the plains of the Po Valley and concentrating troops there—the wonderful result of the Allies' spectacular intransigence. Meanwhile, Pucheu[18] has been arrested and imprisoned in Meknes. Communist Party meetings are no longer outlawed in Algiers. Thirty-five Communist deputies are strutting about there, the same thirty-five who, in 1939, on Moscow's orders, played right into Germany's hands. And that fine fellow Queuille is presiding over the commission examining the records of twenty-five Tunisian civil servants accused of collaboration.

At around 1:30 P.M. twenty-five flying fortresses flew over the Inn Valley at an altitude of 10,000 feet. Impressively, with the greatest of ease, they headed southwest, toward Italy. There was no cannon fire. The sentries gave the alert and the garrison set up their machine guns, but it was a bit of a joke, since they only have a range of 2,500 feet. Some of the soldiers were indignant at seeing their nation's airspace violated so casually. Far off in the distance we could hear the sounds of bombs bursting. At around 2 P.M. everything was back to its usual calm.

7 P.M. I learned on Ankara radio that the Allies had entered Messina, which, according to a German communiqué, had been evacuated by their troops with all their equipment. "A retreat comparable to the most splendid of victories." A few more victories like those …

There is heavy fighting in the suburbs of Kharkov. The Russians continue to move on Briansk.

---

18. Prior to the war, Pierre Pucheu had had close ties with La Roque, then with Doriot. In Vichy, he was successively Pétain's Minister of Production and of the Interior. In 1942, he went to Algiers to join forces with General Giraud. He was arrested, sentenced, and executed by firing squad.

August 20, 1943

Jouhaux came back for dinner from the hospital in Innsbruck, where specialists are looking after his heart. He had seen artillery, tanks, and troops moving on to Italy, and young vigorous soldiers, spirited and well equipped. There were flowers in the barrels of their rifles and artillery pieces. The soldiers were singing joyfully. Both the soldiers and the officers were twenty to thirty-five years old, all of them veterans exuding strength and confidence. While captain Hauffmann was off making a few purchases, Jouhaux saw a truck pull up in front of a restaurant where two employees began loading barrels. Jouhaux overheard one of them say in perfect French argot, "I got a date with a chick at two o'clock at the center," as our little Frenchman, either a volunteer worker or a war prisoner released from a stalag, went on complaining that it was already after two and he was going to miss his date with his chick. Spoke briefly with Jouhaux, who had nothing at all to say about the war, or France, or the future. Visibly soused, Jouhaux claimed that the captain of "the castle" was Bavarian. Now that's important news.

August 23, 1943

The Labor Party has won a landslide victory in the Australian elections. In South Africa, a few days ago, the elections were marked by the overwhelming success of General Smuts's party. People will continue to speak of the decline of the British Empire and the defection of the various colonies, etc. In truth, what stands out most is the incomparable greatness of this community of British peoples. Of course, the soldiers there voted, just as American soldiers will soon be voting in Sicily, North Africa, and England. Can anyone really be that sure that the German Army and the German people would vote for their present government and a continuation of the war? In France in 1918, would we have voted for Clemenceau, and for him to carry on the war to the very end?

Can anyone really believe in all seriousness, even for a second, that those millions and millions of Anglo-Saxons, from Greenland to the South Pole, who have constantly supported the war effort in elections, have been manipulated by the Jews in New York and London? Those Jews would have to be prodigious geniuses to pull that off, in which case they really would deserve to run the world!

In truth, England and America are real democracies, but without class struggles, or rather without the demagoguery that has been corrupting France since 1900. Along with Renan, I believe that the methods and the spirit of Protestantism are among the essential reasons for this profound difference. ... Beyond that, what does it matter if there are "differences between Protestant denominations," which has been the major argument advanced by Catholics since the time of Bossuet?

August 24, 1943

In Germany, it has become impossible to work because of the air raids to which the people are subjected nightly, sometimes at midnight, sometimes at 2 A.M. As soon as the sirens sound the alert, they have to take two suitcases and move into designated shelters. The consequences of these raids are obvious in terms of morale and productivity, which is why the decision was made to evacuate a million Germans, half of them to Poland, the other half to Austria. The government considered withdrawing to Vienna, but in the end only the various Ministries scattered and set up in areas surrounding Berlin.

August 25, 1943

I am beginning to find meals at our guest table unbearable. It's as if we were on a motionless ocean liner. I am going to have to go to Innsbruck for medical care.

September 1, 1943

Nitti[19] and Giorgini have arrived.

19. Francesco Nitti, Italian statesman, several times Prime Minister. An anti-Fascist, he left Italy in 1924. He was incarcerated by the Germans during the war. In 1948, he was reelected Senator.

September 3, 1943

Anniversary of the declaration of war.

At around 5 A.M. Lebrun and François-Poncet arrived. The latter was smiling, looking calm and peaceful as if he were in one of the drawing rooms of his embassy. Lebrun bore the signs of the fatiguing journey; his face was pale, his features sunken. He is seventy-one years old and had traveled all night and part of the following day, beginning on Thursday at 7 P.M., and hadn't had anything to eat.

At 11:30 A.M. last Wednesday, the Italian officer in charge of the surveillance of Lebrun's villa and the troops quartered at the Caisse d'Epargne bank, suddenly came and told him that he was free to go. In La Tronche, at just about the same time, an Italian Colonel was making a similar statement to François-Poncet. He added that once the Italians began their withdrawal from the Grenoble area, he would be pleased to take him to Florence, so as to avoid his falling into German hands, an offer that François-Poncet gladly accepted.

A few minutes later in Vizille, a German officer and several soldiers with submachine guns, arriving directly from Lyons, with an Italian soldier seated next to the driver as their guide, burst into Lebrun's villa. While the German officer went about informing him that he was under arrest and ordering him to come with him without delay, the soldiers kept their submachine guns pointed at him and his family, who had come running up to see what was happening. He was whisked away in a car after barely having had the time to pack two suitcases. The car drove through La Tronche, where they arrested François-Poncet under similar circumstances.

September 7, 1943

Anniversary of my arrest at La Vernue, as well as those of Reynaud and Gamelin. We celebrated with a bottle of cognac that Reynaud had received and a magnificent box of mint and fruit candies that my sister had sent me, along with other wonderful gifts. The candies were a big hit.

September 8, 1943

At 10 this morning Brazzaville radio announced that Italy had surrendered unconditionally. Badoglio issued a statement saying that the superiority of the enemy forces had compelled his government to request an armistice.

At 9:15 P.M. London radio added a few details. The negotiations had begun in a neutral country and been continued in Sicily between Allied and Italian military leaders. Terms had been finalized on September 3, but it had been agreed not to make the signing public until the Allies judged the moment propitious. The military clauses of the settlement have been kept secret. The Italians have committed themselves to respecting political, economic, and financial terms that are to be worked out subsequently. Italy has declared that it is prepared to defend its territory against all acts of aggression, whatever quarters they may come from.

There was joy in Itter castle. Nitti and Giorgini were very moved. Had they remained free just a week longer, they could have tried to make it back to Rome. "I have been in exile, waiting for the collapse of fascism, for the last twenty-one years." Actually, Italy's fate was already sealed when they lost Tunis.

Germany is not about to throw in its hand. They'll organize defensive positions in the Apennines, the Alps, and the Po Valley. But then what will Italy do? Admiral Cunningham has called on Italian ships to move on to Allied ports or to be scuttled.

On the radio and through tracts dropped by plane all over Italy, the Italians are being asked to join the Allies in liberating their country. The appeal to them is cast in sober and moving terms.

At 8 P.M. German radio announced the news of the surrender of the Italian government. At 9, the DNB began heaping abuse on Badoglio and his Ministers.

This is the end of fascism. It is the end of the Triple Alliance. It is the end of an era: the end of arbitrary rule, barbarianism couched in scientific terms, and the deification of brutal strength. This is the twilight of the false gods.

German radio stations are broadcasting a statement addressed to the Italian people by a "national Fascist government" whose seat and makeup remain unspecified. Nitti thinks the leader is probably Farinacci, who voted against Mussolini because he found him too soft. Farinacci had been arrested earlier but escaped to the German Embassy in Rome. While the *carabinieri* were surrounding the building, he made his way out in an embassy car, disguised as a German officer, and went on by plane to Germany. The statement on the radio was made in Mussolini's name and in the name of everything the Fascists had achieved. Badoglio, who was already being held responsible for the defeat, was accused in the strongest terms of being a traitor. They called on the Italians in the Army and the Air Force to continue the fight alongside their brothers in arms to save the honor of the Italian nation. We must fight back in order to save our honor and "drag our country into the war." These words appear to me to speak volumes about the Italian people's desire for peace at all costs. The station played the Fascist hymn, which is none other than the song of the Italian *Arditi*, the Italian assault troops from 1914 who used to sing it as they marched at our side.

The Allies have landed in the area around Naples and in Sardinia, but from my point of view, the Balkans remain the grounds on which to launch a real offensive, if there is a way it can be done.

For our benefit, all the SS radios in the castle broadcast the Fascist hymn all morning long.

Nitti doesn't believe the new Fascist government will be able to do anything. To my mind, this is the final step in giving this world war the look of an international civil war.

London radio recalled the war in Italy in 1940, citing the victorious resistance put up by five French divisions. They mentioned my personal struggle to eliminate the war zone in the Rhone Valley and transfer the divisions in the Alps to the Northeast, and Gamelin's, Georges's, and Prételat's obstinate refusal. Given the movement of the French forces in Belgium, it was incumbent on us to reinforce the pivotal areas. Not doing that was the major mistake, the principal cause of our defeat. How much damage were the tanks and Stukas really going to inflict on fortifications that had been built years before and had been constantly improved? Add to that the incredible overestimation of the Italian forces by our Military

Intelligence in the War Ministry and the Air Force and the overestimation of Belgian forces by the "famous" Colonel Laurent.

September 10, 1943

The day began with a broadcast of the Fascist hymn throughout the building. I can almost sing it now. At 7 P.M. once again on Brazzaville radio, we heard about another great Allied success: their taking control of the port of Taranto, where there were probably only a couple of squadrons left. Actually, the Allies have been taking their time in Calabria, even though the armistice went into effect on September 3, although it wasn't officially announced then. They have barely gotten anything out of it other than a few landings in the area around Naples. Italian naval vessels have remained in their ports, and with the exception of seven ships that made it to Gibraltar, they are being attacked by German airplanes.

No landings have been attempted in Sardinia, occupied Corsica, or the area around Rome. According to a German communiqué reported on Lausanne radio, the Germans continue to occupy Rome, Genoa, Trieste, Dalmatia, and Albania. They are supposed to have disarmed the Italian occupying forces and moved them to detention centers in France, east of Toulon and Nice. The Italians in the Savoie crossed over into Switzerland. On the other hand, the Italians are reported to be holding Turin, Milan, and Venice. Mussolini is said to be imprisoned on Maddalena Island, north of Sardinia, and the Germans are making every effort to free him.

At 8:30 P.M. Hitler gave a speech. I didn't recognize his voice. François-Poncet said he did recognize it but that Hitler was so emotional it didn't sound like him. He praised Mussolini, the great Italian, the creator of the new Italy, and his faithful friend. He mentioned the undying support that he and Germany had given Italy, even though Italy had not honored the Pact of Steel and had not entered the war in September 1939. He had backed the Italian Army in Greece, Africa, Sicily, and Calabria, but he had been betrayed by Badoglio and the Judeo-Masonic forces as early as September 1939. Those forces, he said, were now triumphant, but their triumph was precarious. Nothing had been lost in Russia. Germany was still the master of Europe and was forging new weapons to fight off the terror raining down from the skies. All of Germany was as one with the Führer and the Nazi Party.

Giorgini told us how Mussolini had made a deal with three Greek Generals to buy the war against Greece for 250,000 million. The Italian Army was supposed to march right in without firing a shot—a military cakewalk. Their disappointment, their anger, and the losses they incurred were all the more bitter.

He also told us that while under arrest, Mussolini supposedly wrote to Badoglio to thank him for the consideration he had been shown and offer him his services. So much time has been wasted by the Allies since that July 25 when he was imprisoned.

An article in a German newspaper that we received today refers to "Badoglio's and the House of Savoy's ignoble treason." It says that their betrayal surfaced with the Anglo-American landing in Sicily, which could never have succeeded without the complicity of certain Italian divisions commanded by Generals who were part of Marshal Badoglio's band of traitors. The article went on to say that the second act of infamy lay in waiting for the moment that most favored Europe's enemies before announcing the armistice that had actually been signed on September 3. Badoglio had effectively handed an ally over to the enemy.

September 13, 1943

A German bulletin announced that German paratroopers had rescued Mussolini from the hotel in the Abruzzi where he had been held prisoner. The news sent shock waves through our little community. Mussolini is going to make a triumphant entrance into Rome and take back his place at the Palazzo Venezia. Can anyone explain to me why the Allies left him in Abruzzi? Does this mean that the Italians refused to hand him over, which would in that case honor Badoglio and the King of Italy? More and more I am beginning to think that if England does win this war, it will have to be the work of Divine Providence.

The Americans have run into stiff German resistance forty miles south of Naples. Montgomery's Army went off somewhere south of Calabria to conquer Taranto, Brindisi, and Bari while the Germans were taking Rome and Naples and disbanding Badoglio's Army.

Badoglio and the King of Italy fled Rome on Wednesday September 15 and went to an Italian division's headquarters near Lake Albano. From there, they fled to Sicily on a twin-engine plane. The Germans burst into the headquarters only moments after their departure.

September 20, 1943

A Lieutenant-Colonel doctor came to see me—an astounding visit. We spoke about the way the war had evolved. He stated that the British were fighting for the benefit of the United States and the Soviet Union. Even if victorious, England would come out of the war so drained and would remain that way for so long that it would cease being one of the world's great powers. The British would be abandoned by their colonies, who would turn toward the United States. They would lose India, without which they would be no more than a second-rate power. They would lose their markets abroad and the dominance of the pound.

I answered that the British were confident of their victory and that they probably didn't have the slightest doubt about the loyalty of the nations of the Commonwealth. In any event, I told him, one thing was certain: Either any offer of a peace settlement accompanied by threats and intimidation would be rejected out of hand by the British or I knew nothing about the character of the British people. Similarly, there might well be clashes and problems between the United States and England, but they were of little consequence in terms of the deep-rooted, indestructible solidarity binding the two nations.

The Colonel came back to his idea about a compromise peace settlement with the West. In connection with this, he told me that Laval's government had no backing in France, that although Laval was extremely resourceful, the people had no confidence in him whatsoever, which was an extreme handicap for someone expected to implement a policy of collaboration.

I asked him if he thought that a defeated Germany, occupied by and paying ransom to the victorious nation, forced to turn over to that nation great numbers of her citizens as hostages, many of whom would die facing firing squads or in concentration camps, and stripped moreover of two wonderful provinces and precisely those she held most dearly, if he thought that Germany would agree to collaborate with that victorious nation? He replied that as long as the war continued, painful experiences were inevitable. All of that would disappear, he said, if peace were reestablished with the West, adding that Hitler had been far more lenient than the German High Command had wanted. Moreover, he added, within France, collaboration is associated with politically and socially reactionary ideas that violently conflict with the innermost feelings of the French people, as the Germans realize full well.

The doctor repeated that Laval had no backing whatsoever but that I, in contrast, he said as he bowed, continued to maintain a large following in France. I thanked him, telling him that all the credit should go to Pétain who had sentenced me, before the trial ended, to be deported for life and who, seized with panic, had halted the Riom trial because, in spite of all the precautions he had taken, he found he was becoming its principal focus. I was forced to add that if I did continue to enjoy a certain popularity in France, the German government had also contributed to it by bringing me to Germany as a prisoner, in defiance of international law and of Germany's own commitments.

Today's German press, I went on, is condemning Badoglio and accusing him of having tried to hand Mussolini over to the British. Didn't Pétain hand me over to Germany? Hasn't the Gestapo locked me up in Itter castle? The doctor answered that those were matters he could not discuss and asked me if I had any particular wishes. I answered that I never had any particular wishes and that Epictetus was now my favorite author.

He bowed and saluted, but I reminded him that the examination for which he had come was supposed to be of a medical nature, and that ever since I had arrived in Germany I had been suffering from visual and auditory problems, as I had explained to him. He politely contended that it was far too late to do anything then, for he had to return to Munich immediately, but said that he would come back the following Saturday with his instruments. What was the purpose of his visit? Who ordered it?

Badoglio has given a statement asking the Italian people and the Italian Army to combat the German invader and free the homeland from oppression by fighting alongside the Allies.

I am uneasy about this. This is the same man who, after having signed the unconditional surrender on September 3, was telling his former allies as late as September 8 that the news about his surrendering was a fabrication of British propaganda.

September 25, 1943

François-Poncet was visited today by one of Himmler's lieutenants. His wife had written Mme Göring, who had gotten Himmler to agree to transfer her husband to a villa where he could be joined by his wife and children, but where he has to promise to remain until the end of the war.

October 1, 1943

The September 26 *Parizer Zeitung* carried an article entitled "Benes's Crowns[20] Rolled in the Streets of Paris." The bulk of the article consisted of excerpts taken from the archives of the Czech Foreign Affairs Ministry, which the Germans had seized when they marched into Prague. According to these files, Benes and, on his instructions, his Press Chief, Jean Hajek, were royally subsidizing substantial portions of the French news media. For some twenty years, French newspapers and certain key figures received large subsidies from the Ministry's press and propaganda fund.

Some of the subsidies went to well-known news organizations and journals: L'Agence Economique et Financière, L'Agence Fournier, L'Agence Radio, *L'Ere nouvelle*, *Excelsior*, *L'Exportateur français*, *L'Information financière*, *Le Journal des débats*, *La Presse associée*, *Le Peuple*, *Le Monde slave*, *Les Annales*, *L'Europe nouvelle*, *Liberté*, *L'Information*, *Marianne*, *Messages*, *L'Ordre*, *Paris-Soir*, *Pax*, *Le Petit Parisien*, *Regard*, *Revue bleue*, *Revue mondiale*, *Le Temps*, *Volonté*.

The amount of the subsidies varied for each newspaper and also varied according to the times.

20. Unit of Czech currency.

The article then lists subsidies logged in Benes's hand, under the heading, "For Dr. Osusky in Paris for 1922." M. de Lapradelle, Professor of Public Law, received considerably more money when it was learned that he was the founder and publisher of *Droit international* and *Vie des peuples.*

These payments continued through 1938. In that year of crisis, Benes sent two million crowns to Ministers in Paris and London. Following Munich, it seemed necessary to cut down on expenses. Two days after Benes resigned on October 8, 1938, Hajek wrote Osusky that he was to distribute these moneys only to groups of particular political importance, such as *Le Temps, Les Débats, L'Information,* ... E. Tapounier, X. Vallat, L. Weiss.

Actually, that news pales in comparison with the sensational revelations about the Italian and German subsidies. According to Nitti and Giorgini, Italian subsidies to Frenchmen and French organizations totaled more than 28 million francs in just one year, with the two men receiving the largest amounts being Bailby[21] and Bourrageas.

October 28, 1943

This evening, the news was confirmed in a pompous and pretentious speech by Pierre Bourdan, French radio's strategist in London, "a rout, a debacle, a catastrophe." Jean Oberlé also spoke, denouncing the Munich Agreement on this, the twenty-fifth anniversary of the Czechoslovak Republic, and attacking me personally, "who stood up in his car, like a dictator." This fellow was unaware that I was standing in that car to keep women and children from being struck, as had already happened several times starting from the moment we drove out of Le Bourget Airport. Most important, though, is that a centralized Czechoslovakia was simply not a viable alternative. The system Benes adopted and sustained was a disaster.

October 29, 1943

At 9:15 P.M. Roosevelt announced that the Moscow Conference had come to an end and was a glowing success.

21. Léon Bailby, journalist with *Le Matin.*

November 1, 1943

A Socialist Party meeting was held in Algiers, with Le Trocquer presiding. A motion of sympathy and loyalty to Léon Blum passed by acclamation. They talked of working in cooperation with the Communist Party and creating a multinational organization to prevent all future wars.

François-Poncet commented, "It's funny. These are the same expressions they used in 1918." Nitti added, "I already heard all that at Versailles, and I am just as skeptical now as I was then."

9 P.M. A bulletin from Moscow. After a meeting that lasted twelve days, agreement has been reached on a common approach to shortening the war. I noted in particular the plans to oversee the institution of democratic regimes throughout the world. Those guilty of massacres and atrocities will be handed over to the various Allied nations and judged according to their respective laws. Russia has agreed to act in cooperation with the Allies. Nothing was said about France. There was no word on Poland, and nothing about Japan. We'll have to wait and see.

November 7, 1943

All the mountains are covered with snow. It has been snowing in Itter as well, but I still managed to play ring tennis with Mme Brenklein and Jouhaux. Suddenly we heard a military band and artillery fire. Flags were flying over city hall. They were celebrating their dead from 1914–1918. It brought back memories of November 7, 1918, when I was in the area around Origny-Sainte-Benoite. I remembered the German envoys arriving at a little villa at the outskirts of La Capelle.[22]

When the conditions of the armistice were announced on November 11, the troops were not delirious with joy, as I had expected. They had the feeling that their victory was incomplete; they saw themselves escorting the German Army back to their homes. The peace treaties of 1919 carried

22. As a Lieutenant in 1918, Daladier received the German envoys who had come to ask for an armistice and led them to his superiors. He had begun the war in 1914 as a Sergeant in the Foreign Legion. He was awarded the *Croix de guerre*, three citations, and the *Légion d'honneur.*

the seeds of the following war. The conditions were at once too harsh and too lenient. The gravest error was to strengthen German unity and destroy Austria-Hungary. What will the peace treaties of 1944 herald? A Slavic victory?

The Germans were celebrating their heroes. The people of the village of Itter went to church. Six Privates and two NCOs delegated from the castle garrison went too. What could they all have been thinking, in their little church, as they called forth memories of the national disaster of 1918 at the very moment the Russians had just stormed Kiev and after two consecutive years of German retreat? At 1 P.M. I listened to a highly measured Roosevelt-like speech given by Stalin. No word on the Baltic States or Poland.

Mme V. is in tears. Her brother was killed in Russia.

November 10, 1943

There has been another change in the French Committee of National Liberation. Giraud and Georges are no longer members, but Giraud remains Commander in Chief. De Gaulle is president. He appointed the following *commissaires:* Queuille, Catroux, Philip, Le Trocquer, Marin, Jacquinot, d'Astier,[23] Massigli, René Mayer, Mendès-France,[24] Bonnet, Jean Monnet, et al.

It looks like a third Blum premiership, and once again without the Communists, who will probably go on playing the game they always play. It includes Socialists and Generals who are notorious Laval supporters. That gives us in France, in Vichy, a German party, and in Algiers, on the

23. Emmanuel d'Astier de La Vigerie, founder of the Resistance movement Libération Sud. He went to London in 1942. In 1943, he was appointed Commissioner in the Security Department of the French Committee of National Liberation and in 1944, Interior Minister in the Provisional Government.

24. Pierre Mendès-France, Radical-Socialist Deputy in 1932, Under Secretary of Finance in Blum's second Cabinet. He supported the Munich Agreement in 1938 and was an Air Force pilot in the war. In 1940, he left for North Africa on the *Massilia*, as per the decision of the government in Bordeaux. He was sentenced to six years in prison but escaped and went to London, where he flew missions with the RAF. He was Finance Minister in 1944 and headed other Ministries thereafter. He was Prime Minister in 1954–1955.

whole, a Socialist Party. The irresponsible influence being exerted by the Communists behind the scenes is significant.

I had a talk with Nitti. He is an elderly man of vast experience and great subtlety, in the Italian tradition. He explained that he passed for a Germanophile in France because of his staunch opposition to the Treaty of Versailles as well as to anti-Russian policies. He felt we had to find a modus vivendi with Germany, which remained a strong and populous nation in the very heart of Europe. "We are not going to make them disappear," he said. "We have to find a way to live with them." He felt reciprocal concessions would have to be made by England, Russia, Germany, France, and Italy. He had always had a low opinion of the Socialists, both in France and in Italy, and had been kept fully informed of the Soviets' plans by Carlos Ferrari, a Captain in the *carabinieri* who had gained the Soviets' trust by passing himself off as an anarchist. Nothing had happened since to make the Socialists rise in his esteem. Nitti was highly critical as he listened to the propaganda on the radio. He believed that after the war, England would be terribly weakened, Italy and France would be in ruins, Germany too. He felt there was probably a secret agreement between Japan and Russia and thought there would be an explosion of anti-Semitism throughout the world and above all in the United States, which was good reason for us to remain calm and reflective and not fall into crude traps.

Badoglio was right to refuse the King's offer to abdicate.

November 11, 1943

This should really be our national holiday.

Anniversary of 1918. Deep in thought, thinking about Origny-Sainte-Benoite, about La Capelle, about the future, too. The Gaullist propaganda is becoming more and more incredible. Their methods are unpleasant and have needlessly offended Churchill and Roosevelt.

There was a review of Allied troops in Algiers. Who reviewed them? De Gaulle or Eisenhower? The radio said nothing on that point. Meanwhile, for the first time ever, France has been excluded from the negotiations going on in London, where Russia, England, and America are determining the world's fate. We were defeated in 1814 and 1815 and even invaded and occupied, but France nonetheless played an important part at the Congress of Vienna. De Gaulle hasn't even been summoned to London. Stalin could have insisted that he be present, since he has recognized the Algiers Committee. Our only hope is that Churchill and Roosevelt will still be alive and still be in power when peace arrives.

November 13, 1943

Establishing an international monetary system is a distant goal. The first step is to assign as stable a parity as possible to the various currencies. Our first task therefore will be that of determining the domestic purchasing power of each currency, which will be difficult to do, given that price indexes have lost all real meaning. We also have to see to it that this same domestic purchasing power is not subject to wide fluctuations. A stable exchange rate means stable prices. The prewar period offers numerous examples of price variations. Excessive protectionism, such as that practiced by the Americans, can only weaken the stability of the international monetary edifice.

Moreover, no international monetary system will be possible until we establish definitive parity between the dollar and the pound. Without a definitive solution to that problem there would be no point in holding an international monetary conference.

We could create a single international currency even if gold didn't exist. The only people opposed to doing so are the English, who are major producers of gold, and the Americans, who hold large stores of it. If the Americans continued to buy gold at a fixed price, the metal would have the same fixed exchange rate with the international currency the dollar has. There is no reason then to link the gold issue to the debate over whether to have an international currency.

November 17, 1943

The experience of the American and British landing has shown that it would be equally difficult for them to make headway in Burma or in the Pacific archipelagos that have been lost. Japan is vulnerable only from the air. Stalin, though, far from turning over airfields to his allies in the fight against Germany, has regularly been locking up stranded American pilots.

What decisions were made in Moscow with respect to Japan? Has Stalin secretly committed the Soviet Union to join the fight against Japan if and when Germany is defeated? Or will he remain neutral and leave the door open to a vast propaganda campaign in Nationalist China, where there are still Communist Generals and armies? Will he offer his support to the Japanese if they promise him India and part of China in exchange? China alone represents one-quarter of the world's population. Whatever the case, no valid conjectures can be made as yet about what a peace settlement will entail, at least not until the Anglo-Saxons demonstrate that they have learned something from the lessons in tactics and strategy that were given to them by Rommel and other Marshals of the Reich, and that they are just as good students as the Russians. Nitti agrees with me.

November 18, 1943

As they used to say at the time of the French Revolution, some of the smaller countries, like Bulgaria, Romania, and Yugoslavia, are sisters of the Republic! It is significant, as Goebbels pointed out, that the statement issued after the Moscow Conference mentions Austria's independence but says not a word about Russia. "*Pravda*," Goebbels added, "was right in stating, just prior to the conference, that the western borders of the Soviet Union were of as little a matter of concern for the Anglo-Americans as the borders of Canada and California were for the Soviets." But what would become of Germany then? Driven by despair or by a hatred for democracy even greater than their hatred for the Soviets, overrun by Soviet agitators who would find recruits and supporters among former Communists and among those freed from the concentration camps, Germany too would declare itself a Soviet Republic and become a member of the great federation of the Union of Soviet Socialist Republics, just like the little neighboring states.

In fact, one could well conceive that in the wake of major upheavals within France, Italy, and Spain, all of Europe would gradually join such a Soviet-style European federation, with variations for individual nations; but then one would also have to accept the notion that England and America would stand by idly. But won't they be giving all their attention to the war with Japan?

The importance of Japan's victories in this war has been grossly underestimated. The key Pacific and East Asian positions of the British Empire and America collapsed in just a few days' time. To date, only Chiang Kai-shek's China has held out.

November 19, 1943

Nitti told Giorgini, "If we are shot by firing squad, you'll see how I smile and remain calm."

Had another long talk with Nitti about the war. He dismissed Germany's chances for victory long ago. British and American involvement has been essentially limited to bombings, but the Russians have poured huge numbers of men and huge amounts of matériel into the war. Nitti's thinking is almost exclusively directed at the postwar period. He came back to his major thesis: We can't afford another Treaty of Versailles; this time we have to allow for the existence and the legitimate aspirations of a great German nation living at the heart of Europe. He recalled the errors committed in 1918: the creation of a Czechoslovak nation, the independence granted to an Austrian state that wasn't viable and wished to be part of the Reich, and the "fabrication" of a huge Polish state that included Danzig and Upper Silesia. (In this connection, he revealed to me that Sforza, the son of a low-level civil servant, under the influence of a Polish countess who was his mistress, became a count as the result of a bureaucrat's error at the Ministry.) Nitti sided with Millerand, who disagreed with the way Lloyd George ignored the results of the plebiscite in fixing the line separating Upper Silesia.

I agreed with him; I voted against the Ruhr. In May 1939, I let the Poles know that France would not go to war over Danzig, and it was not over Danzig that France did go to war. And if Germany should be defeated, this victory and the victory of 1918 will have nothing in common, for the victor will be Soviet Russia. Nitti agreed. He said that the real question is, what does Stalin want? The West or the East? I personally think he wants both. To the west, he will put back together the empire of the czars: Finland, the Baltic States, and Warsaw, where he'll resort to well-known means to set up Soviet Republics.

November 21, 1943

Talked with Nitti. He has the appearance of an old man with a serene philosophy of life, not unlike the sages of ancient Greece, philosophizing in the gardens of the Academy with the friends of Socrates or Marcus Aurelius. Only this is Itter. I am very interested in what he has to say about the period following the last war and the French statesmen he met. He spoke about his conversations with Briand, whom he advised to give back the Saar without calling for a vote. Briand refused, citing the opposition of M. de Wendel and company. Nitti admired Briand's intelligence and subtlety and his sensitivity to public opinion. But, he said, "like all Socialists, he only governed to get applause." To my mind, after the curtain calls, this great actor would forget his role as soon as he had his topcoat on. Nitti went on to say that Briand was a liar and that he had corrupted French politics. I would sooner say that through his speeches and his acolytes he was one of the great corrupters of the public mind. His famous rallying cries haven't been forgotten: "Roll back the cannons. So long as I am here, there will be no war." Peycelon[25] handled the corruption end of it and didn't leave himself out.

Nitti cited a conversation he had with Colonel House, a confidant and friend of President Wilson. Wilson told House that if he had been aware of the secret treaty signed by Briand and the Czar in 1916, America would never have entered the war. Nitti mentioned Briand's major speech from 1916: "We don't want German territory, we don't want as much as an inch of it. We are at war with the German government, not with the German people, etc., etc." Briand also spoke about liberating Poland and oppressed nations. At that very moment, Paléologue,[26] who naïvely recalled this in his book on the Romanov's final journey, was meeting with the Czar, on Briand's orders, persuading him to agree to a secret treaty. France would accept all of Russia's claims—the annexation of all of Poland, Constanti-

25. Gilbert Peycelon, one of Briand's close associates.

26. Maurice Paléologue, diplomat and Director of Political Affairs in 1912. He was Ambassador to Russia from 1914 to 1917.

nople, and the Straits—and in return, Russia would agree to allow France to annex the left bank of the Rhine, including close to 14 million Germans. "The Bolsheviks published this treaty and a number of others, provoking President Wilson's ire." Nitti said that greatness in statesmanship required respect for moral principles.

A few days ago, I received a visit from Captain Höner[27] of the Reich's Security Police, who specifically oversees Itter castle and the prisoners here. He was very friendly when he came into my room and inquired about my health. Then, very abruptly, he stated that he had been ordered by the German authorities to insist that I take advantage of the offer that had been extended to me the very day I arrived, to have the company of some friend, or rather some female friend, as two other prisoners at Itter had done. I thanked him for this gracious officer and begged him to convey in turn my thanks to the German authorities for their marked and kind insistence. But I reiterated to them what I had already stated several times: that I consider myself to be what I actually am, a French prisoner, one of the innumerable captives in the stalags and oflags. Do my compatriots have the right to have the company of their wives or their girlfriends? When they do, I'll get back to you.

November 29, 1943

Nitti's departure. Yesterday, Nitti was informed by the Captain that he was to leave for a pleasant hotel where he would enjoy far greater material comfort. Nitti protested and asked to remain at Itter, where he had found spiritual comfort, which was, in his eyes, far more important than material concerns. Today, he was forced to leave in spite of his protests. He was very sad; tears welled up in his eyes. I tried to get his departure postponed by explaining to the Lieutenant of the SS patrol that had come for him that it was cruel to ignore the wishes and the state of health of a seventy-five-year-old man. We were gathered together in Nitti's little room; he had packed. On his bed, which, small as it was, took up almost the entire room,

27. Captain Höner's visit should be seen in conjunction with the doctor's visit on September 20. On orders from Berlin, both adroitly sought to learn whether Daladier would subscribe to some form of collaboration with Germany.

lay a cheap-looking suitcase and a few cartons that constituted everything he owned, he, a man who had several times been Minister and even Prime Minister of Italy.

His departure pains me deeply. I had come to appreciate more and more the gentle wisdom of this courageous old man. Following a cruel period of exile and the loss of a daughter, Nitti had made a reputation for himself throughout Europe with his knowledge of Oriental languages. He had been abruptly abducted from Paris, where he was forced to leave behind his sick and elderly wife and his son, the Director of the Pasteur Institute. He possessed to the ultimate degree that moral resolve that allows man to overcome adversity. Since our nightly chats began and I was favored with all his kindness and courtesy, how many times did I regret never having had occasion in Paris, before our captivity, to encounter this great Italian.

December 4, 1943

The Japanese greeted the statement issued at the close of the Cairo Conference with considerable sarcasm. They pointed out that in spite of the contentions of the Anglo-Saxons, Japan, far from being prepared to surrender unconditionally, has held on to all its phenomenal conquests. Not one of them has been breached or even seriously threatened.

December 8, 1943

Left for Innsbruck at 7:30 A.M. Thick fog and ice on the roads. We stopped at Wözel to get gas. It reminded me of a trip I made long ago with Dulot and our visit with a former burgomaster. We passed truckloads of soldiers and antiaircraft batteries. The stores were open, but the only merchandise in them was in the windows. I reflected on the stupidity of the predictions Gouin and Moch had made in the spring of 1942. We arrived in Innsbruck at 9 A.M., pulling up in front of the Gestapo building. At the hospital that was adjacent to it, I got an impression of cleanliness, order, and discipline. I found myself face to face with the otorhinolaryngologist: a young, dark-haired, kindly fellow, unaffected and polite. Mlle B. served as interpreter. He thoroughly examined my ear and treated it right away. Would it be necessary to operate? First, he wanted to get an X-ray. He handed me a slip for the radiologist in Building 2, directly behind the administration building.

The Gestapo has been worried that I'll be recognized. It finally had taken an order from Captain Höner to get me treated in Innsbruck, after three months of waiting. They're still afraid the British might pull something off. That is why they had given me the name Dietrich. The admission papers I was carrying were made out that way, but there was no first name. Mlle B. christened me Heinrich. So it was Heinrich Dietrich who went off to see the radiologist. A few yards away, I heard someone say in German, "It's really funny how much Dietrich looks like Daladier." I pretended not to hear. They are perfectly capable of turning me into the Man in the Iron Mask the next time. They took several X-rays but said I wouldn't get the results until the following day. Undaunted, I went back to the specialist. He kindly offered me a cigarette and recounted a few things about his area of specialization. He was familiar with the work of an old friend of mine, Maurice Vernet. He said he deplored bureaucratic mix-ups and that he would let me know if an operation were necessary, one way or the other.

December 9, 1943

They have just delivered machine guns and cases of grenades and ammunition to the castle. On the brighter side of things, my ear doesn't hurt anymore.

December 16, 1943

The British government has declared that it is in no way bound to the King of Greece. Hence, the British are leaving Greece to be sovietized. Finland, the Baltic countries, Bulgaria, Romania, Hungary, Yugoslavia, and now Greece. The Russo-Czech agreement is not without interest: It provides the avant-garde, the bridgehead, the platform from which Russia's Air Force can carry out its surveillance and perhaps even its battle missions.

From the Near East and Central Europe to the Adriatic; from the Aegean Sea in the South to the Baltic in the North: a Europe under Russian influence. The Anglo-Saxons have given up the view they had traditionally held.

December 17, 1943

Went back to Innsbruck. As we came into town, sirens sounded. People were hurrying about in the streets. They were coming out of the shelters. The siren had sounded the end of the alert.

This was another false alert, but there have been numerous bombings, the last one from about sixty American planes dropping their bombs from 10,000 feet. The train station and a military hospital were destroyed. There were sixty dead, mostly women and children. In the heart of the city, Marie-Thérèse Street, which had been so gay and welcoming in peacetime, was particularly hard hit, notably the Hotel Marie-Thérèse, where I once stayed with Dulot. Trenches were being dug in the outskirts of the city. Women and children were being evacuated from surrounding areas. I saw no sign of fright or nervousness on their faces, only expressions of calm and resolve. The National Socialist Party leaders have maintained their authority and are leading by example.

Nothing seemed to have changed at the medical center. I got the same impression of orderly bustle in a beehive of activity. I saw the same doctor, and he received me with the same kindness as before. I ran into a young French artilleryman, a prisoner in a khaki uniform, who was just walking about from one room to the next.

On our way back, we stopped at an inn, as we had the first time. Prices were high and there wasn't much choice—potatoes and rye bread—but our ingenious captain had got a pork chop from a farm.

December 20, 1943

There have been a great many radio broadcasts about the execution by hanging, in front of 50,000 people in Kharkov, of the two German officers and the Russians who were sentenced to death for having killed large numbers of people by asphyxiation. They had transformed a truck into a gas chamber. Russian propaganda is using the same techniques the Germans used when they uncovered the mass graves in Katyn Forest.

Maurice Schumann gave a bombastic speech, bombast having become the characteristic sign of the Gaullist radio station that allows you to distinguish it from the others. He extolled the Moroccan, Algerian, and

French troops fighting alongside the Americans in Italy, although to date no battles have actually been fought.

A few outposts are captured and it becomes an exploit worthy of Homer. Their attempts to glorify France make it look ridiculous. They are back promoting the myth of an Army on the Meuse, in May 1940, fighting without equipment. No mention of the panic and the cowardice that had seized them at the time of the opening battles, and at the time of some of the closing battles, too. It is their way of pounding out a mea culpa on someone else's breast.

December 21, 1943

Hungarian radio has announced that the new weapon being built by the Germans is a cannon that fires 12(?)-ton shells that can destroy everything in a radius of thirty miles. These cannons are to be set up on the western coast, supposedly to destroy London. In Russia, Stalin is reported to have decided to change the lyrics of the *Internationale*, which no longer reflect Russia's situation. But the *Internationale*, with these changes, will remain the national anthem!

This evening, the SS garrison celebrated Christmas a few days early so that they could all be together for a dinner among friends before some of them went home on leave. The supply manager had bought them a deer, which the Czech cook spent the day preparing, sending odors of venison wafting throughout the castle, and filling every room in the place right up to the rafters. The dinner was held in a large room on the second floor from which the ping-pong table had been removed. Each man found a little box on his napkin, with jam, fruit, cigarettes, and fifty marks. The soldiers sang until midnight. Most of them sang on key; many had lovely voices. The SS sent us some stewed venison as well. It was excellent.

December 23, 1943

Another trip to Innsbruck. We were on the road by 8:30. We passed a lot of trucks heading in the opposite direction, loaded with beds, furniture, women, and children. It looked like France at the end of May 1940. There were clearly a number of similarities, but this was all done with order and discipline. The German authorities had decided to evacuate the women and the children. We drove through the city to pick up a hundred liters of wine at a store next to the train station. Saw considerable damage everywhere. Here and there, shops and hotels had been reduced to piles of smoldering rubble. I noticed purple placards on all the abandoned houses: "Looters will be shot." Large apartment houses were split in two as if by an axe. Workers and soldiers were already out clearing away the debris. The people looked serious and sad, their faces impenetrable and taut.

The Gestapo said that more than a thousand people had been killed, once again a result of bombs dropped from an altitude of 10,000 feet and intended to work total destruction. If the Germans really do come up with a new and terrifying weapon, which they have been talking about for months now, there will be indescribable joy and enthusiasm throughout Germany. There are signs of collapsed buildings everywhere in the city.

At the clinic, there was a great deal of activity. The specialist asked me, "Why war?" I gave him Dietrich's answer. I was received there with the same open smiles and cordiality as before. At the police station, in contrast, faces were closed.

We went quickly back to Itter, without stopping at the inn, where trucks were parked out front. That evening, we went about exchanging Christmas gifts, as best we could. Mlle B. called out the names. There were flowers from all of us for Mme M. as a gesture of thanks. I had made a few gifts of my own: a bottle of Châteauneuf-du-Pape for the women prisoners who wait on us (they were delighted), a tin of sardines for the waiter, and a bottle of champagne for the Czech cook and the Serbian handyman. I feel a lot closer to them than to some of the others. I gave a few cigarettes to the accountant who had earlier given me some tobacco. I was able to hand out jam and chocolates as well. I could see J.'s face and hear his objections already, once I had my back turned.

It has taken time in a German prison for me to come to the realization that my father-in-law, Dr. Laffont, was right when he would say that only two things motivate men: pleasure and self-interest. My Rousseauian or idealist philosophy is only valid for humble people, not for the false elite assembled here, with two notable exceptions. I should act accordingly, counter to what I have done throughout my life. It is a little late, though, for me to have realized it. I was struck again by what Dr. Heckel told Debeck when he was giving me boxing lessons, "Make him mean."

December 24, 1943

I have continued to have great games of ring tennis with Borotra. I spotted him at 3 P.M. breaking the ice in the courtyard. I went down to help. As they used to say, he is a true gentleman. He'll garner affection and respect for France wherever he goes. Following the enlightened instructions of this wise *polytechnicien*, I began pouring wheelbarrowfuls of sand over the courtyard, which he spread about with consummate skill. We had a wonderful time until nightfall. We played until we couldn't see the ring anymore. It is a game that doesn't cost much and is easy to set up. It should be made more popular. This ring tennis idyll will have been our best distraction from captivity. This evening, I went to the dining room that the women had decorated under the supervision of the German Captain and his wife. They showed great consideration in inviting the French prisoners to their Christmas Eve party. Between the two windows to the east hung a portrait of Hitler. Gamelin was shocked.

Having paid them a visit, I returned to my cell, where I dined alone, as was my custom. Memories surfaced of Christmases of my childhood: mangers with little figures in them. I thought of the molds for Christmas figures that Raphaël Mouletin used to make. I remembered as well Christmas in the little house in Garches, where the fireplace was surrounded by toys for Jean and Pierre; and then, too, Christmas in 1914 in Verzenay, and in 1915 in Arras; and I thought of Canon Desgranges, my friend and war buddy. Christmas 1943 brings the duel between the Slavs and the Huns from which there will emerge, for Europe and for the entire world, a revolution whose form has not yet taken shape, but still a revolution far less important than that of Christ's.

At around 8:30, Granger came over and told me stories of his days in Tunisia and his captivity in Dachau. He's a fine man, highly patriotic and brave, a wonderful example of the average Frenchman. He was highly appreciated in Dachau, even by the SS in his cell block, and all the more so, of course, in his bunker. The stories he tells are fascinating, but he has no desire to write them down. After he had gone, I read Sombart's *German Socialism.*

December 25, 1943

I was awakened at 7 A.M. by a little black-headed titmouse. He comes to the window facing west to pluck seeds out of the little butter box that Susset sent me. The noise of the butter box clinking against my window is my alarm clock. At 1 P.M. we once again exchanged good wishes and thanks. Had soup and starches yet again. This is probably the reason I thought all those women were pregnant—why they're generally so huge. One of them was arrested and beaten for having been seen with Poles. I learned this morning that they had discovered that another of them was here by mistake, but that they refused to release her for fear she would reveal that we were being held here. The Iron Mask again. I have been interested and amused by the SS pamphlets that are clandestinely being circulated throughout the garrison. They are typewritten notes. One of them reads like this: "If Germany is defeated, those SS who bring three new recruits to the Nazi Party will receive permission to resign. Those who bring in six will be given permission to resign and will additionally receive a document certifying that they never belonged to the party. Those who bring in nine will receive a document certifying that they spent time in a concentration camp."

A second pamphlet is entitled, "The Führer's Speech of 1955."

"Given on the occasion of the establishment of a common border with Japan and of the steps taken by Major Churchill and Commodore Roosevelt to have their countries officially admitted as colonies of the Third Reich. Pledges of devotion have come in from Lieutenant Colonel Pétain and Lieutenant Stalin. Rosenberg has been elected Pope under the name of Pius XIII, and Goebbels, who is now living in Jerusalem, has been appointed Grand Rabbi."

1944

January 1, 1944

The snow has been falling for three months, compounding the mournful feeling of loneliness that comes with spending the holidays in captivity. Will this new year bring peace? I think not. Germany is still strong. This year will be decisive, though. In Vichy, there has been another palace revolution. Pétain is now flanked by Darnand and Philippe Henriot.[1]

January 8, 1944

This morning, Captain Vinner told me that he had been ordered to go to the Wörgl train station tomorrow to pick up Clemenceau, the son of the Tiger, and Colonel de La Roque! I was so astonished that I made him repeat it, which he did. Then I burst out laughing. He did too. The noise brought Granger from his room, to find out what was going on.

Granger then explained to the Captain that there was going to be trouble in Itter-city, while pretending to sight an imaginary rifle and yelling, "Bang, bang." Vinner went, "Bang, bang," too, laughed heartily, and left us. I reassured Granger that since La Roque would side with Weygand and Clemenceau with Reynaud, the balance of power would be maintained.

I have never met Clemenceau. I heard a little about him a long time ago, from Ignace and several others. Apparently, the only thing he inherited from his father was his name. I saw La Roque only once, very early one October morning in 1936, in the passageway of the train that was car-

1. Philippe Henriot, the principal radio voice for Vichy propaganda. He was a right-wing Deputy who in 1935 spoke out against the Franco-Soviet Pact. He collaborated with Marshal Pétain in 1940 and was later Laval's secretary. He was executed by the Resistance on June 28, 1944.

rying me back from Biarritz. A short, pale, rather flabby fellow, he was standing outside the door of his sleeping compartment, between two bodyguards, watching the sun come up. After that, he came to the dining car to have his café au lait and smoke a pipe. I concluded that he was not a threat to the Republic.

On the whole, he has had quite an eventful life. He enlisted in the infantry and fought bravely in 1914. He was wounded twice, twice cited for bravery. In this war, one of his sons was killed in air combat over the Meuse, the other was seriously wounded. He founded a political movement whose purpose seemed to be the creation of an authoritarian, antiparliamentarian, hierarchical republic, with the reinstitution of corporations as the basic approach to social issues. Anyway, that is what I could make out of it, that along with something of a neo-Boulangism. Although the movement attracted a number of old reactionaries who had been saddened or grown indignant over the fighting among political parties, it mainly drew on the young middle-class men and women who were victims of the economic crisis. They were fed up with the constant changes in Ministers and the way people carried on in Parliament, and also by the scandals of the time, which, even if they were blown entirely out of proportion and exploited for political gain, were all too real.

La Roque was primarily concerned with keeping control of his movement. Chiappe,[2] Tardieu,[3] and Laval wanted him as their Lieutenant, or Recruiting Officer. He couldn't very well refuse to be a part of the February 6 events, but he participated without enthusiasm, as if he had resigned himself to it. It took no more than some Head Sergeant and a few antiriot policemen posted on Palais Bourbon Square for La Roque and his followers to keep right on moving and abandon the idea of storming Parliament.

2. Although Prefect of Police in 1934, Jean Chiappe was aligned with the rioting right-wing parties. He had been overly indulgent in dealing with Stavisky and those handling the swindler's defense. As Prime Minister, Daladier dismissed him, but Chiappe lent his support to the February 6 rioters.

3. André Tardieu, conservative politician, hostile to parliamentary forms of government, Prime Minister in 1929, 1930, and 1932.

This is why Maurras and Daudet[4] —and they weren't the only ones—accused him of being soft, if not quite a traitor.

After February 6, he became one of Doumergue's close acquaintances. That was his period of greatness. The man was the undisputed master at organizing motorized rallies. He could marshal thousands of automobiles on vast prairies without a single accident or breakdown. The grandeur and the flawless formations of his parades humbled his rivals: Pujo, Doriot, and the Bonapartist Taittinger,[5] who since that time has taken on both a position as city councilman and numerous layers of fat.

Little by little, La Roque's parades attracted the various groups of the splintered political Left. Then the Radical Party broke with Doumergue at their convention in Nantes, in spite of Marchandeau's[6] zeal and the predictions about all the wonderful things the future augured. A few days later, the savior, wearing a beret and escorted by police, sneaked out of his house on the Avenue du Bois by a side door and headed back to Tournefeuille. By July 14, 1935, the Popular Front's marches far surpassed those of the Croix de Feu. La Roque can thus be seen as somewhat of a founding father of the Popular Front, whose members were frequently—in fact, most of the time—not in it voluntarily.

After June 1940, La Roque became a National Adviser and, considerably later, one of the special counsels to Pétain, who borrowed a great number of his stock phrases. La Roque was apparently high on the list of those playing the wait-and-see game. Once the Russian campaign bogged down in 1941, he became convinced that Germany would ultimately be defeated, which provoked Laval's ire and made him suspect in the eyes of the Germans, eventually leading to his arrest.

---

4. Léon Daudet, Alphonse Daudet's son, writer and journalist/editorialist for *L'Action française*. At the time of the February 6 incidents, he published articles supporting the riots and advocating racism and political assassination.

5. Pierre Taittinger, industrialist and conservative Deputy. In 1924, he founded the Fascist Jeunesses Patriotes. He supported Marshal Pétain in 1940 and was imprisoned at the end of the war.

6. Paul Marchandeau was a Radical-Socialist Deputy. He was several times a Minister under Daladier. In 1940, he voted to grant plenary powers to Marshal Pétain.

La Roque's arrival has generated still more talk. Reynaud considers him a traitor, primarily because he waged a vigorous campaign against him in the elections of May 1936, which Reynaud won by a hair, but also because he collaborated with the Marshal. Gamelin follows in Reynaud's step like Saint Roch's dog. Jouhaux hasn't forgotten the insults and the threats that were heaped on him by the Croix de Feu. I was subject to them too. Didn't they call me a murderer and an executioner? Borotra and Granger, who were at one time members of the Croix de Feu, have remained loyal to their former leader.

I was better off listening to the radio. The Russians have continued their powerful push forward. They've moved beyond Poland's 1939 borders. Waldeck-Rochet, a Communist Deputy, gave the kind of speech I had heard many times before, from Grenier, Fajon, Gresa, and others. He talked about uniting all Frenchmen and reaching out to the Catholics. France first! Unite, unite! He must have gotten confused and pulled out one of those all-purpose jobs from May 1936. Or maybe Marty[7] just hadn't sent him his copy of Moscow's latest speech. There wasn't a word in it about purging anyone. Or perhaps in spite of himself, Waldeck-Rochet just couldn't help remembering that wonderful statement that appeared in a July 1940 underground issue of *L'Humanité*, "The Communists are in favor of Franco-German collaboration"; unless it was the one from March 1941, "General de Gaulle and that whole crowd working for Britain's financial community would like the French to go to war for the City." As opposed to what the *roi galant* used to tell us in song, it is not just women who are fickle.

Sunday, January 9, 1944

At around 1:30 P.M. Colonel de la Roque and M. Clemenceau arrived in Itter. Borotra went to greet them, followed by Reynaud. They welcomed them and shook hands.

7. André Marty, leader of the 1919 mutiny on board a French vessel sent to the Black Sea to fight the Bolsheviks. Granted amnesty in 1923, he was subsequently elected to Parliament as a Communist and went on to play a major role in the leadership of the Communist Party. He participated actively in the war in Spain. He left France for the Soviet Union in

A little after 2 P.M. a frenzied Gamelin came running into my room, his face flushed with emotion. Clemenceau had told them that in the camp in Eisenberg, from which they had just come, La Roque had offered the Germans his personal cooperation as well as that of his party, the PSF, in fighting the Communists. He had written to Himmler, the head of the police and the SS, to propose his services. The Germans had circulated copies of the letter at the camp, provoking strong reactions from the French prisoners. On hearing Clemenceau recount this, Reynaud had exclaimed, "If I had known that, I would never have extended my hand to La Roque when he arrived," and Gamelin, whose hands were still unsullied, thank goodness, said that from then on he would refuse to shake with him.

I asked Gamelin if he had seen a copy of the letters to Himmler. I asked him if he, Gamelin, had proposed to Clemenceau that he confront La Roque with these accusations, with us present. He admitted he hadn't. "Go and ask Clemenceau if he stands behind his accusations," I said. "Then we'll so advise La Roque, so that he can have a fair chance to defend himself. Once that has been done, we'll have the right to form our own opinion." Gamelin ran out of my room even faster than he had come in, looking for Clemenceau.

I went downstairs to play some ring tennis. I ran into Mlle Mabire and heard her version of La Roque's act of treason. I asked her if she had seen the letter to Himmler. "No," she said, "but Clemenceau has read it." "Fine, then he can share it with us, but with La Roque present. Short of that, I prefer to withhold judgment, not being one of those who rejoices at the thought that France has yet another traitor in its midst."

Then it was Borotra's turn. He came up to me in his sandals, in the snow: bare legs, shorts, and a polo shirt. I asked him if he was aware of what was being said about La Roque. He said he had been apprised of the situation by Mlle Brenklein. News travels fast in Itter. He had protested to her that it wasn't so and protested again to me, indignantly.

1939 and in 1943 headed the Communist Party's delegation to the French Committee of National Liberation in Algiers. He was excluded from the Party in 1953, in what remains one of the major "affairs" of this kind.

I was about to toss the ring over the net when Gamelin came running up, even more flushed than before. He had spoken with Clemenceau, "that tall old man walking over there, stiffly, holding his head erect as if it were the Holy Sacrament." Clemenceau reaffirmed what he had said but was not prepared to state so publicly, not yet. In effect, he was hedging, but without withdrawing his accusation. I found that reprehensible and said so. Gamelin took off again, going from one person to another to tell them that maybe the new inmate wasn't a downright bastard after all. Borotra was delighted. Had a wonderful game of ring tennis.

Went back to my room and read Lucas-Dubreton's book on Marshal Ney. I was struck by the similarities between the Prussian High Command at the time of Iéna and the French High Command in May–June 1940: the same closed inner circle of old men; the same inability to regain control of themselves on the battlefield; the same panic at the first impact and no desire other than that of laying down their arms. Just look at Weygand's admissions as recorded in the transcript of the Riom trial. Of course, eight years after Iéna, the Prussian Army came marching down the Champs-Elysées.

Somebody was knocking at the door—Borotra—to ask me if I would agree to meet with Colonel de La Roque. Given what had transpired, there was no way I could refuse. How different he looked from 1936. The German prison camp had left its mark; hunger had shriveled him. He had been kept in isolation for months, in cells infested with vermin in Moulins and Fresnes and at Cherche-Midi, without news of his wife or children. Then in the German camp at Eisenberg, he was put on a starvation diet, as were all the other French prisoners. At least he got word there about his wife and three surviving children.

La Roque was indignant in denying what Clemenceau had been saying about him. He stated that on their leaving Eisenberg to come to Itter, General Altmayer,[8] the highest-ranking French officer in the camp, acting under German authority, had assembled all the French prisoners and pub-

8. In 1939, General René Altmayer was Commander of the Tenth Sector. He was relieved of his command in September of that year and returned to active duty on May 21, 1940, as Commander of the Tenth Army. He was a prisoner of war.

licly congratulated the two of them for having offered so fine an example of dignity and steadfastness. La Roque also told me that he had never ceased lodging protests with the Germans for his arrest and that of thirty-five of his Parisian associates who were also in captivity. He is convinced that Laval induced the Germans to arrest him, to keep him away from Marshal Pétain, whom he had seen frequently over the previous months. In this connection, La Roque told me that in his opinion, Pétain had long since ceased believing in a German victory. Pétain was playing it smart. He was making ready to call for the Resistance forces and all Frenchmen to unite, just as soon as the hour of liberation began to toll.

I told him I bought absolutely none of that. For Pétain, the defeat of France was an opportunity to realize political ambitions he had been nurturing since 1934, when, during the premiership of Doumergue, he began mustering the support necessary to take Doumergue's place. That is how he came to sound out Jouhaux for a Ministry. He's a crafty, guileful, and devious man who has been using his military prestige, partially drained now, and, even more so, his image as a true and loyal old soldier to carry out his endless intrigues. He wasn't even above disavowing overly compromised associates, like Commander Loustanau-Lacau,[9] whom I had been forced to relieve of his duty in 1937. After the defeat, Pétain didn't utter a word of protest about the annexation of Alsace and Lorraine, in direct violation of the Armistice. Worse still, right after the Germans violated the very Armistice he had presented to the nation as having been negotiated "with dignity and honor," he went to Montoire to drink his cup of shame right down to the dregs. Similarly, there wasn't a peep out of him when the Germans crossed into the so-called Free Zone on November 11, 1942. It makes for a sorry end to a long life.

9. Georges Loustanau-Lacau conspired within the Army to bring the antidemocratic Right to power through insurrection. He was disciplined by Daladier. He joined the Resistance in London and in France and was eventually deported to Germany. He was elected Deputy in 1951.

Monday, January 10, 1944

La Roque and Borotra came to see me this afternoon to show me copies of the letters the Colonel had sent the German authorities. First I read the one he had sent Himmler, which had served as the basis for Clemenceau's accusations. There was not the slightest trace of the supposed deal: If I am released, I and the thousands of French men and women I lead will collaborate with you in fighting communism. La Roque read the others. They were not very well written; I would have preferred another style too, but they were the letters of a man who held passionately to his newspaper, his achievements, and the leadership of his party and who, above all, wanted to see his image of Pétain redeemed through patriotic resurrection—Pétain, our man of Bordeaux, Montoire, and November 11, 1942!

He persists in thinking that Pétain is shrewdly stringing the Germans along, just as Stresemann once did with the French. That upset me, and I told him so. Nonetheless, I reread those letters and really didn't see anything in them that could be taken for any sort of an offer to collaborate with the Germans. Borotra and Granger agreed.

Then he read aloud two letters from French prisoners in Eisenberg, one of them an admirer of Louis Marin, the other a Communist sympathizer. Both thanked him for having comforted them and spoke of their friendship and the trust they had in him.

As far as I was concerned, the Clemenceau business was finished. It was up to La Roque to share these letters with the "lords" of Itter, if he thought it was worth it. But was it really necessary, given that Clemenceau had chosen not to make a public accusation?

To my mind, the matter was closed, but it took yet another turn after dinner. As the radio broadcast we were listening to was about to end, Paul Reynaud told us that he had seen Clemenceau earlier in the evening and that he had once again repeated his accusations; he stood by what he had told Gamelin. Reynaud added that instead of expressing indignation and protesting strenuously, La Roque was holed up in his room. But why on earth should he protest, if Clemenceau himself had told Gamelin that he wasn't prepared to make a public statement? Whatever the case, this had to stop. I said that the two men should have it out with each other tomorrow so that we could get this over with, one way or the other. The atmosphere was already strained enough. I told Reynaud that the only way to put an end to this business once and for all was for the two men to talk it out face to face, and the sooner the better.

Tuesday, January 11, 1944

Here's the epilogue of our little drawing room comedy. At the end of the evening meal, La Roque stood up to say that he wished to respond, without mincing words, to everything Clemenceau had been saying about him for the last three days. A very emotional Borotra read aloud all the letters that La Roque had written to the Germans. There was disappointment on several faces around the table, ironic smiles on others. Clemenceau rose in turn and said that he had never seen those letters and saw nothing wrong with them. However, he went on, La Roque's attitude at the camp in Eisenberg was highly suspect. That, he claimed, was the opinion of the interpreter and many of the prisoners there.

La Roque responded. He said that he had shown Clemenceau several of those letters before giving them to Altmayer, the French General in the camp. Jehin, the interpreter, had entrusted him with confidential messages. And General de Gaulle's brother, who was also a prisoner in the camp, had hugged him as he was leaving and assigned him several missions. I said to myself that if a de Gaulle, be he short or tall, skinny or fat, svelte or hunchback, had put the stamp of patriot on La Roque, even those who were most difficult to satisfy would salute.

Reynaud, however, after a friendly exordium in the purest Ciceronian tradition, said that the matter deserved closer examination. One reading was not enough; there would have to be more. He suggested that La Roque submit the letters to him, Reynaud, and me for further study. La Roque responded that he stood prepared then and there to reread every last letter involved, and there weren't many of them, and that he would reread them as many times as we wished and answer all questions pertaining to them, but he said he wanted to have it done with, then and there. Nobody could blame him for feeling that way.

I spoke up, saying that my initial reading of those letters sufficed and that I had found nothing in them to support the claims M. Clemenceau had made, first privately, then publicly. He had failed to provide proof of the specific accusations he had made, namely an offer to Himmler of the PSF's cooperation in fighting communism. As for La Roque's collaboration with Pétain and support for his policies, this was clearly not the setting for a debate, with the Germans looking on sardonically. It would be up to the people of France, and to them alone, to judge. Since no one had anything further to say, as La Roque duly noted, everyone went back to his room.

As I was heading back to mine, La Roque, whose room is close by, told me that he and his father had once had a run-in with another Clemenceau: Georges, "the Tiger." Around 1898, Colonel de La Roque's father was what they used to call a Naval Artillery General. It was in that capacity that he had opposed the purchase of torpedoes manufactured by a British company, Armstrong, finding the prices excessively high. Clemenceau violently attacked him in Parliament and the Minister of the time insisted that the order be placed. La Roque's father chose to take a leave of absence.

Much later, in 1918, Clemenceau was on a visit to the French troops in Flanders who had just blunted the German offensive. When he arrived at the division command post to which La Roque was assigned, he inquired about officers deserving medals or promotions. The name of Captain de La Roque, who had already been wounded and cited for bravery several times, was mentioned repeatedly. Hearing the name, Clemenceau winced and refused. La Roque added that he knows Clemenceau's daughter quite well. Mme Lemaire-Clemenceau is actively involved in the social work done by his party, the PSF.

January 14, 1944

L'Humanité makes for highly interesting reading. Since the beginning of the year, Communist leaders have been voicing their displeasure with de Gaulle and Gaullism while continuing to proclaim themselves faithful supporters. This is exactly what they did to the first Popular Front government. They began by praising Léon Blum to the hilt, then criticized his halfheartedness and eventually accused him of inertia, if not quite treason. At the Clichy riots, they shouted, "Do something, Blum." They continued organizing strikes and sit-ins in factories, in spite of the Matignon pact and collective bargaining. "Planes for Spain," they chanted, but in the factories, they worked only thirty-seven-hour weeks and turned out a mere 30 planes a month, while the Germans were producing 600.

They are using the same tactics in North Africa. "Long live de Gaulle!" Deputy Grenier said. "The Communist Party is with you heart and soul!" That's even better than in Blum's days. For the last few weeks, their criticisms, which remain measured and are still more insinuation than indictment, have begun showing through their praise. The Algiers Committee isn't purging fast enough. The traitors are still alive. Nothing changed when cautious Henri Queuille, whose very prudence made him suspect, relinquished his seat as President of the Purge Commission in favor of Communist Charles Laurent, known for his combativeness and for having organized a general strike of civil servants. People have been removed from office, but there hasn't been a single execution. The traitors have to be brought before firing squads. The Communists are demanding a court-martial, probably similar to the one Laval and Darlan organized in France, so that they can pronounce death sentences and without further legal ado execute the guilty parties—those named by the Communist leaders.

January 21, 1944

At Vichy's instigation, a law has been enacted in France creating courts-martial with three-judge panels presiding. Their role will be limited to determining whether "terrorist crimes" have in effect been committed and whether the guilt of those arrested is manifest. If so, the guilty parties are to be executed immediately. In the event of contrary findings, the accused will be judged by the appropriate courts.

A recent decree has given Darnand authority over all police organizations.

January 28, 1944

There follows a list of the principal stages in de Gaulle's relations with the Communists:

> *September 24, 1941:* Stalin declares that should the situation present itself, de Gaulle alone would be France's spokesman.

September 28, 1941: De Gaulle sends a congratulatory telegram to Stalin on the occasion of the anniversary of the October Revolution.

January 13, 1943: Grenier, a Communist Deputy from Saint-Denis, goes to London to offer de Gaulle the support of the Communist Party.

January 15, 1943: Speaking on London radio, Grenier repudiates all non-Gaullist leaders of the North African Resistance.

In February: The Gaullist Committee in London requests and obtains the release of twenty-seven Communist Deputies.

March 30, 1943: Molotov meets with Garreau in Moscow. Their talks deal with the Communists' support for de Gaulle.

May 1, 1943: A Communist Party manifesto issued in London calls on all expatriates to support de Gaulle.

June 24, 1943: An envoy from the Soviet Union arrives in Algiers. The decree dating from September 26, 1939, dissolving the Communist Party, is repealed.

August 27, 1943: Moscow recognizes the Algiers Committee as the official government of France

October 1943: Marty arrives, followed by Vyshinsky.[10]

January 31, 1944

Interesting account of Britain's bombing campaign. Sixty cities have been designated for destruction because of their war industry. Debatable. They added that these bombings have kept the greater part of the Reich's fighter planes in the West and in the skies over Germany, in other words, out of Russia. By doing so, the British have contributed greatly to the success of the Russian advance. The Royal Air Force will thus have played an enor-

10. As Public Prosecutor in the Soviet Union in 1936, Andrey Vyshinsky was the state's principal voice during the prewar purges. He served as Minister of Foreign Affairs from 1949 to 1953.

mous role, first by preventing the invasion of England and, in 1943, by favoring the Russian offensive.

It didn't work that way for France in June 1940, despite Britain's promises.

February 1, 1944

In Italy, General Clark has sent a very fine letter of congratulations to General Juin.[11] Schumann gave a good speech about pan-Germanism and the rifts separating the Allies in 1918.

The weather has been really lovely. I had run out of wood and at 8 A.M. went down to the courtyard to get some. When I got back, I found that unsightly hag in my room. I gave her hell and sent her running.

February 6, 1944

February 6, 1934, remains a significant date in the Fascist press throughout the world and notably in France. I am reminded of what the postman in Orange used to say, "In August 1940, they pulled off the coup they had botched on February 6."

La Roque came to see me at 5:15 P.M. He told me that the attempted coup of February 6, 1934, had been organized by Maurras, Lebecq (President of the National Union of Veterans), Taittinger, Pinelli, and Bunau-Varilla,[12] but not Chiappe. The conspirators, who would brazenly speak to each other on the phone, had decided to exploit the Stavisky affair. When I removed Chiappe as Prefect of Police, they realized that they would have to make their move immediately or run the risk of being indicted.

11. General Alphonse Juin (subsequently promoted to the rank of Marshal), Commander of a mechanized division in 1939, the French Forces in North Africa in 1941, and the French expeditionary force in Italy in 1943. He was named Chief of Staff for National Defense in 1945.

12. Maurice Bunau-Varilla, Editor in Chief of the all-powerful *Le Matin.* The Germans authorized the newspaper to begin publishing again as of June 17, 1940. When Bunau-Varilla died in 1944, he was replaced by his son. After France was liberated, *Le Matin* was outlawed and its presses confiscated.

La Roque met with them several times in a cafe near the Hôtel de Ville, but he wasn't interested in marching on the Chamber of Deputies. He didn't think his organization was strong enough. He had only a few thousand men behind him and the movement hadn't yet taken root nationwide. In Toulouse, for example, he had enlisted only seven or eight members. Most of his recruits were from Paris.

He decided to demonstrate separately from the other groups, on the Left Bank, and maintain his group's identity and freedom of action. He was flabbergasted when he learned that Lebecq's men had joined with the Communists in a plan to storm Parliament. The other conspirators were planning to force their way into the Chamber of Deputies and proclaim a provisional government. They thought they could get in through the catacombs and the sewers,[13] which come up between the Chamber and the War Ministry. La Roque's refusal came as a disappointment to Maurras, who would subsequently accuse him of treason!

Late 1937: The same men, abetted by new accomplices, had put together offensive and defensive plans to ward off the Communists. They had organized a coup d'état and intended to set up a new government under the presidency of Marshal Franchet d'Esperey. Pétain had preferred to wait and "see what the future would hold"; Weygand had turned them down.

Alibert (the same fellow who would be seconding Pétain in Vichy), Lémery,[14] Tardieu, Vallat, and the rest of the bunch had hoped that La Roque would provide the troops. Commander Loustanau-Lacau (Marshal Pétain's Chief of Staff) served as liaison between the protagonists.

La Roque refused, which incensed Tardieu; then he bought *Le Petit Journal*, which drew Bailby's wrath. That is why Tardieu set about cutting him down, first by attacking his military record, then by claiming that he had received money from slush funds. Ybarnegaray got various Interior Ministers to state that La Roque had never received secret funds. Pétain himself said that "La Roque's citations for bravery were for him sufficient

13. This was the plan that had been worked out by the CSAR (the Cagoule).

14. Henry Lémery, Deputy and Minister of Justice in the Doumergue government in 1934. In Vichy in 1940, he voted in favor of granting Pétain plenary powers and was appointed Minister of the Colonies.

and conclusive response enough." Weygand refused to speak out against La Roque, who had been a member of Foch's command staff from 1920 to 1922. At a huge rally held in the Vélodrome d'Hiver, Ybarnegaray triggered an outpouring of enthusiasm by quoting Pétain's expression of esteem for La Roque. That's when Tardieu and his fellow schemers took their indignant protests directly to the Marshal. At two in the morning, a journalist working for the Havas News Agency warned La Roque that Pétain had sent them a letter stating that he had never personally had La Roque in his command and was thus incapable of evaluating his true merit. La Roque retaliated with a scathing letter addressed to Pétain and an article in *Le Petit Journal* published along with a letter from Pétain expressing his friendship for La Roque and the confidence he had in him as well as an autographed photograph of the Marshal with words of praise and affection for La Roque. Tardieu then raised the issue of secret funds and La Roque took him to court.

Basically, I think La Roque wanted to create a national movement and assume power legally, with the idea of instituting an authoritarian, corporate state.

In 1938, he approved the Munich Agreement, once General Debeney explained to him that we were not militarily prepared to defend Czechoslovakia on our own and that England was at best reluctant and incapable of undertaking any action elsewhere than at sea.

In 1939, he tried to get in to see me on several occasions. He met a number of times with Arago, who had gone to him on my behalf. He wrote me and later expressed his indignation at not having received an answer. He was summoned by Laval, who told him that according to his count, he would have 120 deputies in 1940. I can't believe that, unless Laval was including the seats of some of Marin's friends.

In Bordeaux in June 1940, Ybarnegaray offered him a position as executive officer of his two Ministries, Health and Family. La Roque said he would only accept if the job were not remunerated and if Pétain and Weygand concurred. But once again, Pétain demonstrated that he was not one to forget the past; he refused to give his assent.

La Roque went back to Pau and decided to take direct control of his newspaper in Clermont. He refused to have his troops incorporated into the Legion. Pétain came little by little to make his peace with him and borrowed a great many of his slogans, in particular the well-known "Work, Family, Country." They discussed plans for arms caches, but Pétain never followed through on them.

Laval can't stand La Roque's relationship with Pétain and is undoubtedly responsible for La Roque's misfortunes.

February 7, 1944

La Roque came back to talk to me about the lawsuits he filed against Tardieu for having accused him of receiving secret funds.

La Roque read aloud to me what he had written about this period of his life, which had been painful for both him and his family. I was interested in finding confirmation for the accounts of certain events that I had long judged suspect. The Republic never really had political police. I have often wondered what they actually do in the Interior Ministry.

"The accusations of corruption lodged against me represent an attempt to dishonor me, resulting from my refusal to participate in an illegal rebellion and lend the services of the members of the Croix de Feu, later known as the PSF, to the overthrow of the republican regime."

A violent press campaign was unleashed by Maurras and Daudet in *L'Action française* and by Bailby, Tardieu, Vallat, Henriot, and others. La Roque noted, "I refused to collaborate with L'Action Française. We were demonstrators, not rioters."

In 1929, La Roque created an Air Defense Committee, later to become the Air Defense League, with the aim of alerting the population to the dangers of aerial bombardment. He was financed by a modest 30,000 franc annual subsidy provided by Michelin. At the time, Marshal Pétain was Inspector General of Air Defenses. La Roque was on good terms with him, but in 1933, he "respectfully" criticized certain memos circulated by Pétain and recommending the purchase of gas masks that had not been thoroughly tested. General Laure, Pétain's Chief of Staff, then offered La Roque sizable subsidies from the Foundries Committee, the coal mining industry, and the Air Force and War Ministries, but with the proviso that La Roque devote himself exclusively to the League, accept Colonel Picot as one of its leaders, and above all withdraw from the Croix de Feu. Anyone could have seen through that. La Roque rejected their offer and even quit the League, despite Pétain's efforts to prevent it.

After February 6, 1934, in an attempt to exploit the aftereffects of the riot, a coalition of Fascist and Royalist organizations known as the National Front was formed. When La Roque declined to participate, Pétain, then War Minister in Doumergue's Cabinet, canceled his nomination for promotion to the rank of Colonel in the Reserves and removed his name from the list of those to be considered for promotion.

In 1935, however, Pétain renewed his overtures to La Roque. They began meeting frequently, every two months. The Marshal shared with him his political aspirations and his ideas for reorganizing the government, ideas he intended to put into effect as soon as he became Prime Minister.

Pétain's political ambitions came to life in the immediate aftermath of February 6, 1934, and expanded rapidly. He realized that given the Radical Party's opposition and the worsening economic crisis, the fall of Doumergue's government was inevitable. He set about taking steps to find the support he would need to accede to power. He got word to Jouhaux that he would like to meet with him and his associates. With me, he became so extraordinarily amiable that I found it excessive. In the Chamber of Deputies, he supported a bill limiting military service to one year, which Weygand staunchly opposed. Since his political objectives would bring him the support of the Right in any event, he was trying to appeal to the Left. But when Doumergue's government did fall, Pétain failed in his attempts to replace him. He chose to lie in wait for a more favorable occasion and discreetly offer his services, with his customary prudence, as head of a national, broad-based government.

He made it a point to be introduced into every possible circle and to place some of his people in all of them. He concerned himself with overcoming the obstacles that lay in his path and neutralizing whatever opposing forces he could not win over to his side. He didn't actually exclude the possibility of eliminating outright those opposed to him, if ever the situation were to present itself without incurring great risk, but violating laws and the use of force was never seriously considered. He was rather counting on the antagonism among political parties and their overall ineffectiveness. It was his wish to appear on the scene at some point as a conciliator draped in glory, with the discreet support of business groups and the boisterous enthusiasm of certain veterans' associations.

In his talks with La Roque in 1936, Pétain told him that the Popular Front's victory would be short-lived, that the Left would inevitably go too far, and that the reaction of the farmers and the middle class would prove fatal. The hour would then be at hand for the victor of Verdun to come to the fore as a moderating force.

Those were the Marshal's words, but the acts of some of his associates belied them. Commander Loustanau-Lacau, for example, was involved in mobilizing an insurrection.

In April 1937, La Roque learned that under the pretext of fighting the Communists, officers in the garrison in Nice had secretly formed their own defense unit. He informed the Marshal in writing. No later than April 15, Loustanau-Lacau, accompanied by Captain Bonhomme, Pétain's orderly, came to tell La Roque that his letter had not been passed along to the Marshal. Loustanau-Lacau then informed him that he had organized a supramilitary intelligence group to handle surveillance of the Communists and asked La Roque to participate. As he explained it, the Communists were preparing a takeover; he had proof of it. The Popular Front government was either powerless to stop them or an accomplice to it. The situation called for a union of the large national political organizations—Doriot's PPF, Maurras's Action Française, the Republican Federation, and La Roque's PSF—to be supported by major business groups. To avoid possible rivalries, they would create a National Committee on which each group would be represented by its leader, but under the presidency of a great military leader, that is, Marshal Franchet d'Esperey, since Marshal Pétain wasn't available. Either General Brécard[15] or General Altmayer would serve as Secretary-General. The organization would reach into every province. After serious and thorough preparation, on D day at H hour, the National Committee of this united Freedom Front would assume power to save France from the Communist peril. Commander Loustanau-

15. General Charles Brécard, former Cavalry Inspector who became the war chronicler for right-wing and far-right-wing newspapers: *Candide*, *Le Jour*, *L'Echo de Paris*, all of which were published with German authorization and oversight.

Lacau was insistent in trying to get La Roque to sign on, but the latter refused to take part in an operation tantamount to civil war.

A short time later, the Freedom Front was created. When La Roque failed again to respond positively to overtures made by Loustanau-Lacau and Bonhomme (both of whom were on Pétain's staff), they unleashed violent attacks against him, with Tardieu, Bailby, Abel Bonnard, Gillouin, Alibert, and Maurras proving especially caustic.

When, on July 14, 1937, La Roque announced that *Le Petit Journal* had become the property of his party, the PSF, the Freedom Front's attacks intensified. Bailby distinguished himself as the most vicious of all. La Roque mentioned once again the relentlessness with which Tardieu maligned him. He clearly represented the principal obstacle to the plot's success. There could be no united front without his followers. Tardieu, and the National Committee along with him, accused La Roque of accepting bribes and corrupting officials, with Tardieu claiming that as Prime Minister, he had personally handed La Roque money from secret funds. La Roque sued Tardieu for slander. That was the beginning of a series of lawsuits and an unusually violent press campaign.

Time went by. I became Prime Minister. My Minister of the Interior never once mentioned this secret organization called the Freedom Front. However, my military advisers informed me that General Gérodias,[16] Deputy Chief of Staff, had sent a message to Army corps and military sector commanders that included the translation of an old Spanish Communist Party paper. The paper described the ways in which to neutralize an army by overpowering its officers, as preparation for an insurgency. Gérodias's message said that these tactics would undoubtedly be employed in France. I expressed surprise and indignation that such a note could have been circulated without its having been communicated to me, General Gamelin, and General Colson. It had been intended to unsettle officers and their families and possibly draw them into political movements. I immediately ordered an investigation.

16. Paul-Henri Gérodias was Deputy Chief of Staff in 1936.

General Gérodias said that the message had been brought to him by Commander Loustanau-Lacau, acting on Marshal Pétain's behalf. He said he hadn't understood its political nature and had simply passed it along for its informational content. When Marshal Pétain claimed that he had never seen it, I decided to place General Gérodias on inactive duty, in spite of his personal merits; in effect, during this past war, he commanded his division brilliantly. I also decided to remove Commander Loustanau-Lacau from office. On learning of my decision, Pétain simply said, "I had been noticing for some time that he had been seeing too many people."

Near the end of 1939, La Roque was visited by Lémery, whom Pétain had dispatched to find out what La Roque would do if Pétain were to seize power, which he was seriously considering, with the approval of Laval and other political figures. It was their intention to negotiate a separate peace agreement with both Germany and Italy, with Spain serving as intermediary. The plan wasn't made public until June 1940, in Bordeaux, when it was put into effect. This had been Pétain's idea as early as May 25, 1940: Use the defeat to seize power. After Reynaud's downfall, Pétain emerged unopposed as the master of France. He immediately called on the men from the Freedom Front and the Synarchie: Laval, Baudouin, Lémery, Bouthillier, Brécard, and so on. He made peace with La Roque when he found he needed him, and made him his confidant. Of course that didn't prevent him from letting La Roque be deported.

Is that the final chapter of this story? I rather doubt it, given that, in spite of everything, La Roque remains devoted to Pétain. He just can't believe that behind the ignoble attacks on him lay a carefully concealed Marshal Pétain. Does he at least believe that Pétain knowingly let it all happen? Not even that. In his view, Pétain was duped.

February 15, 1944

Von Rundstedt has given Gamelin and other French Generals a lesson in warfare. He stated that the Maginot Line, because there was no depth to it and because its rigidity made it difficult to defend, was poorly conceived. Neither the fortifications nor the arms had been designed in response to the firepower of Germany's weapons. Above all, the line could be outflanked since it stopped in the middle of eastern France.

I remember the protests voiced by Pétain, Weygand, and the Supreme War Council when I expressed concern over this gap and suggested that we continue building further north. Pétain considered the Ardennes impassable. He even wrote that it was.

Von Rundstedt will have huge resources at his command. To repel an Anglo-Saxon landing, Hitler will strip the Russian front, if he has to.

March 4, 1944

Pucheu's trial opened today in Algiers. Prior to the war, he was a member of the Synarchie, along with Baudouin, Bouthillier, Barnaud, and others. Their idea was to establish relations with Germany and Italy, with a view toward the economic and financial domination of Europe. Their plan, or plot, probably began as early as 1936–1937. They were also very likely allied with the group that has stupidly been called the Cagoule. Pucheu and other members of the Synarchie had close ties with certain members of the Joint Chiefs: Prételat and Franchet d'Esperey.

They obviously played a significant role at the time of the Armistice, but once the golden age of the Bank of Worms came to an end in Vichy, probably as a result of setbacks in their relations with Germany or on Pétain's advice, these boys decided to try out the Americans. Even that vile creature Baudouin wanted to go to Africa, to join up with Darlan, and later Giraud, but either he couldn't manage it or he was overly wary.

Pucheu took the same route taken by Peyrouton and others who had been in Vichy, but he didn't have the support of the Anglo-Saxons. That support wasn't enough to keep the others from losing their positions, but at least it kept them out of a military courtroom, which is where Pucheu finds himself now.

What standing does this court have? General Weiss is serving as Public Prosecutor. I wonder what Blum's lawyer, Le Trocquer, thinks about it, given that he challenged the legality of Riom's Cour Suprême.

In my opinion, this trial should be held after the war, in an official court of law, with a lot of other men facing charges, too. The verdict, whatever it is, will have no value. It's probably just one of the many bones being thrown to the Communists. However despicable I may find the men of the Synarchie, I place the law and respect for the law above that.

Pucheu is charged with conspiracy against the nation and high treason. He is also charged with having carried out illegal arrests, abuse of power, and abuse of authority. As he stood accused, calm and in perfect control of himself, he began by challenging the court that was trying him. Having been asked questions relative to the request for an armistice and its acceptance, he tried to explain his position at the time, but he was not allowed to, his feelings being deemed irrelevant. Then he accused Laval of having committed the offenses that were being imputed to him. He stated that he had always been anti-German and that he had had some success in defending France's industry against German businesses. He claimed that he had ordered the arrest of members of the Gestapo. He had no response, however, to the charge that he had allowed the Gestapo and the SS to set up their offices in Vichy.

March 6, 1944

Huge Russian offensive north of the Ukraine. The rail link between Lvov and Odessa has been cut. Large amounts of matériel have been seized.

Pucheu's trial is still going on. We were given a long communiqué about the defendant and his statement. General Weiss claimed that Pucheu's position in Pétain's Cabinet was proof of "his complicity in the policies of collaboration." Pucheu replied that in 1941 the majority of Frenchmen supported Pétain and that Admiral Leahy and a representative of the Soviet Union were still at their posts in Vichy. Weiss shot back that that was no excuse for serving in Pétain's government.

At the second court session, they read a memo circulated by Pucheu, ceding control of France's textile industry to the Germans, and so on. None of this has anything to do with the execution of the hostages in Châteaubriant. Pucheu always made a distinction between the Gaullists and the Communists.

Pucheu stated that he had crossed the Pyrenees and gone to North Africa in answer to a call from General Giraud and that he had left behind his wife and children, who had since then been arrested by the Germans. It seems to me that the timing of this trial is particularly poor.

At the third court session, Giraud and Béthouart[17] appeared as witnesses for the defense. I have seen only an extremely brief and rather slanted summary of their testimony. On the other hand, the prosecution witnesses, most of them Communists—Grenier, Laurent—are quoted directly. They often got involved in violent disputes with the other witnesses, with the two groups lobbing accusations of lying back and forth. The Communists accused Pucheu of having handed Party members over to the German authorities and of having set up special courts. They also held him responsible for the Châteaubriant killings. The Communists admitted that they had no proof, but, they said, "We can smell it!"

March 8, 1944

There has been a terrifying daylight bombing of Berlin. There is talk of 3,000 Allied aircraft involved. These air raids bring back memories of the German bombings of London in 1940. Anglo-Saxon convoys are now making their way to Russia and the Mediterranean unobstructed.

Fourth courtroom session for Pucheu. Highly favorable testimony was given by Captain Begbeder, a former member of his staff, and by Giraud, who took the stand yesterday to state that it was at his official request that Pucheu had been called back to North Africa. Giraud and Pucheu had at times been very close.

In a terribly violent closing statement, General Weiss called Pucheu "the nazifier of France," "the pivotal man in the enslavement of the country." "He is the enemy of Stalin's men … and yes, we owe our thanks to Stalin's followers, those men who are supposedly devils. I love those supposed devils, because they are saving our country." Weiss called for the death penalty.

Pucheu was found not guilty of plotting against the nation and its form of government. Conversely, he was found guilty, with no mitigating

17. General Maurice-Emile Béthouart commanded the expeditionary force to Narvik and thereafter the military zone in Rabat. He went to Algiers in 1942 and was Commander of the First Army Corps in 1944.

circumstances, of conspiring with the enemy, to which he had handed over our economy and our police. The charge of having chosen and/or turned over hostages was dropped. He was sentenced to death, and all his assets are to be seized. He has appealed the verdict. The summary of the closing statements presented on the radio was insufficient and skewed. All the arguments raised at the trial were mediocre. It was just so much nit-picking, with no greatness to it at all. The closing statements were feeble.

March 17, 1944

British artillery and aviation have reduced the ancient remains of Cassino to rubble. Once again, I find confirmation of Armengaud's theory that well dug-in troops can withstand aerial bombings.

Speech by Lord Halifax: "France shares with my country the honor of having taken up arms to meet its international commitments and defend freedom." "Our thoughts and our prayers are with the people of France. We are convinced that a strong, free and proud France will rise once again." "Whatever the future government of France may be—and that is for the French people themselves, when the time comes, to decide—we are glad to have in Algiers a body of Frenchmen who, working together, form a remarkable symposium of French opinion, insofar as that opinion can, in present circumstances, be vocal."

March 27, 1944

In Algiers, the National Resistance Council had the unusual idea of issuing a reminder that "France's principal goal is the struggle against the invading forces" along with a series of warnings aimed at "people circulating lists of collaborators, people writing letters informing on others and sentences handed down by kangaroo courts." It was followed by a plea for people not to do anything that might jeopardize the union of all Frenchmen. … This comes clearly in reaction to Pucheu's trial.

The Consultative Assembly in Algiers—the government had chosen not to participate so as not to impede discussion!!—has decided on the structure of the future legislative body even though it was not itself mandated by universal suffrage.

March 31, 1944

The Russians are moving on Odessa.

Of particular note is the economic agreement between Japan and the Soviet Union over fossil fuels and the fishing grounds at Sakhalin. Japan has agreed to an increase in the fees they pay to fish there.

April 1, 1944

There have been new aerial bombings of Germany; the Russian Army continues to drive forward. The bombings are clearly helping them advance, by drawing away the greater part of Germany's fighter planes. The second front is in the sky. The Germans have understood the gravity of the situation along the southeastern front and are aware of its consequences.

Italy: Russia has recognized the government headed by Badoglio and King Victor Emmanuel, much to the dismay of the Anglo-Saxons, who weren't notified beforehand, and probably of the fiery Sforza, the Communists' ally. That explains why the Communist leader Ercoli, extending a hand to the Catholics and the military brass, gave a speech reminiscent of those Thorez used to make before he deserted: "The new government must include members of all the non-Fascist parties. In no instance, can we yield to the desire to wage vendettas. We cannot make the mistake of allowing for the massive elimination of officers. We need them to forge a union of all Italian people."

April 9, 1944

A beautiful sunny day. I watched people stroll by in the ravine, girls with soldiers, women, and children. Itter must have been a vacation spot before the war. There are traces here of religious customs that predate Christianity and that have survived over the ages.

The tribe (Reynaud, Weygand, et al.) held a banquet. Jouhaux didn't get back until 5 P.M., all lit up and giddy. I prefer to have my meals alone.

April 10, 1944

At 2 P.M. I learned that the Russians had reached Ruthenia, a former Czechoslovak province that was ceded to Hungary after Munich. They raised the Czech flag. There was a commemorative ceremony in London and speeches by Benes.

Ever since the retreat from Russia, the German garrison at the castle has been growing increasingly discouraged. An old veteran of the War of 1914–1918 said to me, "Don't they realize that the war is lost and that they have to make peace?" One officer said that he would take to the mountains with provisions; another that it was time to get out his civilian clothes. The younger ones, though, remain fervent and confident.

April 12, 1944

In a recent speech, Lord Vansittart stated that originally, the Entente Cordiale of 1904 was merely a mutual declaration of goodwill generated by the multitude of incidents that had been occurring daily. At the time, England had no wish to conclude an alliance, but had that alliance, to which they did ultimately agree, been forged then, there might never have been a War of 1914–1918. He added that the fruits of the victory of 1918 were lost because the Americans refused to grant France the guarantees that it sought concerning the Rhine.[18] Then the Americans stupidly withdrew, claiming it was not their province to intervene, and the British followed suit. During the French occupation of the Ruhr Valley, the British protests were fully as vehement as those of the Germans. Lord Vansittart added that in 1940, England was spared France's misfortune because it was separated from the continent by twenty miles of sea. France was condemned to suffer its horrible fate as a result of errors of which England was not entirely innocent.

He concluded by saying that it would be folly, and fatal on the part of the Allies, to undertake to reestablish order in the countries soon to be lib-

18. At the Paris Peace Conference, Lloyd George and Wilson did not support France's demand to occupy the left bank of the Rhine (see diary entries for November 11, 1942, and September 29, 1944). They agreed instead to the demilitarization of German territories west of the Rhine (the left bank) and a strip thirty miles wide east of it (the right bank). When Germany violated this provision of the Versailles Treaty by remilitarizing the Rhineland in 1936, England and the United States did nothing.

erated, for the people living in those countries have suffered far more than we have. He said that each of us must refrain from offending our friends by paying too much attention to the words of our enemies.

April 23, 1944

Spring has made a modest appearance in the Tirol; the light is playing upon the snow-covered mountaintops. What a wonderful morning! Suddenly, at 10 A.M. there was an explosion in the village. From behind my barred window, I watched as a villager in a deserted street prepared to fire another round from the cannon they use to signal the joyous or painful events that mark village life. More blasts shook the air. I learned that the cannon shots had been occasioned by the news that two of their sons had died on the battlefield. Then the church bell began to toll. I understand that the priest gave a moving talk and that all the women gathered in prayer were in tears. Itter has a population of only 400; 12 of them are now dead. Proportionately, that works out to 2 million deaths for Germany.

Last night, in one of the village inns, the castle garrison celebrated Hitler's birthday. One of the soldiers told me about their party: beer, wine, and to top it off, a Roman-style orgy with eight women playing the role of bacchantes ... of course the SS do it standing up.

April 25, 1944

The bombing of Europe continues on an increased scale. Airfields in Dieppe, Metz, Nancy, and Dijon were hit. In Itter, yesterday, sirens sounded the alert all day long. Fires have been raging through Ludwigshafen, Mannheim, and Munich. The "Sanitär" got a postcard from his family. "All we can say is that the only thing we have left is our lives." He is a good man and was terribly shaken by the news.

Aerial reconnaissance missions are being flown from the Baltic to the Danube. I also heard stories about the exploits of the French Resistance, much of that news false or grossly exaggerated. Were we not told that in the Ain, the Germans lost 500 men and had 700 wounded, whereas there were only 74 French deaths?

April 26, 1944

The massive bombings have continued without letup. There is fierce fighting between Lvov and the Carpathians. Meanwhile, in London, a ceremony was organized at the Alliance Française. Benes was received by Dejean,[19] the Algiers Committee's delegate in London, and by Viénot, and General Kœnig was present. Dejean condemned "the servility with which the governments who signed the Munich Agreement had backed down; backing down was to become the program of the Vichy government." Benes deplored the fatal error of all those who considered the negotiations at Munich to be of limited import. Then he praised de Gaulle for having raised anew a French flag that had been betrayed.

The Czechoslovak government was pleased to recognize the Liberation Committee as the true representative of France, which, he said, in a liberated Europe would regain its place of strength and honor among the leading nations of the world. Then Viénot concluded by lauding Benes. He attributed the error of Munich to "a feeble-minded government devoid of courage and foresight." Viénot himself voted in favor of the Munich Agreement! Apparently neither the United States nor Great Britain was represented at the ceremony.

April 27, 1944

In London, Pierre Dac, who, prior to the war, was a well-known humorist, was heard threatening collaborators with the death penalty. There is no shortage of surprises, that's for sure.

As for Pétain's tour of France, it has been learned that he spent the night in Melun. Then he went to Notre Dame for the funeral rites of the victims of the Anglo-Saxon bombings of Paris's 18th Arrondissement. The trip was announced twenty-four hours beforehand, allowing the Prefects time to alert the staffs of the collaborationist parties and get out the Pari-

19. Maurice Dejean, career diplomat, one of Paul Reynaud's associates in 1939. He was Director of Political Affairs for Free France and National Commissioner of Foreign Affairs from 1940 to 1942. In 1944, he served as French delegate to the Allied governments based in London.

sian population. By 9 A.M. the French flag was flying over the Hôtel de Ville and a large security force was in place. Pétain left city hall a little before ten, in a huge procession heading for Notre Dame, where he was met, naturally, by a huge crowd. After the ceremony, he returned to the Hôtel de Ville for lunch, then began receiving various delegations, notably the beef porters from the Halles market. Following that, he went out onto the balcony and addressed the assembled crowd. He spoke about Paris in mourning, the confidence the government and the people must have in each other, and the day when peace would return. It was a perfect example of how not to commit yourself. There wasn't a single word in it that could have failed to draw applause from patriots.

May 10, 1944

Massive bombings are continuing with no letup over France, Belgium, Luxembourg, and the Gulf of Genoa. This is today's heavy artillery preparing the ground for battlefields to come. So many flourishing cities will be reduced to formless ruins. How can anyone not be heartsick at the thought of the women and the children there? These are wars of mass destruction; real hell is being wrought on a scale equal to that of our technological advances.

Addressing the House of Commons, Churchill stated that 6,670 American airplanes, 5,050 British tanks, and large amounts of matériel have been delivered to the Russians. England has lent them 80 million pounds, following a tradition set by Pitt, the banker of coalitions. Add to that the American aid, in the form of lend-lease.

"Jeremiah" Schumann has spoken out violently again against Pétain and his trip to Paris. That was followed by a series of official communiqués that formed a tangled web of contradictions.

May 11, 1944

Emmanuel d'Astier de la Vigerie spoke in Algiers about the Resistance and how they see their role in the coming landing. The forces inside France are to be called the FFI. He noted that in the time since the Armistice was signed, 20,000 Frenchmen have been executed by the Germans. He threatened Monzie, Bonnet, and Frossard, who remain staunch supporters of the Marshal and are preparing to install a new republic in Paris. Once again, d'Astier is striking out at shadows.

May 14, 1944

Joan of Arc Day. The new successes won by the French fighting in Italy, in spite of the desperate counterattacks launched against them, are the best commemoration possible.

May 15, 1944

Both the British and American press are filled with heartfelt praise for the French troops commanded by General Juin. His performance has been excellent.

May 16, 1944

Spoke with La Roque about the Synarchie. He talked to me about a plan that Le Roy Ladurie of the Bank of Worms, Pucheu, Baudouin, Bouthillier, Barnaud, and others had devised in 1937. The idea of these anti-Communist promoters of Anglo-Saxon capitalism was to rally political moderates to collaborate with the Synarchie under the leadership of a well-known military leader. Offers were extended to Pétain, who turned them down, and Weygand, who likewise refused. Franchet d'Esperey accepted. It is quite possible that Pétain remained a substitute choice, since Loustanau-Lacau, who was on his staff, monitored these events closely. La Roque refused to be a part of it. He told me that Pucheu had at first been inclined to side with Doriot, but that he dropped him as soon as he had proof that Doriot was being subsidized by the Italians.

May 28, 1944

Lisbeth and Andrea said good-bye to me. They had come to work at the "castle" after having first been deported to a camp; now they were being sent back. Lisbeth is German. She was imprisoned for having married a Jew prior to 1933. After Hitler came to power, she sought refuge in France, in Paris and Lyons. She is about forty-five years old and very bright. She is frail in appearance, with a look that is intentionally closed and lifeless. She finds the Bolsheviks as criminal as the Nazis. Andrea is a young blond-haired woman from a good family, married to a Russian Jew. She is meeker and less intelligent than Lisbeth. Lisbeth said to me: "La Roque is a Fascist! Why did they arrest him?" Then she said: "I hope you'll get to return to France. I know how much they love you there." Going back to the camp is hard on both of them.

Louis Marin spoke on the radio. Finally a speech from a patriot whose only thoughts are for his country.

June 4, 1944

After violent street fighting in the suburbs of Rome, the Eighth Army entered the city, where they encountered no resistance whatsoever. How grand an event this is, and how many memories it evokes! I spent several years in Rome, working on my thesis on the cities of Renaissance Italy. German columns have been sighted north of Rome, in disorderly retreat. The Allies have seized the Alban Hills and the road from Rome to Pescera, on the Adriatic. They took full control of the capital last night. General Clark made the following statement, "It is thanks to the fighting men of France, Britain, and America that this day has come." And thanks to General Juin's men, the shame brought on us by Huntziger, Georges, and Gamelin, if not entirely erased, will at least have been largely offset. In Europe's eyes, thanks to these men, France looks like a warrior again. Clark added that Germany's Tenth and Fourteenth Armies had been defeated. In Rome, delirious crowds cheered the Allied soldiers, above all the French soldiers. They are France's finest ambassadors. The friendship the people of Italy hold for France is alive again, now that the Fascist gangrene has been eradicated. The two countries will have to work together during the peace negotiations. The Pope made an appearance on a balcony at the Vatican. This has also been a victory for the spirit of Christianity, if not for the Christian religion. There is greatness in this historic moment. The only thing missing was the splendid presence of Nitti.

Pétain traveled to Lyons. France's Fascists have left him in the dust, as they have Laval. Now their sole allegiance is to Darnand, Henriot, and

Déat. They no longer take the Vichy government seriously. In the absence of an Allied landing, the continued bombings have had an obvious effect on morale.

According to Monte Carlo radio, Mendès-France, who has been in Washington since May, has resigned, having failed in his negotiations.

Won't the principal Allied landing take place in Italy, where they hold sixty miles of coastline and control the entire country?

June 6, 1944

The Allied landing began in Normandy at midnight, with thousands of airplanes filling the skies. They met neither antiaircraft fire nor German planes. Four thousand boats are advancing behind smoke barriers, in spite of the presence of high-speed gunboats. There is talk of bombings carried out by waves of 10,000 planes dropping 10,000 tons of bombs. The landing took place at 7 A.M. on the left bank of an estuary of the Seine, between Villers-sur-Mer and Carentan. They have moved several miles inland. There is fighting around Caen. That they were able to take the Germans by surprise has been attributed to the effectiveness of previous bombing runs that destroyed communications throughout the coastal zone.

June 8, 1944

Intense battles continue to be waged south of Bayeux and on the outskirts of Caen. American reinforcements have been sent to the area around Carentan. The fighting seems to have been limited to the German troops already in the area and the Allies who landed the first day. Neither German reserves nor the greater part of the landing forces have yet to be engaged. The Germans are expecting a larger-scale landing elsewhere. After four days of combat, the Anglo-Saxons have not been thrown back into the sea. In fact, they have managed to make significant progress inland.

June 11, 1944

The Americans have made great advances in the Cotentin peninsula. British columns are moving beyond Bayeux onto Caen. Other British units have joined up in the vicinity of Carentan with the paratroopers who landed on the peninsula.

The Allies have made a major push north in Italy, halfway to Florence. And they have sealed the Moroccan border facing Spain. In anticipation of a massive landing in the Gulf of Genoa?

There has been considerable British and American news coverage describing the joy and the emotion in the areas that have been liberated. There was a huge demonstration in Bayeux, in spite of the fact that the Germans were still close by. People put on tricolored armbands with the Cross of Lorraine and shouted de Gaulle's name.

In an interviewed with F.I.,[20] de Gaulle strenuously objected to Eisenhower's statement denying his representatives the right to govern the liberated parts of France. It is a violation of French sovereignty, de Gaulle said; the people have already spoken.

It has been raining outside, but oh, the joy in our souls!

June 13, 1944

10:30 A.M. The alert sounded. Bombers and fighters flew over the mountains, some on to Munich, others toward Innsbruck. ... More women and children about to be killed. Another alert sounded at 10:30 at night. We watched them as they flew over the "castle" and then again on their way back around 3 A.M.

June 23, 1944

According to Sottens, the Russians have launched their offensive.

Spoke with La Roque, who told me that at the time of his lawsuit with Tardieu, his former commanders, Pétain and Weygand—who is currently imprisoned with us here—pretended not even to know him, the same Weygand who used to have lunch at the home of Pozzo di Borgo.[21] When the Armistice was signed, La Roque was at odds with the Marshal. He said

20. L'Agence Française Indépendante

21. Pozzo di Borgo, rich Corsican landowner. He and General Duseigneur founded the Union des Comités d'Action d'Extrême Droite. His resignation from the executive committee of the Croix de Feu caused considerable fuss. He was closely aligned with François Coty.

he suffered more under the Vichy government than he did with the Popular Front.

June 25, 1944

The sun has finally come out again.

Bernanos has addressed a message to the "people of France," just a simple little message to the entire nation. Is there anyone these days who isn't addressing messages to "the people of France"? This one is solemn and as vague as they come: spiritual values … economic injustice … noble Normandy. A slew of stock images squeezed into a few lines. The unbelievable conceit of all these expatriates in America and elsewhere.

Fortunately, the events actually unfolding are far more palatable. Saw a review of the British press and articles from the *Times* and the *Manchester Guardian*. Bands of patriots in Occupied France, and in particular in Normandy, are risking their lives attacking the Germans. Resistance groups have been paralyzing the movement of their armored divisions. Many of their members had been imprisoned during the Occupation; and there were others who were executed. Read an excellent article in the *Sunday Times* about the simple and prideful dignity with which French patriots welcomed their liberators. Their war correspondent wrote that "there were no hysterical scenes. Standing before the ruins of their homes, the people were calm and proud. They talked with the Canadians and the British and expressed their admiration for England, for having held out in 1940. The British, they said, had been saved by the Channel, for they were not armed or ready to fight. Then Hitler got the insane idea of invading Russia." This article has led to a series of others in which people admit to having underestimated the French. Have the Anglo-Saxons finally begun to see things clearly? They still have to explain where their Air Force was during the Battle of France.

June 28, 1944

Philippe Henriot was assassinated by men pretending to be militiamen come to protect him. He was killed in his bedroom, with his wife looking on. Laval made a speech about it and Pétain sent his widow a letter, all of four lines long. Pétain hasn't said a single word implying that he and Henriot were in any way aligned, although Henriot was his Minister of Information. The man's ego is monstrous, politically as well as personally. It wouldn't surprise me if he were busy cutting a deal with the Americans.

July 9, 1944

A milestone would appear to have been reached with today's events. The Russians are advancing on eastern Prussia and Poland. The push stretches over a front three hundred miles long.

In Italy, several miles outside of Ancona and Livorno, the Allied advance has intensified.

In Normandy, they have taken Caen.

It would appear that the Germans waited too long to cut loose and evacuate some of the territory they occupied. They are suffering today from an inferiority of the worst kind, one that will cost them the war: inferior numbers of men.

In Normandy, it was inevitable that the Allied advance would stall, given the hedgerows, the marshy terrain, and the sunken lanes. This is a war for infantrymen, and the Germans have had much more practice at it.

I had thought the Allied landing in the Cotentin was only a first phase designed as a cover for the real landing: in Flanders or the Gulf of Genoa, or both.

July 14, 1944

Another July 14 in captivity, the most painful of them all, when I consider all the tragedies that have befallen my country. There's something terribly oppressive in the silence of these mountains, in this peacefulness, in the solitude. It has been a day spent in despondency.

This evening, I learned that Mandel had been assassinated. The German government had handed him over to the French, probably to be held as a hostage following the assassination of Henriot. According to Vichy, he was killed during an escape attempt contrived by "resistance fighters" as he was being transferred to some prison. Memories of Mandel have been racing through my mind. He was present throughout my political career.

While in Morocco, both of us tried to win General Noguès over to the side of the Resistance; and both of us tried, in vain, to reach London. We were imprisoned together and brought to Germany together.

July 15, 1944

Jean Oberlé gave a thoroughly mediocre funeral oration for Mandel on British radio; Monte Carlo radio has been spewing forth vile remarks about him. His assassination hasn't given rise to a single statement of protest, neither by the United Nations[22] nor in any of the capitals of the nations allied in the fight against Nazism, although Nazism is what killed Mandel. During the last war, he was Clemenceau's secretary, and he adored the man. He even took a bust of Clemenceau with him when he went to prison. I can hear a dispute going on between the son of the "Tiger" himself and Jouhaux. Michel Clemenceau is a horse's ass; there's just no way around that. I am more and more struck by how narrow-minded he is and by his inability to see that there's anything in this world other than himself.

René Payot has moved his chatter over to Swiss radio. He is now as pronounced a Gaullist as he was a Pétainist. He spoke of the "disaster in the East"—those were the words he actually used.

Von Rundstedt has given up his command for reasons of health. Actually, there was a difference of opinion: Rommel wanted to attack the Anglo-Saxons as soon as they landed and push them back into the sea; Rundstedt wanted to wait until they had moved further inland. His error has proven fatal. Almost the entire German High Command has been replaced.

July 17, 1944

According to an SS who was there, yesterday's air raid in Munich was carried out by several hundred planes. It was the fourth one over the last five days. The city is in flames. The losses were even more horrible than they

22. The twenty-six signatory states, which in their Declaration of January 1, 1942, resolved not to make peace separately and to form an international organization to replace the League of Nations.

might have been, and more cruel, because the evacuation of children had just begun when the bombers appeared in the sky. It was a dreadful spectacle.

In eastern Germany, the population has begun fleeing before the oncoming Russians, who are only fifteen miles away. Great numbers of Germans are making their way out of the Baltic States.

July 18, 1944

The Captain went to Munich to attend funeral services for his brother. The city had been devastated; there were no buses and no cars. He had walked through the debris for two hours to get to the improvised morgue where his brother's remains lay when more bombs fell and razed it to the ground, with all the dead bodies pulverized in the explosions. No services were held. He returned to Itter totally demoralized.

Mandel was handed over to Vichy when the Resistance kidnapped Chevalier, a former Minister and Dean of the Humanities division of the University of Grenoble. The man was half senile, but Pétain was very attached to him, which is why they offered Mandel as a hostage.

Jouhaux pointed out to me that Renan and Nietzsche, starting from totally opposite points of view, both concluded that the creation of a unified Europe was a necessity. We would be wise to get at it soon, or there will be nothing left of it: no cities, no industry, no universities, no museums. Even as we spoke, the sky above us filled with hundreds of American bombers and fighters.

After the Allies took Ancona and Livorno, General Kesselring, the Commander of the German forces, was awarded "oak leaves." Apparently, every army has its strange customs. The Germans are now in serious trouble in the Baltic, and eastern Prussia is threatened with imminent invasion. They have made the same mistake Napoleon made when he failed to pull out of Spain before heading down the road to Moscow. How could Germany have expected to prevail on so many different fronts?

July 21, 1944

It has been a beautiful, sunny day. After a while, the contrast becomes oppressive, but what can be done about it?

Last night, there was a dynamite attack on Hitler's headquarters. A bomb went off about six feet away from him. He escaped with just a few bruises, although several members of the High Command were wounded. He went right back to work and met with Mussolini. A little later, Göring arrived. The news has had a major effect on the prisoners in Itter, both the men and the women, but it's impossible to discern any sign of it on their faces. Living in the camps has taught them to say nothing and remain impassive. Some of them have been tortured.

A. described various forms of torture: a pail clamped over a prisoner's head and pounded with a hammer, the strappado, as many as three days straight without bread or water, slow death by starvation and exhaustion, crematoriums, gas chambers. I would never have believed that there could be such abominations in Europe. Centuries of effort and progress have been wiped out. We've gone back to the Inquisition and the Wars of Religion.

Hitler made a statement following yesterday's failed attack on his life. It involved, he said, "a small clique of unhappy Generals." The architect would appear to have been General Von Beck, who has apparently been executed. Göring made a statement, too. As for Goebbels, he feels it was the work of the Intelligence Service. A report from the DNB lists the names of the Generals who were seriously wounded and those who were wounded only slightly. It was followed by a long article on the men really responsible for the attack: the various Secret Services, Roosevelt, and his two accomplices, Churchill and Stalin. "That they are forced to resort to murder is proof that they are powerless militarily." No mention in this long article of the Generals Hitler and Göring denounced, neither Von Beck nor the others.

The importance of this plot is obvious, and the timing highly significant. These were, moreover, Generals who had been decorated by Hitler himself, some of whom had distinguished themselves during the war. Himmler, the head of the domestic forces, has ordered Germans to shoot any suspect resisting arrest or attempting to flee.

July 30, 1944

The Russian Supreme High Command is actually concentrating the greatest part of its resources, not in those areas that protrude into eastern Prussia, but in Poland, along a front stretching 120 miles from Brest Litovsk to Bomberg. In Grodno and Hannas, they are holding their positions without attempting a breakthrough. The Russians intend to cross the Vistula and attack Warsaw. Their aim is to:

1. Cut off the German retreat in the Baltic states;
2. Enter eastern Prussia;
3. Outflank Warsaw;
4. Cross the Carpathians and move into Slovakia.

The *maquis* have clearly been effective in disrupting German operations behind the lines in France. De Gaulle's efforts and those of the Resistance have been far from futile. Dissension remains, however, this time between the Communist *maquis* and the others, and for the British these divisions are a matter of concern.

August 3, 1944

At 8 P.M. a glowing Jouhaux came and announced the capture of Rennes and Dinan. Is there another Westphalia Treaty in the making, with Stalin taking the place of Louis XIV? Or will there be a democratic settlement that will really bring us peace?

The breakup of the German states is a very real possibility. Once the Prussian cement is gone, they might well revert to independent nations. Anything can happen as a result of or during the invasion of Germany. The opposite possibility can't be overlooked either: that of a German nation holding to its unity and "going Bolshevik" to preserve it.

Jouhaux continues to emphasize the overriding importance of economic issues in the postwar period. I tend to attach greater significance to psychological elements, like the sense and spirit of nationalism and, above all, the Soviet Union's desire to exert a preponderant influence over Central Europe.

The Americans have taken Rennes, where the German garrison surrendered. In spite of their lack of experience, the Americans have made their landing a success, but they won't be able to organize a second one in Flanders, as I had hoped. It hardly came as a surprise that Turkey has broken off diplomatic and economic relations with Germany.

In the "castle," anger and dismay are rife among the SS, while the deportees are experiencing a secret joy.

August 6, 1944

There was just one sunny spell throughout the entire gloomy day, a break in the cloud-filled sky. But Granger told me that the Americans are fighting just outside of Brest and that they have reached the Loire.

La Roque told Reynaud that he has learned from a very reliable source that the Germans have decided that whatever happens, neither Reynaud, Weygand, nor I is to be harmed. I find it all quite amusing. How people reveal their true selves in times like these! To my mind, given the cataclysm that is now imminent, I can't imagine how our lives could be spared. But what does that matter, if Nazism is destroyed.

August 15, 1944

The Anglo-Saxons landed between Toulon and Cannes this morning.

August 19, 1944

The German Army has met disaster in Normandy, as a result of the overwhelming superiority of Allied air power. This is precisely the reverse of the situation in the spring of 1940. Similar causes have produced similar effects.

The German Seventh Army is almost entirely encircled in a pocket around Falaise. They are trying to break out.

The coastal fortifications in Provence were no more successful at stopping the Allies than the Atlantic Wall.

De Lattre de Tassigny is making his way up the Rhone Valley. Little by little, Marseilles, Toulon, and Hyères have been turned and outflanked.

August 20, 1944

It has been a wonderful sun-filled day, but in Paris patriots are battling with the Germans. Images flash through my mind of the Paris I saw on March 31, the skeptical Paris just before the war, and the working-class Paris, once so antimilitaristic. So many strangely different looks in the space of a few years, each of which has proven equivalent to centuries.

August 21, 1944

In the Vaucluse, Perthuis has been liberated.

The Resistance has taken control of Vichy; I heard it on the radio. Their playing the "Marche Lorraine" is a little much. There was a speech on the peacetime organization of France. It sounded like Cassin's[23] voice. Laval's Cabinet is apparently in Belfort. There hasn't been a word about Pétain. What a way to end a life.

August 22, 1944

The noose around Paris is tightening. The Allies have taken 50,000 prisoners in Normandy and 15,000 in Provence. What would happen if the Allies were to mount a drive on France's eastern border?

Toulon, Hyères, Bandol, and La Ciotat—towns that bring back memories of various periods of my life—have all been liberated.

Bouisson[24] was taken prisoner by the Resistance forces in his villa in Saint-Raphaël. The radio broadcast claimed that he had confessed to receiving 30,000 francs a month from the Germans. How strangely naïve of him, and how implausible it seems for a man as cynical as he. His role in gross cases of corruption did terrible damage, as did the petty insolence he displayed as President of the Chamber of Deputies and his obsequiousness

23. René Cassin (1887–1976) joined de Gaulle at the time of the Armistice. He was a member of the Consultative Assembly in Algiers in 1944.

24. Fernand Bouisson, industrialist, Socialist Deputy, and President of the Chamber of Deputies from 1927 to 1935. He was Prime Minister for seven days in 1935. He sided with Marshal Pétain in June 1940 and voted in favor of granting him plenary powers.

toward those who held power. Few men have done as much as he and Tardieu (both of whom were seconded by Laval) to bring about the decline and discredit of parliamentary government. He was very close to Laval and played a thoroughly despicable role at the National Assembly in Vichy. "I want the names of everyone who has abstained to be published in the *Journal officiel,*" he is reported to have said. What surprises me most is that he decided to wait out the storm in Saint-Raphaël. What delusions could he have had about the hatred the Communists have for him, not to mention the contempt he has inspired in every loyal patriot for so long now?

August 23, 1944

Paris has been liberated after three days of street fighting led by the French Forces of the Interior. Ordinary policemen have taken over the Prefecture. Jouhaux claims the Commune is having its revenge, and there's some truth in that. This will go down as one of the great dates in French history.

August 25, 1944

Leclerc's division has marched into Paris.

August 26, 1944

Cavaillon, Avignon, Carpentras, and Orange have been liberated; I have put on my Sunday clothes. De Gaulle gave an excellent speech.

August 29, 1944

Following the arrests of Taittinger and Paris's city councilmen, Sacha Guitry, Stéphane Lauzanne, and Carcopino are now behind bars as well.

September 1, 1944

Five years from the day the Germans marched on Poland. In spite of the appeals being made by the insurgent Polish forces in Warsaw and the Poles now in England, the Russians have done nothing to supply them with weapons, ammunition, or food, although they are just a few miles away.

For me, today marks the anniversary of Verdun. My thoughts go back to the fighting in 1916. In Verdun, even though we were pounded by the bombings, we were able to crawl out of our holes and repel their attacks. What a monstrous bloodbath it was.

September 3, 1944

Five years to the day I declared war on Germany. Cause for meditation.

September 4, 1944

At 8 A.M. Gamelin came into my room to bring me news of the American advance, news I had already heard the night before. Then he switched to the arrests and shouted, "What they're doing there is stupid because we are the ones who are going to pay for it." Now there is a cry straight from the heart!

The Germans won't be able to hold out more than a few weeks longer. They have turned to challenge the Allies too late, like a boar who has already lost too much blood. Which means that the second half of the great human tragedy is about to get under way. Who will win out? The authoritarian approach to organizing a society, Moloch's cruel and unfeeling new State, or men who are free but disciplined? We're into one more round of Athens versus Sparta, Rome versus Carthage, the great confrontation that has taken on a look of the eternal. Will we see an authoritarian state ruling over enslaved men or a land of the free? The latter is worth dying for.

September 5, 1944

Rumor has it that the Nazi leaders have taken refuge in Madrid.

September 6, 1944

Now it's de Gaulle who is being compared to Joan of Arc on every radio station. Not a word about Pétain. There are more and more arrests. Maurras is behind bars.

September 15, 1944

The Russians have finally decided to help the Warsaw insurgents.

Brazzaville radio has been abject in commenting on Maurras's arrest. They had the nerve to say that the Third Republic should have outlawed L'Action Française!

A warrant has been issued for Pétain's arrest.

September 17, 1944

London is celebrating the fourth anniversary of the RAF's victory over the Luftwaffe. In 1939, I thought that the British Air Force and, above all, their fighters were very powerful. But what does one make of Vuillemin's extraordinary inability to do anything during the Battle of France?

September 18, 1944

Baudouin (enthroned by Reynaud) played a decisive role in the surrender in Bordeaux; they were all at his house when the decision was first made. He betrayed his own Prime Minister in the very midst of the fighting; he glorified Pétain on the radio, and Pétain kept him on as Minister, relieving him simply of his position as Chief Executive Officer of the Indochina Bank. It's interesting to compare his fate with that of Carcopino, who has been arrested.

September 19, 1944

Some people in Itter would like to see a new Treaty of Westphalia, but a pact like that could work only if we went back to the demographics of the time, when France had the largest population of any country in Europe, twice that of Germany. It's absurd to imagine France annexing the Saar Valley and the left bank of the Rhine. Today, there is a strong sense of national unity in Germany. Moreover, a Germany broken up into small pieces would run the risk of being sovietized. We would see Russia's domination spread throughout Europe. Stalin would succeed where Hitler has failed. A federated German nation is not inconceivable.

September 24, 1944

Le Roy Ladurie and Worms[25] have been arrested. Now we have reached the inner circle of plotters. I think that prior to the war, out of their hatred or fear of communism—which, as of late 1938, no longer posed any sort of threat at all—these two men were laying the political groundwork within France for an alliance with Germany. They wanted to install a regime grounded in Nazism. And of course they were prepared to leave Germany free to reign over Central and Eastern Europe. I am convinced that their group—Le Roy Ladurie, Worms, Lémery, Alibert, Brécard, Loustanau-Lacau, which is to say Pétain, and some adviser from a line of Protestant emigrants with a French-sounding name that I can't remember—was working in close contact with the German Embassy. The war offered them a magnificent opportunity, "a divine surprise." Pétain wanted an armistice immediately, as early as May 19, and Weygand by May 25. The Worms group had links with the Synarchie—Bouthillier, Devaux,[26] Leca,[27] and Baudouin—as well as with people in Reynaud's entourage, who trusted them. These weren't traitors in the ordinary, traditional sense, but rather men eager to accept defeat. Emigrés in their own land.

Needless to say, Dormoy and after him Sarraut knew nothing and did nothing about any of this. In the time since the end of the other war, with the sole exception of Schrameck,[28] France has never had a real Minister of the Interior.

25. Hippolyte Worms, Director of the Worms conglomerate: banking, munitions, and brokerage. He was a Pétainist in Vichy, a collaborator in Paris, and a Gaullist in London.

26. Gilbert Devaux, Finance Inspector and Assistant Director of Public Accounting. He was Paul Reynaud's Deputy Chief of Staff.

27. Dominique Leca, Finance Inspector. He was twice Reynaud's Chief of Staff, first in the Finance Ministry (1938), then when Reynaud became Prime Minister.

28. Abraham Schrameck, Senator and Minister, first of Justice and later of the Interior (1925). When Ernest Berger was killed, Schrameck began legal proceedings against Charles Maurras, who had made death threats against Berger. In Vichy, in 1940, Schrameck voted in favor of granting Pétain plenary powers.

September 25, 1944

For the last few days, snow has begun covering the top half of the mountains. The cows have moved back down from the elevated pastures to the plains. I now hear cow bells jangling in the night. It makes me think I am back in Provence.

In Holland, the Germans have launched a counterattack against a British airborne division in Arnhem. The British have put up stubborn resistance west of the Rhine, between Aix and Cologne, and along the Moselle, in the gap at Belfort.

Fierce fighting continues in Warsaw.

September 29, 1944

Churchill made an important speech in the House of Commons: "I have not forgotten that the promise of aid that Britain and America made to France in 1919, which led France to give up its demand for a border on the Rhine, was not ratified by the American Senate, and that peace failed as a result. I know that France, with her small and declining population, stood across from a powerful neighbor.

"In the course of the twenty years that followed the first war, my opinion regarding the vital necessity of maintaining the alliance that unites France and England never wavered."

October 2, 1944

Resistance in Warsaw has ceased. The city is being evacuated. Having been abandoned by the Russians and having had terrible difficulty establishing links with the British, the decimated insurgent groups have given up the fight. The repercussions felt in the United States and Britain will be painful. General Bor has been taken prisoner.

October 7, 1944

I watched the SS go rushing about the "castle." Red flares went off. It was all either preparation to ward off a commando raid or a positioning exercise in anticipation of an attack from the village or from down in the valley.

The maneuvers lasted two hours, and enlisted men and officers alike went through them in dead seriousness.

Peyrouton, Flandin, and Bergeret have been indicted for treason.

October 9, 1944

The Dumbarton Oaks conference has ended with the creation of an organization for international security: the United Nations. It will feature a Security Council with five permanent members, one of which will be France. Resolutions will require a two-thirds majority. The organization will have at its command a military air force as well as a sort of council made up of the head military leaders of various nations. ... In short, after thirty years of mistakes and debates and after another world war, the ideas Léon Bourgeois promoted as France's representative in 1918 have finally won out. If the Anglo-Saxons had adopted them in 1919, the fate of the world would not have been the same.

The present war marks the end of a period of history that began in 1792—the era of independent nations. Nations will now have to be integrated into federations and, above all, vast economic systems. The well-being of the masses will have to be assured. The partitioning of Germany, which certain Britons and Americans have been talking about, is an absurd proposition. Once the war is over, the Anglo-Saxons will be anxious to demobilize. England has already called back its miners and many of the workers in its major industries. We can't be drawn into playing the role of world gendarmes.

October 11, 1944

In a recent speech, Goebbels was remarkably effective in turning to his advantage various articles and statements calling for the Allies to flatten Germany, apportion its territory, occupy it up to the Elbe in the East and the Rhine in the West, and deport millions of its workers.

I have seen a great many trains go by the last few days, but they are often pulled by steam-powered locomotives.

October 14, 1944

In a radio broadcast, de Gaulle hammered away at the same themes we heard in Nancy, Lille, and Rouen. He appealed to everyone to keep working; the war isn't over yet. He appealed to people's sense of discipline. He was trying to reach the more committed members of the Resistance and above all obtain the support of people in the middle. The truth is that a choice will have to be made between furthering the cause of a social revolution or putting an end to it. Probably the only thing de Gaulle can do right now is evade the issue.

For example, with regard to the way the various parties will be represented in a broadened Consultative Assembly, there is talk of using a sort of proportional system: seven Communists, fifteen Socialists, twenty-three Radicals and Christian Democrats. Why the strange coupling of Radicals and Christian Democrats? And why weren't seats allotted to every Member of Parliament who voted against Pétain or abstained? This all smells of backroom deals, and history shows that machinations of this kind have a short life span. Just look at the *Directoire.*

As for the reality of our situation here, it was brought home to us by the Captain. He told us that any prisoner attempting to escape during an air raid would be shot.

October 17, 1944

Twenty-four new SS and three NCOs showed up, carrying machine guns and ammunition. They dug trenches around the "castle" and positioned their weapons. Then they established visual communications with the garrison in Wörgl, about two or three miles from here as the crow flies, where an SS battalion is stationed. Everything was done with speed and discipline. Do they fear an Anglo-Saxon commando raid or an insurrection from the Tirol?

In this autumn season, there remains the contrast with the beauty of nature: the gold of the maple trees and the birches amid the darker colors of the pines, all of it enveloped in a light mist. There is a magnificent maple tree just beneath my window. The snow has begun to cover the lower parts of the mountains. Soon, it will blanket the "castle" and its courtyards. Another winter to be spent here.

October 19, 1944

The trade union convention and the speeches made by Morgenthau and Cripps have strengthened the Nazis' grip on their people and firmed the nation's resolve. They have got the Germans convinced that their cities will all be destroyed and that they're going to be deported. Yet Stalin handled Romania and Bulgaria so skillfully.

October 20, 1944

The Captain got drunk tonight. He threatened the Czech cook, telling him that he'd be the first to get it and that we'd be next in line. Instead of a cooked meal, he made him serve us tiny bits of meat and leeks, a portion of rubbery paté, and a few dried-out potatoes.

October 21, 1944

It has been reported that on his trip to Moscow, Churchill agreed that henceforth the Soviet Union would control certain areas once under French influence: Romania, Greece, Poland, Yugoslavia, etc. This agreement has to be seen in the light of the one Churchill worked out with Belgium and Holland.

October 22, 1944

A delegation including Vincent Auriol went to see Jeanneney to protest the highly unusual methods he had used to exclude from the Consultative Assembly certain Members of Parliament who had voted against Pétain in Vichy. I'd be interested to hear what Jeanneney had to say, he *not* being one of those who voted against Pétain.

October 25, 1944

De Gaulle has been complaining in the Paris press that the Allies have failed to give the French the amounts and kinds of weapons they need to wipe out the remaining pockets of German resistance. He is right. The situation is paradoxical. There are still 60,000 Germans in Lorient, La Pallice, and Le Verdon.

The Cabinet has decided to grant Algerians the same rights enjoyed by French citizens living in Algeria. That reminds me of Proudhon's well-known comments from 1848 about according universal suffrage to Frenchmen. There are 900,000 French citizens and 7 million native Algerians. Of course, the French there have always opposed reforms every step of the way. These are just stalling measures, not real progress.

October 27, 1944

All around me, I have been watching the SS hurriedly work to reinforce their defenses, setting up machine gun nests and felling trees to block the routes leading up to the "castle." There have been practice alerts. The Captain informed us that they would be using two different alarms: one to signal aerial bombings—in which case it would be up to us to decide whether to take shelter in the cellars, with the understanding that if we didn't, it would be at our own risk—and another to signal a ground attack—in which case we could either go down to the cellars of our own accord or be taken there by force.

October 28, 1944

Roosevelt has announced a major naval victory and a successful landing in the Philippines. A few days ago, Churchill decided to send part of the British fleet to operate in conjunction with the United States in the Pacific, against Japan. Shows the importance of Asia. De Gaulle has issued an order for the creation of a volunteer force for the liberation of Indochina.

November 2, 1944

All Souls' Day. Soon I too will be in Père Lachaise, resting in peace. The Captain has taken away our radio to stop us from listening to short wave broadcasts. Now we'll only be able to get German stations.

November 5, 1944

Reynaud was visited by the fat German girl who used to be his reader. They had lunch together with Mlle Mabire, who was not entirely thrilled about it. Later, we watched them stroll by: Reynaud, with a woman on each arm, and Gamelin solemnly bringing up the rear, as the Germans looked on and chuckled. They repeated their laughable performance later in the afternoon.

November 7, 1944

Gertrude is a prisoner working in the "castle." She has just received a letter from her lawyer informing her of her release, scheduled for mid-November. The poor girl is delighted, but she is sensitive enough to hide it so as not to depress those around her who haven't been so fortunate. Gertrude hopes to go back to Leipzig and move as close to Weimar as she can, to be near her French boyfriend, who is a prisoner there.

The Germans continue to stage military operations to defend the "castle." Now they are busy fighting off paratroopers camouflaged with tree branches, sneaking in through the ravines.

November 10, 1944

Churchill and Eden continue to repeat mechanically their pat phrase demanding Germany's unconditional surrender. Yet even now the Allies are giving refuge to Germans who used to run the country; these men could govern the country again. In his dealings with Finland, Romania, and Bulgaria, Stalin gave them an expert lesson in subtle diplomacy—and what a lesson it was! Are we witnessing the intellectual decline of Britain's ruling class and the Foreign Office?

November 21, 1944

A major French victory: The French have reached the Rhine. Eisenhower has sent congratulatory telegrams. The Americans have broken through twenty-five miles of the Siegfried Line in an area around Cologne. Gertrude, who is still here, said to me, "It is terrible to find yourself rejoicing over the misfortunes of your own country."

November 23, 1944

The French have entered Strasbourg.

November 28, 1944

De Gaulle has arrived in Moscow with Bidault and Palewski. He has begun talks on a Franco-Soviet pact and participated in others dealing with the breakup of Germany. He is distancing himself from the British.

November 29, 1944

I dreamed a great deal about my son Jean last night.

There has been street fighting in Brussels. The Communists have been demonstrating against Pierlot, who has demanded that they turn in their weapons.

December 4, 1944

According to Paris Radio, Germany, acting through Switzerland, informed the French government that the lives of French hostages held in Germany would be directly linked to the fate of the collaborators in France.

The Russians have reached Lake Balaton.

December 6, 1944

Last night, Churchill spoke to the House of Commons about the events unfolding in Greece. The Communists have taken a number of steps designed to bring them to power: organizing general strikes, attacking and taking over police stations, preventing trucks and boats from unloading food supplies, and so on. Churchill declared that Greece must move forward with a general election under fair conditions, and that until such time, Britain would unflinchingly assume the burden of maintaining stability. He added, "Left-wing elements and the Communists are responsible for the bloodlettings."

December 8, 1944

Following Churchill's speech on the events in Greece, his government was forced to call a vote of confidence. He won out, with 270 in favor and 30 opposed, but the majority of the Labor Party members abstained, which is a good indication of the extent to which the policy of improved relations and cooperation with Moscow has gained in popularity.

As for the Americans, they have ruled out any form of intervention in the internal affairs of Greece.

December 11, 1944

A moving ceremony, chaired by Joliot-Curie, was held at the Sorbonne to commemorate the role played by intellectuals who had given their lives. The American press, above all the *New York Times*, has been just as enthusiastic as yesterday's *Times* over the Franco-Soviet military alliance and the mutual aid agreements that have just been signed. They see them as a complement to the pact between Britain and the Soviet Union—a guarantee against future German acts of aggression that is in perfect harmony with the goals of a broader, international peace organization.

Whatever the case, there has been a change in the Anglo-Saxon attitude toward France, so it's just as well. Now they will probably indulge us a little more when we ask for ships, tools, and supplies. I read an excerpt from an article in which Lippmann, who had just returned from Europe, paid homage to the people of France. The fellow has improved a little. Others will begin changing their tune as well. No one is saying what General Smuts said a few years ago, that France was a second-rate nation with no influence. We have once again become, in Churchill words, "one of the world's leading powers."

Still, it's Greece that has really been drawing my attention. The Communists have taken over the greater part of Athens and said that they will not lay down their arms until Papandreou resigns. There is talk of 10,000 armed Communists in Athens.

At the Labor Party convention, Bevin staunchly defended Churchill's policies. "You don't govern with sentiment." They deem the situation in Greece intolerable. The Communists signed an agreement, then went back on it. The leadership of a country cannot be left in the hands of a bunch of armed men. Greece is effectively our first test.

December 14, 1944

On his return from Europe, Walter Lippmann wrote a long article in New York sharply criticizing Churchill's policies with regard to Greece and Belgium. As is his wont, he also offered a little instructive advice to Europeans and every government around. I find his tone highly objectionable. He added, "The governments in power in 1939 failed in their duty to defend the independence of nations." Another prime example of American impertinence. Why didn't the Americans intervene in September 1939 or June 1940 instead of waiting to be attacked by the Japanese? Of course, at the time, isolationism was a virtue. Actually, elections should have been held immediately in every liberated country. Lippmann is sarcastic in belittling the growing influence of communism throughout Europe. A few months from now, he will be able to measure the validity of the theories he expressed, with his usual conceit, in 1943. He still hasn't understood that at this very moment a powerful movement is at work, drawing Europe toward communism.

December 17, 1944

The terms of the Franco-Soviet pact have been made public. There is the standard phrasing one finds in all mutual aid pacts, but it also includes a twenty-year military alliance, similar to the one with Great Britain. They have agreed to counter any German attempt to extract revenge, or even any semblance of such an attempt, which is to say that they reserve the right to intervene in the makeup of future German governments. So as to avoid the appearance of a bilateral treaty, they have chosen their words carefully and made constant reference to the United Nations. Even so, there is also an unusual clause, the fifth or sixth one, that prohibits both countries from entering alliances formed against either of them. That can hardly benefit anyone other than the Russians. What kind of coalition could conceivably threaten them in the future, and for what reason? They must have in mind a coalition including Britain or the United States, or even both of them, that might be formed in the event of some serious conflict in Asia. Russia can hardly be considered vulnerable other than from within Europe, where an Anglo-German-French coalition could pose a serious threat. Is this clause the work of a highly cautious man or is it an indication of Russia's political designs over China? Doesn't the wording suggest that there are secret appendixes? It certainly seems strange that so brief a document required de Gaulle to spend all that time in Moscow, engaged in lengthy negotiations. There are probably secret agreements about the Rhineland, the Saar Valley, eastern Prussia, Poland, and perhaps the Dardanelles and the Balkans.

I have just this moment heard that the Germans have broken through the Allied lines south of Aix-la-Chapelle and driven fifteen miles forward, in a wedge twenty miles wide. They have moved into Belgium and Luxembourg. There were violent air battles, in which they are reported to have lost 130 planes.

December 19, 1944

The Germans continue to drive forward. They have moved beyond Stablot in Belgium, which represents an advance of twenty miles, and are supposed to be using new weapons. General de Lattre gave an eloquent speech about the French Army retaking Alsace—a sober, moving speech, elegant in its very simplicity.

Stettinius, the American Secretary of State, has issued a statement about Poland that is pathetically hypocritical. He claimed that the United States never guaranteed any European country's borders. According to him, we would do better to put these matters off until after the war, when they can be taken up in the United Nations. Yet he knows well that Russia has just recognized the Lublin Committee as Poland's sole representative.

In Teheran in 1942, did the British reach agreement with Stalin over Russia's new western borders? In all events, that is what Molotov now claims. The Polish Cabinet in London has refused to enter into any form of agreement with the Lublin Committee.

December 20, 1944

The Senate met in Paris and approved the Franco-Soviet pact by unanimous vote. There was a lot of talk and a lot of enthusiasm, but few direct references to the document itself. As I suspected, the important part is the one that did not appear in the Moscow texts: the agreement over the partitioning of Germany.

Russia's hold will stretch over Central Europe and the Balkans—it will be the greatest sphere of influence on the European continent. Populations will be shifted about as they were in the days of the Pharaohs.

The German offensive that began six days ago into Belgium and Holland has been stopped by the Americans, north and south. Eisenhower's objective: to transform the German offensive into a nightmarish defeat.

At the Radical-Socialist convention, Chautemps, Bonnet, Palmade, and Mistler were excluded from the party.

December 24, 1944

Christmas Eve. Just as they did last week, squadrons of bombers continue making their way to Innsbruck and Munich. There isn't a cloud in the sky.

Several speeches were given tonight, notably one by Roosevelt, but it was the Pope's address to the College of Cardinals that really caught my attention. The text of the speech was given on Swiss radio. The Pope:

1. Offered praise for true democracies but said there were countries whose system of government, although claiming to be democratic, was totally alien to democracy;
2. Condemned dictatorships;
3. Said that while armies were carrying out their work of destruction, men were joining together to lay the foundations for a future peace. He paid homage to the efforts of these men;
4. Recognized that the peace settlement to come would necessarily include war reparations, but said it must not lead to the permanent enslavement of the vanquished peoples, which would run contrary to our efforts to bring justice to the entire world;
5. Recognized the legitimacy of the punishment to be meted out to individuals guilty of criminal acts, but said that there must not be wholesale condemnations of groups.

In its broadcast out of London, the BBC omitted the fourth point and the second part of the first one, in other words, all that might be construed as casting doubt on the democratic nature of the Soviet regime. Who would have believed that the Pope would one day be censored by the BBC?

December 25, 1944

It now appears that the Americans have completely halted the German offensive in the West. I note, however, that after four years of war, and although opposed by an Army of overwhelming superiority, supplied with great amounts of equipment, tanks, and planes, the Germans were nonetheless able to unleash a surprise attack of unexpected violence, over particularly difficult terrain in the Eifel region, and drive the Allies back forty miles in just a few days. The analogy to be drawn with Sedan is obvious. This should put a clamp on the criticism that has been lodged against the French Army, criticism which was particularly bitter in American newspapers under Walter Lippmann's byline.

December 29, 1944

Churchill and Eden have returned. They are going to ask the King of Greece to accept Papandreou's resignation and the institution of an Archbishop-led Regency.

1945

January 2, 1945

We have had even heavier snowfalls; twenty inches of snow blanket the courtyard. A few groups of SS have gone about cutting a narrow path through it, while others have been clearing off the roofs that might otherwise collapse under the weight, all of it accompanied by playful laughter and shouting and horseplay as old as time itself. The sky is clear and the sun is shining on the mountaintops.

The lead-in to the speech was dramatic: All boys sixteen and seventeen years of age are now officially members of the Army; almost all of them enlisted voluntarily. The youth of Germany have long been prepared to make the supreme sacrifice, and now that time has come.

He began speaking. I could barely recognize his voice. It had once been so powerful, so modulated too, as it would alternate in throaty tones between moments of pathos and moments of irony, before culminating with a burst of triumphant fanfare; that forceful voice of his that from town to town, over a period of ten years, won over all of Germany. This evening, that voice revealed fatigue and deep concern. As I listened, I wondered whether it was really his.

He explained that he had not addressed the people of Germany since the attempt made on his life on July 20 because all his energies had been devoted to organizing the military campaign. "During this past summer, we altered the course of fate." He reminded his listeners of what he had said at the Reichstag on September 1, 1939: Germany will *not* be defeated. The Allies had predicted that the war would end this winter; they had even worked out details for the partitioning of Germany; that was because they don't know what Germans are made of. "We are prepared to make every effort necessary; we shall never surrender," he said, indulging in some predictions of his own. And as is the case with all oracles, this one invites comment, too. I actually do not believe that Hitler will ever surrender. He will either die leading his last remaining troops in battle or put an end to his own life. He won't bring dishonor on himself by taking flight, as William II did.

He went on to lash out at the Allies' tactics—the bombing of cities, the coldly conceived, premeditated massacre of women and children, intended to break down the morale of the country and its fighting men. He reviewed the casualty figures, and he could not hide the fact, he said, that they had made a powerful impact on him, too. But German industry is continually producing new weapons, he said. Their new fighter planes have firepower and fly at speeds heretofore unknown. Then he unleashed a resounding condemnation of the free enterprise system and glorified the new, egalitarian state that would demand sacrifices of the German people and necessitate further suffering. Finally he launched into his grand conclusion, but what a disappointment it was! Belief in miracles and faith in God Almighty, who would bring victory to "those who deserve it most" by virtue of the purity and dignity of their sentiments and their thoughts. The people of Germany will reshape the world. The speech lasted all of twenty-five minutes.

He concluded his program of operations for the military with a similar appeal to God Almighty: "We are fighting now for the very existence of the German people. The Jews and the plutocrats are seeking to wipe our country off the map, by reducing us to slaves and sending 15 to 20 million Germans to Siberia, and by making our western provinces part of France and our eastern provinces part of a sovietized Poland. Morgenthau, that Jew who is Roosevelt's Secretary of the Treasury, actually wants to destroy Germany's industry. ... Their monstrous plans stand as justification for everything I have done.

"The fighting will become more and more intense. The setbacks we have suffered are the result of a series of betrayals and the collapse of the Italian-Hungarian front on the Don in 1942. The July 20 attempt on my life marks a turning point. That conspiracy will be the last. There will never be another November 9. ... Our enemies would do well to understand that they will pay for every inch of German soil with torrents of blood. ... I have never been as confident as I am now." Then he threatened to annihilate anyone within Germany who attempted to weaken or undermine the magnificent resistance of the German people. He followed that once more by an appeal to divine Providence.

All of Germany was listening tonight—the soldiers on the front lines, the old men and the women in the ruins of their bombed-out cities, the peasants in their peaceful villages or in their isolated farmhouses. For six months they had been waiting—first in stunned impatience, then with a kind of anxiety—for word from the man who had so frequently brought them news of victories, those won in the fight against unemployment and the war on poverty, and those of the Reich's triumphant entrance into capital after capital of the nations of Europe.

Rumors had been spreading that Hitler was paralyzed or dead. He had to go on the air, but the voice that the people had been waiting to hear for so long had changed; it was almost a monotone. He brought them not one single reason to hope.

To be sure, the German Army will fight on heroically, as long as their leaders choose to lead them into battle. But on this the first night of the new year, are there not among them, and among the leaders of Germany's economy as well, some who are wondering whether the moment hasn't come for Germany to follow a different path, not the road to death and despair that Hitler has just laid out for them?

Before listening to Hitler's speech, I picked up some news items. A committee of Polish Communists, most of whom had been living in Moscow for quite a while and who had returned to Poland with the Soviet Army, has just set itself up in Lublin as the country's provisional government. A Polish newspaper printed in London, the organ of the Peasant Party, has protested both against Russia's annexation of Lvov, Poland's great industrial center, and the fact that armies of a foreign power have established a government without the Polish people having spoken. They called for a free and independent Poland. The Polish government-in-exile in London has also protested. The British, however, have remained silent, whereas France has gone as far as to assign this provisional government, if not an official Ambassador, an Observer, which amounts practically to the same thing. It has been the subject of scandal in many British newspapers, where de Gaulle and his government have come under sharp attack. The United States has not recognized the government in Lublin, but that has not kept the people in power there from routinely going about their work. After having expressed their gratitude to the Russians—which was only natural—and labeled the Polish émigrés in London Fascists—which was inevitable—they have begun dividing up large estates among poor peasant farmers—which is far more serious.

Saturday, January 6, 1945

Last night, I listened to the Swiss journalist René Payot's weekly program on political and military events. He spoke about France as if he held some veiled official capacity. Gamelin told me that in 1940 and later as well, *Le Journal de Genève* ran a number of Payot's articles on the military that, without ever naming Gamelin, were clearly indictments of him. Through mutual friends, Gamelin provided Payot with documents that proved that the figures he had been using were erroneous. Payot refused to give them credence, saying only that he had got *his* figures from General Weygand. Now he has a job as a Gaullist propagandist in French-speaking Switzerland.

Payot praised statements made by de Gaulle at a recent session of the Consultative Assembly. Another speaker there had attacked Jeanneney for having supported the naming of Marshal Pétain as Prime Minister in Bordeaux, at the most dramatic moment of our nation's history. The speaker attacked Jeanneney further for having later praised Pétain on the Senate floor in Vichy, and for having matter-of-factly chaired the National Assembly session and personally called for the vote, without voicing the slightest objection, that gave Pétain plenary powers and allowed him to destroy the Republic. In covering for the former President of the Senate, who has since been named one of his Junior Ministers, General de Gaulle maintained that in June 1940 there were several different views of what the best interests of the country entailed. Given the Army's refusal to continue the fight from North Africa, suing for an armistice was a legitimate option. In every one of his previous speeches, de Gaulle had been saying exactly the opposite.

Tuesday, January 9, 1945

Over the last few days, the situation in Alsace has become one of great concern. The Americans have been drawing off units from the Saar Valley, in all likelihood to support their slowly progressing counterattack in the Ardennes. The Germans have taken advantage of the situation and gone on the offensive; they are now threatening Strasbourg. They have crossed the Rhine to the south of the city and are only fifteen miles away. The news has left France terribly shaken.

Vladimir d'Ormesson,[1] writing in *Le Figaro*, and Paul Bastid,[2] in *L'Aurore*, among others, have been reminding people that the war is not over yet, and that all our efforts must be subordinated to the work of liberating the country. But what can France do if the Allies won't arm and equip French soldiers? How is it possible for them not to want to make forty French divisions battle ready? If Strasbourg were to be lost again, it would be a national disaster.

The Polish government in London has protested the methods it claims are being used by the Communist government in Lublin: the tyranny of a police state, the suppression of all democratic freedoms, and, behind the lies proffered for the press and the international community, the institution of a despotic reign of terror. The Lublin government has retorted by issuing a decree stripping "the Fascist leaders of the expatriate government" of their Polish nationality. The Poles are fighting among themselves amid the ruins of their homeland. It is a terribly sad story for all of us who admire the courage and patriotism of this martyred people, who truly appear to be victims of fate.

How is one to know what is best for them? Only truly free elections, jointly organized by the three major powers with all the necessary guarantees, could have allowed the Polish people to express their preferences.

1. Vladimir d'Ormesson, conservative journalist, named Ambassador to the Vatican in 1940 but dismissed by Vichy. He was named Ambassador to Buenos Aires in 1945 and to the Vatican in 1948.

2. Paul Bastid, lawyer, Deputy from the Cantal, and Commerce Minister in Léon Blum's government in 1936. He was a member of the National Resistance Council in 1943–1944. Editor in Chief of *L'Aurore*.

Most likely, a coalition government would have emerged. But for at least the last two years, Great Britain, clearly, and the United States, apparently, have abandoned Poland to the powerful sphere of Soviet influence and allowed it to be reduced to a veritable protectorate. With the dictatorship of the proletariat and the physical destruction of the middle class, we shall soon be told once again that "order reigns in Warsaw."

Thursday, January 18, 1945

Last Sunday, January 14, the Russians began mounting another formidable offensive along a front 250 miles long, stretching from eastern Prussia to Silesia. If you include the men still involved in the siege of Budapest, that would make 5 million men, organized into seven separate armies, marching from the Baltic to the Danube. I am now convinced that the war will come to an end this year, perhaps before winter.

More and more, Germany's leaders have resorted to terror as a means of governing the people. In Vienna, the Gestapo is supposed to have fired on factory workers demonstrating against the decision to remove machines from Austria and send them to Germany. During their retreat from Poland, the Germans summarily executed civil servants. And last Friday, in an act of unprecedented cruelty, five Frenchmen were shot, in retaliation for the execution of collaborators in Alsace and elsewhere in France. German radio stated that there would be similar acts of reprisal as long as the execution of collaborators continued. On Tuesday, Algiers radio replied that "the work of French justice would not be delayed." Isn't this absurd? Are French patriots currently held by the Germans going to die because French traitors are being sentenced to death? Is that what justice demands? Of course not. This is just one more reason, and there are a great many of them, for postponing the greater number of these trials until the end of the war, when they can be held in official, legally constituted courtrooms, after calm and order have been restored.

At a time when present circumstances have nothing in common with those that France faced in 1793, there is far more urgent work to be done than this parody of a revolutionary tribunal. They might as well make executions public again! I am surprised that certain former deserters haven't been demanding it.

Churchill gave an excellent speech to the House of Commons. He reiterated the Allies' demand for an unconditional surrender, but, he added, "We are not monsters and we have no intention of destroying Germany or enslaving its people." I am absolutely convinced that if the German people had a clear idea of the conditions under which the Allies were prepared to make peace, unrest might very well break out within Germany. Obviously, they have to be anticipating terribly exacting conditions. Still the phrase "unconditional surrender" is too humiliating and too vague. It has allowed Nazi propaganda to raise the specter of the total destruction of the country, to refer constantly to the Jews' desire to annihilate the Germans, and to maintain, unopposed, that there is no other way out for Germany than to defend itself desperately, to the bitter end. Death is to be preferred to the slow, agonizing tortures to which the Allies are preparing to subject them. Churchill was absolutely right to say what he did. The term "unconditional surrender" doesn't really mean anything.

From the details Churchill provided about England's contribution to the war effort, there would seem to have been only sixty-seven divisions of British soldiers engaged in combat on all fronts combined. In 1918, there were sixty-two divisions just on the front lines in France. Now in 1945, there must be ten British divisions in India, twenty or so in Italy, and five or six in the Middle East, which would leave only thirty divisions fighting in France, not counting, obviously, Canadian troops.

To be sure, these figures reflect only their ground forces; the numbers of men engaged in action in their Air Force and Navy are surely quite high. Nonetheless, it is highly unlikely that the British and Americans can mount and sustain a major offensive in the West without increasing their numbers significantly. As of now, there are probably no more than 100 divisions in all. In 1940, France alone had 110 divisions in action. British losses would appear to be similar to those of the Americans: 300,000 wounded, 57,000 dead. It is clearly the Russians who have suffered the heaviest casualties, with numbers beyond comparison with those of the Allies.

Saturday, January 20, 1945

It was extremely difficult to bring in anything on the radio today. Fortunately, I had two copies of *Das Reich*, from December 24 and 31. I know of no European political weekly that is as lively, as diversified, or as well documented about international affairs. Obviously, its function as a tool for spreading Nazi propaganda has to be kept in mind, but even with that, I always find it extremely interesting. In these two issues, Goebbels examines the passivity with which Churchill and Roosevelt have gradually allowed Stalin to achieve the domination of Europe, not to mention Poland, Romania, Bulgaria, Yugoslavia, and Czechoslovakia, which are just so many more or less—and generally not very—disguised Russian protectorates. The pressure being exerted by the Bolsheviks is increasingly strong, even in countries liberated by the Allies.

The Anglo-Saxons had hoped to use Russia to bring down Germany, but Germany's downfall has effectively led to the triumph of the Soviets in Europe. The Franco-Soviet agreement totally nullifies the pact among Western nations that England had been seeking. Even if victorious, Great Britain will be reduced to a second-rate power. Of course Dr. Goebbels has yet to explain why Germany entered into an agreement with the Bolsheviks on August 23, 1939.

Wednesday, January 24, 1945

They are fighting in the suburbs of Posen. The Russians are now only 150 miles outside of Berlin.

Thus, in one of those dramatic reversals of which history offers so many examples, the Slavs are invading the vast eastern plains that had for centuries been subjected to callous and implacable German colonization. We have entered that period of history that Renan had predicted in letters written to his "master" Strauss, during the war of 1870. East of the Elbe, and even more so east of the Oder, one still finds Slavic place names, typically Slavic settlements, with their characteristic villages organized around a large circular plaza lined with houses opening directly onto the fields, and large estates, all of them spoils of Germanic conquests. There can be no doubt that the Russian and Polish Slavs will divide eastern Prussia among themselves or that the new Polish nation, Russia's western outpost, will occupy territories stretching westward up to the Oder, and the ethnic Germans living there will be forced to leave their homes and settle in a defeated, dismembered Germany. For geographers, the Oder has always marked the border separating the two Germanys: one to the west with deciduous trees, one to the east with evergreens; one with small farms, one with the huge estates of country squires; the Germany of the ethnically pure and the other Germany in which, in spite of repeated conquests and domination, Slavic islands attached to the *Lander* have survived intact. Nothing will remain of the achievements of the Knights of the Teutonic Order, or of the accomplishments of the great Margraves of Brandenburg, whose statues are still traditionally visited by the schoolchildren of Berlin, where they line one of the principal paths in the Tiergarten.

The day before yesterday, the Germans reported that after they took the bodies of Marshal Hindenburg and his wife to Berlin from the crypt of the monument in Tannenberg where the two lay, they destroyed this grandiose memorial to Hindenburg's victory over the Russians in 1914 and the liberation of eastern Prussia. The news of that destruction will echo painfully in the hearts of the German people. It marks the end of a great period of both German and European history. After centuries of the Germanic race's expansion toward the East, after centuries of accumulating wealth and glory, the hour of the Slavic expansion toward the west is at hand. It won't be long before Moscow's soldiers come marching into Berlin, but this time the period of military occupation will be a long one.

The Germans are withdrawing in the West, too, driven back by the American counteroffensive. They have been forced to give up the territory they had won back in the Ardennes. Obviously, this is nothing like the generalized, precipitous retreat in the East. West of the Rhine, which remains a formidable barrier, the Germans have retained the vast fortified zone incorrectly called the Siegfried Line.

To break through these powerful fortifications, or to neutralize and move beyond them, the Allies will have to commit greater numbers of men and matériel. They apparently thought last summer that the Germans were exhausted and prepared to lay down their arms. The Americans then mounted a powerful offensive in the Pacific, against Japan. They won't be able to launch a general offensive on all fronts until next spring, and it alone can bring Germany to surrender.

Heard quite a bit about France this evening; unfortunately all the news is sad. France is suffering from hunger and cold and cruel deprivation.

There are more than half a million unemployed in France and more than a million people reduced to part-time work, even though 2 million Frenchmen, the youngest and the hardiest, are either prisoners or workers in Germany. In this major crisis, which has spared no one, gravest of all is the almost total absence of virtually every means of transportation. The winter has been harsh, but coal remains piled in the mine shafts because there are neither locomotives nor coal cars to transport it. Similarly, agricultural regions are finding great difficulty shipping their produce to urban centers where people are starving. But what can the Ministers who are being criticized be expected to do? Or the prefects who are being blamed, or the civil servants who are being taken to task, given the almost total lack of locomotives and railroad cars? It seems to me that all our efforts should be aimed at obtaining some from the Americans and the British, whatever the cost. This is not the time, to say the least, for the political controversies we so often get embroiled in with them.

The efforts to supply food and fuel have generated considerable criticism, but judging from press releases and the debates in the Consultative Assembly, apparently not so much as what has been called "the foot-dragging in the purges." François de Menthon[3] has come under attack a number of times. He has been accused, if not quite of being overly indulgent, of being a "moderate," although judging from his speeches, he sees himself as a direct descendant of the uncompromising likes of Fouquier-Tinville. In the Consultative Assembly, they have made no effort to temper their expressions of displeasure. They find him timid and lazy in meting out justice and characterize him as a man who simply goes by the book. Yet it doesn't seem to me that the fellows on the firing squads have been especially affected by the general crisis in unemployment.

3. François de Menthon, who had left France to join forces with de Gaulle, was the French Committee of National Liberation's Commissioner of Justice and then Minister of Justice in 1944. During the purge trials, he proved to be scrupulously conscientious.

On the radio today, they gave out specific figures: Forty thousand people accused of crimes and collaboration with the enemy have been languishing in French prisons for the past several months. Two thousand people have been tried, and 1,800 of them were convicted, including 340 who were sentenced to death. The activities of 20,000 of the people now being held are under investigation. The 114 courts set up specifically to handle purge trials hand down 60 sentences a day. At this rate, it will take two years to bring to trial all the people held, that is, if some of them are not previously released and of course assuming there aren't additional arrests.

Given that timetable, it is understandable that people have grown impatient. But it is equally understandable to hear complaints and objections of violations of basic human rights from men who have been living piled together for months in prison cells or internment camp barracks, without knowing exactly what they have been charged with, without ever having met with the Investigating Magistrate, and at times without there even being an actual case file on them.

Treason is the most abominable of all crimes. Any Frenchman who turned over other Frenchmen to the Gestapo deserves the death penalty. Many of the contemptible traitors who participated in the enslavement and the oppression of their own country have managed to flee to Germany. Some of them have been pointed out to me right here in the towns around Innsbruck, militiamen and "French" (sic) Volunteers Against Bolshevism, who have put their uniforms back on and gone back to spying and informing on people, this time for the Tirolean Gestapo. They have seen to it that some of the poor souls in the camps have ended up facing firing squads. But if they don't return to France after the war, there will be no way to punish them.

Everyone who was able to get out of France before the Liberation did so. In view of that, couldn't we quickly sift through the cases of the 40,000 currently in French prisons and hold over for trial only those who have criminally conspired with the enemy?

Of all our wounds, this is the most painful and the most grievous of all, which is why it should be lanced, without delay, so that the healing process might begin, without delay. It seems to me that the only possible approach is to separate crimes from misdemeanors and quickly mete out punishment for the former even if it means that those guilty of the latter benefit from a relative indulgence. Whatever is decided, it is thoroughly unacceptable for France to allow people to be held in prison without trial.

January 28, 1945

I wouldn't be at all be surprised if the policies the Soviets will soon be implementing were conceived and elaborated long ago. Their plans call for the Red Army to enter Berlin and remain there as an occupying force. They are probably holding a friendly German leadership in reserve. They will set them up in power immediately following the military collapse of the Reich. It will naturally include leaders resigned to the annexations and harsh conditions that come with military defeat: the annexation to a sovietized Poland of states to the east and southeast of the Oder; the Rhine as the military frontier of France; devastating war reparations in the form of raw materials, machines, and laborers. As a Soviet satellite—and the Soviets will have need of Germany's conversion industries—the German government will be able to save whatever there is to be saved and preserve their future. It wouldn't surprise me to see the war end that way, with Russia the master of Europe. The Allies would protest, you say? Nothing would be easier than to present this new Russophile government as the will of the people, which is to say, the workers and the farmers. Even though the concept of universal suffrage is totally foreign to the Soviet regime, they're very good at working it and using it to their advantage.

What is more, I think that the idea of a treaty with Russia, even one involving tough conditions such as these, would very quickly find considerable backing in Germany. Germans admire the power that dominates them, even the power that crushes them. It would have been so easy for France, in 1918, to arrive at a practical settlement with Germany. Stalin is not about to let the chance slip away. It will allow him to achieve the domination of Europe without firing another shot. Even if Churchill and Roosevelt have foreseen these grandiose schemes, and that is far from certain, they don't have the means to prevent him from carrying them out. This would mark the end of Great Britain's place as one of the world's leading powers. England would be reduced to a leading position among the nations of the second tier, and British influence in Europe would wither.

Such could well be the result of the overblown rhetoric and the short-sighted vision that have framed the Allied approach. In the place of realistic and humane terms, the Allies have demanded unconditional surrender and threatened to reduce Germany to so many potato fields. Whatever happened to Britain's legendary tact and the political flexibility of yesteryear, when balance and moderation were foremost in British minds? It is as if their political leaders had adopted the style and the spirit of an Ezekiel or a Jeremiah, along with the belief that maledictions and threats are enough to bring order to this, the most prodigious of world revolutions since the fall of the Roman Empire.

Tuesday, January 30, 1945

This is the twilight of the gods; there is utter consternation in Itter castle, our prison. All the radios have been locked up in the Commandant's office for the last few days, probably to keep the garrison's morale from caving in, but in spite of all the precautions, disastrous news reports continue to filter through. The SS can see the clenched jaws and the faces of their two commanding officers; their strained and downcast looks tell them just as much as they could ever learn from listening to field communiqués.

An officer arrived sometime during the night, a relative of the castle warden. He has difficulty getting around on his two canes, the result of wounds sustained on the Russian front. He has been assigned to the quartermaster corps. He arrived in so frenzied a state that all the soldiers were soon buzzing around him. He had just returned from a mission to Prague, where he had found the situation extremely tense. The Gestapo were on edge and unable to keep up with events. The cafes and all other public establishments had shut down. In short, Prague was a city on the verge of revolting against its oppressor. The SS were deeply stirred by the grim images conjured up by this disabled veteran, now convinced that two years ago his blood had dappled the snows of Russia to absolutely no purpose at all.

This morning, as I was cautiously making my way over the ice-covered ground, I could see dejection on the faces of the sentinels and consternation in the eyes of the soldiers as they busily went about their chores, as they do every day. In the kitchen, where I occasionally go to chat with the young Czechoslovak cook, the four women prisoners who assist him were beaming, as if they could already feel the winds of freedom caressing their faces. The young Czech who waits on the SS and hears and sees everything told me that we had to be on our guard. Some of the SS were talking about suicide. Others planned to seize all the food supplies, drink all the beer and the few bottles of wine that are kept in the cellar, get drunk, and shoot us. The two faces of Germany.

I heard a summary of the French press on the radio. It is generally felt that the final offensive won't be launched until the spring. The military experts—a race I had thought extinct, but that has apparently been given a new lease on life—laid out plans for the Russian Army and offered advice, with all the authority that their war school diplomas and armchairs confer on them. First the Russians will make this move, then they'll follow it with this one. These experts should have learned from the almost five years of war that boldness is the principal asset of Russia's military leaders, just as it was of France's revolutionary Generals.

If they have a chance to march on Berlin, you can be sure that they are not going to wait to hear from Churchill and Roosevelt. It won't be long before both of these gentlemen realize the irreparable error they committed in failing to rearm France these last six months. There should be fifty French divisions along the Rhine right now. But that is another story.

Thursday, February 1, 1945

Caught in the vise. The news we heard last night was of considerable moment, and it was confirmed this morning. The vise is squeezing them ever more tightly.

Goebbels has been given command of the defense of Berlin. How is he going to stop them when everywhere else the most formidable fortifications have crumbled under the Soviet onslaught? Riots are on the verge of breaking out in the major metropolitan areas. Starving refugees from eastern Prussia have been pillaging food stores, and the SS have opened fire on them, spilling the first drops of blood. Will Berlin be able to hold out as Leningrad and Warsaw did? Or as Budapest is still doing even now? Whatever Goebbel's personal energy, whatever the fanaticism of the Nazis, what can they possibly do to hold back the storm?

With the same admirable political skill that they have demonstrated throughout the war, skill that stands in such stark contrast to the total disregard of psychology in the Anglo-Saxon camp, the Russians have been appealing to the German people to rise up against the Nazis, whom Soviet propaganda has already begun differentiating from the rest of the German population.

The Committee for a Free Germany, which the Soviet government set up in Moscow, with General Paulus and other high-ranking officers at its core, has been operational for a long time. You can be sure that they'll move into Berlin on the heels of the Red Army, just as the Polish Committee in Moscow followed the Red Army into Lublin. And you can be just as sure that they will do everything they can to sovietize Germany. This is the beginning of a new chapter in world history, but to judge from the summary of the news I heard, the incredible events unfolding on the battlefield don't seem to have captured the attention of the French press. For them, the main issue is whether France's provisional government and the provisional National Assembly, both of them self-appointed, have the right to implement structural reforms that would rework the nation's social fabric.

Le Monde claims that they don't have that right, that the people of France must be given a voice. They feel it legitimate to assume that many Frenchmen chose not to join Resistance groups precisely because they were opposed to the revolutionary changes being proposed. They see a clear distinction between patriotism—the fight against a foreign oppressor—and social revolution. *Combat* and another newspaper, *Le Populaire*, which is the organ of the Socialist Party, have vigorously attacked *Le Monde*'s position.

One could hardly have expected otherwise, given that France is now going through a period when "legality is on leave," the period Léon Blum thought would be so highly favorable to the establishment of a socialist system.

In *Combat*, they wrote that "a revolution in social conditions is a necessity." In *Le Populaire*, they said we have a unique opportunity to revolutionize France from the top down, in orderly fashion, whereas later we shall find ourselves obliged to make revolutionary changes from the bottom up, with nothing orderly about it at all.

Thus do they call for the nationalization of banks, electric companies, insurance companies, the transportation sector, and heavy industry. After all, aren't the people in the Resistance the real France? In any event, such are the issues of the heated and engaging debate now going on in France, which have the added virtue of making us forget that the war is still going on. Nationalizations don't frighten me. In fact, I nationalized the arms industry and paved the way for the nationalization of the railroads. But I find nationalizations outdated. There are more flexible and efficient ways in which to shape a new economy.

Even though I have no fondness for *Le Monde*, which is little more than a revamped version of *Le Temps*—the voice of the prewar cliques of the privileged and the powerful, with little new other than a change in its discredited name and its defeatist publishers—I agree that the people alone can make such decisions. There should have been elections within the three months following the Liberation. More than ever, I am a supporter of democracy, a believer in its spirit and its methods. The people writing in *Combat* and *Le Populaire* are "totalitarians" who don't dare acknowledge it. No one has spoken about the revolution in values, although it underlies the other one.

The National Front's convention is still going on. Two million Frenchmen of the most varied leanings are represented there, with speakers as different as Jacques Duclos[4] and Debu-Bridel,[5] François Mauriac, and Joliot-Curie.

I have seen excerpts from speeches calling for a wealth tax and the replacement of old banknotes with new ones, with the idea of holding down inflation, at least partially, by asking those with cash savings to make con-

4. Jacques Duclos, Communist Deputy whom the Party put in charge of various surveillance missions. He was sentenced to three years in prison in 1932. When the pact between the Soviets and the Germans was signed in 1939, he was called on to bring Party members to accept it. He was active in the Resistance and regained a seat in Parliament after France was liberated. He went on to play a major role in Communist Party affairs.

5. Jacques Debu-Bridel joined the Resistance as a moderate in the group Libération and was a member of the Consultative Assembly.

siderable sacrifice. There have been speeches in support of nationalizations and the farmers' movement as well. We'll have to wait and see what they resolve to do in the end.

Of all the French newspapers, at least from what I can gather, the Communist *L'Humanité* is the only one exclusively concerned with the war. They keep calling for the creation of a large French Army. And they are right. There is simply no way to overstate how deplorable it is that Free France is not now a presence on the Rhine, with fifty divisions or more. But that was up to the Allies.

Did the Allies actually believe last summer that the war would be over in a matter of weeks? Were they alarmed by the suddenness with which the French and the Soviets concluded a separate agreement? Whatever the reason, it is too late now.

As for fielding a large army of occupation forces on the Rhine, that is another problem altogether. It will require little more than a large police force. If all the able-bodied youth of France are sent to keep watch on the Rhine, who will be left to rebuild the nation?

February 2, 1945

The battle for Berlin rages on. The Russians have brought in reinforcements and the Germans are busy digging antitank trenches and shelters.

More than a million Germans from Silesia and Pomerania are making their way back to the capital in below-zero temperatures. They are blocking roads, paralyzing troop movements, and sowing panic along the way.

Yesterday, the Russians were sighted just forty miles outside of Berlin. The Nazis are determined to defend their cities in house-to-house fighting, if it comes to that.

Word has it that the foreign diplomatic missions have left the city and that German government services have been moved into either Bavaria or the Tirol.

Here too, it is possible that we will forced to evacuate Itter "castle." We might well be transferred somewhere near Berchtesgaden, so that as the tragedy winds down to its conclusion, we, too, can play our role. Hostage or victim?

The progress made by the Russian troops has quite naturally exalted the Communists and promoted their cause everywhere. Marcel Cachin commemorated the liberation of Stalingrad. Along with the Anglo-Saxon landing in North Africa, the liberation of Tunisia, and the landing in Italy, that victory marked the turning point of the world war.

I am convinced that de Gaulle entered into agreements with Blum and the Communists as early as April 1943. In fact, he made a speech at that time that I heard while I was in Weimar.

Le Monde and the economist Charles Rist[6] have been attacked in an article in *Le Populaire*, Blum's mouthpiece, for having dared to criticize the wealth tax. In 1932 and 1934, Rist erred totally in opposing devaluation at a time when it was unavoidable. He himself admirably admitted his error in his testimony at the Riom trial, an event so rare that it is worth noting. I think he is wrong again now. The issue is neither the desirability of a wealth tax nor the various problems it would generate. It is rather a matter of whether there exist any other effective means for cleaning up the nation's financial situation and whether there is any way to avoid such a tax. To my mind, this tax is both inevitable and insufficient.

Finally, in *L'Ordre*, Emile Buré[7] has taken his turn at playing the biblical Jeremiah: "Woe unto the bourgeoisie should they oppose these reforms; woe shall befall them, just as nobles and clergymen suffered at the time of the Revolution." The bourgeoisie has heard all this before.

In contrast, the Communists are going about skillfully reassuring public opinion, most notably the middle class, where people become so quickly alarmed whenever they feel their property or savings are being threatened. The Communists are looking to win majority support by pre-

6. Charles Rist, free enterprise economist, Deputy Governor of the Bank of France from 1925 to 1929.

7. Emile Buré, Socialist journalist with extremist views. He joined Clemenceau's camp before World War I. In the period between the wars, he ran *L'Eclair*, then *L'Avenir*, then founded his own newspaper, *L'Ordre*, which was centrist but staunchly anti-German. He was hostile to Daladier. During World War II, he took refuge in the United States, where he started a newsletter, *France-Amérique*, with Henri Torrès. (See the February 21, 1945, entry for one of the reasons for Buré's hostility toward Daladier.)

senting electoral slates in combination with the Socialists, the Christian Democrats, and others, after which, little by little, they'll take full control.

To get the votes of those who are not Communists—since the votes of Party members are not in doubt—all you have to do is avoid frightening them. After all, you don't catch fish by blasting your hunting horn on the riverbank. You catch fish by cleverly preparing your bait. Or as Captain Traint, one of the first French Communists, used to say: "When you want to pluck a chicken, you don't go chasing after him, there are too many risks involved; it's a lot smarter to offer him a little tasty chicken feed. Then there's no problem later on, when it's time to pull out the knife."

That's why Duclos, Billoux,[8] and others have been all sweetness and light since the Liberation. As Orgon said in *Tartuffe*, "What gentility!" Look at what Duclos and Billoux told a gathering of Communist physicians in Paris. There wasn't a single word about the Soviet regime and not the slightest mention of a social revolution. They said that there would have to be true democracy in France, that reforms would have to be carried out "in an orderly way, in compliance with the law, and by authority of the government." Then these wolves in sheep's clothing presented a moderate program of political action designed specifically for Mr. Average Frenchman, whose incurable naïveté and unflappable penchant for gullibility are well documented. Duclos and Billoux even spoke out against "carrying nationalizations too far" and in favor of the farmers, just as Stalin did—right before he shipped them off either to Siberia or those agricultural barracks they call *kolkhozy*. Better still, Duclos and Billoux criticized attempts to fiddle with our currency, which should be enough to reassure the people holding banknotes, at least long enough for the Communists to win a majority. On the other hand, when it comes to patriotism, there is no holding them back. They are intransigent, almost fanatical:

8. François Billoux. Communist Party member as of 1925, elected Deputy in 1936. In 1940, he was arrested for pacifist activity and condemned to five years in prison. He volunteered to testify against Daladier at the trial in Riom. He made his way to North Africa, where he was a *commissaire* on the French Committee of National Liberation and a member of the Consultative Assembly.

The Franco-Soviet pact takes precedence over everything. I can just hear the ecstatic little bourgeois nationalist joyfully murmuring, "Ah, that Duclos ... say what you will, he's really a good man."

Thus does Captain Traint's chicken lick his lips as they bring him his feed, without ever considering the terror reigning in Poland, Bulgaria, and the Baltic. ... As the British press has been saying, "These regions are now shrouded under an impenetrable veil of mystery and silence."

February 5, 1945

The Americans have captured Manila. The Anglo-Saxons have turned matters around in their fight against the Japanese; they would like to finish them off without having to turn to the Russians for help. They have made considerable progress in Burma, where the old Silk Road has been reopened. Their victories will have tremendous impact throughout the world, at least on those who understand that the ultimate goal, of both the Anglo-Saxons and the Slavs, is the domination of Asia.

In a ceremony recently held in Moscow, amid great pomp and pageantry, the famous Alexis was anointed Patriarch of All the Peoples of Russia. Alexis had first sided with the Soviets years ago, bringing "religion's workers" into the Party ranks. Orthodoxy has thus become an effective tool in the Russians' drive for the domination of Eastern Europe.

The French press continues its commemoration of the victory in Stalingrad. Jean Richard Bloch sees that victory as proof of the superiority of Marshal Stalin and the Bolshevik system over the Nazis! By playing superpatriot, the Communists have stifled the few protests that have been voiced over the Party's role in 1940 and before. Time will bring matters into perspective.

For the moment, there has been no word on Paris, American, or British radio about the countries "liberated" by the Russians.

Is Soviet Russia using the war to pursue its goal of world revolution? Is it actually possible to reconcile Western humanism and Russian communism?

The only information I have comes from excerpts from the Allied press reprinted in quotation marks in German newspapers.

VB[9] published parts of a telegram to the *New York Times* that their Sofia correspondent was able to cable to New York only after he had gotten out of the country: "A government including representatives from all four major parties has in fact been formed, but it is actually the Communist Party, which has control over the police, the militia, and the Ministry of the Interior, that holds the reins of power."

Terror reigns in Sofia. In two special courts set up in the capital, they have been putting on trial not only the Regents and Ministers who had collaborated (along with most of Parliament, in fact) but also democrats like eighty-year-old Mouchanov and seventy-year-old Bourend, both of whom had been fighting the Germans these last several years.

No one is talking about referendums or free elections.

Terror reigns in Poland as well. The British have offered to grant citizenship to Polish soldiers who fought in the Allied ranks and now wish to return to their homeland. That "protection" says it all.

It is the same story in Romania. The fact is that Churchill intervened only in Greece, where he prevented the Communist ELAS[10] from seizing power. Churchill is reported to have put out an official report detailing the atrocities committed by the Communists there.

The reports coming in remain to be confirmed, but there can hardly be any doubt about the general tendency.

Whatever happened to the Atlantic Charter and all the solemn declarations made by the Allies? If the point of this war was to defend democratic freedoms from the threat of Nazi dictatorship, doesn't it follow that it remains the Allies' duty to reestablish these freedoms in the liberated nations?

9. *Völkischer Beobachter* (People's observer), daily newspaper that served as the semi-official organ of the Third Reich.

10. The Army of the EAM, the National Liberation Front.

February 12, 1945

The woman who serves as quartermaster for the "castle" went to Magdeburg, where her house had been destroyed. When she got back, the horror was still visible in her eyes. Her stories make you shudder.

At 11:30 P.M. I heard a communiqué detailing the Yalta Conference. I took notes. The fundamental principles were stated clearly and unanimously: "The Premier of the Soviet Union, the British Prime Minister, and the President of the United States have jointly examined the matter of the political and economic reconstruction of Europe, including nations that were allied with Germany. They have agreed to aid these nations, through democratic means, in resolving whatever economic and political problems they may have. These nations must be allowed to establish democratic institutions. ... All three nations are committed to bringing about free, secret-ballot elections and universal suffrage."

February 21, 1945

In particular, the Yalta Agreement calls for a strong, free, and democratic Poland. In Britain, twenty-two Conservative deputies offered an amendment: "The House of Commons would like to express its regret at not having been able to prevent the transfer of the territory of an Allied nation to one of the great powers, this transfer being contrary to several treaties as well as to Paragraph 2 of the Atlantic Charter. The House regrets as well that the government was not instituted through free elections." Twenty-five Members of Parliament voted in favor of the amendment, 396 against. In contrast, the Yalta Agreement was approved unanimously.

The *Daily Telegraph* would like to know why, after the signing of the Yalta Agreement, mass arrests were carried out in countries "occupied" by the Soviets.

There has been a Roosevelt–de Gaulle incident. Every French newspaper has backed de Gaulle's refusal to go to Algiers to meet with Roosevelt, at the latter's request, on his return from Yalta. De Gaulle considered it humiliating for France. I am not so sure.

Roosevelt sent back a stinging response; Churchill's was sharper still: "We met to discuss our own affairs. The three powers that have been bearing the brunt and burden of this war over the last four years are not about to grant anyone a say as to whether they can meet whenever and wherever they wish or take joint action to bring about an end to the war."

As for Poland's independence, I don't think Churchill seriously believes there is "freedom and independence in today's Poland." The Red Army set up a Polish government after a sham general referendum. Poland will become Russia's western outpost. It would be more honest and straightforward to say that without Russia's participation in the war, Poland would have remained off the map. But that is still a far cry from the democratic pronouncements contained in the Atlantic Charter.

The same people who continue to criticize the Munich Agreement of 1938 are accepting annexations that are far more serious and definitive, and at a time when they, as opposed to us, are *not* in a position of weakness. Quite the contrary.

The meeting being held in Alexandria is of major consequence. Churchill and Roosevelt have brought together the Emperor of Ethiopia, the King of Egypt, and representatives of Syria, Lebanon, Iraq, and Saudi Arabia. These regions are of vital importance to the British Empire. Should there ever be a Third World War between Russia and Great Britain, the Middle East will be one of its principal theaters.

The British have resurrected their grand designs for a pan-Arabic confederation, now that the French have been chased out of Syria and Lebanon. Syria and Lebanon were never of vital interest to France anyway.

The French press has been speaking with virtually one voice. Before the war, the French press was corrupt, but as a rule newspapers acted independently. There wasn't a single Prime Minister or Minister of the Interior or Foreign Affairs who would have been so crude as to withhold from newspaper publishers who attacked his policies the monthly subsidies he received from secret funds. Occasionally, very rarely actually, and even then only temporarily, when attacks got too violent or became too personal, they would hold back an envelope or two. Even I had that experience, with Emile Buré, who never forgave me for it. Still, the truth is that newspapers followed their own political line—that of their party, or their publisher, or the business group that owned them. No one was ever required, as has often been claimed, to back government policy, not even those who were being subsidized regularly from secret funds. In this respect, the ministerial musical chairs that they used to play back then worked to strengthen the custom of noninterference.

I have no idea how things actually work today. It seems as if there are more papers than there used to be, even though there are fewer readers, as a simple result of the deportation and imprisonment of some 2 million Frenchmen still in Germany. The higher cost of everything can't have failed to have repercussions on the cost of running and printing a newspaper. Consequently, it is highly likely, in fact inevitable given present circumstances, that many newspapers could not survive without financial assistance from the government. Censorship remains, and not only in military matters, at least to judge from the vehemence with which it has come under attack. Still, given that no newspaper could have made it onto, or back onto, the stands without the government's approval, and given that most of them could not continue to publish if the government were hostile to them, the reality of the situation is that the greater number of journalists have to be considered bureaucrats. Only when peace is restored will freedom of the press really return, if it ever does return, along with other human freedoms that tend to atrophy when systems of law are in recess. So it is that the entire French press has endorsed General de Gaulle's refusal to meet with President Roosevelt in Algiers. The Information Minister deserves to be congratulated on the discipline he has instilled and the impressive united front the press has shown.

Could the war have been won without the involvement of the United States, which the French press tends to overlook? They should have a look at what the German press has to say about it: Despite the resistance of American isolationists, Roosevelt managed to convince his nation to throw its people and its resources into the battle for freedom. The official reasons given for turning down the invitation to Algiers are so sordid that several papers have strained to find others: It would seem that the head of the provisional government has foiled a plot against the nation, that although France had not been asked to participate in the Yalta Conference, they tried to enlist de Gaulle's support by getting him to go to Algiers. That is clearly not the issue. Generosity and gentlemanliness are often more productive than prideful self-righteousness.

March 1, 1945

Roosevelt's speech to Congress is first and foremost a display of his consummate skill as a statesman. He would like to avoid the stumbling block that proved Wilson's undoing. Wilson presented his work as that of the Democratic Party. At Versailles, he surrounded himself exclusively with Democrats. Then the bill he sent up to Congress failed to pass by a mere six votes. Roosevelt has been careful to point out, over and over again in fact, that peace cannot possibly be the work of one political party, that it is the work of every American, and that it requires the sustained efforts and understanding of everyone who participates in America's democracy. He was careful to include Republicans in the delegation going to San Francisco.

Moreover, American public opinion has apparently shown no restraint in criticizing what the Soviets are doing in Finland, Poland, and the Baltic States. Soviet expansionism throughout the world has become a cause for concern in American industrial and financial circles.

Unlike Churchill, Roosevelt was not about to accentuate the problems; on the contrary, he tried to minimize them. But he was careful to emphasize, tactfully, the agreement reached by the three major powers for the establishment of democratic institutions in liberated countries, an agreement that also stipulated that there would be no zone of influence dominated by any one of them. But are these statements reflected in the reality of the situation? The speech was apparently very well received by the Congress and the press. Roosevelt stated in particular: "It was Hitler's hope that we would disagree, but never before have the major Allies been more closely united. All our military plans were worked out together in detail. ... From now on, we shall be engaging in the massive, systematic bombing of Germany in direct support of Soviet Armies. ... We appeal to the German people to understand that unconditional surrender does not mean the destruction of Germany. It rather means an end to Nazism and militarism, the punishment of war criminals, and war reparations in kind." Roosevelt said nothing about forced laborers. "We have reached thoughtful agreement on Germany, Poland, and peacetime arrangements. ... Poland is a good example of our joint action. The Polish government will be reorganized and then recognized, after which general elections by secret ballot will be held."

He concluded by pointing out the need for the United States to accept its responsibility in creating a peaceful world order. "Ours must be a new era in the history of mankind."

March 3, 1945

Paris is mired in tedious debate. There is controversy on all sorts of issues, with voices coming from all quarters.

Germany is marked by panic and despair, and by its relentless determination as well—a fight to the death. Courts-martial are being held with only one outcome: the death sentence. The choice that remains is that of the means: firing squad, beheading, or hanging. Goebbels said that he would prefer to die and see his children die rather than become a slave. They are stirring up fears of catastrophe, destruction, and mass deportation.

According to rumors circulating around here, the German Army is preparing to mount a last-ditch resistance and concentrate its forces in two areas: one in the North, in an area including Hamburg and the Jutland; one in the South, in Bavaria and the Tirol. So in ancient Germania did they circle the wagons, with their wives, their children, and their war trophies inside.

April 12, 1945

2:35 P.M. A squadron of twelve planes flew over the "castle" at low altitude. I didn't see a single woman out working in the fields. Calm was restored by 3 o'clock. Jouhaux came to see me. He had set out for the hospital in Innsbruck yesterday at 5 A.M. It is just a short distance away, but he didn't get there until 4:15 in the afternoon.

The chaos in the train stations is terrifying. Women and children refugees are piled on top of each other, without either food or facilities. Sometimes the stations are bombed, and they all dash madly for the shelters and the trenches. The tracks have been cut at several points along the line. The railroad cars are old and dilapidated, with broken windows. Jouhaux overheard an old *Feldwebel,* wearing an Iron Cross, say that it was all over, that there wasn't a single officer left on the front lines, and that it was criminal for the government not to sue for peace.

April 13, 1945

Roosevelt is dead. Death came at three in the morning, following a cerebral hemorrhage. The commentary by the British was excellent. Roosevelt was a true believer in democracy, a man who served humanity. The goals he set forth in 1942 have almost all been reached. His wonderful voice will long be heard throughout the world. Along with Lincoln, he is one of the great figures of modern times. I remember his phone calls, his attempts to strengthen our Air Force, his words of encouragement as he told me to hold on until he could convince his countrymen to go to war against the Nazis. His associate, my friend Bullitt, proved to be the most faithful and most helpful of friends.

April 14, 1945

M. and Mme Cailleau arrived in Itter last night. Her maiden name is de Gaulle; she is apparently the sister. This morning, Mlle Mabire paid her a visit at the earliest hour propriety allowed and promptly launched into a diatribe against the traitors in Vichy.

Just as Mme Brenklein was coming up to offer her services as well to our newly arrived guests, Mme Cailleau began sharply replying that in June 1940 Frenchmen could very easily have had a different view of what their duty to the nation was, whereupon Mlle Mabire quickly moved on to praise General de Gaulle and the Prime Minister (Reynaud), who was the first to argue in favor of mechanizing the Army, who supported de Gaulle, etc., etc.

This afternoon, I was out for a walk with Jouhaux when I spotted our new prison mates. Mlle Mabire and Reynaud were still clinging to their sides. Mme Cailleau is a distinguished and very personable woman. She spoke in measured terms of the fatigue and suffering she had gone through following her arrest. She had been separated from her husband throughout the ordeal, he having been sent to Buchenwald. But Mme Cailleau didn't have a chance to say anything further. Reynaud and his companion led her off for a walk around the ramparts, hanging on her every gesture, drinking in her every word. As Mazarin said long ago, the Frenchman is a born courtier. Now that battle lines have been drawn in the war to win her over and influence her, the twists and turns of it just might offer us a little amusement. M. Cailleau, the mere prince consort, stood peacefully by throughout; he wasn't snapped up the way she was. He was playful and spirited in describing his experience in Buchenwald, although it must have been excruciatingly painful. While in Saint-Etienne, he had done volunteer work with the prisoners there, in an attempt to ease the hardship of their captivity. "I never once suspected," he said, "that I would come to know similar conditions firsthand, and all the worse for me."

When they were transferred, in the heart of winter, the Germans left them nude in their cattle cars to make sure they wouldn't escape and gave them practically nothing to eat.

The camp was located a few miles outside of Weimar, Goethe's city. There was even a statue of the great German poet right outside. What he described to us in the most measured terms was absolutely horrifying. Twenty thousand deportees subjected to starvation, illness, beatings, and humiliations, and at times outright torture. Most unbelievable of all, the Gestapo set up a whorehouse right next to the camp. On Christmas Day 1944, after lunch, the block leaders were asked over the camp loudspeakers to supply a list of people who were interested in going there. Will anyone ever be able to fathom the German mind?

April 20, 1945

It's Hitler's birthday today, a national holiday if there ever was one. But this year, all we got was a speech by Goebbels stating that Hitler never wanted anything other than peace, that all he had ever been looking for was a place in the sun for Germany. Then he said: "The evil coalition of Bolsheviks and plutocrats is about to collapse. Fate has intervened to remove the head of this enemy coalition, just as it had earlier intervened to spare the Führer so that he might continue the work Providence had called upon him to carry out." The word Providence came back seven times. … This was followed by the placid description of what life would be like after the war—after Germany's victory in the war. Such was the first part of the trilogy. Events were to furnish the other two.

Looking out my barred window these last few days, I have been watching the exodus down the road that leads from Wörgl to Hofgarten:

automobiles with mattresses on the roofs, people on foot loaded down with Tirolean knapsacks, and frazzled women dragging starving children by the hand. Sometimes the women stop at farmhouses and ask for a piece of bread, but the farmers just raise their hands to the sky. They have nothing left to give them. When traffic gets bottled up, people simply lie down in the ditches on the side of the road; when it clears, they get up and start out again. Millions of people are fleeing over the few German roads that remain open, down through the narrow corridor that, for a few days more, will carry them from the North to Bavaria. Other roads, both to the east and the west, are already under Allied control. Soon all of Germany will be occupied by Allied troops. Thus has the grand dream of dominating all of Europe come to its disastrous end.

Germany has been defeated. All countries come to know the whims of fate, or as Frederick the Great used to call it, His Majesty Chance.

Then there's the third part of the trilogy. For the last few days, London radio has been describing the horrors of the concentration camps with tragic sobriety. General Eisenhower has issued orders to have all the civilian authorities in neighboring towns led through them, so that no one can remain ignorant of the cruel and sadistic acts that were committed there, both during the war and well before it. Germans suspected of being anti-Nazi were probably tortured even more than those deported from other countries. The stories of those who escaped and the photographs taken of the camps have been met with prolonged shrieks of horror. In a cruel twist of fate, the proof of these ignominious atrocities has been released throughout the world on the very day Hitler is celebrating his birthday, in the company of the few handfuls of fanatic Gestapo and party members that remain. The documentation is so unimpeachable that even the Germans will be forced to recognize the truth.

Germany's defeat appears everywhere as the great liberation of mankind. Hundreds of thousands of prisoners, people deported from every nation, have set out to regain their homelands.

Here in Itter, confusion and fear are running rampant. Lieutenant Stephen can already see himself in Siberia. The woman in charge of the female German prisoners has been pouring out her distress to them. She's preparing herself for life in a Russian prison camp, where she'll have to put on the same kind of convicts' clothes her prisoners have been wearing for the last four years.

The SS and the soldiers of the Wehrmacht have been eyeing each other hostilely. It seems that Germany will be spared a civil war only because of the presence of foreign occupation forces.

Evidence keeps pouring in. They have seized concentration camp logs, interviewed eye witnesses, and taken photos.

The description of the camp at Dachau that appeared in the British press corresponds exactly to what I heard, when I came to Itter, from prisoners who had been held there. The Nazis had institutionalized concentration camps and torture long before the war; it was one of their tools of government. Thereafter, they introduced them throughout whatever parts of Europe they conquered. As the war progressed, as the setbacks they suffered worsened and the restrictions on food supplies tightened, they left their prisoners with just enough rations to starve by.

In Buchenwald, the Americans were able to evacuate some 5,000 people who were gravely ill, but there remain all those poor souls who can't be moved, who are dying at a rate of 40 a day from tuberculosis, typhus, and harrowing physiological deficiencies.

In the camp at Belsen, the Americans discovered corpses of women piled almost 6 feet high, in a row 250 feet long. A hundred other women and countless children stricken with typhus and tuberculosis were found lying on lice-infected wooden floors. Here, as in all the other camps, in what was clearly part of a calculated plan, the Nazis carried cruelty and sadism to new heights, by seizing every available opportunity to humiliate and degrade their captives.

In other camps, as the Allies closed in, prisoners who attempted to escape were shot by the hundreds or died in barracks set aflame by the SS. But the worst might yet be to come when Dachau, the camp near Munich, is liberated.

April 24, 1945

The names of the prisoners held in Itter "castle" were picked up on a German pirate radio. The hairdresser in Hofgarten told Mme Brenklein, adding, "We can only remember one of them, Daladier." When did the hairdresser hear this broadcast? What does one make of it?

April 25, 1945

This is the sixth day of tremendous street fighting in Berlin. They are even fighting in the subways, where the Germans have set up machine guns and even field artillery. The resistance they have put up borders on the fanatical; sixteen-year-old boys have been thrown into the battle. They are being bombed from the skies; artillery shells are raining down on them. To the east, the city is in flames.

Patton is now just forty miles outside of Munich. The French have reached Lake Constance.

April 29, 1945

At 5 P.M. I learned that Mussolini had been executed by firing squad, along with his mistress and seventeen Fascists. His body lies exposed in the street.

It is a sun-filled evening; the cherry trees are in blossom. Wisps of smoke mount skyward from mountain chalets. The Americans are now only forty miles outside of Innsbruck, not very far away at all. There is fighting in Munich between the Nazi authorities and the civilian population. The climax is at hand.

I went downstairs at 6:30 and ran into Borotra, who greeted me with, "Have a nice walk, Prime Minister." Ten seconds later, a blast went off. I ran to the parapet, as did Borotra, but then he scaled it and started running madly down the hill. The SS began firing at him from a few yards away. He took the barbed wire in stride as more and more shots rang out and the SS began their pursuit. 7:20 P.M. Borotra was brought back. He had probably twisted an ankle, given the way he was limping. He had once tried a nighttime escape, on a Sunday about a month ago.

The "castle" was in an uproar during the night. Violent fights broke out around three in the morning. I saw the captain go down and begin shouting orders. It was impossible to sleep.

April 30, 1945

The Russian flag is flying atop the Reichstag.

Last night, the Commandant of the camp at Dachau came to Itter with his direct subordinates, their wives, and their children. Before fleeing the camp, he had had 2,000 people shot. He is obese and apoplectic, with the face of a brute. His second in command is tall and fat, a real thug.

May 2, 1945

The Commandant from Dachau had barely settled in when he committed suicide. Ever since Hitler's suicide,[11] the garrison is like a body without a soul.

May 3, 1945

At 6:30 this morning, a little titmouse came into my room and started fluttering around me, as if to say good-bye.

At the time of his arrest, Pétain said, "I was never involved in politics." The comedies and tragedies of life.

I learned that the body of the Commandant from Dachau was put in a pine box, but the box was too big for the doorway to his room. Four soldiers removed his boots and dragged his corpse across the floor. On the ground floor they put the body in a sack and stuck it in the coffin. This morning, the priest from Itter refused them permission to bury him in the village cemetery.

May 4, 1945

They are actually fighting right near us, in Wörgl. The SS Commandant of the "castle" had me informed that as part of their retreat, the Germans would make a stand at Itter. He asked me if I wanted to leave with them. I refused. They put on civilian clothes and took off on bikes, after having handed me a corporal's pistol. Around 3 P.M. I took advantage of our jailers' departure and went for a walk in the village. Large numbers of soldiers passed by in orderly fashion. A lot of them were very young. None of them

11. Hitler committed suicide on April 30.

showed any signs of despondency, even less of disaster. I spotted the priest, not in religious dress, and a very beautiful young blond girl. In an inn, a young man in civilian clothes introduced himself as a German officer in charge of an antiaircraft battery. "This is the second time the Jews have won out," he said, "but we'll get them next time."

At around 5 P.M. I came upon Borotra and La Roque in the village. We met a young, very nice and very intelligent airman, twenty-three years old. ... He was worried about our safety. He was afraid that the SS who were falling back would try to take the "castle" and kill us. Horns started honking from within the "castle" walls. We ran to see what was happening and found an American captain there with five or six other men, in a tank. A German major with fifteen soldiers also appeared on the scene, having come voluntarily to protect us. Lee, the American Captain, was crude in both looks and manners. Gangel, the German Major, on the other hand, was polite, dignified, and distressed. If Lee is a reflection of America's policies, Europe is in for a hard time. There were toasts and a good deal of bustling about. We were joined by two Austrian resistance fighters wearing armbands and toting guns. Quite a strange gathering.

For the help we got, and maybe even for our lives, we owe our thanks to Andrea, the German deportee who worked at the "castle" under the Quartermaster. When the Germans took off and released their prisoners, instead of taking flight and hiding out, Andrea headed for Wörgl by bike. A battle was being waged there between the Americans and the SS. Everything was in utter confusion, but that didn't seem to faze Andrea, who went to see the German Major and explained our situation to him. The Major made contact with the American Captain and they both left for Itter to help us. In any other circumstances, a story like that would be unbelievable.

May 5, 1945

This morning, two bullets whistled by my ear and landed in the wall behind me.

At 10 A.M. I was walking in the courtyard with Jouhaux when they began lobbing shells into the "castle" from the South: Austrian 77s or 88s. They honored us with about fifteen of them. One of them went through Gamelin's room ... and was followed by machine gun fire. We hurried back inside the "castle." All the phone lines were cut. The American Captain set up machine guns along the wall, but his tank was destroyed by a shell, as it sat on the stone bridge. The German Major deployed his men and set up his machine guns and his armored vehicle. A lull in the action prompted the Major to move into the doorway to observe the situation. Suddenly, he slumped to the floor. A bullet had gone through his heart. It had struck him dead on the spot. His right hand trembled a bit, then fell motionless. The nobility of this man, this German for whom the war was over! He had risked his life to help French prisoners, his enemies.

The situation was getting worse. At around 12:30 P.M. Captain Lee gave Borotra information about American troop movements and sent him off to try to bring back reinforcements. Clemenceau and La Roque busied themselves firing randomly into the woods, although they hadn't actually seen any Nazis.

I went up to the second floor where two of the German soldiers who had come with the Major had taken up positions, with their rifles resting on the window sills. They pointed out German soldiers firing at the "castle" from a few hundred yards away, near the little electric plant, on the edge of the forest. The two soldiers returned the fire. I took advantage of a moment of calm to exchange a few words with our defenders. They told me in German that they were Polish. When I told them that I was French, one of them started shaking my hand while the other pulled a bottle out of his coat and offered it to me. It was a bottle of Fernet Branca; where the devil did he ever get that? I drank a bit; it was really bad. Then he laughed and told me that Hitler was kaput.

Suddenly he stopped laughing and shouted, "Panzer!" Five tanks were approaching. We watched them turn onto the road leading up to the "castle." The SS attackers vanished; these tanks were American. They had been alerted and guided by Borotra, who was now wearing an American uniform. The unit with him was a company, maybe a little bigger. The American Colonel appeared, a big, strong, nice fellow. We greeted each other cordially. As we were thanking him, war correspondents from American newspapers began taking photographs. Then we introduced the German soldiers who had fought to help us, and the corpsman with them. They were immediately released. Other French prisoners began arriving, they too having been liberated by the Americans. One of them recognized me and said that we had once been together at a branding in the Camargue, back in the days when they were still marking wild bulls.

Then we all moved down toward the tanks and the automobiles. The people from the village had gathered in the town square. Austrian flags were hanging from the windows. An old antiques dealer from Berlin, who had taken refuge in the area with his daughter, told us, "We have been liberated, too." I noticed that Resistance fighters from Wörgl were there as well.

At 7 P.M. we headed down to Innsbruck, free at last. We were shown to the Command Post of the General leading the 103rd Division, Anthony McAuliffe. That was the heroic division that had been surrounded in Bastogne. The General had in fact been on leave at the time, in the United States. He immediately had himself flown back and parachuted into the middle of his troops. His encircled division eventually broke out. He greeted us in princely, kindly fashion and honored us with a candlelight dinner in his Tirolean villa.

May 7, 1945

The General called the Army and asked for a plane to carry us back to Paris, but the First French Army insisted on handling our transportation. That is why we ended up leaving by car for Augsburg, where Patton's Seventh Army headquarters was located. We moved from the enthusiasm of the Tiroleans, joyous in spite of the bombings and the buildings reduced to rubble, to the hostility of the Bavarian population, mainly old men, women, and children. Their hostility was written on their faces. Many of them turned their backs as soon as they sighted American vehicles.

Augsburg is a city rich in palaces and churches, one that played a major role in the history of civilization and intellectual history, above all in the fifteenth and sixteenth centuries. The city had been subjected to massive bombings. A flood of trucks, cannons, and tanks were making their way through it, heading for the front.

We arrived at 7 P.M. and went to the Seventh Army headquarters, but no one was there. Our convoy set out again, this time for the suburbs. We stopped in a neighborhood of lower-class housing. German officers, now prisoners, could be seen standing at windows. We strolled around a playing field to pass the time. At 8:30, Captain Lazare showed up, sporting a fine red garrison cap. He didn't say much, laughed a lot, and told us he would try to find an apartment for us. We didn't see him again. We went back to Headquarters, where a French captain set us up at the Kaiserhof, which was practically deserted. Captain Lazare reappeared and informed us that we would be leaving the following morning at 10 A.M. sharp for the Headquarters of the First French Army at Lindau, on Lake Constance.

May 8, 1945

At 11:30 we were still waiting. After having paced up and down the sidewalk, I went to sit down in the officers' mess in the Kaiserhof. As I glanced toward the door, I saw my son Jean. I hadn't had word from him in almost two years. I thought I was hallucinating, but it really was Jean. This was the most wonderful moment of my life.

General Patton, one of the greatest commanders in the American Army, came in. He was unaffected and cordial. I expressed France's admiration and gratitude for all that the Americans had done. "No need to, not at all," he said. "You were the ones who showed us the way in 1917."

We left for Lindau. News of our liberation had been spreading. Ribet, my lawyer, was there to greet us, along with Soupiron, a reporter from Lyons who had followed the Riom trial, published accounts of it, and written *Bazaine contre Gambetta.* I remember having shouted at one point during the trial, "The way things are today, Gambetta would be in prison and Bazaine would be an official in the government."

Then I saw Bullitt, wearing a French Commander's uniform. We hugged each other. Oh the memories that awakened!

At 10 P.M. I had a friendly chat with General de Lattre. He left me to talk at length with Weygand. Two planes had been brought in: one for us, one for Weygand, La Roque, and Borotra, whom they intend to put on trial upon their return to France.

I went off peacefully on my own, in my son Jean's car. We went to his regimental Command Post.

Jean had joined a *maquis* in the Jura Mountains, where he had been shot in both legs. He was helped out by patriot farmers, then finally picked up and attended to by Dr. Charlin, a good man who helped him get across the border into Switzerland. Jean later returned to France to join the Alsace-Lorraine brigade, commanded by my good friend Jacquot.[12]

We had lunch at Jacquot's Command Post, in the company of his officers, all of whom were from *maquis* in the Corrèze and Dordogne. They told deeply moving stories.

We left the following day with my son and Jacquot and passed trucks carrying deportees and former prisoners, rolling along now in joyous song. A lot of them were very young. At Brisach, we took a pontoon bridge over the Rhine. There we stopped. There were young soldiers all around. As we set foot on French soil, a Lieutenant bid us welcome to France. Some of the men recognized me, men from Fos-sur-Mer and the Gard. We stood and chatted together on the banks of the Rhine. They were all volunteers. One of them, who had been a *maquisard*, had been tortured by the Germans.

Alsace is everywhere bedecked with French tricolor flags, just as it was in 1914. In Mulhouse, I saw Alsatian women in traditional dress, some of them very beautiful. Crossed the Vosges via Bussang Pass, drove through the streets of Remiremont, lined with the blue, white, and red colors of France. Stopped at a farmhouse to fill the car with water. Having recognized me, a man came up to us with his sons and daughters. "Welcome, welcome," he said. "We still love you … more than ever."

We stopped around 10:30 P.M. in Vrécourt, in front of Jacquot's house. His mother was expecting us, a sturdy, energetic woman, seventy-five years old. She told us gripping tales in the simple words that befit the stark occupation years. Then she cracked a few eggs and served up two delicious omelets.

We got back on the road. It was dawn when we arrived in Paris, a silent Paris whose symbols of victory were still illuminated, a deserted Paris, perhaps more moving than it would have been had the streets been filled with joyous crowds.

12. This is the same Commander Jacquot who had come to visit Daladier, in the prison in Riom in 1942, dressed in military attire.

Appendix A
France's Principal Modern Weaponry

Weapons	June 1, 1936	Sept. 1, 1939	May 1940
60 and 81 mm Brandt mortars	450	7,500	9,980
25 mm antitank guns	1,280	3,800	6,000
Tracked armored vehicles	700	3,800	6,000
47 mm antitank guns	0	411	1,280
Blockhouse antitank cannons	0	518	[a]
12 ton Renault, Hotchkiss, FOM tanks	0	1,780	2,665
20 ton SOMUA speed tanks	0	261	416
16 ton D1 tanks			150
20 ton D2 tanks	17	50	260
30 ton B, B1, B1[b] power tanks	17	172	387
Machine guns: AMR (7 ton), AMC (7 ton), and AMD	0	407	866
Fortified defense weaponry	0	96	[a]
Small caliber (20, 25, 40 mm) anti-aircraft weapons	0	321	2,140
Modernized 75 mm antiaircraft weapons	25	400	[a]
Modernized 105 mm antiaircraft weapons	0	124	[a]
New 75 mm antiaircraft cannons	38	392	[a]
90, 94, 100 mm antiaircraft cannons			40
13.2 mm antiaircraft machine guns			1,360

[a]Production terminated.

[b]Second series.

Source: Document furnished by Edouard Daladier after the war to Parliament's fact-finding commission.

Appendix B
The Riom Trial

Jean Daladier

[*Directives for the Press*[1]

All newspapers are to publish excerpts from the Riom indictment preceded by an appropriate introductory paragraph, no later than April 26. These excerpts are to be taken from the brochure previously distributed to the media and outlining the principal charges. This press release is intended to spur sales of the full-length version of the prosecution's indictment, soon to be made available in bookstores.

Be sure to emphasize the prosecution's arguments.]

The Riom trial[2] was one of the most shameful and one of the saddest trials in our history. It was shameful in that Marshal Pétain sentenced Daladier and his codefendants to life in prison simply on the basis of a recommendation made by the Political Justice Committee chaired by Perretti della Rocca, whom he, Pétain, had appointed (see the diary entry for October 14, 1941).

The Vichy government then set up a tribunal to hear the case. Daladier was to answer to the principal charge of having declared war on Germany! The pretrial investigation was actually conducted along these lines for months. The charge was later changed to having failed to prepare France for war. With the exception of General Gamelin, who would, incidentally, refuse to say a word during the trial, only civilians were indicted.

1. Addressed to journalists by Vichy government bureaucrats. Throughout the trial, Vichy issued directives to the press as well as to many witnesses and magistrates. This is the directive dated April 24, 1942.

2. See Frédéric Pottecher, *Le Procès de la défaite* (Paris: Fayard, 1980).

All facts predating 1936 were barred from the courtroom, which is to say, all facts pertaining to the period when Pétain was War Minister and a member of the Supreme War Council.

Most pathetic of all, the trial ended when Hitler publicly demanded that it be suspended, at a time when Vichy could already sense how counterproductive it had been.

Quite a sorry business, this trial. I was there. After each session, newspapermen were given directives to be followed under threat of penalty. They were not to mention Pétain or his associates; not to mention Free France or certain Generals. The trial was especially sad in that men who had acted bravely in 1914 took the stand to deny any responsibility whatsoever, as per the script that had been written out by Vichy. Because they were not allowed to consult their notes, a number of these witnesses were shown to be mistaken or lying and ended up looking like fools.[3]

At the beginning, people were lining up to testify—career officers, politicians, even Communists. But after Daladier virtually took over the first few sessions, volunteers were hard to find.

Very few men—and they are all the more noteworthy for it—took the stand and simply told the truth as they saw it, as did for example M. de Moustier,[4] whose opinions in fact conflicted with Daladier's. As for the rest, what hatred and incompetence they displayed. What base flattery they showed toward Vichy, what scorn for the British, what blindness in their estimation of Germany's strength.

As soon as his cross-examination began, Daladier revealed unusual audacity in the face of the Germans present in the courtroom. "Germany intends to use the sentences pronounced against us for propaganda purposes, and demand admissions of guilt from its victims. ... France should be the one admitting its guilt. ... The way things are today, Gambetta would be in prison and Bazaine would be an official in the government." That set the tone for the rest of the trial. The man who stood accused was to become the principal accuser.

3. Roger Génébrier, *Le Procès de Riom*.

4. A Deputy and a member of the Resistance. He was deported and died in the camps.

Daladier had to bear the burden of practically the entire trial, since he alone had command of all the facts and knew all the people involved.

During a subsequent court session, he declared: "Germany met its first defeat when it proved incapable of invading England. It has met a second defeat in Russia. Germany will be defeated, that is now inevitable. We must not let our confidence waver."

When the Presiding Judge interrupted, Daladier pretended to yield to his point, but he held the floor and came back even stronger.

Tanks and Antitank Weapons

Presiding Judge: There were only 2,848 tracked infantry vehicles; we needed 3,765 of them.

Edouard Daladier: On May 1, 1940, we took delivery of 6,200 tracked vehicles. According to General Picquendar, 1,200 of them remained in storage depots and were never used, like the 500 tanks the Germans captured in Gien, along with considerable amounts of other matériel.

Bruzin, the prosecuting attorney, shifted the questioning to tanks. "Production figures refer to 3,446 tanks."

The Presiding Judge reiterated the myth, debunked by both France's Military Intelligence (Colonel Rivet) and German Generals, to the effect that the German Army had between 7,000 and 8,000 tanks. (They actually had around 3,000 tanks.)

Daladier stated that when he was appointed War Minister in 1936, France had only 34 tanks! In 1940, 3,500 had rolled off factory lines, including the 2,800 tanks that were in combat position, along with 500 other armored vehicles. The Germans attacked with only 3,000 tanks. (General Guderian confirmed these figures.)

Our tanks were split between the infantry and the cavalry. They were not used to capacity; they were even used to protect bridges; 2,400 tanks were assigned to the infantry, the remainder to the cavalry.

Daladier went on: "General Doumenc was the first to suggest a modern-day strategy for using tanks, as early as 1928. General Guderian adopted his ideas in 1934."

In fact, the Army adopted Marshal Pétain's theories. "Our approach is the correct one," Pétain said. "Tanks are best used in support of infantry. There is no point in throwing armored vehicles into the wilds."

General Georges, the Commander in Chief, and General Dufieux, the former Tank Inspector, agreed with him. For example, the High Command halted the construction of thirty-ton tanks. Certain appropriations were never spent.

Several Generals voiced their opposition to these outdated theories, but they were not heeded. Daladier mentioned that General Billotte had warned that the Germans would deploy five armored divisions, either in Lorraine or west of the Meuse, and use the same strategy they had put into effect in Poland. Billotte stated: "We have at our command one armored division, three heavy-armor units, and more than forty light-armor battalions. Technically and numerically, our superiority is clear." [*At the end of this court session, the press was instructed to omit these comments.*]

Although the Military Command had sole power in determining the weapons they used and the quantities they required, Daladier noted that he had gotten them to create one armored division. It had taken two years to decide on a field for military maneuvers near Nancy, and Daladier actually had to go there himself to get it done. "Our tanks were spread out everywhere, and thrown into battle in little bunches," he said in conclusion. "The problem wasn't our matériel; the problem was our approach to conducting a war."

After a series of exchanges, Daladier made a similar demonstration for our antitank weaponry. "There were 15,000 antitank guns," he said. "Many of them remained in storage dumps. After the Armistice was signed, we handed over 2,500 cannons and 1,200 armored vehicles to the enemy."

Then the Presiding Judge accused the defendant of responsibility for the insufficient number of mines.

Edouard Daladier: It was the High Command that put an end to the production of mines! Now they are trying to hold me responsible for it.

The prosecutor himself had to admit that it was so.

At a later session, General Keller, the Tank Inspector, was called as a witness for the prosecution. He repeated that the Germans had attacked with 6,000 tanks (as we have seen, historians have shown this figure to be erroneous) and said that given that imbalance, there was nothing our military commanders could have done.

Edouard Daladier: Is the witness aware that in 1935 the Chiefs of Staff scrapped an order for thirty tanks, and that in 1936 they simply neglected to order them from the Renault Company? The witness has no knowledge of these facts? Then maybe the witness is aware that the Chiefs of Staff put off placing orders for Hotchkiss tanks for over a year?

General Keller: Undoubtedly for lack of funds.

Edouard Daladier: They had all the funds they needed, in particular 300,000 francs that had to be carried over to the following year because no one had spent them. It was the same story with the 1937 cannon, the 1938 model. Its production was delayed two years because the people in the Tank Division were six months late in making a decision.

General Keller: Then you'll have to put your question to those people.

Edouard Daladier: I'll ask my questions whenever I like; I don't answer to you. To these figures we should add 600 British tanks.

General Keller flashed a smile.

Edouard Daladier: The mention of British tanks brings a smile to your face, does it? We have just seen what they can do in the area around Tripoli. Go ahead and laugh if you want, we'll see who'll be laughing ten or fifteen months from now! Did you, General Keller, communicate to your superiors the same black picture you've painted for us here?

General Keller: Of course.

Edouard Daladier: To whom did you communicate it?

General Keller: General Gamelin.

General Gamelin, indignantly: You never told me that. Do you hear me, never!

Court was adjourned. General Keller waited for General Gamelin and moved forward to greet him. Gamelin refused his hand, saying: "I shall never shake hands with you again. You're no man at all."

When Colonel Perré, whose tank division had fought brilliantly, took the stand, he testified that he was satisfied with the tanks, satisfied with their sturdiness, their armor, and their speed. However, he criticized the radio equipment, saying that there were too many different models.

Presiding Judge: M. Daladier, do you have any questions to ask of the witness?

Edouard Daladier: I have no questions to put to real military commanders.

The matter of a conspiracy within the Army surfaced during the cross-examination of General Gérodias, who had conducted himself ably. He mentioned, in particular, having been sanctioned by Daladier for having circulated throughout the Army a memorandum outlining a Communist putsch that directly threatened military officers and even their families.

When asked by the Presiding Judge where the memorandum had come from, the witness replied, "From Commander Loustanau-Lacau, of Marshal Pétain's staff." His response electrified the courtroom.

Fortifications

Daladier was accused of having been shortsighted in the area of fortifications. He answered by stating that he had committed 2.5 billion francs to building fortifications, adding, "I tried to have their construction continued further north on several occasions, but the Supreme War Council rejected the proposal each time, adopting the motion of its Vice President, Marshal Pétain.

"In spite of the opposition, I managed to have funds set aside for fortifications as early as 1933. When I was back in the War Ministry in 1936, I had an additional 300 million francs put in the budget for 1937, even though Belgium had backed out of its alliance with us. I made on-site inspections of everything that was being built and personally brought the matter to the attention of the High Command, but Marshal Pétain stated that the enemy would never be able to advance over this sector. [*Directive to the press: Delete the passage referring to Marshal Pétain's statement about this sector.]*

Similarly, in Parliament, each time deputies moved to have our fortifications extended further north, Marshal Pétain succeeded in blocking them. His hold over Parliament was undeniable.

Better still, in 1939 and 1940, General Billotte pointed out our vulnerability in this sector. The High Command took no notice of it.

An airman was called to testify. On May 8, 1940, he had flown over the Ardennes and spotted hundreds of German tanks moving on France, headlights ablaze.

Subsequently, Commander Caillet would affirm that in 1940, he had sealed off the two roads over which the Germans would later advance, by building walls and laying oak trees over them. On May 5, just a few days before the attack, he was ordered by the Second Army's Headquarters, commanded by General Huntziger (Pétain's War Minister at the time of the trial), to dismantle these barriers.

It was by these same two roads that the Germans reached the Meuse.

Conduct of Operations

The Chiefs of Staff believed neither that the Germans would attack with armored divisions nor that they would choose to attack through the Ardennes. One of the witnesses, General Etcheberrigaray, was in command of a B Series division (reserves) in this area. Two other B Series divisions were based at the point where the Germans attacked. The regular Army troops remained either in Alsace or in the East.

One further example: Our troops moved into Belgium in the daytime rather than at night, as military regulations stipulate. Daladier, who was there, said: "I didn't see a single German airplane, not one sign of an armed intervention. I thought that we had fallen into a trap."

General Prioux so notified his superiors, to no avail.

The errors committed by our military commanders surfaced again and again throughout the trial.

During the sixteenth court session, one of the prosecution's own witnesses, General Hering, acknowledged that Daladier's accomplishments were considerable, whereas the Ministers who had preceded him had done nothing.

In answer to a question from the defense attorney, Ribet, Hering stated that during a meeting of the Supreme War Council, Daladier had advocated the use of armored divisions and air power in combined operations. Unfortunately, the Council wasn't even able to reach agreement on what should constitute an armored division.

Aviation and Antiaircraft Weaponry

Guy La Chambre, who was Air Force Minister from 1938 to 1940, was called to testify. "In 1937," he said, "our industry was turning out only thirty-five planes a month. It was a craft industry; I even had to order machines from abroad. The High Command didn't really take aviation seriously. For example, we were forced to reduce our work force by 50 percent.

"In 1938, M. Daladier offered me the most useful kind of support there is, namely appropriations of 5 billion francs. The result was that by June 1940, we had 2,500 warplanes."[5]

General Massenet de Marencourt took the stand. "The Chiefs of Staff had locked up all our planes in hangars. I took it upon myself to put together fighter patrols. I even found the turret guns and machine guns we needed in Châtellerault." The witness gave other examples as well.

With regard to the planes ordered from the United States, Guy La Chambre said that "for reasons of security, the High Command asked us to have them delivered to Casablanca rather than to France, although there were neither assembly plants nor adequately trained personnel in Casablanca." Everything had to be improvised. Daladier was not even notified of the decision, although it was on his initiative that planes had been ordered from the United States.

5. It is generally agreed that there were 2,176 airplanes on the front lines, in addition to 550 British aircraft, not including the planes based in England. The Germans had approximately 4,500 aircraft. In 1940, France was producing 500 planes a month. That, taken together with the British output, meant either that the Allies were already outproducing the Germans or that they would outproduce them sometime in 1941.

Antiaircraft Weaponry

General Marescaux, a former Commander of antiaircraft defenses, testified about the major deficiencies in his units. He said that he had brought the seriousness of the situation to the attention of his three superiors: the Artillery Inspector General, the Director of Artillery, and the Inspector General for National Air Defense.

Marescaux said, however, that Daladier was not made aware of the situation until May 1938, at which point he immediately called Marescaux in. Within a few days' time, a 2.5 billion franc program for the construction of antiaircraft pieces had been launched. Then it was the experts' turn to show themselves incapable of reaching agreement. In the end, an exasperated Daladier had to impose the choice of a 90 mm cannon that had been designed in 1932 and that eventually proved to be an excellent weapon.

Nationalizations, Organization, and Legislation

Presiding Judge: You have been accused of failing to apply existing labor laws.

Edouard Daladier: France was stricken with an unemployment crisis. Many factory owners were offering their workers only thirty to forty hours of work a week. Moreover, in 1938, when I became Prime Minister, 130,000 workers were on strike. I negotiated with them; that was my duty. I appealed to public opinion; then I evacuated the factories without spilling a single drop of blood.

That ended the general strike.

Presiding Judge: But the strikers were hired back.

Edouard Daladier: It was a time to demonstrate generosity and unite all Frenchmen. We couldn't afford to lose men with expertise. As it turned out, by the end of 1938, half of the equipment had already been built. There were no production delays, quite the contrary.

Presiding Judge: You elected to nationalize certain industries for political reasons.

Edouard Daladier: I nationalized only ten factories. I also proposed government investment in private industry. M. Dautry, the Arms Minister, stated that "thanks to the retooling underwritten by the government, factories were able to provide the equipment needed at the time of the mobilization." In 1936, we appropriated 6 billion francs to stockpile industrial machinery and metals. We set up state plants. I tripled the number of new machines purchased from the United States. Working together with manufacturers, we created veritable industries in aluminum, cobalt, and magnesium. Similarly, after the general mobilization, output continued to increase, even though, without my knowledge and contrary to my instructions, skilled workers were called up who should have been left at their jobs in the factories. The production of equipment was three to four times what it was at the time of the mobilization.

The Presiding Judge cited a statement by M. Dautry characterizing France's industrial output as meager.

Edouard Daladier: If things were that bad, how does M. Dautry explain the rise in the productivity curve?

Colonel Rinderknech, writing to General Gamelin on June 2, 1940, stated that "there would be no reductions in munitions and matériel."

Of course, getting them to the front lines was something else!

Prosecutor: But you were the War Minister, weren't you?

Edouard Daladier: Once war was declared, the Supreme Commander was no longer under my authority. You'll have to put your questions to General Georges and the Army's commanders. What demands for matériel did they make? They should have created commissions to determine the state and quantities of our war supplies.

(On August 6, 1945, General Picquendar testified that in October 1940, he had seen equipment sitting in depots and even out in the fields. That matériel, with an estimated value of between 15 and 18 billion francs, could have outfitted twenty-four divisions—enough to arm three hundred thousand men. A full third of this equipment, the General said, fell into German hands when they invaded the Unoccupied Zone in November 1942.)

As of the twenty-fourth court session, Marshal Pétain issued a decree suspending the trial. Of the three hundred witnesses who were to appear, only thirty-six had been called. It had become clear, both in France and abroad, that those actually responsible for the defeat were Marshal Pétain; his War Minister, General Huntziger; and our military commanders, since they alone were in charge of defining strategy, directing operations, and choosing the kinds and quantities of weaponry to be used.

It had been shown that the French people and their civilian Ministers had provided the military with all the moneys that they had requested, and more.

The tribunal that had been created by Marshal Pétain and his government decided to release Guy La Chambre, the head of the Air Force; and Jacomet, who in his capacity as Secretary-General of Arms was in effect the head of France's ground forces. In view of the decision to drop the charges against these two men, how could one maintain that Daladier and Blum were responsible for the defeat?

How does one explain the fact that Daladier and Blum remained in prison, if not by a desire to appease Hitler and Vichy? In 1943, Marshal Pétain and his government would hand both men over to the Gestapo, who had them imprisoned in Germany.

And once again, how does one explain the fact that, even today, what were revealed to be lies and errors during the trial in Riom are still given credence by a great many Frenchmen?

Appendix C
Biographical Timeline

1884	Born in Carpentras, into a family of craftsmen, originally peasants, who had settled in the Vaucluse region of France in the seventeenth century. Attended middle school and high school in Lyons, on scholarship. Received the highest score ever achieved until then on the *agrégé* examination in history.
1909	Appointed to a position as a history teacher in Nîmes.
1911	Elected Mayor of Carpentras on the Radical-Socialist ticket at age twenty-eight.
1913	Founded a far-left, republican newspaper, *Germinal.*
1914	Having volunteered, served as a Sergeant in the Foreign Legion. Was awarded the *Croix de guerre,* three medals for bravery, and the *Légion d'honneur.* Promoted to Lieutenant in 1918.
1919	Elected to Parliament on the Radical-Socialist ticket.
1923	Voted against Poincaré's decision to send French troops to occupy the Ruhr Valley.
1924–1926	Appointed Minister several times, including Minister of War in 1925.
1932	Published the first paper calling for the nation to rearm (one in a collection of papers).
1933 (Jan.–Oct.)	Prime Minister. Won support for the nation's first rearmament program. Toppled by the Socialists, who opposed his rearmament program, and the Right, who criticized his social reforms.

1934 (Feb.)	Appointed Prime Minister a second time. Stood up to the rioters, who failed in their attempt to storm the Chamber of Deputies. Failed to win adequate support for his proposed stand against them. Stepped down in the absence of a majority in Parliament.
1936	Regained the leadership of the Radical-Socialists and, by supplying the party's support, brought about the victory of the Popular Front. Launched the first vast rearmament program as War Minister in Léon Blum's government.
1936–1938	Served as Minister of Defense on several occasions.
1938 (Apr.)	Appointed Prime Minister for a third time. Signed the Munich Agreement in September.
1939	Declared war on Germany on September 3.
1940 (Mar.)	Resigned.
(Mar.–May)	Minister of Defense, then Minister of Foreign Affairs, in Paul Reynaud's government.
(June)	Left for North Africa with Mendès-France, Campinchi, Mandel, and several Members of Parliament to carry on the fight from there.
(Sept.)	Forcibly brought back to France and imprisoned.
1942	Sentenced to life imprisonment, then tried in Riom.
1943	Imprisoned in Germany.
1945 (May)	Liberated.
1946	Reelected to Parliament from the Vaucluse.
1946–1958	Served concurrently as a Member of Parliament and Mayor of Avignon.
1958	Resigned from all political offices.
1970	Died in Paris.

About the Book

The French Prime Minister who signed the Munich Agreement in 1938 and who one year later led his country into war against Hitler's Germany, Edouard Daladier was arrested by the Vichy regime and imprisoned in France and Germany until the war's end. As a pastime and a catharsis, Daladier wrote.

He wrote about what had happened to him and to his country, about day-to-day conditions in captivity, and about what he could glean of the anti-Nazi war effort through newspaper accounts, from the visits of his friends and family, and from his well-hidden radio receiver. He wrote of the accusations made against him by his former protégés and comrades-in-arms; and of his trial, during which the charges oddly metamorphosed from having declared war on Germany to not having sufficiently prepared France for battle (the charges were of little importance, as the verdict had been previously decided).

Ever the statesman, Daladier wrote most of all about his hopes and fears for France and Europe—which hung so heavily, at first, upon the battlefield successes of the British, American, and Allied forces; and later, upon the Allies' refusal to recognize in Soviet power the danger of the very totalitarianism that they had been fighting to eliminate. At the war's end, witnessing the devastation of Germany, Daladier wrote with a poignant sympathy that is unexpectedly moving.

Daladier's notes remained forgotten and unpublished until twenty years after his death, when they were discovered and compiled by his son Jean. They are presented here in English for the first time. By turns sorrowful, enraged, humorous, and philosophical, this lively narrative gives fresh insights into the tangled politics of the era.

Edouard Daladier was born in Carpentras in 1884. He was elected to Parliament as a member of the Radical-Socialist Party in 1919 and named War Minister in 1925. Thrice named Prime Minister (1933, 1934, and 1938), it was he who signed the Munich Agreement for France in September 1938. From March to May 1940, Daladier was successively Minister of War and of Foreign Affairs in Paul Reynaud's government. When France was overrun in June 1940, Daladier left for North Africa with the hope of carrying on the fight from there. He was forcibly returned, arrested, and imprisoned by the Vichy government, which brought him to trial in Riom in 1942, then handed him over for deportation to Germany in 1943. Daladier remained in captivity there until he was liberated by the Allied forces. After the war, he was reelected to Parliament and served as Deputy and Mayor of Avignon from 1946 to 1958. He died in Paris in 1970.

Jean Daridan, who provided most of the annotations to the original French edition, was a good friend of Edouard Daladier and remained close to him during the war. A diplomat who began his career in 1932, he was also a member of the staffs of two Prime Ministers, Edouard Herriot and Joseph Paul-Boncour.

Arthur D. Greenspan is Professor of French at Colby College.

Index

Abetz, Otto, 31–34, 36, 43, 123–125, 135, 158
Abrial, Admiral, 104, 143
Abyssinia, 73, 107
Achard, 76, 134
Achenbach, 31–35
Action Française, 190, 264, 290
Action française, L', 13, 24, 30, 62, 104n, 249(n4), 262
Addresses to the German Nations (Fichte), 185
Africa, 164, 169–172, 176, 182, 186, 202. *See also* North Africa
Afrikakorps, 202
Agrarian Party, 134
Air Defense Committee, 262
Air Defense League, 262
Alexandre, Serge. *See* Stavisky, Sacha
Algeria, x, 103, 169–170, 183–184, 296
Algiers, xii, 104–105, 180, 186–187, 190, 206–207, 219, 231–233
Algiers Committee, 234, 257, 258, 274
Alibert, Raphaël, 23, 25, 32–33, 135, 150, 260, 265, 291
  and Laval, 39, 154
Alsace-Lorraine, 111, 123, 151, 253, 301, 309
Altmayer, René, 252, 255, 264
Anti-Bolshevik Legion, 92
Anti-Jewry Board, 75
Aosta, Duke of, 56
Asia, 25, 195, 296, 300, 324
Atlantic Charter, 325, 327
Auriol, Vincent, 26, 295
Australia, 132, 220
Austria, 221, 235
Badoglio, Pietro, 214, 216, 218–219, 223–224, 226–229, 233, 271
Bailby, Léon, 230, 260, 262, 265
Baltic States, 185, 218, 236, 240, 329
Bank of Worms, 134, 137, 267, 276
Baraveau, 63, 119
Barnaud, 267, 276
Barthe, Edouard, 23
Barthélemy, Joseph, 51, 73, 80, 92, 93, 108, 124–125, 142
  and executions, 141, 152, 156–57
  and prisoners, 95–96, 168, 191
Bastid, Paul, 309
Baudouin, Paul, 20, 23, 43, 97, 103, 106, 135, 266–267
  and Mussolini, 161, 215
  and Reynaud, 77, 202
  in Synarchie, 267, 276, 291
  and Vichy government, 25, 290
Begbeder, Captain, 269
Belgium, 120, 155–156, 161, 217, 275, 299, 301–302
Belin, René, 20, 91, 137, 202
Belsen (concentration camp), 334
Bénazet, Henri, 208
Bénazet, Paul, 75, 109–110, 143
Benes, Edward, xi, 210, 229–230, 272, 274
Benoist-Méchin, Jacques, 76, 78, 89, 159
Bergeret, Jean, 180, 185, 293
Bergery, Gaston, 85, 89, 124, 138
Berl, Emmanuel, 12
Bernanos, 280
Besse, René, 157–158
Béthouart, Maurice-Emile, 269
Bichelonne, Jean, 151
Bidou, Henri, 64
Billotte, General, xx
Billoux, François, 323

Bineau, Henri, 32, 162
Bireau, 179
Bismarck, 66
Bloch, Jean Richard, 324
Blum, Léon, 11, 52–57, 127–128, 153, 197, 256
  arrest of, 16–19
  in Bourassol prison, 37(n64), 78, 131, 146, 168
  in Buchenwald, 208, 201(n11)
  communications with, 66, 69–70, 81, 86, 98, 114, 161
  and Daladier, 18–19, 102
  and Darlan, 65–66, 178
  on Dormoy assassination, 82
  and de Gaulle, 160, 197, 207, 322
  German deportation of, 174, 180, 181, 189, 193, 199
  and Germany, xii, 130, 145–146
  government of, xvii
  illness of, 121
  on Iraq, 59–60
  and Jacomet, 141
  and La Chambre, 60, 116
  marriage of, 210
  optimism of, 51, 56, 60
  and Pétain, 80, 85
  and Popular Front, xviii
  in Le Portalet prison, 92, 94, 101
  and Riom trial, vii, xi, 101–102, 120
  Royalist attack of, 104
  and Socialist Party, ix, 204, 231, 319
  and United States, 196
  on World War II, xii, 121–122
Blum, Renée, 71, 80, 84, 114
Blum, Robert, 153
Blumel, André, 131–132
Bois, Elie, 129
Boissier, Gaston, 83
Boisson, Pierre, 171, 179, 186
Bolshevik Legion, 151
Bonhomme, Captain, 264–265
Bonnard, Abel, 124, 265
Bonnefoy, René, 177
Bonnet, Georges, xi, 11–13, 23–24, 46, 52, 137, 140, 232, 302
  as collaborator, 142
  and Pétain, 275–276
Borie, André, 3, 4
Borotra, Jean, xii, 201, 214, 250–252, 254–255
  in Itter prison, 201, 208, 244, 335, 337, 338, 340
Boucoiran, Jeanne, 75–76
Bouisson, Fernand, 287–288
Bourassol prison, vii, 37(n64), 80, 121, 152
  conditions at, 70, 110, 168
  and German occupation, 166–168, 170–174, 183, 189, 192–193
  military buildup in, 64–65, 67
Bourdan, Pierre, 230
Bourend, 325
Bourgeois, Léon, 293
Bourrageas, 230
Bourret, General, 178
Bousquet, René, xiii, 136, 151, 153–155, 160, 168, 181
  and Bourassol prison, 170–171, 186
  and Daladier, 171, 193
  Génébrier talks with, 145, 176
Bouthillier, Yves, 76, 97, 106, 202, 266
  and Synarchie, 267, 276, 291
Brandt, 75, 125
Brécard, Charles, 264, 266, 291
Briand, Aristide, 40, 185, 237
Bridoux, Eugène, 130, 150, 203
Brinon, Fernand de, 33, 35, 37, 42, 82–84, 124–125
Brochet, 4
Brossolette, Pierre, 159
Bruzin, 87, 118, 140
Buchenwald (concentration camp), 201(n11), 331, 332, 334
Bulgaria, 56, 185, 235, 240, 295, 297, 312
Bullitt, William C., 13, 19, 45, 136, 167n, 207, 331
  and French war declaration, 33–37
  friendship with, 47, 75, 340
Bunau-Varilla, Maurice, 259
Buré, Emile, 322, 327

Cachin, Marcel, 322

Cagoule, xvii, 25, 27(n54), 64–65, 72, 83, 106, 260(n13), 267
Cailleau, 331–332
Cairo Conference, 239
Camelots du Roi, 72
Campinchi, 178
Canada, 24, 120, 212–214
Candide, 24
Caous, 102, 140, 156–160, 186, 191
Carbuccia, Horace de, 27, 135
Carcopino, Jérôme, 288, 290
Cartel des Gauches, viii
Cartier, General, 87
Cassagneau, 89, 191
Cassin, René, 287
Castelnau, 74
Cathala, 162
Catholic church, xvii, 106, 121, 133, 151, 160–161, 190, 196
Catroux, Georges, 25, 79, 176, 232
Caziot, 135
CGT. *See* Confédération Générale du Travail
Chamberlain, Neville, x–xi, xix, 8, 173, 215
Champoille, Fabien de, 85
Chapoulié, Bishop, 190
Châteaubriand, 72
Chatel, 180
Chaumié, 109
Chautemps, Camille, ix, 11, 30, 75, 77, 103, 120, 182, 205, 302
Chauvel, Henry, 50, 53–54, 58–59, 69, 84, 125, 130
  and Daladier sentencing, 88–89
  and Pétain, 78–80
  visits by, 64, 77–78, 96, 152
Chavin, 6, 17, 21, 52, 60
Chazeron prison, 4–5, 8, 21, 94
Chevalier, 38, 283
Chiang Kai-shek, 131, 236
Chiappe, Jean, 248, 259
Chichery, Albert, 137, 143, 157
China, 25, 131, 148, 235, 236, 300
Christian Democrats (France), 294, 323
Churchill, Winston, xxii, 8, 15, 24, 202, 210, 284
  and Daladier escape, 186n
  Edinburgh speech of, 161
  and France, 143, 173, 174, 205, 233–234, 292, 318
  on German surrender, 297, 311
  and Greece, 298, 299, 303, 325
  and the Philippines, 296
  and the Soviet Union, 275, 295
  and Stalin, 312, 316
  on Yalta Conference, 326–327
Ciano, Galeazzo, 13, 107, 161
Ci-devant (Monzie), 109
Clapier, Marcel, 63, 178
Clark, Mark, 259, 277
Clemenceau, Georges, xix, 8, 89, 166, 186, 220, 256, 282
Clemenceau, Michel, 247, 250–252, 254–256, 282, 338
Clémentel, 94
Collin, Paul, 198
Combat, 132, 319, 320
Comité France-Allemagne, 42
Committee for a Free Germany, 319
Communist International, 204
Communist Party (Algiers), 219
Communist Party (France), ix–x, xvii, 29, 71, 74, 260, 264, 322–324
  and de Gaulle, 232–233, 256–258, 322
  and party system, 197, 294
  and Popular Front, xviii, 18
  and Socialist Party, 204, 231
Communist Party (Germany), xvii
Communist Party (Greece), 298, 299, 325
Communist Party (Poland), 307, 309
Confédération Générale du Travail (CGT), ix, x, 17(n34)
Corap, General, 53, 111
Council of Political Justice, 142
Cour Suprême de Justice, 4(n3), 6
Crespi, 215
Cresteil, 116
Cripps, Sir Stafford, 119, 131, 295
Croix de Feu, 18, 249, 250, 262
Croquez, 49, 65, 155–157
Crouzet, Guy, 131
Cunin, 83–84
Czechoslovakia, vii, xxii, 7, 12, 212, 229–230, 236, 312

and France, xix, 261, 274
and the Soviet Union, 120, 271–272

Dac, Pierre, 274
Dachau (concentration camp), 211, 244, 334, 336
Daily Telegraph, 326
Daladier, Edouard, vii–xiii, xvi–xx, xxii–xxiii, 1, 37(n64), 240
British rescue attempts for, xvi, 2(n4), 186n
liberation of, xxii, 338–341
in World War I, viii, xvi, 231
Daladier, Jean, 4–5, 69, 105, 160, 298, 340
and Daladier escape plan, 189
letters from, 119, 199
in Resistance, 340–341
visits by, 17, 19–21, 24–25, 28, 55, 82–84, 87, 98–99, 110, 137, 163, 170–172
Daladier, Marie, 66, 87, 114
Daladier, Pierre, 5, 66–67, 82
visits by, 72, 87, 163, 164, 167, 168, 184
Daridan, Jean, 52, 59, 77, 146–147, 174–175, 190
Darlan, François, xii, 1(n2), 2, 68–69, 73–74, 84, 93, 140
in Africa, 129, 171–172, 176, 180, 190
in Algeria, 169
assassination of, 178, 180
and Baudouin, 267
and Clapier, 63
dislike of, 61, 173
and Gamelin, 70, 163
and Hitler, 44, 50, 66
and Pétain, 78–79, 81, 125, 129, 179
political rise of, 50, 65–66, 178–179
and Riom trial, 51, 155
and Tunisia, 171, 212
Darnand, Joseph, 140, 149, 247, 257, 277
d'Astier de la Vigerie, Emmanual, 232, 275–276
d'Aubagne, Gence, 96
Daudet, Léon, 249, 262
Dautry, Raoul, 74
Davis, Norman, xvi
Déat, Marcel, 13–14, 83, 89, 124, 135, 182, 278
and Laval, 39, 40, 176
popular opinion of, 72–73
and Royalists, 62–63
Debeney, General, 261
de Brinon, 54
Debu-Bridel, Jacques, 320
de Castelnau, General, 165
de Flore, Joachim, 67
Degrelle, Léon, 156, 198
Dejean, Maurice, 274
de Kérillis, Henri, 206
de Labradelle, 230
de Lattre de Tassigny, General, 286, 301, 340
Deloncle, Eugène, 25(n48), 74
Democratic Party (U.S.), 329
Dentz, Henri, 65, 76
Desgranges, Canon, 85–86, 121, 137, 244
Deshuses, 149
d'Esperey, Franchet, xvii, 25(n48), 260, 264, 267, 276
Devaux, Gilbert, 291
d'Harcourt, 115
Diard, 105
di Borgo, Pozzo, 279
Dillard, Reverend Father, 133, 146, 160
Dommange, 83
Doriot, Jacques, 62–63, 124–125, 135, 138, 150–152, 249, 264
and Granger arrest, 211
Italian subsidy of, 276
Doriotists, 63, 72, 140, 149–150, 177
d'Ormesson, Vladimir, 309
Dormoy, Jeanne, 82
Dormoy, Marx, 26, 27(n54), 81–82, 291
Doumergue, Gaston, ix, 19, 40, 249, 253, 263
Dreyfus affair, 9, 28
Droit international, 230
Duclos, Jacques, 320, 323
Dufieux, Julien, 29–30
Dulot, Charles, 17, 21
Dumbarton Oaks conference, 293
Du Moulin de Labarthète, 125, 131, 140
Durand-Viel, Admiral, 66, 178

Eden, Anthony, 171, 186, 297, 303

Egypt, 59–60, 132, 147, 164, 327
Eisenhower, Dwight D., 171–172, 233, 279, 297, 302, 333
England. *See* Great Britain
Entente Cordiale, 272
Epictetus, 228
Ercoli, 271
Esteva, Admiral, 203
Europe, postwar, 273–275, 283, 300

Fabre, Francisque, 59, 160
Fabry, Jean, 11, 22, 206
Farinacci, Roberto, 93, 224
Farnoux, Abel, 163
Fascist Party (France), xvii, 11, 277–278
Fascist Party (Italy), 214–216, 223–224
Faure, Paul, 138
Ferrand, Clermont, 49
Ferrari, Carlos, 233
Fichte, 185
Filhol, 65
Finland, x, 236, 240, 297, 329
Flandin, Pierre-Etienne, 18–19, 38, 40, 43–44, 50, 130–131, 190, 293
Foch, Ferdinand, 89, 96, 97, 165, 181, 186
Fonck, René, 125
Foreign Legion, xvi
Forneret, 104
France, xv, xvii–xviii, 161, 322
  Air Force of, xxi, 11–12, 22, 48, 111, 115–117, 153–154, 191
  in Algeria, x, 270, 296
  Allied support of, 173–175, 309, 311, 318
  Armistice in, xv, 1, 2(n5), 91, 103, 164–165, 169
  Army of. *See* French Army
  Battle of, 54, 280, 290
  and Belgium, 217
  collaborator trials in, 315–316
  Consultative Assembly in, 294, 295
  coup attempts in, 259–260, 264–265
  and Czechoslovakia, xix, 261
  economy of, 314
  executions in, 120, 275, 310
  German negotiations with, 32–37, 40, 43–44, 58–59, 61, 84, 103, 123–124, 127, 151, 176–177
  and Germany, xix, 53, 77–78, 287, 298
  and Great Britain, 7, 34, 55, 102, 108, 117, 259, 272, 280, 299
  and Italy, 105–108, 215, 276
  and Japan, 81
  and Lebanon, 327
  liberation of, 278–280
  military leadership in, 48, 91, 109–111, 115–116, 162
  Navy of, xxi, 171, 188
  North African plan of, xv, xxi, 1–2, 82, 103, 106–107, 129, 148
  Occupied, 6, 111, 127, 158, 280
  party system in, 197, 294
  and Poland, 7, 23–24, 117, 236, 307–308
  postwar, 196, 290
  press in, 327–328
  provisional government of, 319–323
  rearmament of, xi, xvi–xx, xxii, 7, 11, 22, 48, 102, 148
  Resistance in. *See* Resistance
  and the Soviet Union, 71, 92, 237–238, 298, 299. *See also* Franco-Soviet pact
  and Syria, 65, 76, 327
  Third Republic of, vii–xiii, 4(n3)
  in United Nations, 293
  and United States, 45, 47–48, 86, 102, 136
  Unoccupied, xxi, 38, 53, 136, 138–139, 165–169, 174–175
  Vichy government of. *See* Vichy government
  and Yalta Conference, 326, 328
France Soir, 13
Francisque, 149
Franco, Francisco, 201
François-Poncet, André, 107–108, 222, 229, 231
Franco-Soviet pact, 298–301, 312, 321, 324
Freedom Front, 264–266
Free French Resistance Forces, 25(n47), 126
Freemasons, 65, 85, 104, 109, 129, 143

French Army, x, xv, xxvii–xxii, 7, 107, 138–139, 301, 335
in Africa, 2, 154, 169–70, 176
Allied support of, 309, 321
in Italy, 224–226, 242
leadership of, 49, 53, 91, 146, 162
in U.S. press, 303
French Army of the Armistice, 49
French Committee of National Liberation, 209, 232
French Forces of the Interior, 288
French National News Bureau, 118
French People's Party (PPF), 62(n18), 138, 149, 211, 264
French Social Party (PSF), 18(n35), 212, 251, 256, 262, 264–265
Frère, General, 30, 138–139, 150, 169
Frossard, Ludovic-Oscar, 14, 205, 275–276

Gabolde, 142
Gaboriau, 9, 163
Gamelin, Maurice, vii, xi, 52–53, 71, 191, 265, 277
on Allied landing in Sicily, 213
arrest of, 9, 22, 222
and Badoglio, 214
in Bourassol prison, 9, 12, 29–30, 37(n64)
Catholicism of, 67–68, 133, 146
and Daladier, 8–9, 68, 106
and Darlan, 70, 179
and French Army, 8–9, 12, 29, 209, 224
on French arrests, 289
on French defeat, 198
on Georges, 205–206, 217
in Itter prison, 181, 189, 200–201, 208, 244, 297, 337
and La Roque, 250–252, 254
and Maginot Line, 266
and North African plan, 106
and Payot, 308
in Le Portalet prison, 92, 94, 96
in Riom trial, vii, 115, 163
Gasnier-Duparc, 65, 74, 178
Gaulle, Charles de, viii, xii, xxi, 21–22, 180, 234, 295–296
and Africa, 25, 172, 173
and Algiers, 187, 207, 232
ambition of, 205
and Benes, 274
and Blum, 160, 322
and Churchill, 174
and Communist Party, 256–258, 322
criticism against, 209
and Daladier escape, 186n
and Darlan, 171, 176
and Eisenhower, 279
in Franco-Soviet pact talks, 298, 300
and French isolation, 210
on French liberation, 288
and Giraud, 180, 204–205
as Head of the Provisional Government, 197
and Noguès, 2(n5)
and Payot, 58, 308
and Pétain, 79
and Peyrouton, 212
popular support for, 289
and Resistance, 285, 294
and Roosevelt, 326, 328
and Stalin, 257–258
in Syria, 68–69
and Vallin, 159
Gaullists, 109, 153, 184, 190, 256–257
propaganda of, 177, 233
Gazette de Lausanne, 76
Génébrier, Roger, 22, 54, 86, 139–140, 151, 193
and Bousquet, 136, 145, 176
and Riom trial, 113
visits by, 51–52, 59, 71, 90, 149
George, Lloyd, 236, 272n
Georges, Joseph, 9, 27, 30, 140, 163, 205–206, 224, 232, 277
criticism against, 209, 217
Gerbe, Le, 72, 198
Gerlier, Cardinal, 90
German-Soviet Pact, 45, 74
Germany, 46
Air Force of, 117
Army of, 78, 110, 138, 154, 181, 185, 192–193, 220, 286, 305, 330
and Bourassol prisoners, xiii, 174, 181, 189, 191–195. *See also* Itter prison

in Churchill's address, 311
Communist executions by, 133, 141
concentration camps in, 333, 334
Daladier's policy toward, x, xii, xx
defeat of, 117, 182, 236, 289, 333
and Great Britain, xix, 7, 53, 79, 81, 147–148
in Franco-Soviet pact, 300
French citizen executions in, 275, 310
French collaboration with, 40, 43–44, 315
and French draft, 176
French factory orders of, 53
French hostages of, 298
French Jews arrested by, 141
French negotiations with, 32, 34–36, 58–59, 61, 84, 103, 123–124, 127, 129, 151, 169, 176–177
French workers in, 131, 137, 144, 151, 183, 196
High Command replacements in, 282
industrial capacity of, 46
and Italy, 106–107, 146, 216, 218–219, 223, 225–228, 277
and Laval, 58–59, 123–124, 137
Mézières attack of, 27
and Nazism, xvii, 185, 198, 295, 310
partitioning of, 293, 301, 313
postwar, 77, 285, 290
Prussian domination of, 146
rearmament of, 19, 148
and Riom trial, 108
and the Soviet Union, xvi, 235, 316
in Unoccupied France, 165–169, 174–175
and U.S. war intervention, 126, 302–303
if victorious, 90, 145
in World War I armistice, 231–232
Yugoslavia executions by, 161
Gérodias, Paul-Henri, 265–266
Gestapo, 123, 124, 150, 310
Gillouin, 265
Giorgini, 221, 223, 226, 230, 236
Giraud, Henri, 2(n4), 130, 150, 171, 184, 204–207, 232
in Algiers, 186
and Baudouin, 267
and Churchill, 202
criticism against, 209
and de Gaulle, 180, 204–205
and Laval, 179
and Pétain, 169, 187, 190
and Peyrouton, 212
and Pucheu, 268–269
in Vichy cliques, 137
Goebbels, Joseph, 126, 175, 185, 235, 284, 293, 330
in Berlin defense, 318
Hitler birthday speech by, 332
on Soviet Union, 189, 312
Göring, Hermann, xxi, 93, 110, 125, 184–185, 284
Gort, Lord, 175
Gouin, Félix, 204, 239
Gouraud, 30
Granger, Marcel, 211–212, 244–245, 247, 250, 254, 286
Great Britain, xxi–xxii, 12, 45, 111, 201, 234
colonies of, 220
and Daladier, xvi, 1, 2(n4), 3, 21, 70(n22), 87(n42), 105, 240
as democracy, 120–121, 221
Expeditionary Force of, 175
and France, xv, 7, 20, 32–35, 37, 102, 259, 272, 280, 299
French military cooperation with, 55, 108, 117, 173–174
and de Gaulle, 298
and Greece, 56–57, 240, 298, 325
and Hitler, xvii, 117
and Iraq, 60
and Italy, 215
and Japan, 236
and La Roque, xii
and Laval, 38, 42
Navy of, xxi, 66
in North Africa, 105, 322
and pan-Arabic confederation, 327
Pétain on, 79
and Poland, 301, 307, 310, 325–326
postwar, 233, 293, 316
rearmament of, xviii–xix

Royal Air Force (RAF) of, 15, 24, 55, 117, 258–259, 280, 290
and Soviet Union, 298, 299
survival of, 119
and United States, 7, 47–48, 60–61, 174, 227
and Vichy government, 13
and war victory, 162, 227
Greece, 55–56, 225–226, 295, 303
Communist Party in, 298, 299, 325
and Great Britain, 56–57, 240, 298, 325
Grenier, Fernand, 207, 257, 258, 269
Gringoire, 24, 27(n55), 65, 104n, 116
Grumbach, Salomon, 26
Guariglia, 214–215, 217
Guillermet, 104
Guitry, Sacha, 288
Guy, Edmonde, 158

Hajek, Jean, 229–230
Halifax, Lord, 12, 270
Henriot, Philippe, 247, 262, 277, 280
Herr, Admiral, 70
Herriot, Edouard, viii–ix, 1, 45, 64, 86, 103, 134, 193
arrest of, 159
in North African plan, 129
restrictions against, 181
and Reynaud, 202, 205
Hesse, Prince of, 161–62
Himmler, Heinrich, 93, 229, 251, 254–255, 284
Hindenburg, Paul von, 313
Hitler, Adolf, 62, 98, 110, 130, 218, 273
Blum on, 55
and British invasion, 79, 117
and Chamberlain, xix
and Darlan, 44, 50, 66
defeat of, 93
and Flandin, 40, 43
and France, xv, 7, 92, 123, 138, 151
and headquarters bombing, 284
and Italy, 106–107, 225–226
and Laval, 32, 34, 66, 124
and Mussolini, 284
1945 address by, 305–307
1945 birthday of, 332
and Pétain, 34, 40, 65
and Poland, vii, x
and Soviet Union, xx, 70, 71
and Stalin, x, 107
strategical error of, 185
suicide of, 336n
and Vatican, 133
Höner, Captain, 238, 240
Hood, 66
House, Edward, 237
Hull, Cordell, 86
Humanité, L', 250, 256, 321
Humbert, Charles, 125
Hungary, 56, 240
Huntziger, Charles, 10, 43–44, 49, 76, 169, 277
and Roosevelt document, 31(n59), 32–33, 37

India, 119, 227, 235, 311
Indochina, 25, 296
Information, L', 229, 230
Inonu, Ismet, 76
Internationale, 242
Iraq, 57, 60, 155, 327
Ironside, William, 217
Italy, xvi, 7, 42, 177, 271
and France, 105–108, 215, 224–225, 276–277
French press subsidies by, 230, 276
and Germany, 106–107, 146, 216, 218–219, 225–228, 277
and Great Britain, 215, 311
morale in, 213
Navy of, 55
rationing in, 147
and Riom trial, 120
Soviet recognition of, 271
surrender of, 223–224
Itter prison (Germany), 208, 213, 237, 317, 334–335
Daladier in, vii, xii–xiii, 200, 222, 238, 286, 321, 338–339
liberation of, 338–339
military operations in, 240, 292–294, 296, 297, 336–339

Jacomet, Robert, 60, 74, 119, 127, 135, 146, 163, 193
arrest of, 87, 181
imprisonment of, 58, 61, 83–84, 153, 186–189, 192
and Laval, 130
and Riom trial, 140–141
Vichy treatment of, 75
Jacquin, Colonel, 48
Jacquinot, Louis, 204, 207, 232
Jacquot, Pierre-Elie, 49, 53, 71, 116, 139, 347
Jael, 140
Jallu, Olivier, 157
Japan, 24, 79, 126, 132, 234, 239
and China, 25, 131, 236
and Soviet Union, 56, 189, 233, 235, 271
and United States, 56, 98, 126, 296, 313, 324
Vichy negotiations with, 81, 122
Jardin, Jean, 31, 147
Jassa, 89
Jean Bart, 170
Jeanneney, Jules, 45, 103, 129, 148–149, 295, 308
and Daladier, 105–106, 108
and Reynaud, 202, 205
Jerome, Saint, 61–62
Jesuits. *See* Society of Jesus
Jews, xiii, 35, 141, 220–221, 306, 311
and Catholic church, 151
Legion hatred for, 143
Pétain scapegoating of, 129
press articles against, 65
Joffre, Joseph, 11, 96, 166, 186
Joliot-Curie, Frédéric, 299, 320
Josselme, Albert, 84
Jouhaux, Léon, ix, 193–96, 204, 282, 231, 250
and de Gaulle, 197, 207
in Itter prison, 201, 208, 220, 231, 271, 330, 337
on Paris liberation, 288
and Pétain, 253, 263
and postwar Europe, 283, 285
Jour, Le, 16, 17
Journal, Le, 17
Journal de Genève, Le, 69, 74, 308
Journal officiel, 85, 118
Jouvenel, Bertrand de, 109
Juin, Alphonse, 259, 276, 277
Juvanon, 85

Kayser, Jacques, 140
Kesselring, Albert, 283
Kœnig, Pierre, 126–127, 274

Laborde, Admiral, 2
Labor Party (Australia), 220
Labor Party (Great Britain), 298
La Chambre, Guy, 60, 111, 135, 153, 181
in Bourassol prison, 37(n64), 146, 159–160, 168, 186–189, 192
and Riom trial, 110, 115–116
Lagarde, 23, 51, 63, 73, 81, 84, 86, 102
and Daladier indictment, 88–89
and prison visitors, 66–67, 70
Lagardelle, Hubert, 137, 151
Lamoricière, 103, 105
Lamoureux, Lucien, 124, 157
Landry, 83
Langeron, Roger, 51
La Roque, François de, xii, 18, 62, 212, 276, 279
arrest of, 249, 253
on French coup attempts, 259–260, 262, 264–265
in Itter prison, 247, 250–252, 254–256, 286, 337–338, 340
and Laval, 248, 249, 253, 261–262
and Pétain, 249–250, 253–254, 256, 260–264, 266, 279–280
political rise of, 247–249, 261–262
Lassguiwer, 131
Laure, Emile, 140, 150, 162, 262
Laurent, Charles, 146, 225, 257, 269
Lauzanne, Stéphane, 288
Laval, Pierre, ix–x, 19, 22, 85, 93, 128, 140
arrest of, 154
Benoist-Méchin dismissal by, 159
and Bourassol prisoners, 168–169, 173–174, 181, 186–187, 191
and Bousquet, xiii
and Chautemps, 120

and Chichery, 143
and Daladier, xii, 144–145, 193
and Darlan, 179
dismissal of, 38–40, 42–43
and French Resistance, 287
and German negotiations, 123–124, 151, 164, 174–177, 179
and Germany, 58–59, 137, 161, 190–91
and Henriot assassination, 280
and Hitler, 32, 34, 66
and La Roque, 248, 249, 253, 261–262
and Le Trocquer, 181
and Mussolini, 124, 215
personality of, 6, 144–145
and Pétain, xviii, 6(n8), 44, 79, 125, 129, 177, 266
and Peyrouton, 184
political rise of, 40–42, 90–91
and Pucheu, 268
and Riom trial, 33, 135, 139, 143–144, 155
and Roosevelt, 31–33, 35–37, 175
Stalin pact with, 130
in Stavisky affair, 110
support for, 132, 227–228, 277
and Third Republic, 7n
in Vichy cliques, 65, 137–138, 147, 150, 210, 288
Lazare, Captain, 340
League of Nations, xix, 42, 45, 282n
Leahy, William D., 268
Lebecq, 259–260
Lebrun, Albert, ix, 8, 9, 11, 39, 103, 129
in Itter prison, 222
and Reynaud resignation, 202, 205
Leca, Dominique, 291
Le Chatelet, General, 115
Leclerc, General, 288
Lecoin, 14
Lefèvre, Colonel, 64
Legion of French Volunteers (LVF), 62, 73, 86, 89, 149–150, 152, 203
as Nazi party, 93, 97
propaganda of, 143
Legion of French Volunteers Against Bolshevism, 125–126
Legueu, 67, 162
Lemaire, 142
Lémery, Henry, 260, 266, 291
Lenclud, General, 122, 158
Léonard, Roger, 53, 71
Le Portalet prison, 88, 92, 94–95, 99(n47), 101, 135, 142
Lequerica, de, 93, 103
Le Roy Ladurie, Jacques, 134–135, 151
Le Roy Ladurie, Gabriel, 134, 276, 291
Lesueur, 63
Le Trocquer, André, 51, 159–160, 168–170, 173, 181, 231–232, 267
Leygues, Georges, 178
Liberia, 164
Libya, 2, 98, 126, 131
Liebknecht, Karl, 145
Lippmann, Walter, 299–300, 303
Littorio, 55
Lorraine, Sir Percy, 108, 215
Lorraine Corporation, 75
Loucheur, 90
Loustanau-Lacau, Georges, xvii, 25(n48), 253, 260, 264–266, 276, 291
Lublin Committee, 301
Luchaire, Jean, 72–73, 131
Luxembourg, 275, 301
Luxemburg, Rosa, 145
LVF. *See* Legion of French Volunteers

Mabire, Christiane, 211, 251, 331
McAuliffe, Anthony, 339
Madagascar, 122
Malaysia, 98
Mallet, 131
Malvy, 90–91, 93
Mandel, Georges, 75, 90, 135, 199, 202
assassination of, 14(n31), 201(n11), 281–283
imprisonment of, 14, 22, 51, 201(n11), 208
Mandel, Louis Georges. *See* Mandel, Georges
Marchandeau, Paul, 249
Marianne, 229
Marin, Louis, 175, 176, 232, 277
Marion, Paul, 83, 124, 179
Maroselli, André, 191, 204, 207

Marquet, Adrien, 4–5, 80, 97, 124, 135, 202
Marquis, Admiral, 2
Marshall, George, 47
Martin, Glenn, 15
Martin, Henri, 65
Marty, André, 250, 258
Masaryk, Tomas, xix
Masse, Pierre, 141–142
Massenet, 115
Massigli, René, 232
Massilia, 1, 103, 129, 179
Matignon pact, 17, 121, 256
Matin, Le, 65, 259(n12)
Matsuoka Yosuke, 56
Maulnier, Thierry, 123
Mauriac, François, 320
Maurin, Joseph, xix, 11, 22
Maurras, Charles, 30, 78, 90, 182, 259–260, 264
  arrest of, 289–290
  and La Roque, 249, 262, 265
Mayer, René, 232
Mazé, Pierre, 4–5, 49–50, 53, 86, 105–106
  and Daladier escape plans, 87, 186, 188–89
  during Riom trial, 113
  visits by, 17, 20–21, 24–25, 28, 46, 59, 69–70, 83, 99, 108–109
Mazzini, Giuseppe, 215
Mendès-France, Pierre, 232, 278
Ménétrel, Bernard, 78, 80, 140, 144, 150, 210
Menthon, François de, 314
Menzies, Robert, 132
Metal Workers' Union, 18
Michel, General, 1
Middle East, as future theater, 327
Midway Islands, 126
Millerand, Alexandre, 236
Mistler, Jean, 91, 137, 302
Mitterand, François-Maurice, xiii
Moch, Jules, 26, 239
Mollet, 31–37
Molotov, Vyacheslav, 127, 218, 258, 301
Monde, Le, 319, 320, 322
Moniteur, Le, 37, 175
Monnet, Jean, xviii, 8, 206–207, 232
Montagne, La, 17, 84, 160
Montcalm, 188
Montigny, Jean, 39, 42, 89, 129
Monzie, Anatole de, 14, 91, 93, 124, 137, 158
  at Chaumié trial, 109
  and North African plan, 202
  and Pétain, 275–276
Morgenthau, Henry, 295, 306
Morocco, vii, xxi, 1–2, 6, 103–104
Moscow Conference, 230–231, 235
Mouchanov, 325
Mouton, 90
Moysset, 85
Munich Agreement, vii, xi, xix, xxii, 230, 261, 274, 327
Mussolini, Benito, 13, 38, 93, 130, 175
  in Alexandria, 147
  and Daladier, 161–162, 215
  execution of, 335
  and Flandin, 43
  and France, x, 107
  and Hitler, 284
  imprisonment of, 225–226
  and Laval, 42, 124
  resignation of, 214–216
  in Sardinia, 125
  and the Vatican, 133

Napoleon I, 64, 101, 110
National Front (France), 263, 320
National Resistance Council (Algiers), 270
National Socialist Party. *See* Nazi Party
Nazi Party, xvii, 20, 121, 146, 185, 241
  and Bonnet, 142
  and Doriot, 150
  and Pétain, 84–85
  postwar, 131
  and Royalists, 63
Nehru, Jawaharlal, 119
New York Times, 299, 325
Nitti, Francesco, 221, 223–224, 230–231, 233, 235–239, 277
Noguès, Charles-Auguste, 1–3, 66, 104, 169, 179–180, 186
  in Africa, 171

in Morocco, 282
resignation of, 207
North Africa, 129, 182, 322
as French base, 15, 55, 82, 154, 176
French plan for, vii, xv, xxi, 1–3, 103, 106–107, 148
Norway, 8, 120, 124, 161
Nouveaux Temps, Les, 72(n24), 73, 131

Oberlé, Jean, 230, 282
Œuvre, L', 17, 24, 65
Offie, Carmel, 75
Ordre, L', 229, 322

Paléologue, Maurice, 237
Palestine, 155
Palmade, 302
Papandreou, 299, 303
Papen, Franz von, 132
Paris (Bidou), 64
Paris, Count of, 92, 97, 136, 140, 143–144, 150, 184, 190
Passemard, 38, 50, 62, 66, 81, 152
execution of, 87(n42)
Patton, George, 335, 340
Paul-Boncour, Joseph, 30, 97
Paulus, Friedrich, 319
Payot, René, 58, 282, 308
Perchot, Claude, 163
Perré, Colonel, xxi, 30, 122
Perretti della Rocca, 88, 89, 142
Perrin, Paul, 33, 85
Pétain, Philippe, vii, ix–x, 67–68, 70, 78–81, 84, 139
and armistice, 119, 165, 291
arrest of, 290, 336
Bordeaux conspiracy of, 202
Cabinet of, 11(n20)
and Catholic church, 121, 190
and Communist Party, 141, 193
and Consultative Assembly, 294, 295
and corruption, 147
and Daladier, xii, 73, 80, 202, 228, 263
Daladier sentencing by, 91, 102, 113, 142
egotism of, 60
and the Jews, 129, 141
and French liberation, 289
and French rearmament, xvii, 11, 96
and French troops in Africa, 170
on Gaullist forces in Syria, 79
and German negotiations, 50, 124, 165–166, 168, 174, 253
and German victory, xxi
and Great Britain, 13, 79, 205
and Hitler, 34, 40, 65
and Maginot Line, 267
Marquet's removal by, 5
as Minister of War, xvii, 115
Monck comparison with, 26
National Assembly violations by, 149
and Nazi Party, 84–85, 96
and 1937 coup attempt, 260
and North African plan, xxi, 129
Paris trip of (1944), 274–275
plenary powers of, 2
police force of, 111
and Le Portalet transfer, 88–90, 95
as Réal Del Sarte, 123
and resignation rumors, 98
and Resistance, xxii, 287
"return to the land" promotion of, 5(n6)
and Riom trial, xxii, 4, 51, 80, 93, 129, 135
rise of, 263–264, 266
and Roosevelt document, 31(n59), 32–33, 35–36
and Sedan attack, xx
and Soviet Union, 79
speeches of, 92, 101, 103, 128–129, 162, 166, 177, 179, 182
support for, 277–278
and Synarchie plan, 276
as Tartuffe, 129–130
and Third Republic accountability, 9
trial of, xxiii
and Tunisia, 212
and United States, 79–80, 85
Versailles base of, 165
and Vichy cliques, 137, 140, 210
See also individual persons, and Pétain
Peter II (king of Yugoslavia), 54
Petit Journal, Le, 16, 17, 260, 261, 265
Petit Parisien, Le, 17, 229
Peycelon, Gilbert, 237

Peyrouton, Marcel, 5–6, 7, 10, 36, 51–52, 182–184, 190, 267
Granger on, 212
indictment of, 293
and Laval, 39, 154, 184
and Pétain, 187
U.S. support of, 186
Philip, André, 232
Picot, 262
Picquendar, 54, 61
Pierlot, 155–156
Piétri, François, 11
Pilori, Le, 65, 72
Pinelli, 259
Pius XII, 177, 302
Platon, 210
Poincaré, Raymond, 89, 96
Poland, xii, 185, 236, 295
executions in, 161, 310
and France, 7, 117, 236, 307–308
and Germany, vii, x, xx, 12–13, 23–24, 107, 199, 310
and Great Britain, 307, 310, 325–326
and Lublin Committee, 301
provisional government of, 307–310
and the Soviet Union, 281, 285, 288, 290, 310, 312, 316, 327, 329
and the United States, 301, 308, 310
in Yalta Agreement, 326
Political Justice Committee, 88, 89
Pomaret, Charles, 19, 103
Populaire, Le, 319, 320, 322
Popular Front, ix, xiii, xviii, 4, 249, 264
and Communist Party, 18, 197, 256
creation of, 18, 130
Porquerolles (island), 80–81, 88(n43)
Portmann, 91
Pourpre, Némorin, 94
PPF. *See* French People's Party
Prételat, 29–30, 224, 267
Prince, Albert, 41
Protestant church, 196
Prouvost, Jean, 103
PSF. *See* French Social Party
Puaux, 207
Pucheu, Pierre, 219, 267–270, 276
Pujo, 249

Queuille, Henri, 204, 207, 219, 232, 257

Radical Party, viii–xi, xiii, 26, 31, 59, 294
and Doumergue, 249, 263
Radical-Socialists, 302
Radio Paris, 81
RAF. *See* Great Britain, Royal Air Force of
Ragaine, Commander, 159
Reibel, Claude, 75, 97, 125, 138, 206
Republican Federation, 264
Requin, 29, 127
Resistance, xiii, 15, 132, 273, 285, 295
Chevalier kidnapping by, 283
and French provisional government, 319–320
in Occupied France, 275, 280, 287
and Pétain, xxii
Revers, General, 147, 163
Revue des deux mondes, La, 61, 66, 67
Reynaud, Paul, vii, x–xi, 106, 135, 179, 247, 280–291
in Bourassol prison, 28, 51, 62
and French rearmament, 15, 148n
and Gamelin, 8–9, 12
and Germany, xxi
and Giraud, 186
and Great Britain, 173–174, 205
at Itter prison, 201, 208, 214, 222, 271, 286, 296–297, 331
and La Roque, 250, 251, 254–255
and Monnet, 207
and Pétain, 106
resignation of, 202, 205
and Vichy government, 38, 42, 77, 102–103, 129, 266
and Weygand, 97
Rhineland, xix, 14, 205
Ribbentrop, Joachim von, 31(n59), 34, 46, 110, 123, 138, 203, 217
Ribet, Maurice, 26, 28, 51–52, 58, 80, 108–109, 142–144, 340
and Daladier file, 32, 35–37
and Mandel defense, 75
during Riom trial, 115, 118

visits by, 46, 49, 51, 65, 72–73, 90, 109, 141
Richelieu, 188
Riom trial, vii, xxii, 3, 23–24, 26–28, 30, 33, 73, 92–93
adjournment of, 118–120, 135, 181–182
and Bazaine trial, 128
Bénazet testimony at, 109–110
Daladier testimony at, 113–115, 117, 135
French Army Generals in, 184
Gamelin testimony in, 163
German involvement in, 108
international reaction to, 120
La Chambre testimony at, 115–116
and Laval, 139, 143–144, 155
Perré on, 122
Perretti della Rocca at, 142
and Pétain, 88, 129
press coverage of, 118
public effect of, 140
Rist testimony at, 322
and Roosevelt document, 37
and Vichy government, 51, 131
Rist, Charles, 322
Rivet, Colonel, 54, 71
Romania, 185, 235, 240, 295, 297, 312, 325
Romier, Lucien, 85, 108, 124
Rommel, Erwin, 147, 155, 164, 181, 235, 282
Roosevelt, Franklin D., xvi, 79, 133, 210, 302
and Darlan assassination, 180
death of, 331
and French rearmament, xviii, 47, 318
and French war declaration, 31(n59), 34–35, 37
and de Gaulle, 326–328
and Gaullists, 233–234
Goebbels on, 284, 312
and Great Britain, 61
and Laval, 175
and Monnet, 207
and Moscow Conference, 230
and Peyrouton, 184
and the Philippines, 296
reelection of, 37, 45
and Stalin, 316
and U.S. intervention, 45, 47–49, 172, 328
and Yalta Agreement, 329–330
Royalists, xvii, 11, 39, 63, 104, 124
Rundstedt, Karl von, 165, 168, 266–267, 282
Russia. *See* Soviet Union
Russo-Czech agreement, 240

Salengro, Roger, xvii, 104
Sarraut, Albert, 14, 67, 291
Sarraut, Maurice, 59
Saudi Arabia, 327
Scandinavia, x
Schrameck, Abraham, 291
Schumann, Maurice, 241, 259, 275
Secret Committtee for Revolutionary Action. *See* Cagoule
Sedan (France), xx–xxi, 10, 27, 303
Semard, Pierre, 120
Sentimental Journey (Sterne), 66
Service d'Ordre de la Légion (SOL), 135–137, 149
Sforza, 213, 215, 236, 271
Sikorski, Wladyslaw, 210
Sino-Russian pact, 56
Smuts, Jan, 220, 299
Socialist party (France), viii–ix, xvi, 40, 41, 204, 231–233, 294, 323
Society of Jesus, 121, 133, 140
SOL. *See* Service d'Ordre de la Légion
Soupiron, 340
South Africa, 220
Soviet Union, 56, 120, 231, 300
executions in, 161
and France, xv, xvii, 71, 237–238, 258, 289, 299. *See also* Franco-Soviet pact
and Germany, xix–xxi, 316
and Great Britain, 275, 295, 298, 299
and Japan, 56, 189, 233, 235, 271
and Poland, 288, 290, 301, 310, 312, 316
and postwar expansion, xii, xxii, 235–236, 240, 285, 290, 295, 301, 312–313, 316, 324, 329
and Riom trial, 120
and Russian Army, 76, 77, 81, 82

U.S. aid to, 275
war casualties in, 311
Spain, 2, 93, 107, 131–132
Spanien, Samuel, 54, 89, 150, 160, 168, 170
Stalin, Joseph, x, 128, 153, 210, 218, 232, 234
and Bulgaria, 295, 297
and France, 71, 234
and de Gaulle, 257–258
and Germany, 70, 71, 74, 316
Goebbels on, 312
and Hitler, x, 107, 284
and *Internationale* lyric change, 242
and Laval, 130
Matsuoka treaty with, 56
and Romania, 295, 297
if victorious, xxii, 190, 197, 236
Stavisky, Sacha, 41
Stavisky affair, ix, 90, 110, 259
Sterne, Laurence, 66
Stettinius, Edward, xviii, 301
Stimson, Henry, 61, 177
Stinner, Hugo, 146
Stora, 41–42
Stresemann, Gustave, 185
Stulpnagel, Karl von, 148
Sudetenland, xi, xix, xxii
Suhard, Cardinal, 190
Sûreté, 3, 5, 6, 21, 24, 104
Susset, 81, 138
Switzerland, 76
Synarchie, 134(n18), 266–267, 276, 291
Syndicats, 20
Syria, 61, 65, 68–70, 76, 79, 155, 327
and France, 65, 68–69, 76, 79

Taittinger, Pierre, 249, 259
Tardieu, André, 248, 260–262, 265, 279, 288
Tavera, 178
Temps, Le, 134–35, 229, 230, 320
Théry, 53–55, 186
Thierry, Amédée, 61, 154
Thorez, Maurice, ix
Times (London), 299
Timoshenko, Semyon, 132, 139, 157, 164, 198
Tirol fortress. *See* Itter prison
Tixier-Vignancour, 42
Torrès, 90, 110
Touchon, General, 30
Toute La Vérité (Montigny), 42, 129
Treaty of Versailles, xvi, 77, 185, 236, 272n, 290
Tricolor Legion, 138
Tripartite Pact, 103
Tunisia, 2, 59, 107, 124, 164, 171–172, 198, 203, 322
Turkey, 60, 76, 132, 286

United Nations, 282, 293, 300
United States, xvii, 56, 111, 201, 234
arms production in, xviii, 47, 49, 60, 86, 148, 181
aviation industry in, xxi, 2, 46–48, 148
Constitution of, 122
and Daladier, xvi, 145
as democracy, 221
economic power of, 196
and France, xviii, 34–35, 37, 45, 86, 102, 136
in French press, 328
in German media, 126
and Giraud, 186
and Great Britain, 7, 15, 24, 61, 174, 227
and Greece, 299
isolationism of, xix, 15, 45–49
in Itter prison attack, 337–339
and Japan, 24, 56, 236, 324
and League of Nations, 45
and Poland, 301, 308, 310
and Riom trial, 120
and Soviet Union, 275, 329
and war victory, 162
and World War I, 237
Vichy relations with, 42, 79–80, 83, 85

Vallat, Xavier, 260, 262
Vallin, Charles, 89, 159–160, 207
Vansittart, Lord, 272–273
Varenne, Alexandre, 17, 160(n36)
Verdier, Cardinal, 121
Vernet, Maurice, 240

Veterans' Legion. *See* Legion of French Volunteers
Vichy government, vii, xi–xiii, xviii, 2, 4(n3)
  and Canada, 120
  cliques in, 137
  and Communist Party, 74
  Constitutional Act revision by, 51, 53–54
  demonstrations against, 138–139
  and Free French forces, 25(n47)
  and Germany, xiii, xv, 71, 147, 169
  and Great Britain, 13
  Jacomet's treatment by, 75
  and Japan, 81, 122
  and Laval, 130
  and Riom trial, xi, xxii, 51, 131
  and Royalists, 39
  stupidity of, 101
  and "terrorist" executions, 257
  U.S. relations with, 83
  See also France; Pétain, Philippe
Victor Emmanuel III (king of Italy), 214, 216, 226–227, 233, 271
Vie des peuples, 230
Vienna Congress, 77
Viénot, Pierre, 207, 274
Vingré Martyrs, 102
Völkischer Beobachter, 325
Vomécourt, Pierre de, 186n
Vuillemin, Joseph, 60, 73, 116, 140, 173, 179, 290
Vyshinsky, Andrey, 258

Waldeck-Rochet, 250
Wallace, Henry, 196
Watteau, General, 90
Weiss, General, 267–269
Welles, Sumner, 83, 128
Weygand, Maxime, xxi, 10–12, 29, 84, 141, 260, 276, 291
  arrest of, 169
  and French Army, 16, 22, 29, 267
  in Itter prison, 202, 205, 271, 286, 340
  and La Roque, 247, 261, 279
  and Laval, 39
  and Payot, 308
  and Pétain, 79, 137, 263
  retirement of, 96–97
  and Reynaud, 77, 106
  at Riom trial, 23, 252
Whitman, Walt, 119
Wilkie, Wendell, 34
Wilson, Woodrow, 165, 237–238, 272n, 329
World War I, viii, x, xv–xvi, 231–232
World War II, xii, 45, 49, 120–122
Worms, Hippolyte, 291

Yalta Conference, 326, 328
Ybarnegaray, Jean, 260, 261
Youth Camps, 160
Yugoslavia, 55–56, 120, 161, 235, 240, 295, 312